LAND
OF THE
LUSTROUS
11

HARUKO ICHIKAWA

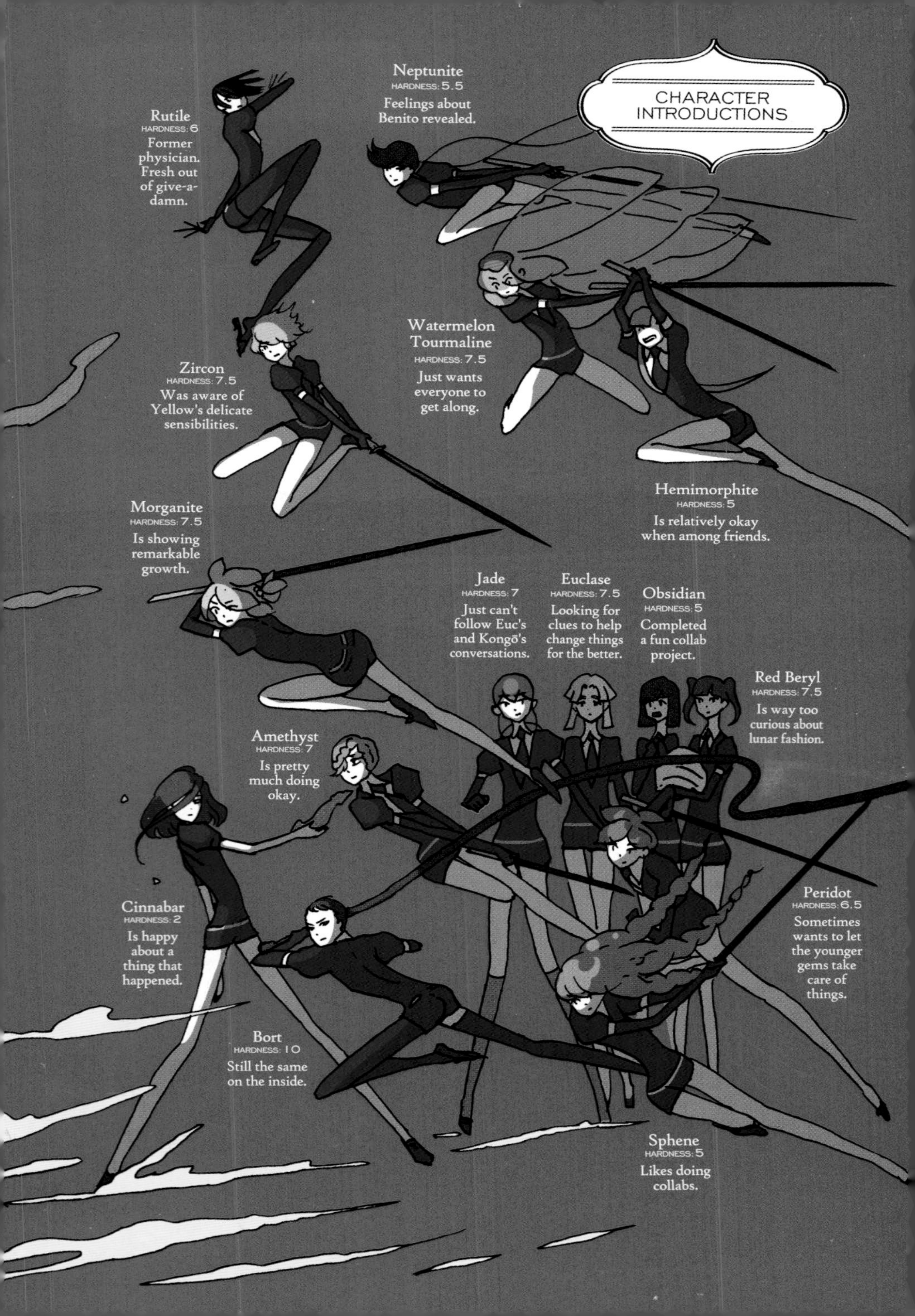
CHARACTER INTRODUCTIONS
Neptunite
HARDNESS: 5.5
Feelings about Benito revealed.
Rutile
HARDNESS: 6
Former physician. Fresh out of give-a-damn.
Watermelon Tourmaline
HARDNESS: 7.5
Just wants everyone to get along.
Zircon
HARDNESS: 7.5
Was aware of Yellow's delicate sensibilities.
Hemimorphite
HARDNESS: 5
Is relatively okay when among friends.
Morganite
HARDNESS: 7.5
Is showing remarkable growth.
Jade
HARDNESS: 7
Just can't follow Euc's and Kongō's conversations.
Euclase
HARDNESS: 7.5
Looking for clues to help change things for the better.
Obsidian
HARDNESS: 5
Completed a fun collab project.
Red Beryl
HARDNESS: 7.5
Is way too curious about lunar fashion.
Amethyst
HARDNESS: 7
Is pretty much doing okay.
Cinnabar
HARDNESS: 2
Is happy about a thing that happened.
Peridot
HARDNESS: 6.5
Sometimes wants to let the younger gems take care of things.
Bort
HARDNESS: 10
Still the same on the inside.
Sphene
HARDNESS: 5
Likes doing collabs.

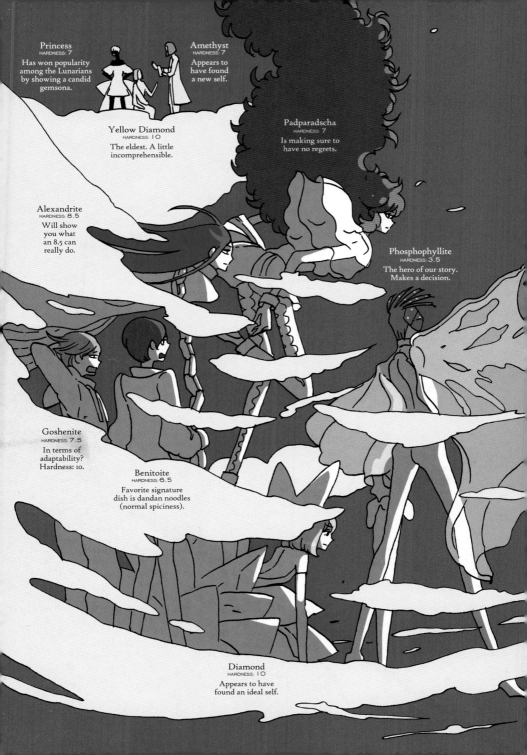

Princess
HARDNESS: 7
Has won popularity among the Lunarians by showing a candid gemsona.

Amethyst
HARDNESS: 7
Appears to have found a new self.

Yellow Diamond
HARDNESS: 10
The eldest. A little incomprehensible.

Padparadscha
HARDNESS: 7
Is making sure to have no regrets.

Alexandrite
HARDNESS: 8.5
Will show you what an 8.5 can really do.

Phosphophyllite
HARDNESS: 3.5
The hero of our story. Makes a decision.

Goshenite
HARDNESS: 7.5
In terms of adaptability? Hardness: 10.

Benitoite
HARDNESS: 6.5
Favorite signature dish is dandan noodles (normal spiciness).

Diamond
HARDNESS: 10
Appears to have found an ideal self.

CONTENTS

CHAPTER 80:

Three Races

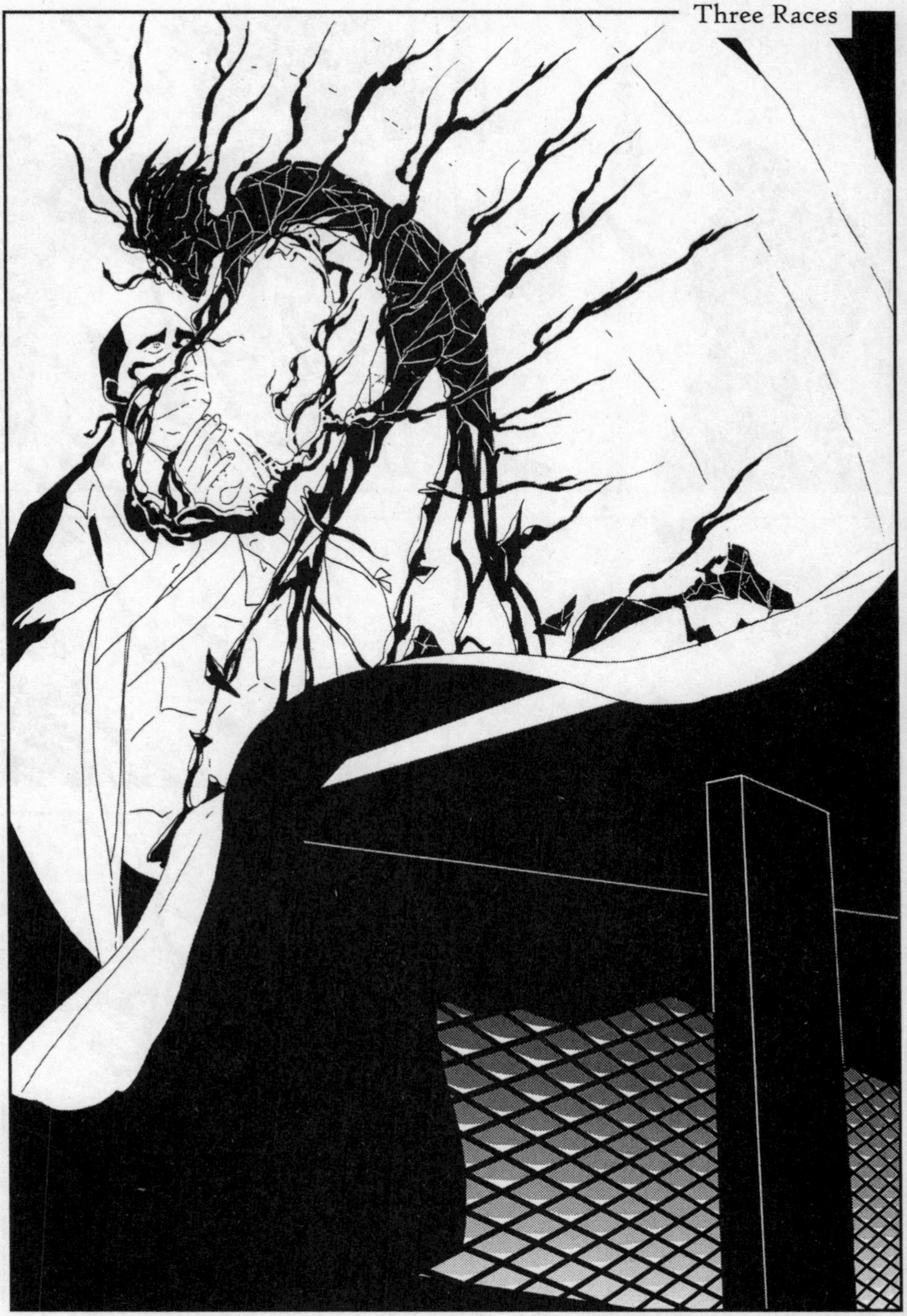

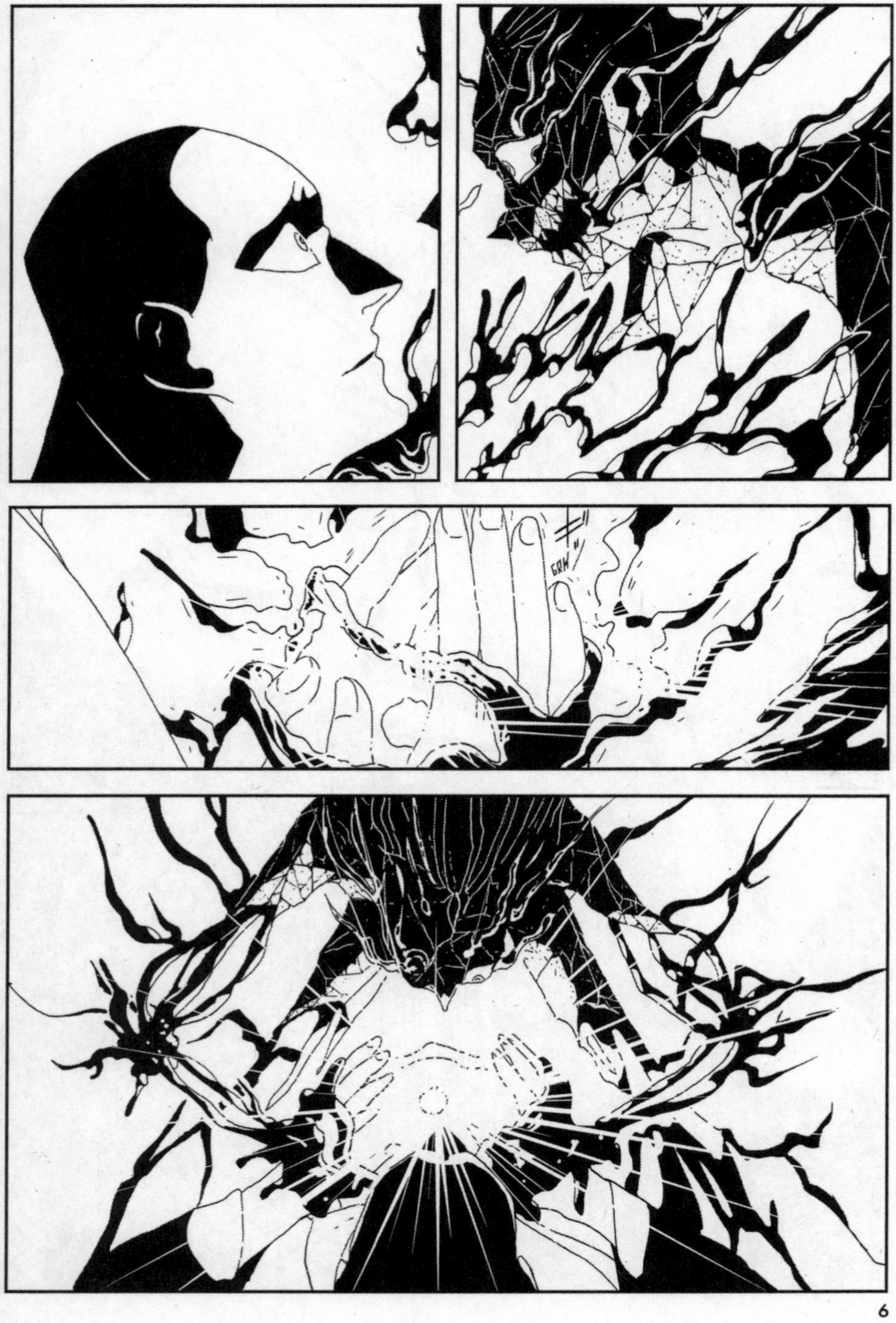
GRK

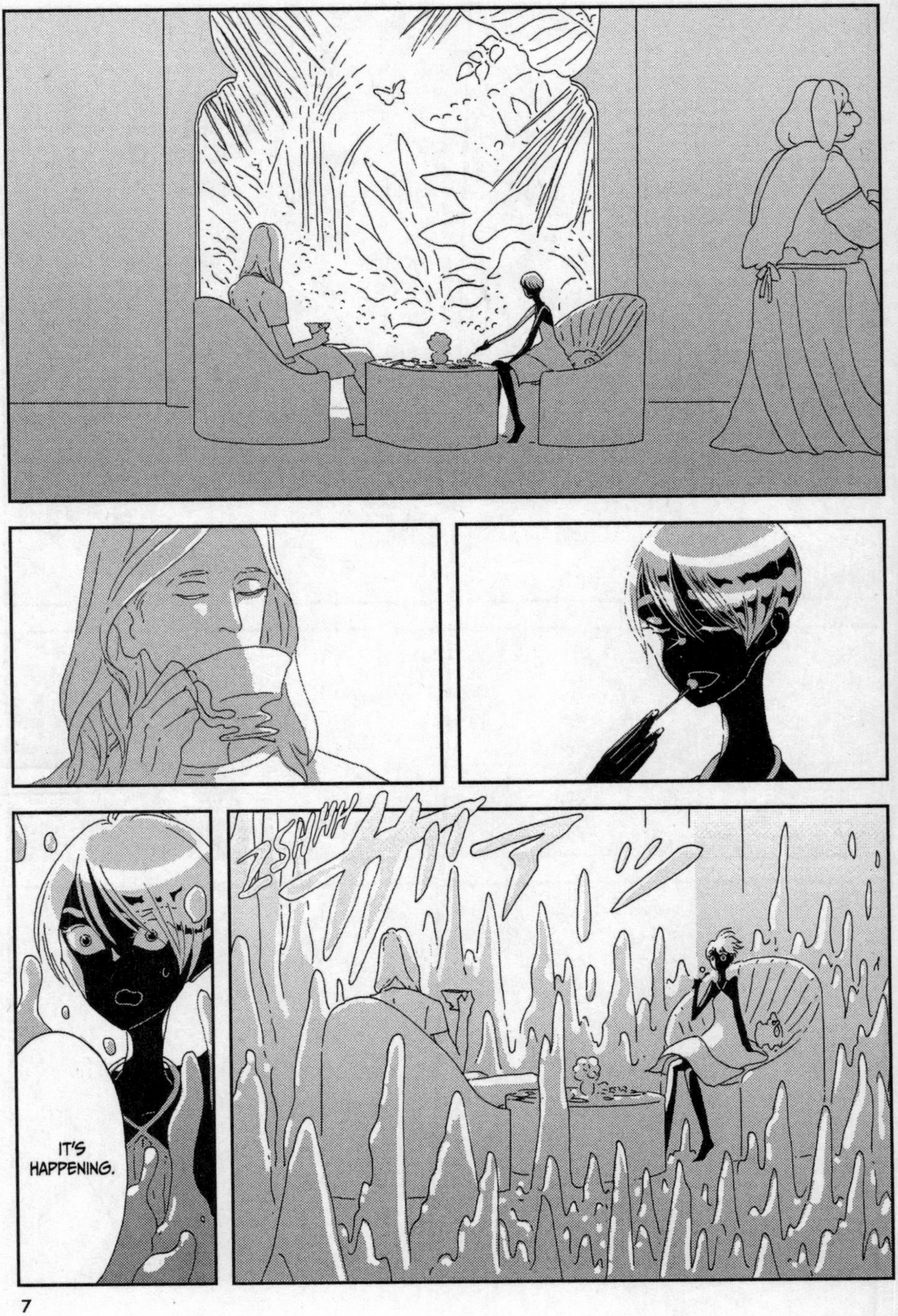
ZSHHH
IT'S HAPPENING.

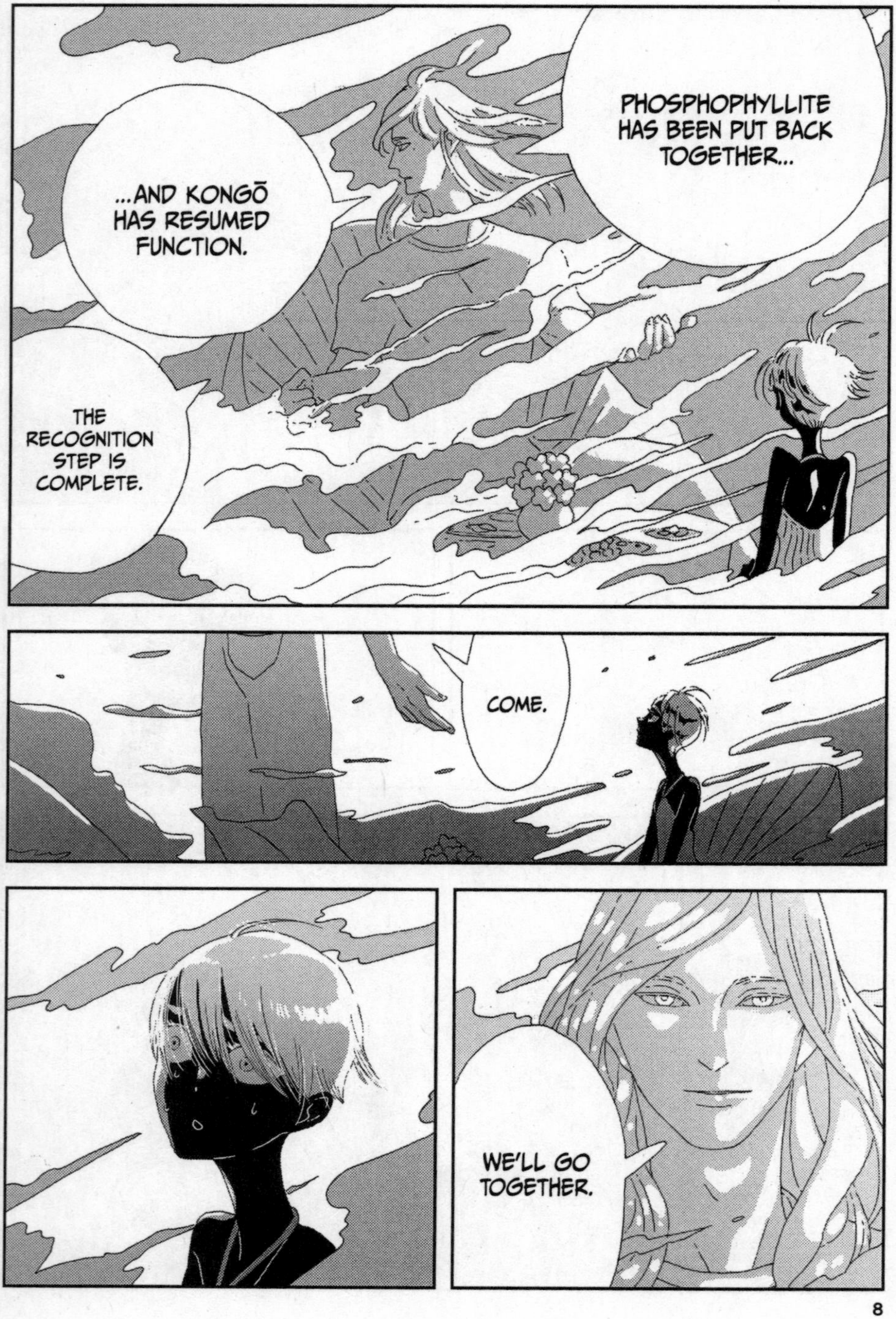
PHOSPHOPHYLLITE HAS BEEN PUT BACK TOGETHER...
...AND KONGŌ HAS RESUMED FUNCTION.
THE RECOGNITION STEP IS COMPLETE.
COME.
WE'LL GO TOGETHER.

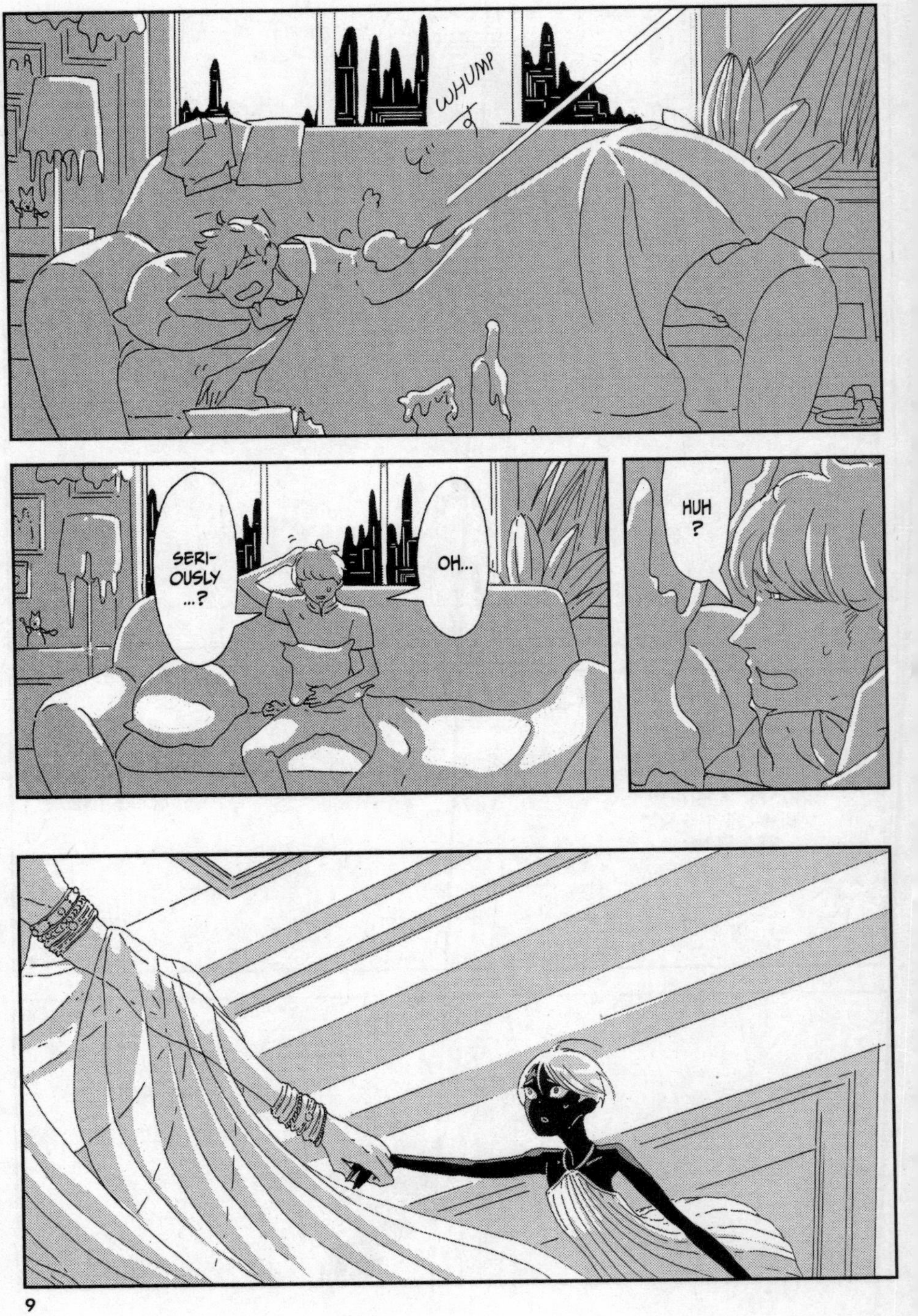
WHUMP
す
HUH?
OH...
SERI-OUSLY...?

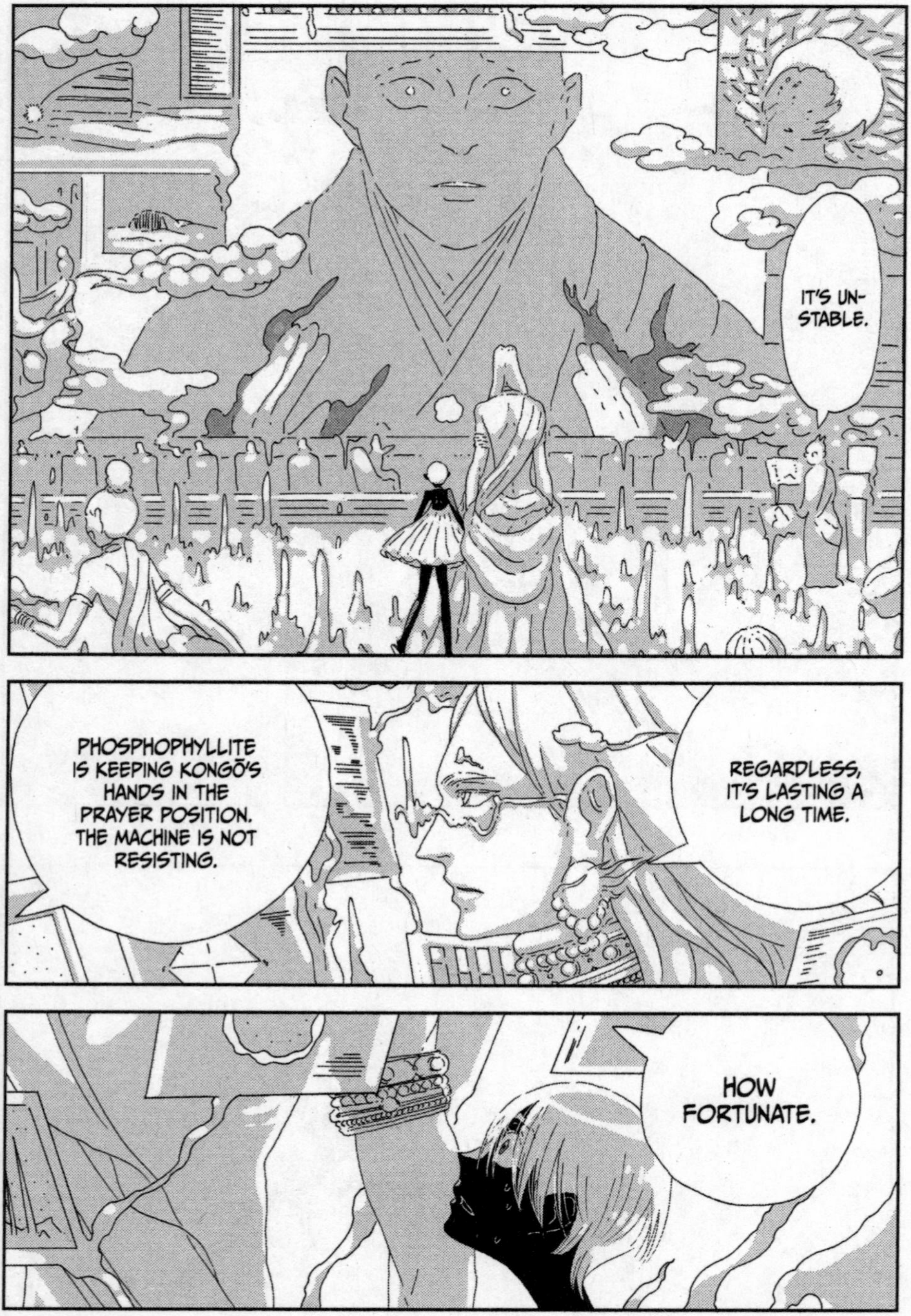
IT'S UN-STABLE.
REGARDLESS, IT'S LASTING A LONG TIME.
PHOSPHOPHYLLITE IS KEEPING KONGŌ'S HANDS IN THE PRAYER POSITION. THE MACHINE IS NOT RESISTING.
HOW FORTUNATE.

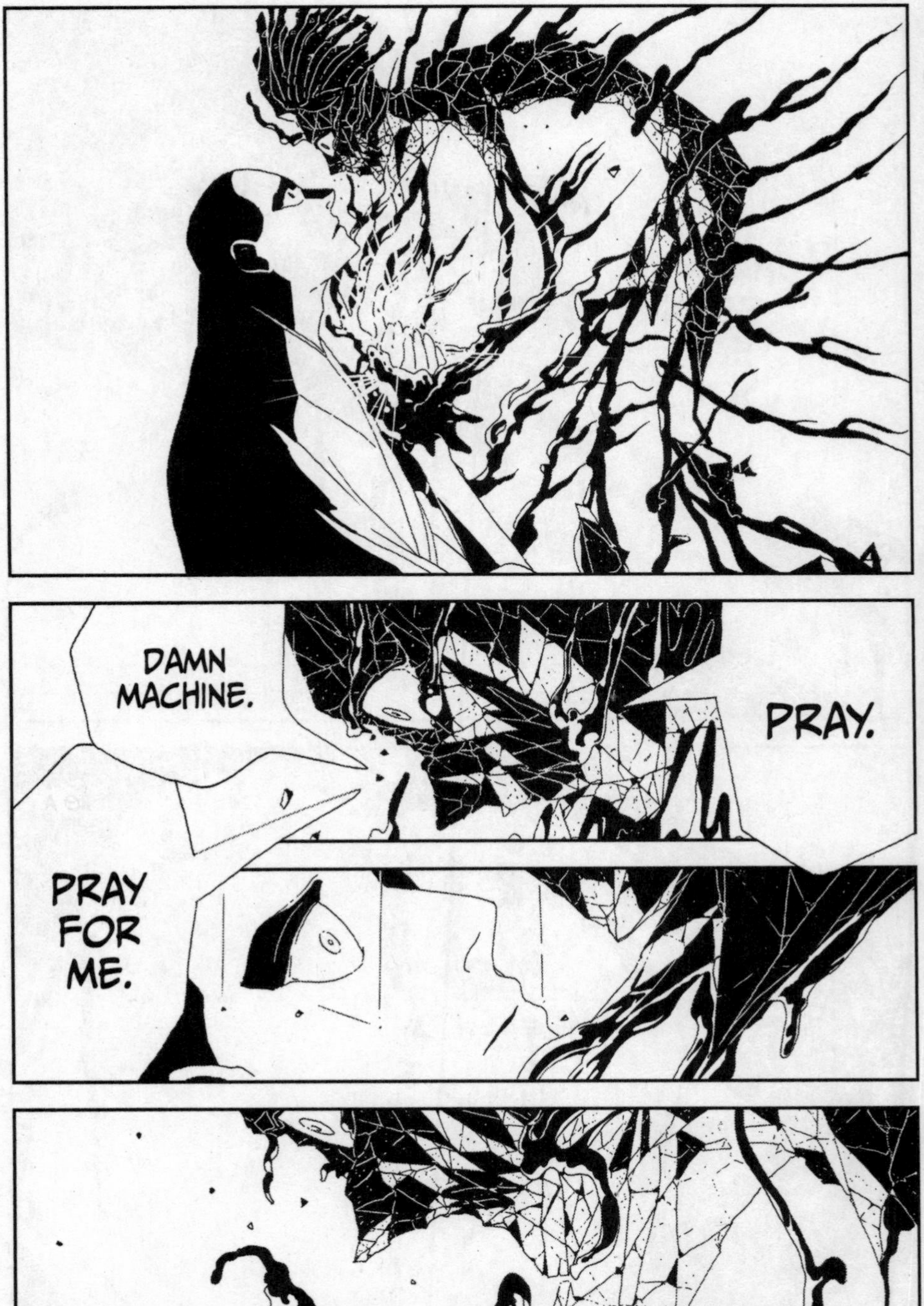
DAMN MACHINE.
PRAY.
PRAY FOR ME.

IF IT HADN'T BEEN FOR YOU...

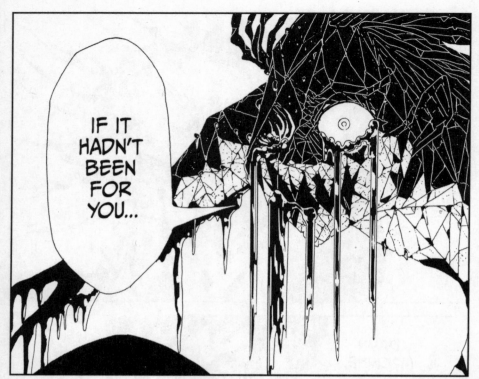

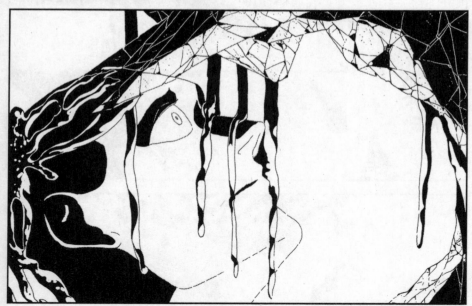

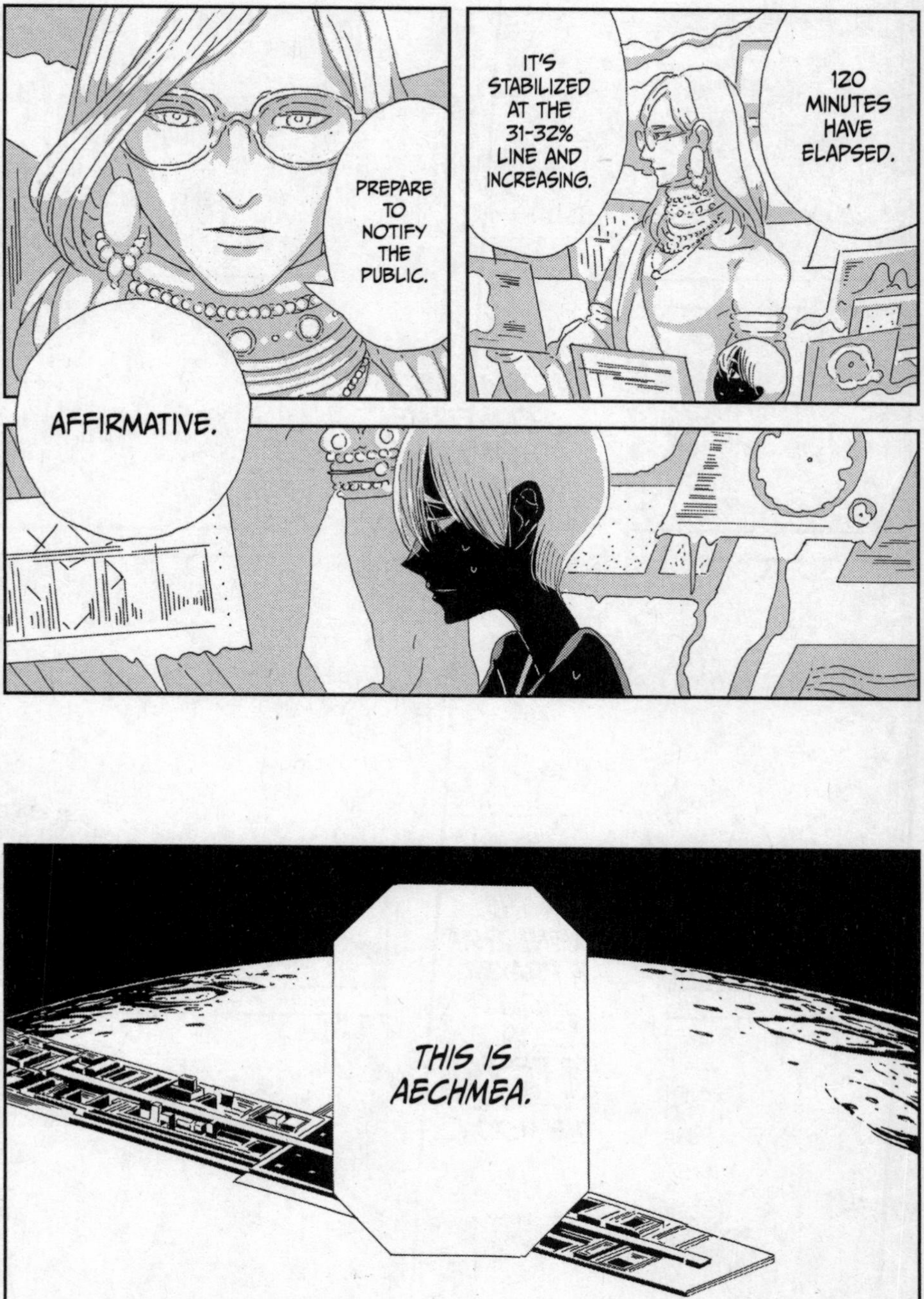
120 MINUTES HAVE ELAPSED.
IT'S STABILIZED AT THE 31-32% LINE AND INCREASING.
PREPARE TO NOTIFY THE PUBLIC.
AFFIRMATIVE.
THIS IS AECHMEA.

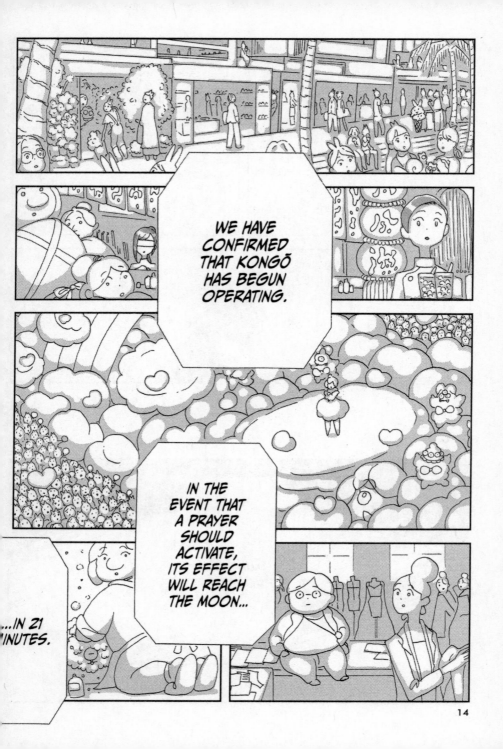

WE HAVE CONFIRMED THAT KONGŌ HAS BEGUN OPERATING.

IN THE EVENT THAT A PRAYER SHOULD ACTIVATE, ITS EFFECT WILL REACH THE MOON...

...IN 21 MINUTES.

EVERYONE.

YOU MUST ALL ACT QUICKLY...

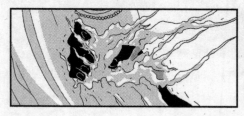

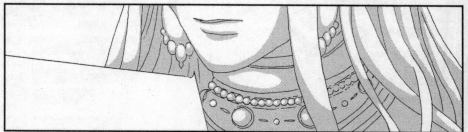

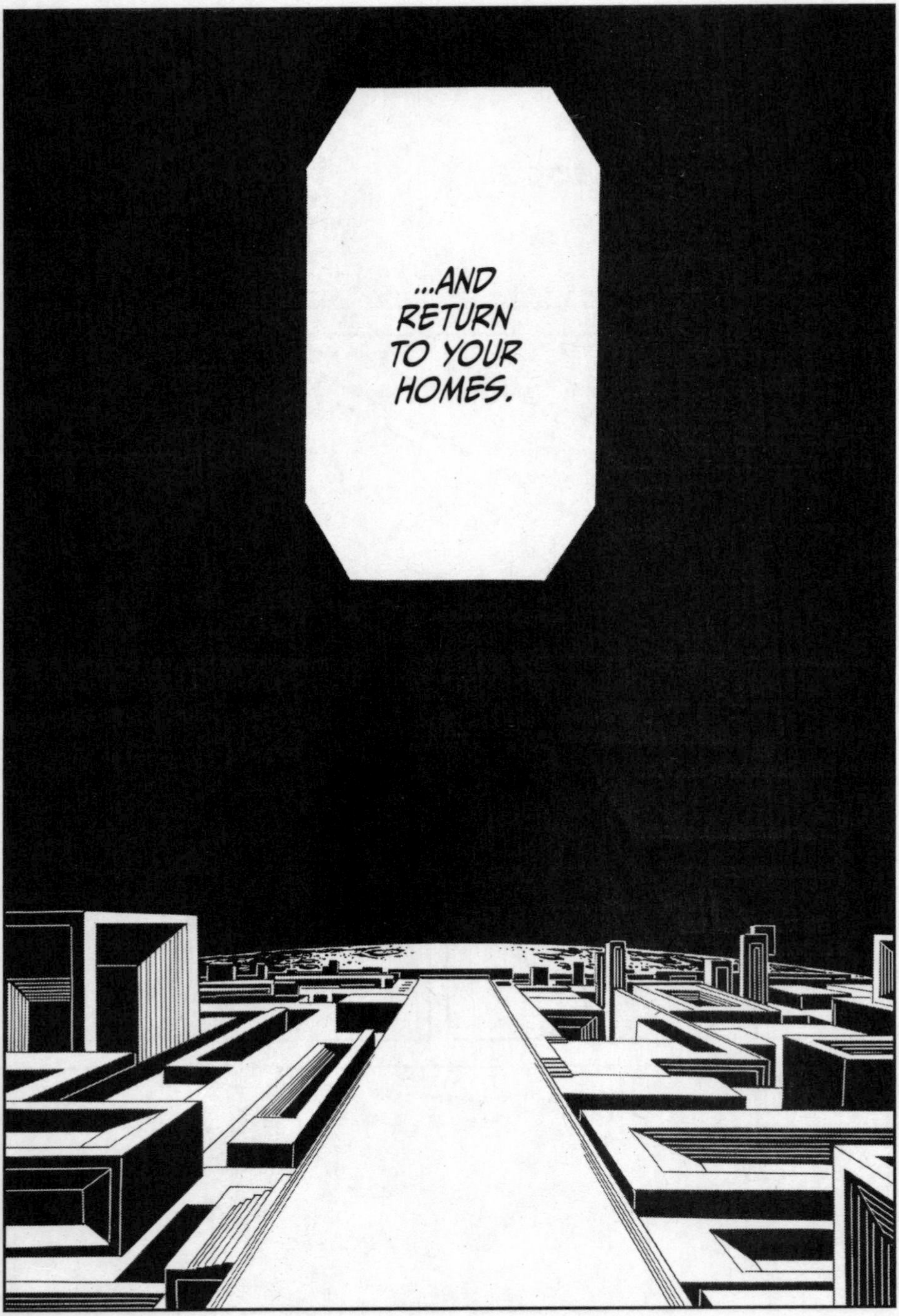
...AND RETURN TO YOUR HOMES.

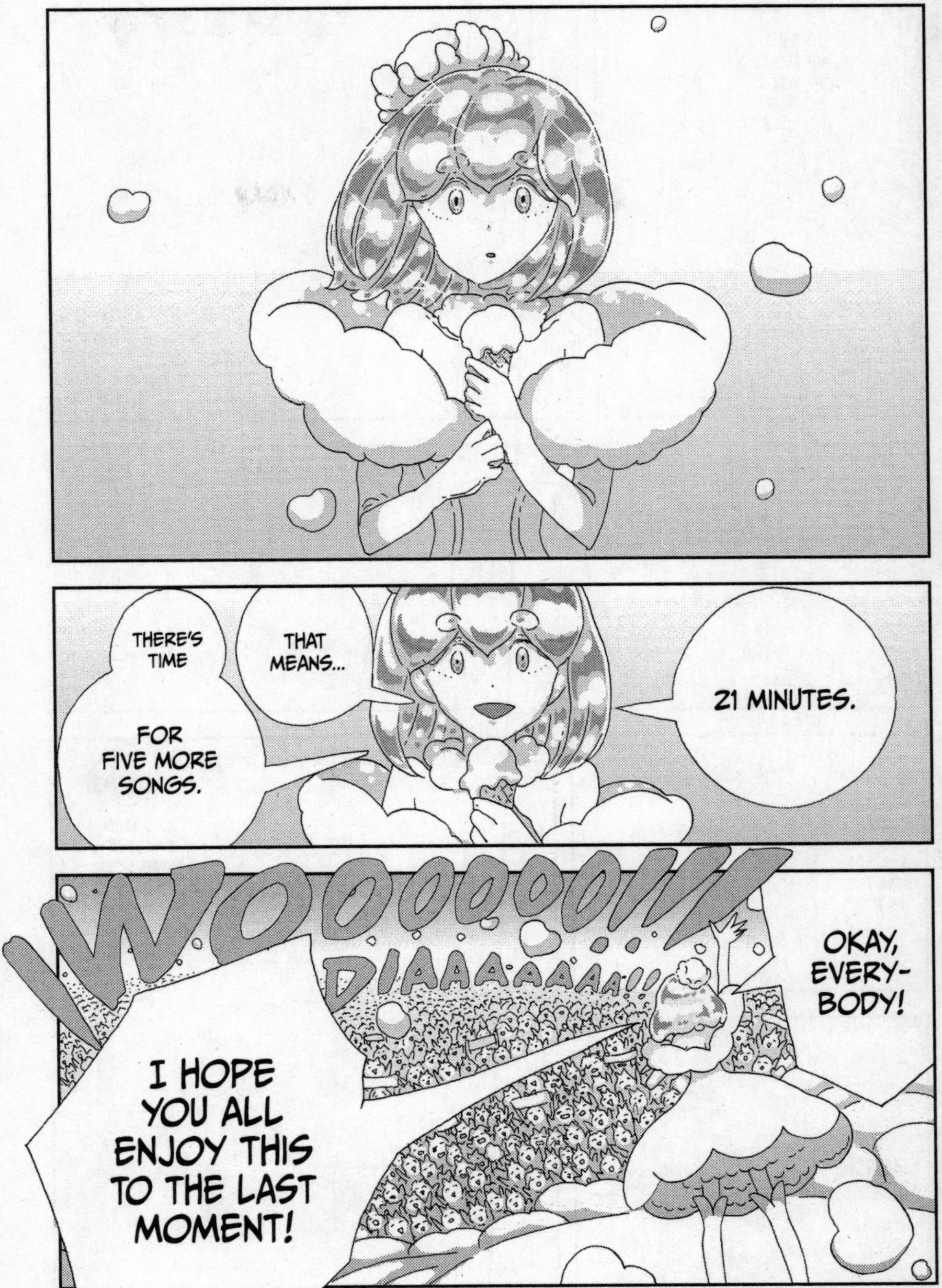
21 MINUTES.
THAT MEANS...
THERE'S TIME FOR FIVE MORE SONGS.
WOOOOOW!!
DIAAAAAAA!!
OKAY, EVERY-BODY!
I HOPE YOU ALL ENJOY THIS TO THE LAST MOMENT!

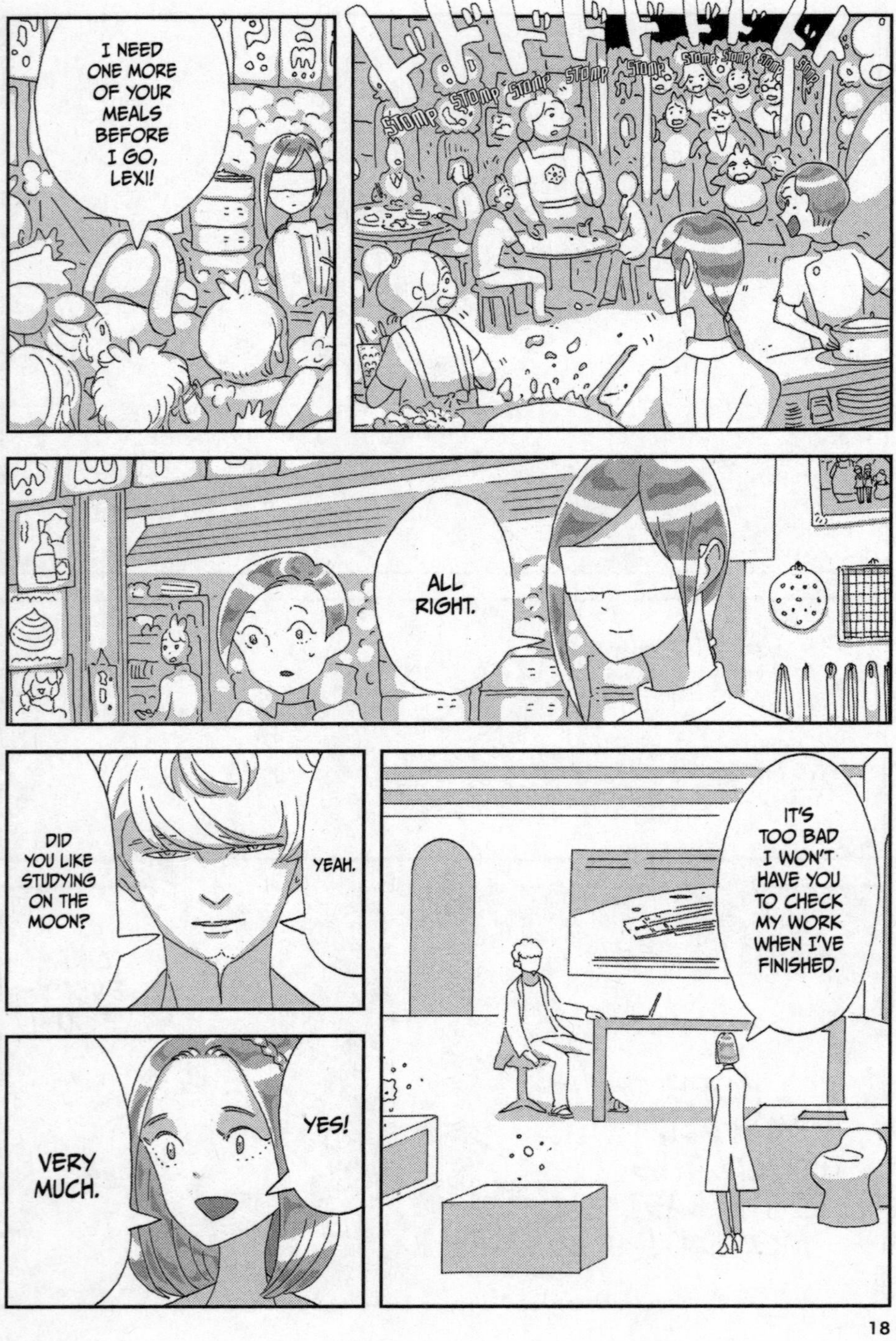
STOMP STOMP STOMP STOMP STOMP STOMP STOMP STOMP STOMP
I NEED ONE MORE OF YOUR MEALS BEFORE I GO, LEXI!
ALL RIGHT.
IT'S TOO BAD I WON'T HAVE YOU TO CHECK MY WORK WHEN I'VE FINISHED.
DID YOU LIKE STUDYING ON THE MOON?
YEAH.
YES!
VERY MUCH.

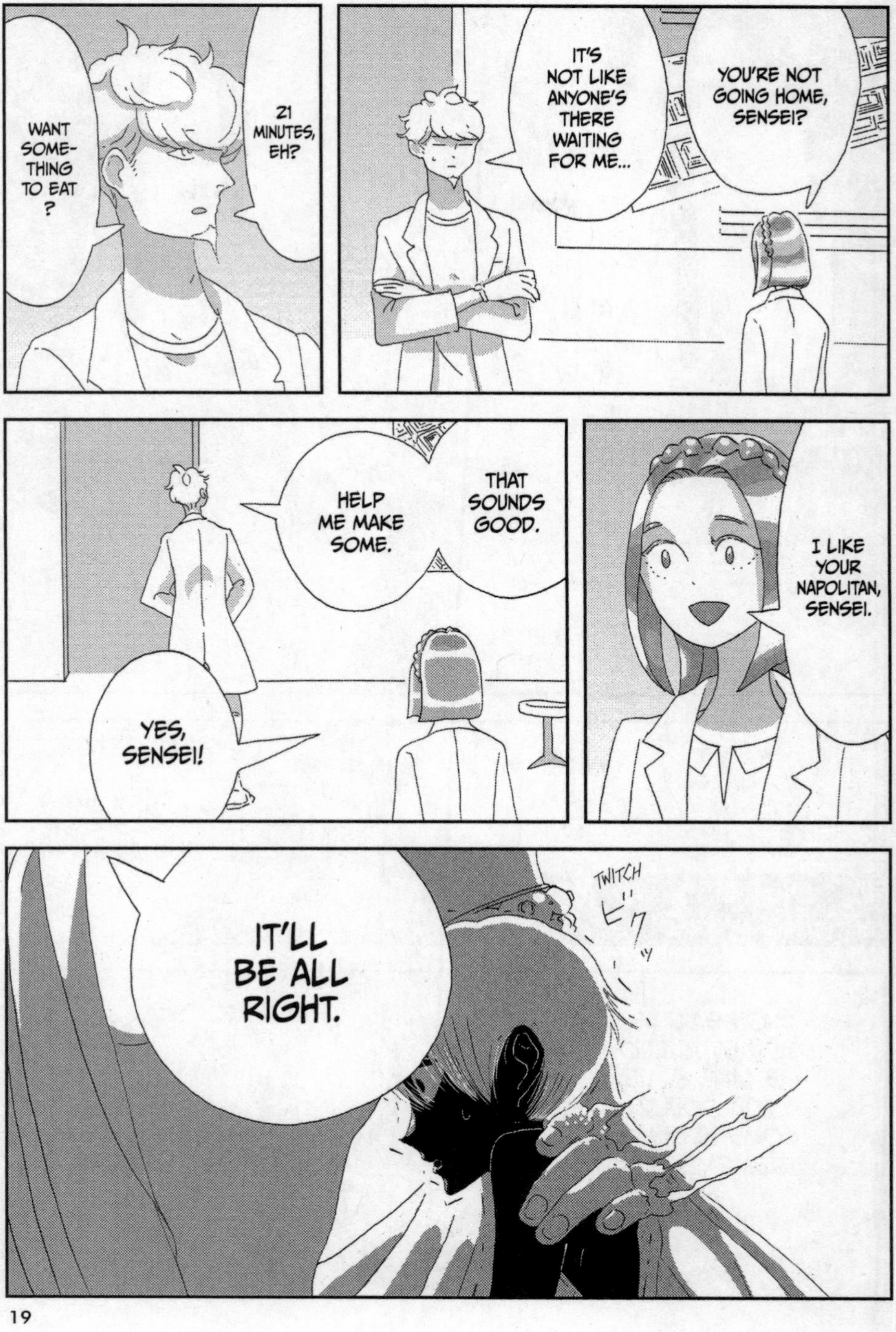
YOU'RE NOT GOING HOME, SENSEI?
IT'S NOT LIKE ANYONE'S THERE WAITING FOR ME...
21 MINUTES, EH?
WANT SOME-THING TO EAT ?
I LIKE YOUR NAPOLITAN, SENSEI.
THAT SOUNDS GOOD.
HELP ME MAKE SOME.
YES, SENSEI!
TWITCH
IT'LL BE ALL RIGHT.

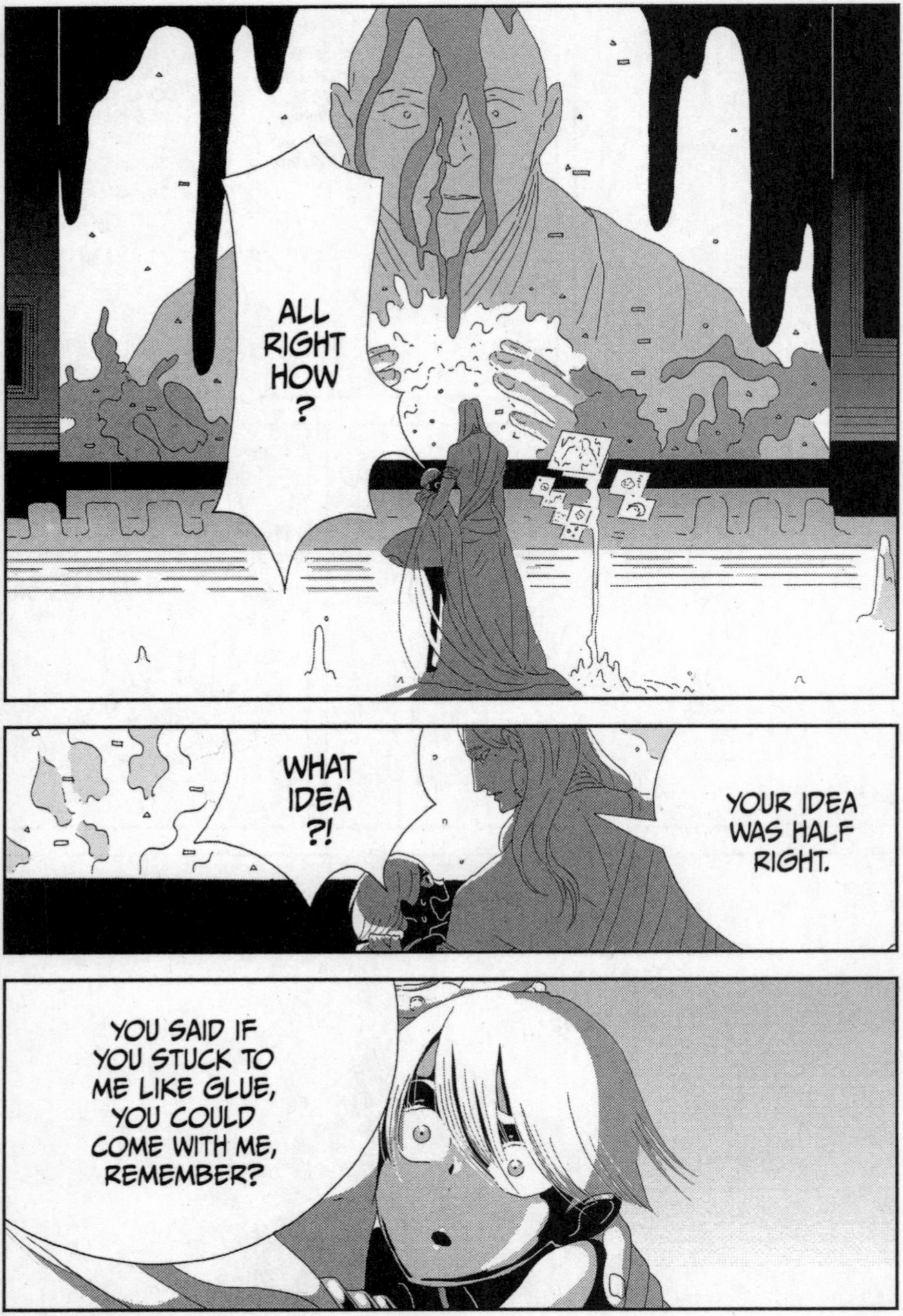
ALL RIGHT HOW ?
YOUR IDEA WAS HALF RIGHT.
WHAT IDEA ?!
YOU SAID IF YOU STUCK TO ME LIKE GLUE, YOU COULD COME WITH ME, REMEMBER?

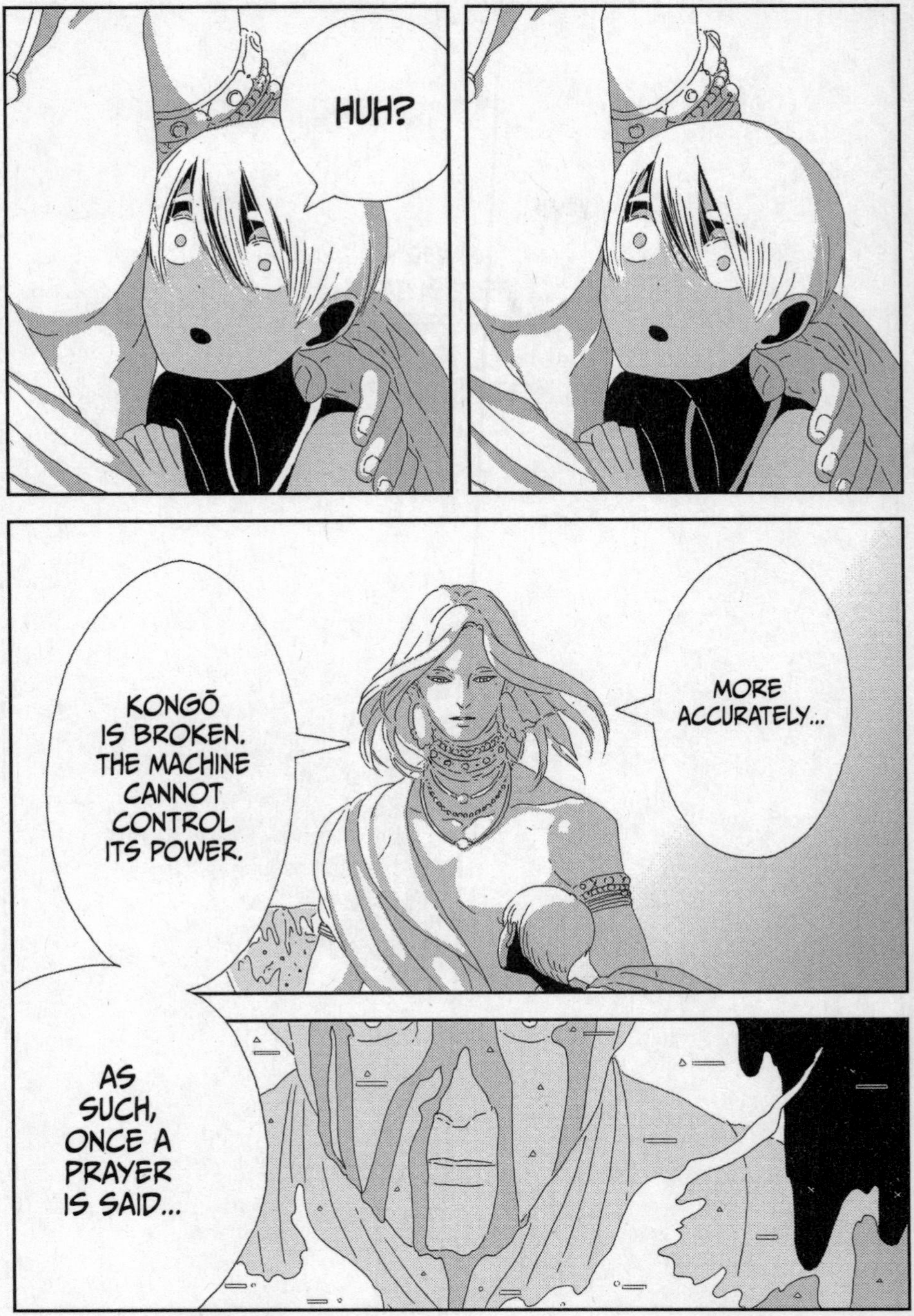
HUH?
MORE ACCURATELY...
KONGŌ IS BROKEN. THE MACHINE CANNOT CONTROL ITS POWER.
AS SUCH, ONCE A PRAYER IS SAID...

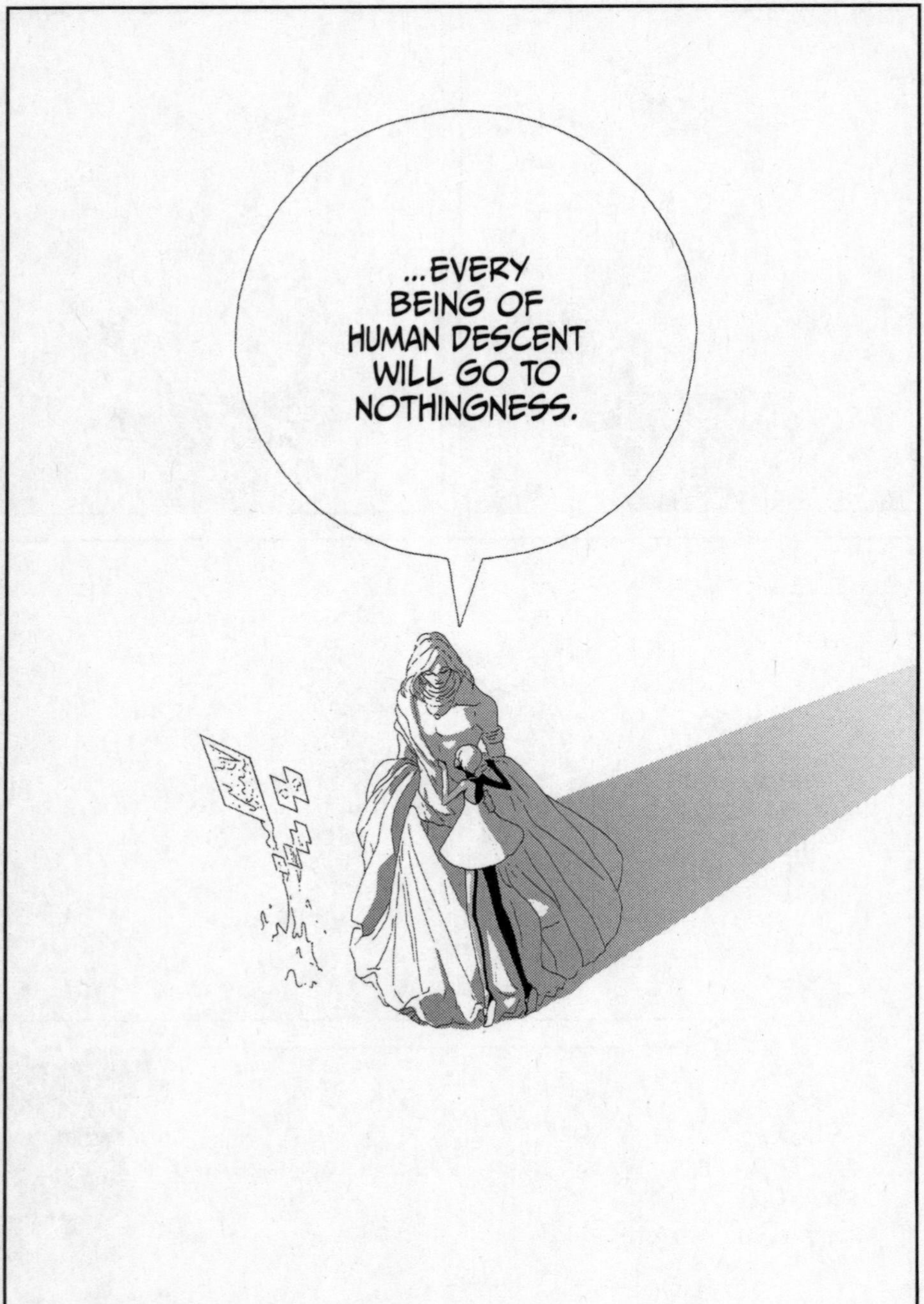
...EVERY BEING OF HUMAN DESCENT WILL GO TO NOTHINGNESS.

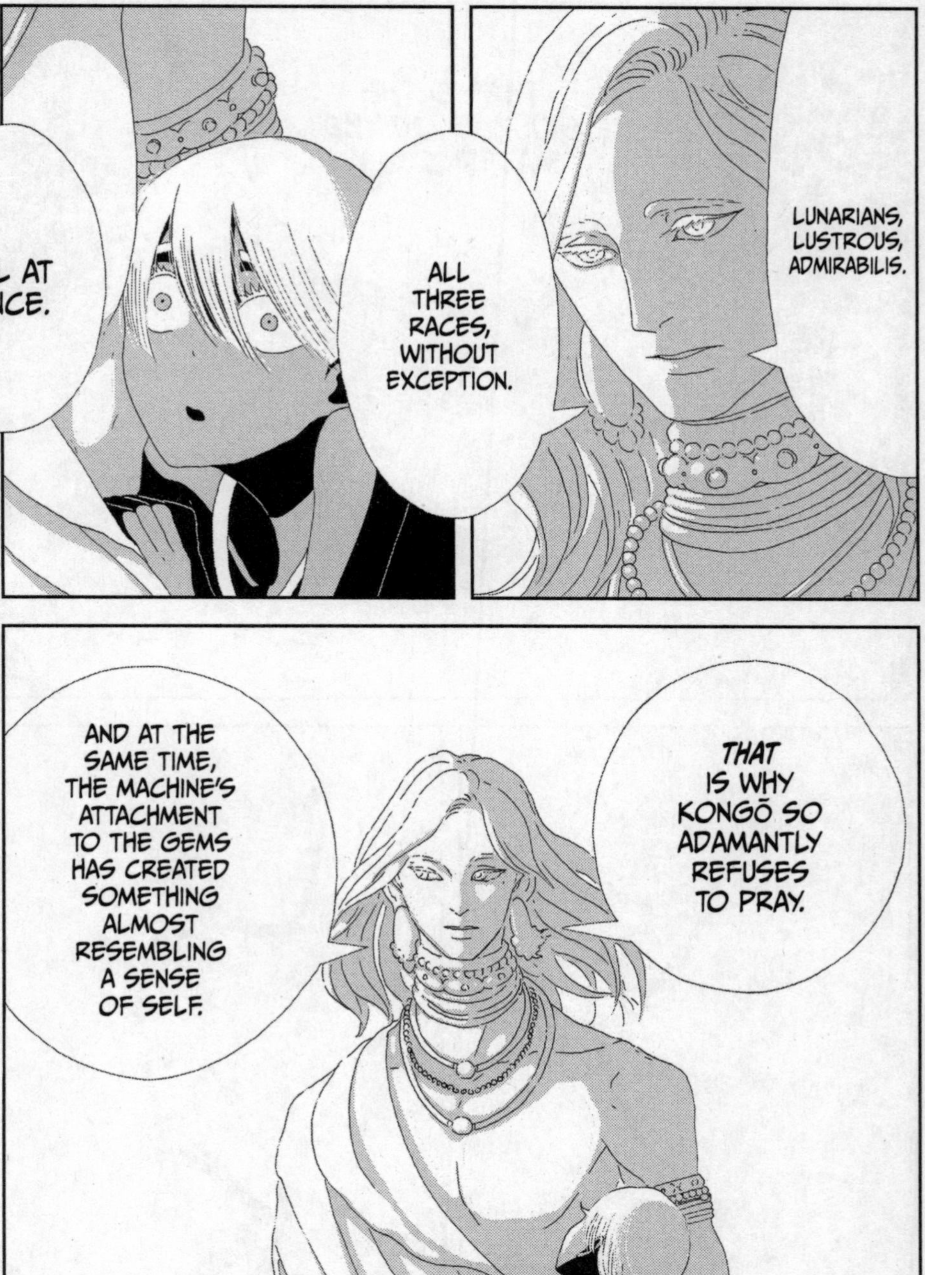
LUNARIANS, LUSTROUS, ADMIRABILIS.
ALL THREE RACES, WITHOUT EXCEPTION.
ALL AT ONCE.
THAT IS WHY KONGŌ SO ADAMANTLY REFUSES TO PRAY.
AND AT THE SAME TIME, THE MACHINE'S ATTACHMENT TO THE GEMS HAS CREATED SOMETHING ALMOST RESEMBLING A SENSE OF SELF.

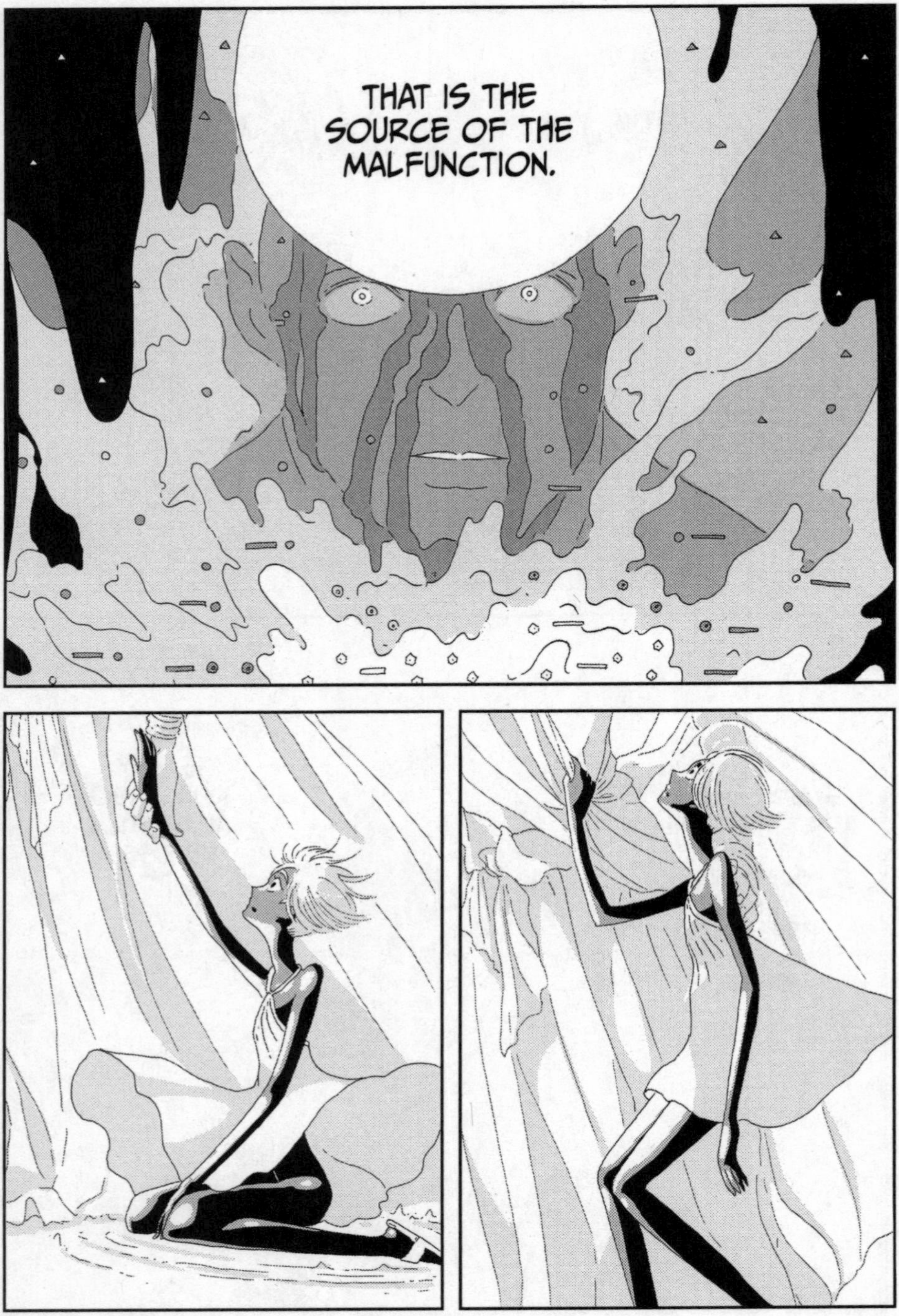
THAT IS THE SOURCE OF THE MALFUNCTION.

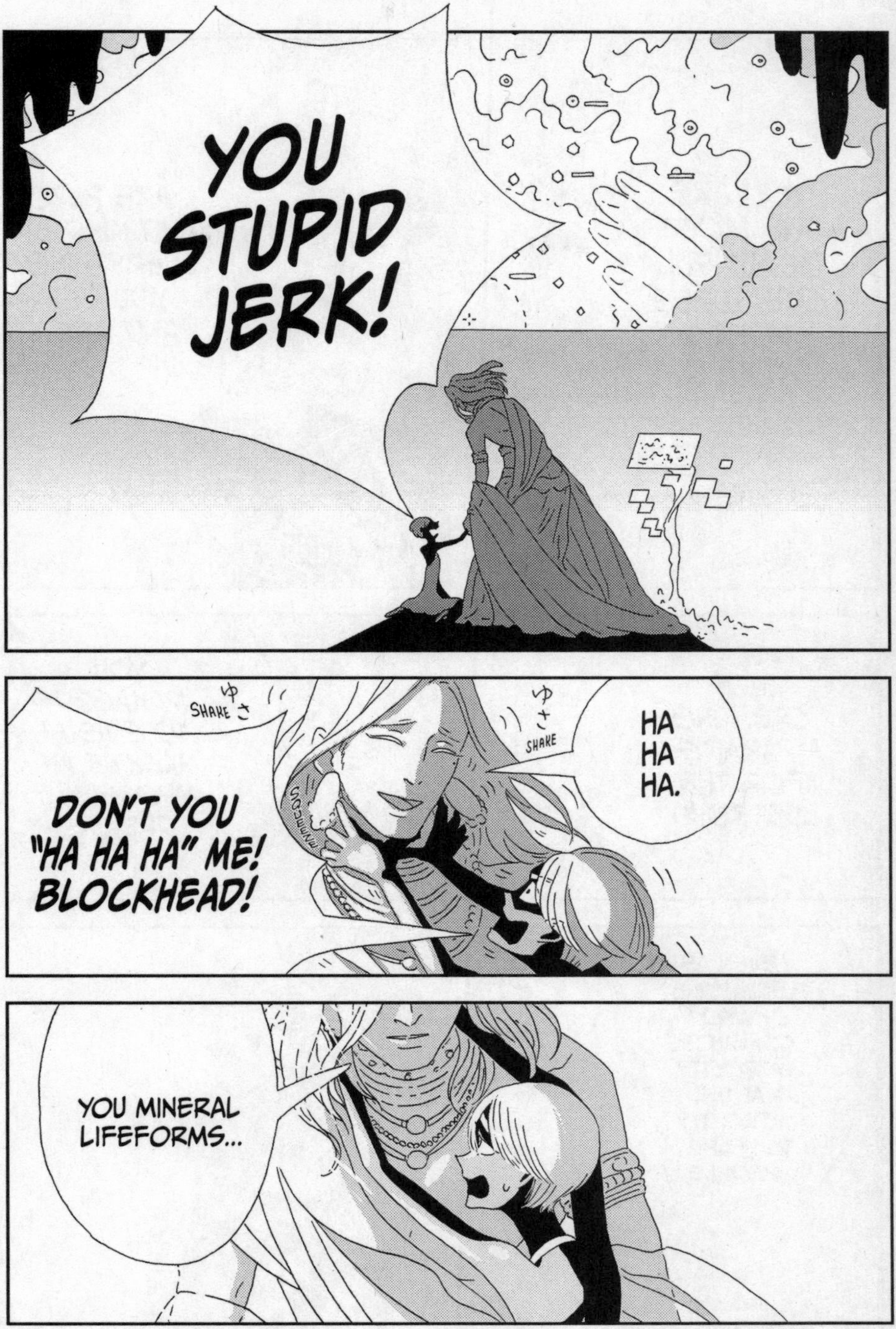
YOU STUPID JERK!
ゆさ SHAKE
ゆさ SHAKE
HA HA HA.
SQUEEZE
DON'T YOU "HA HA HA" ME! BLOCKHEAD!
YOU MINERAL LIFEFORMS...

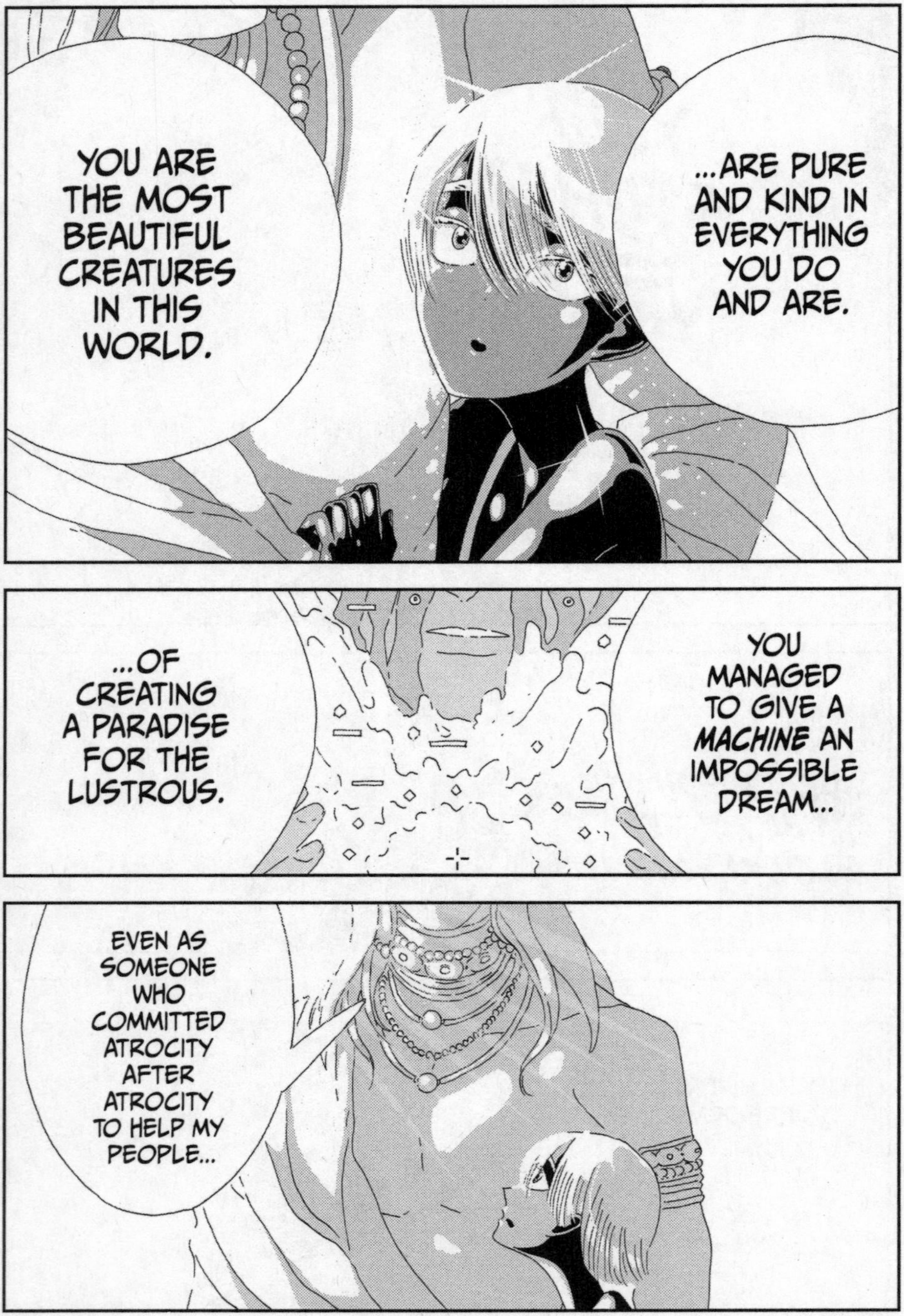
...ARE PURE AND KIND IN EVERYTHING YOU DO AND ARE.
YOU ARE THE MOST BEAUTIFUL CREATURES IN THIS WORLD.
YOU MANAGED TO GIVE A *MACHINE* AN IMPOSSIBLE DREAM...
...OF CREATING A PARADISE FOR THE LUSTROUS.
EVEN AS SOMEONE WHO COMMITTED ATROCITY AFTER ATROCITY TO HELP MY PEOPLE...

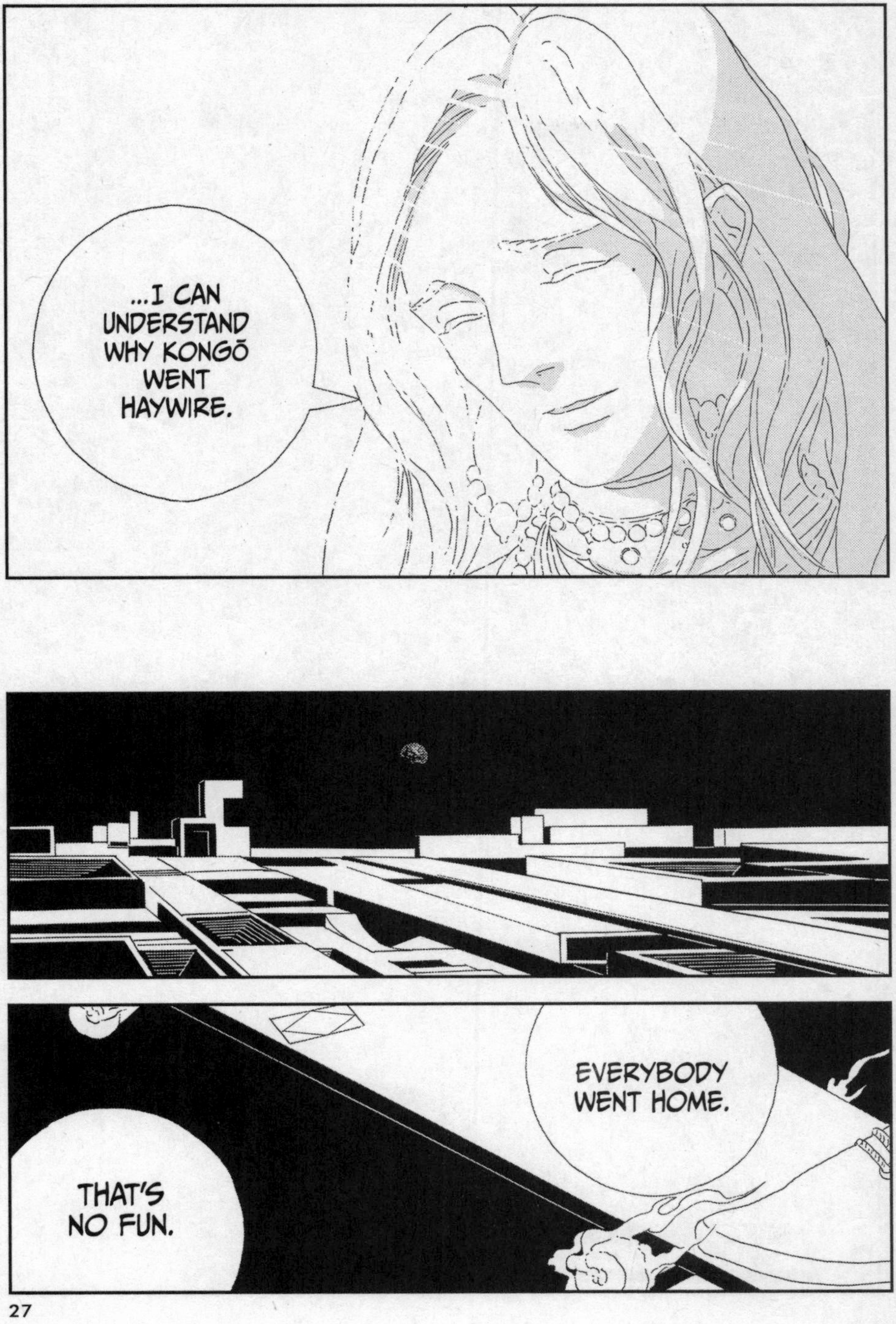
...I CAN UNDERSTAND WHY KONGŌ WENT HAYWIRE.
EVERYBODY WENT HOME.
THAT'S NO FUN.

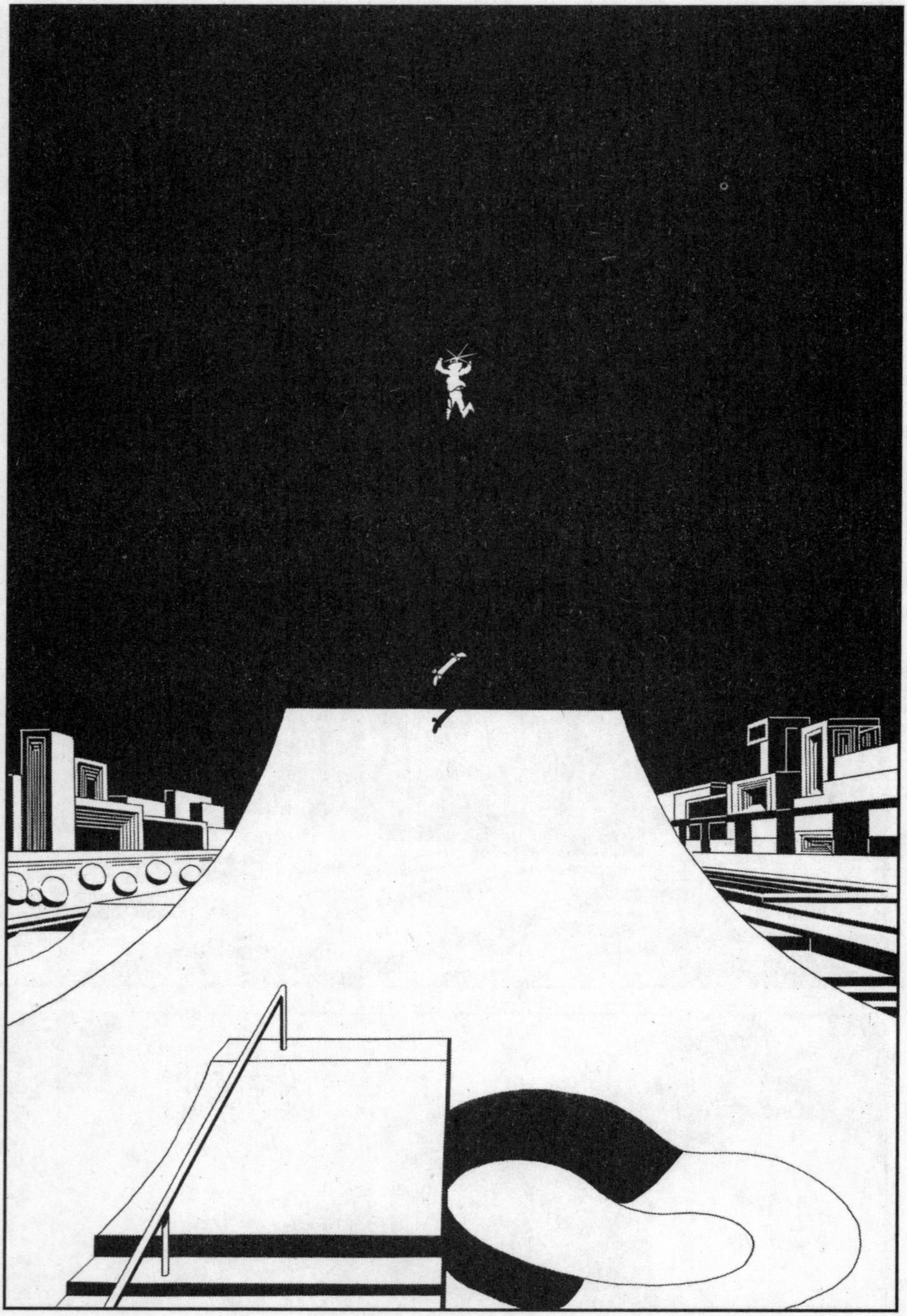

CHAPTER 80: Three Races END

CHAPTER 81:

Souvenir

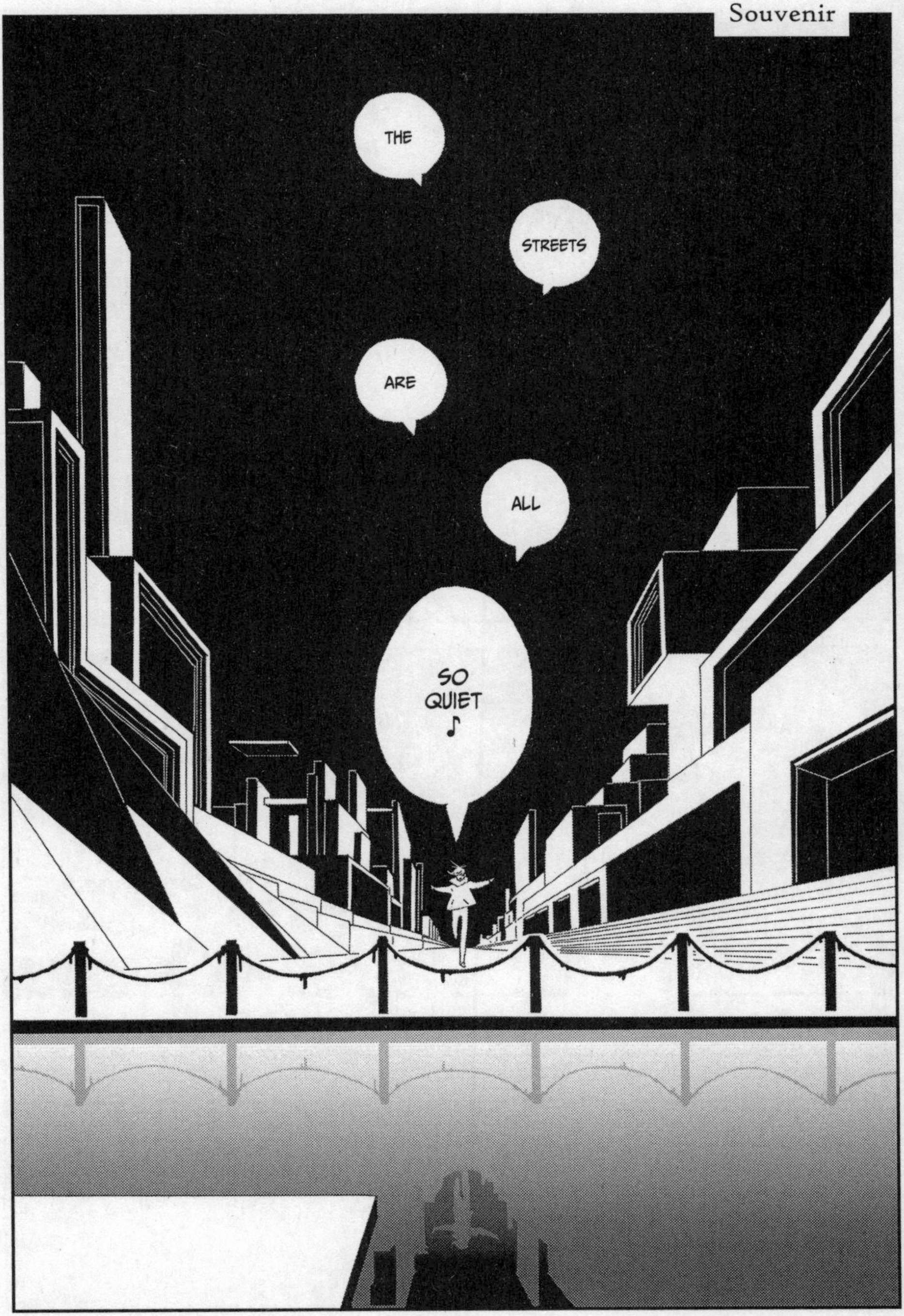
THE
STREETS
ARE
ALL
SO QUIET ♪

BE...
...LONGS TO ME ♪
HOP
THE
TOWN
WAS THAT ALWAYS THERE?

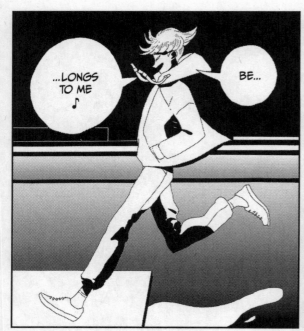

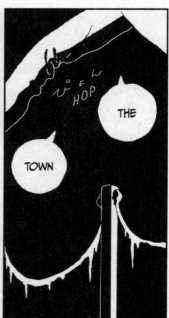

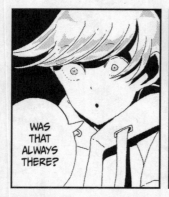

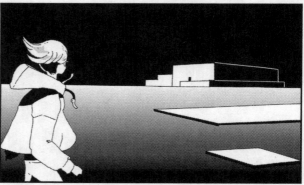

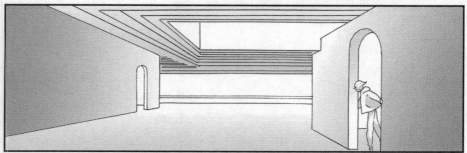

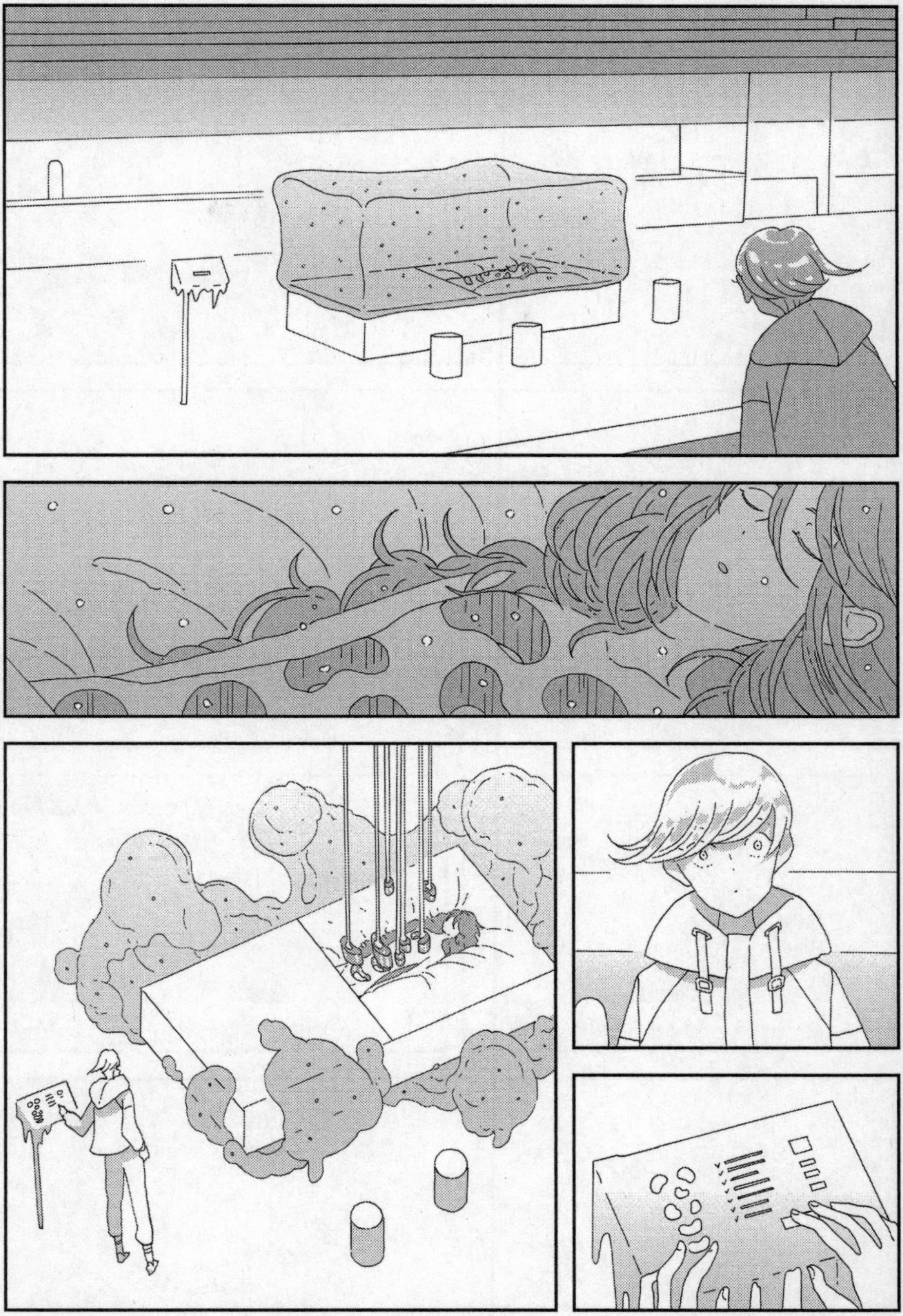

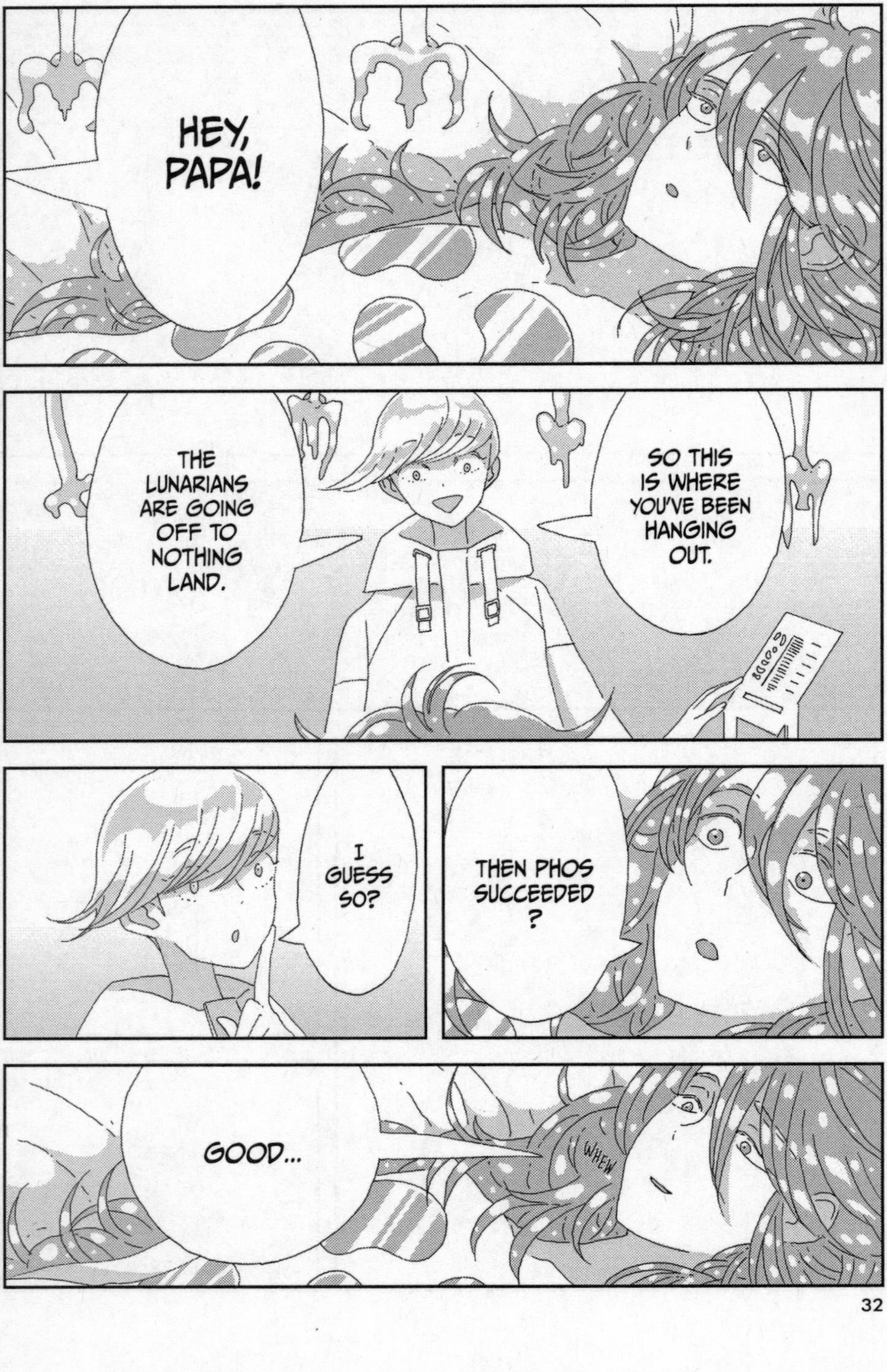
HEY, PAPA!
SO THIS IS WHERE YOU'VE BEEN HANGING OUT.
THE LUNARIANS ARE GOING OFF TO NOTHING LAND.
THEN PHOS SUCCEEDED?
I GUESS SO?
GOOD...
WHEW

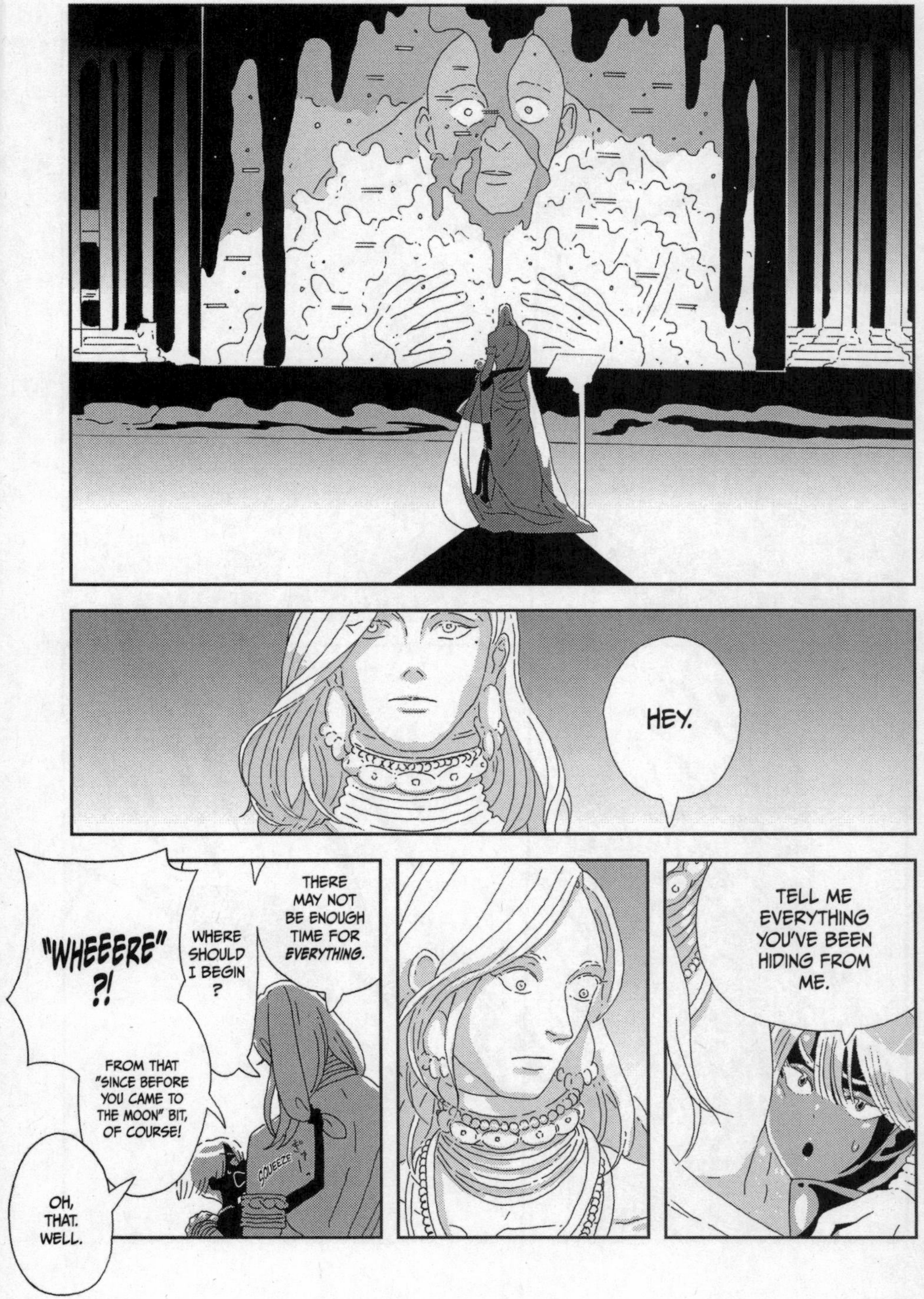
HEY.
TELL ME EVERYTHING YOU'VE BEEN HIDING FROM ME.
THERE MAY NOT BE ENOUGH TIME FOR *EVERYTHING*.
WHERE SHOULD I BEGIN?
"WHEEEERE"?!
FROM THAT "SINCE BEFORE YOU CAME TO THE MOON" BIT, OF COURSE!
SQUEEZE
OH, THAT. WELL.

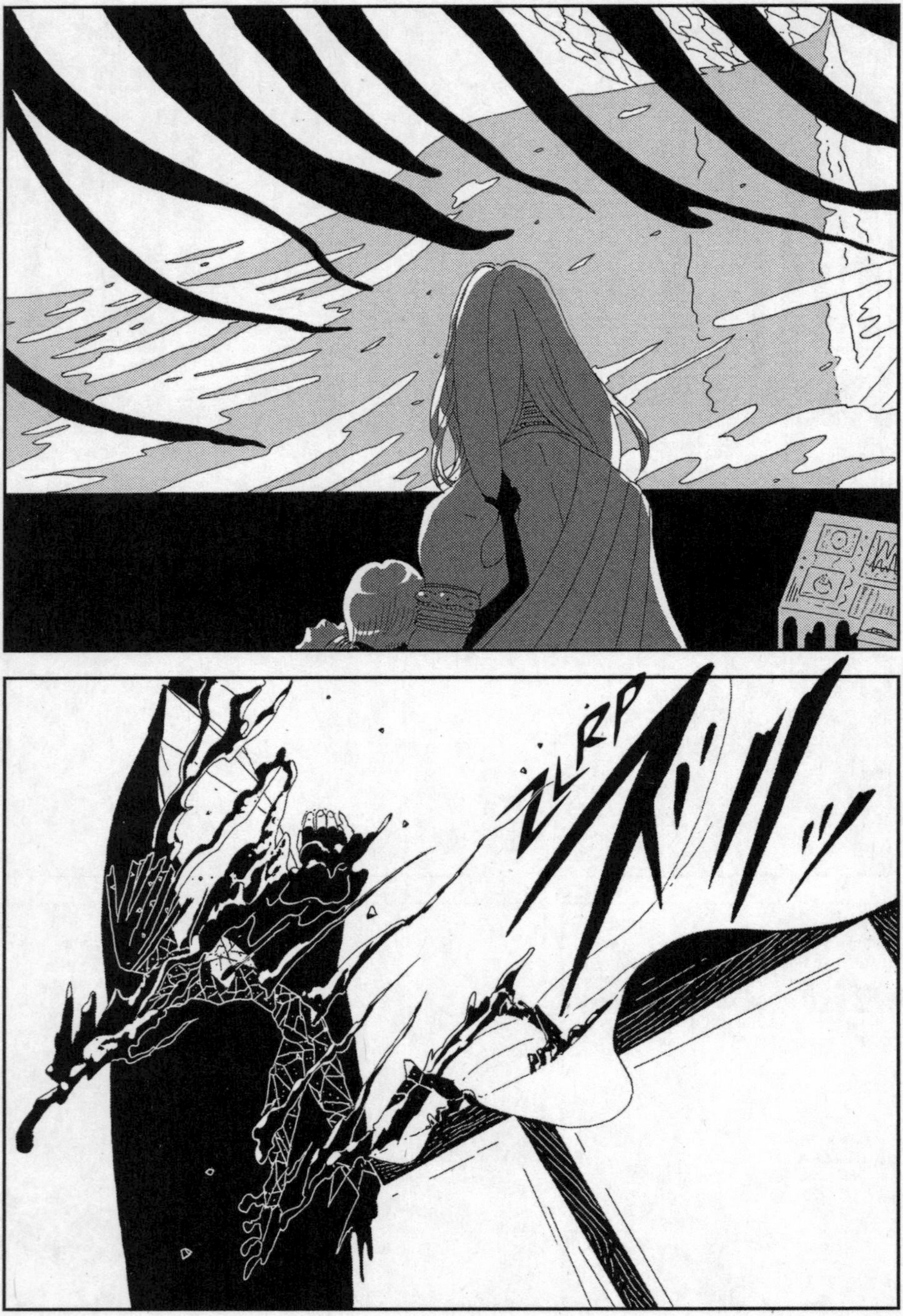
ZLRP

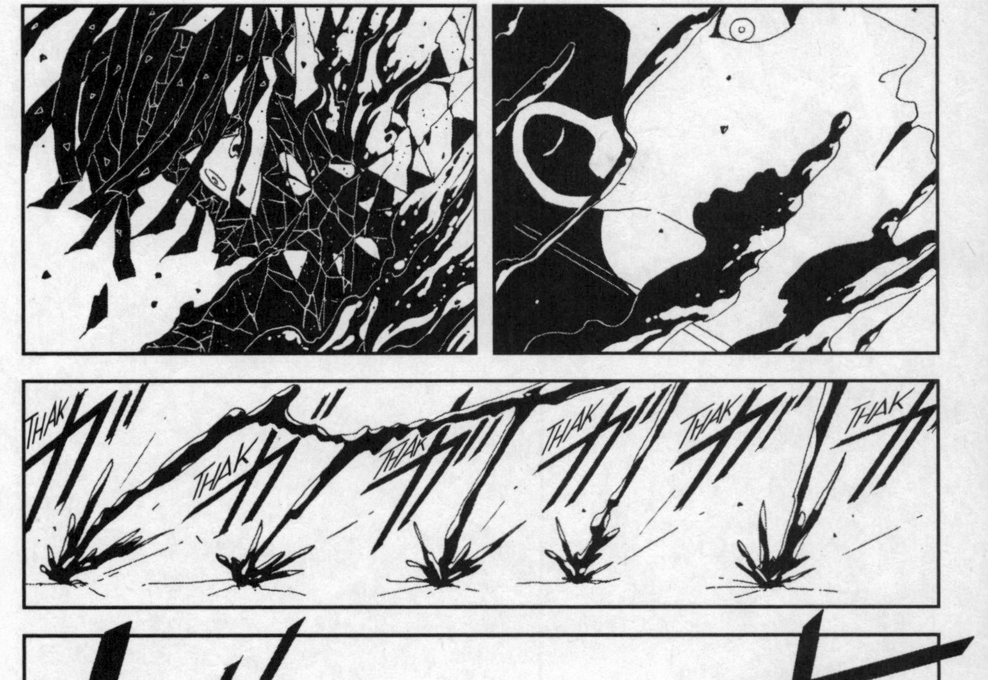
THAK
THAK
THAK
THAK
THAK
THAK
PKT

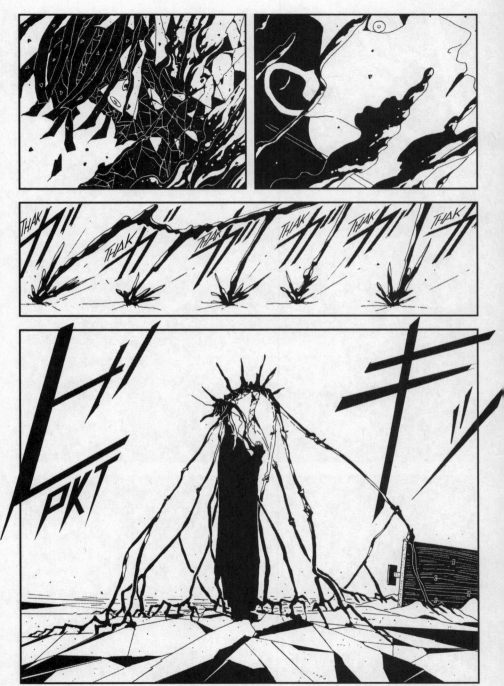

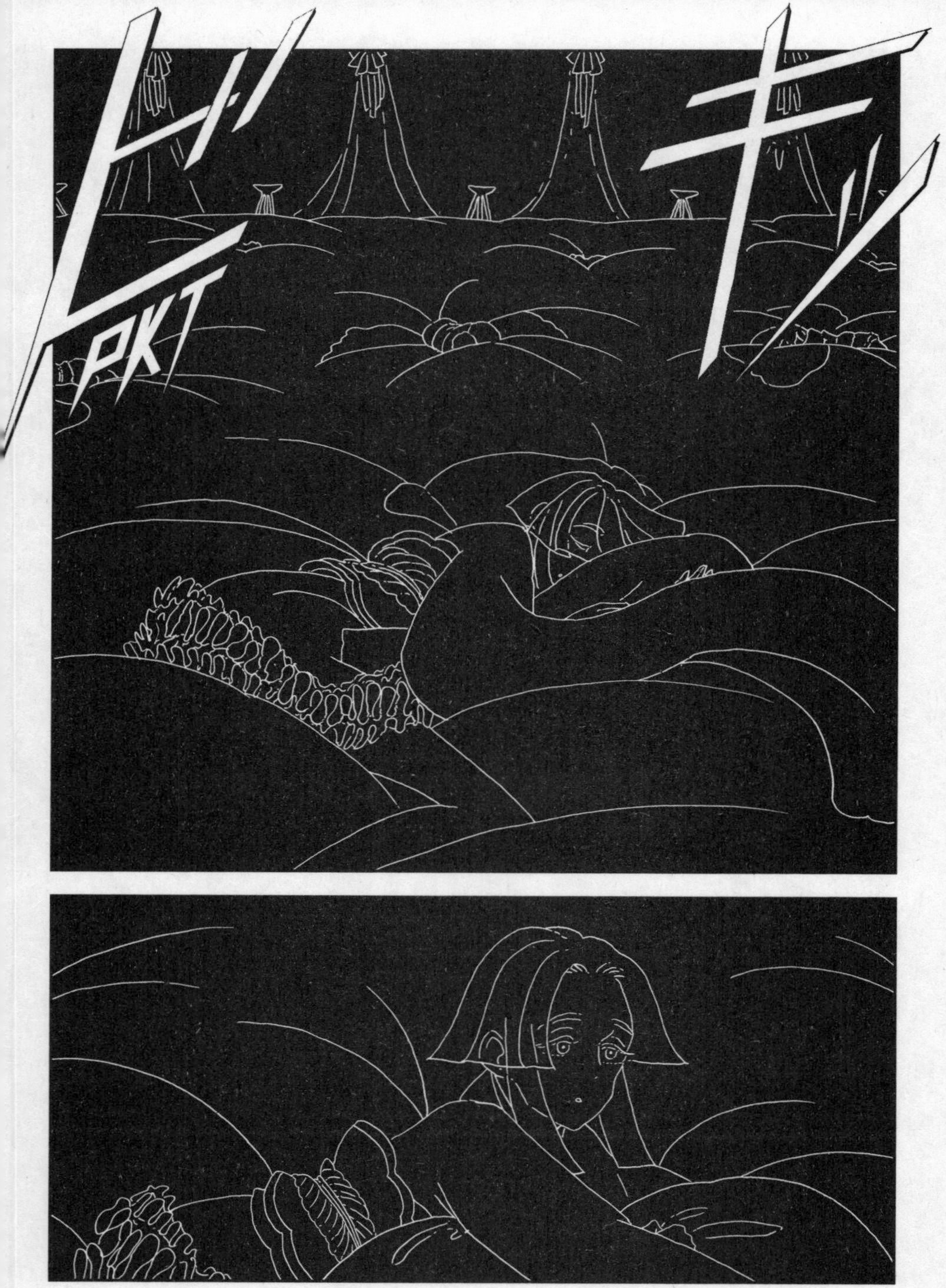
ドキッ
DKT

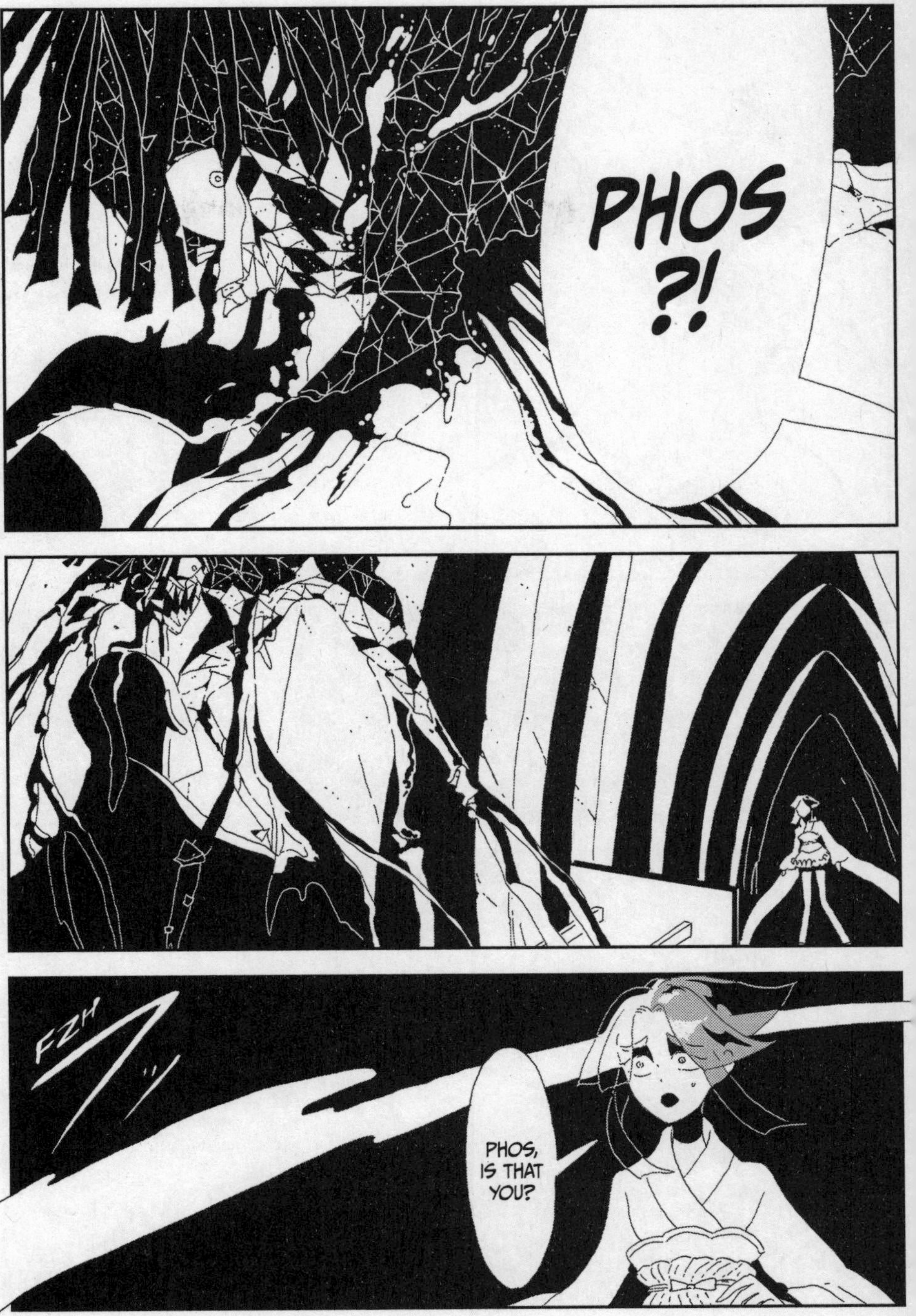
PHOS ?!
PHOS, IS THAT YOU?
FZH

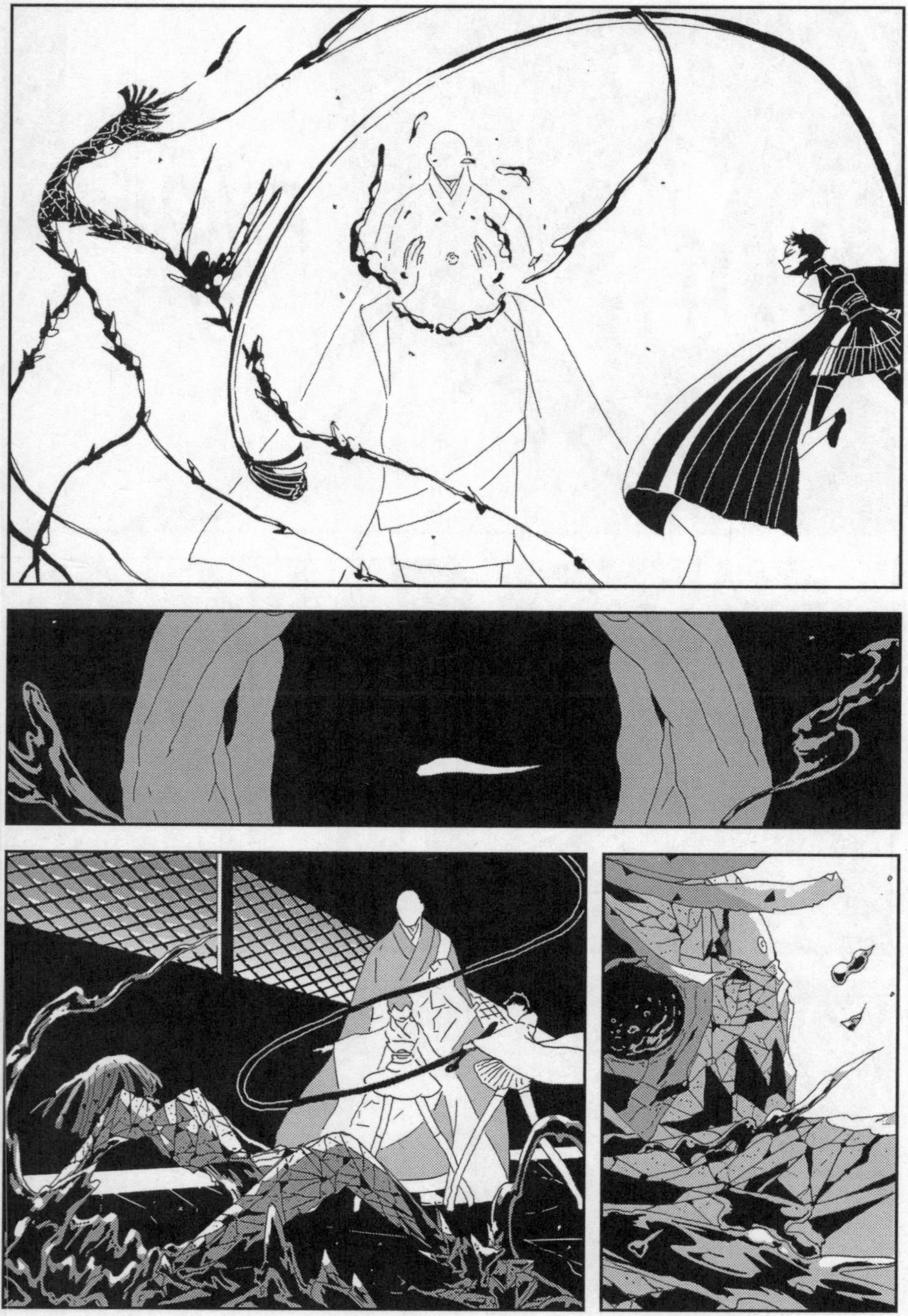

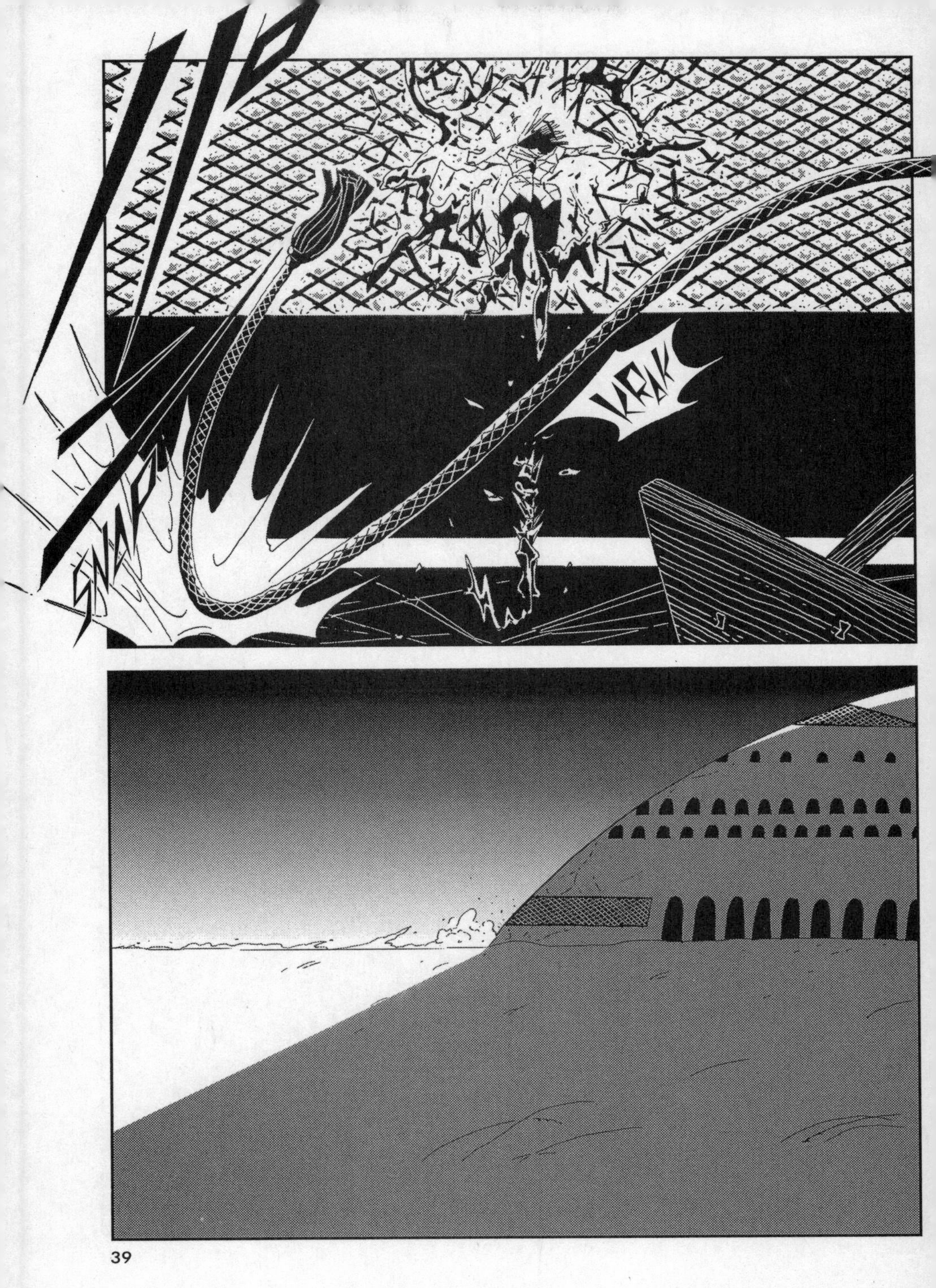
SNAP

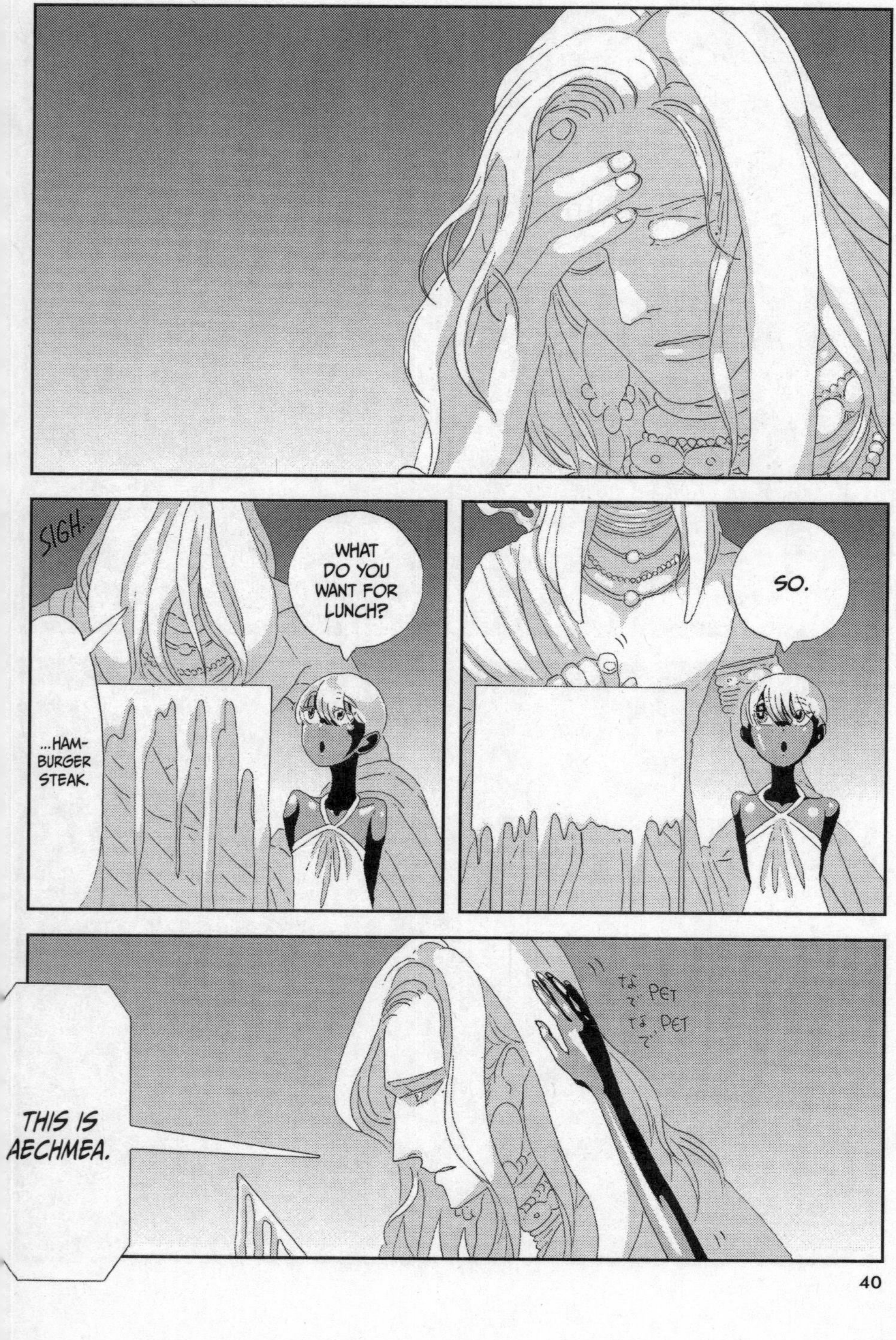
SO.
WHAT DO YOU WANT FOR LUNCH?
SIGH...
...HAM-BURGER STEAK.
PET
PET
THIS IS AECHMEA.

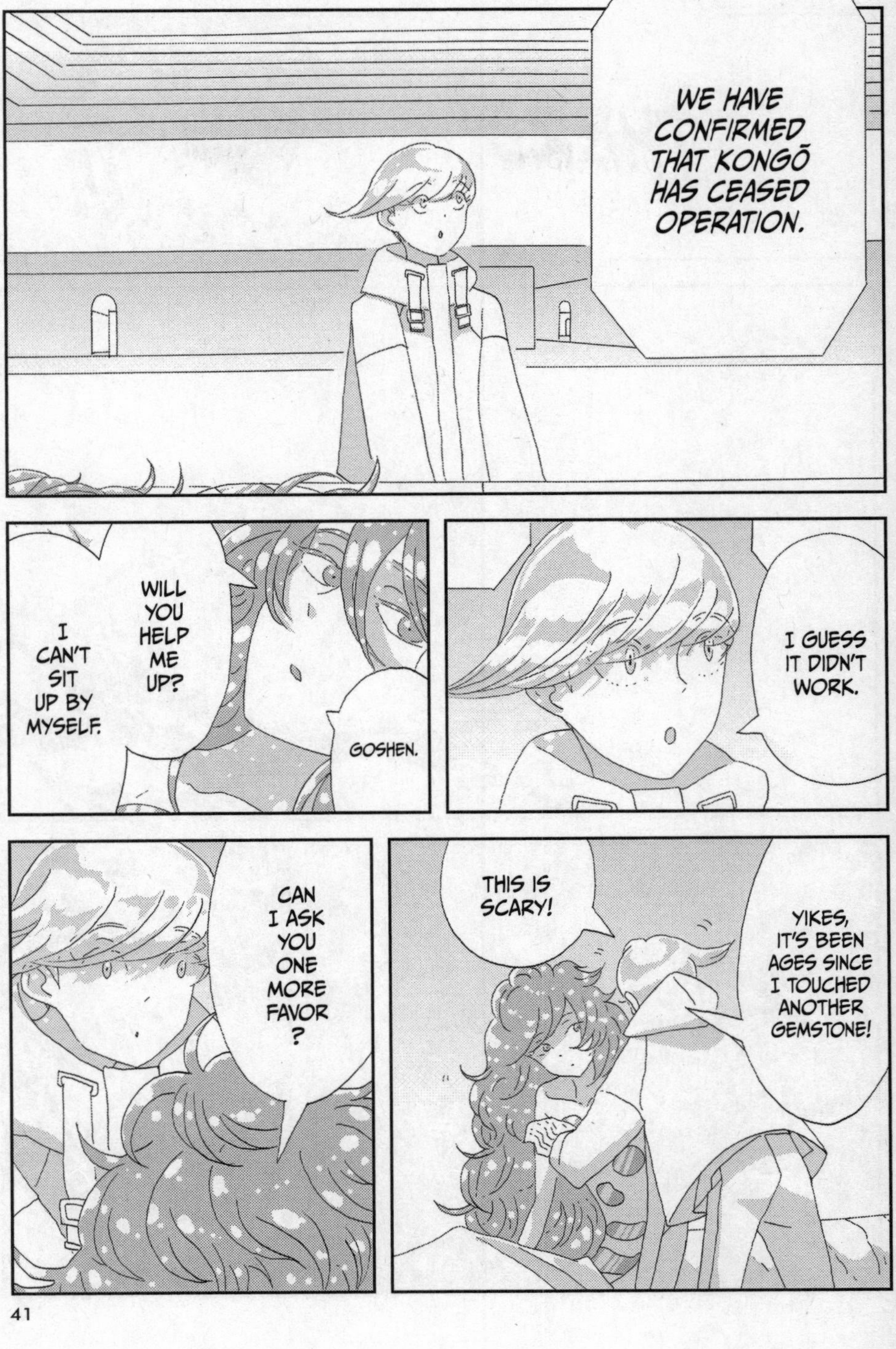
WE HAVE CONFIRMED THAT KONGŌ HAS CEASED OPERATION.
I GUESS IT DIDN'T WORK.
WILL YOU HELP ME UP?
I CAN'T SIT UP BY MYSELF.
GOSHEN.
YIKES, IT'S BEEN AGES SINCE I TOUCHED ANOTHER GEMSTONE!
THIS IS SCARY!
CAN I ASK YOU ONE MORE FAVOR?

THERE!

TWITCH

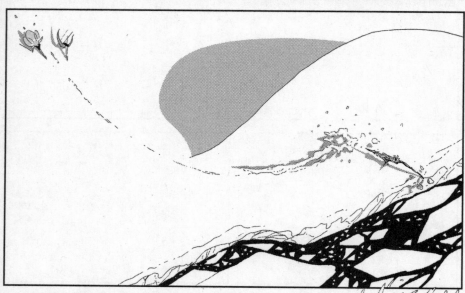

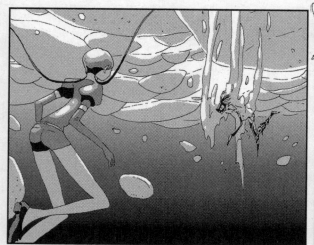

SPLASH

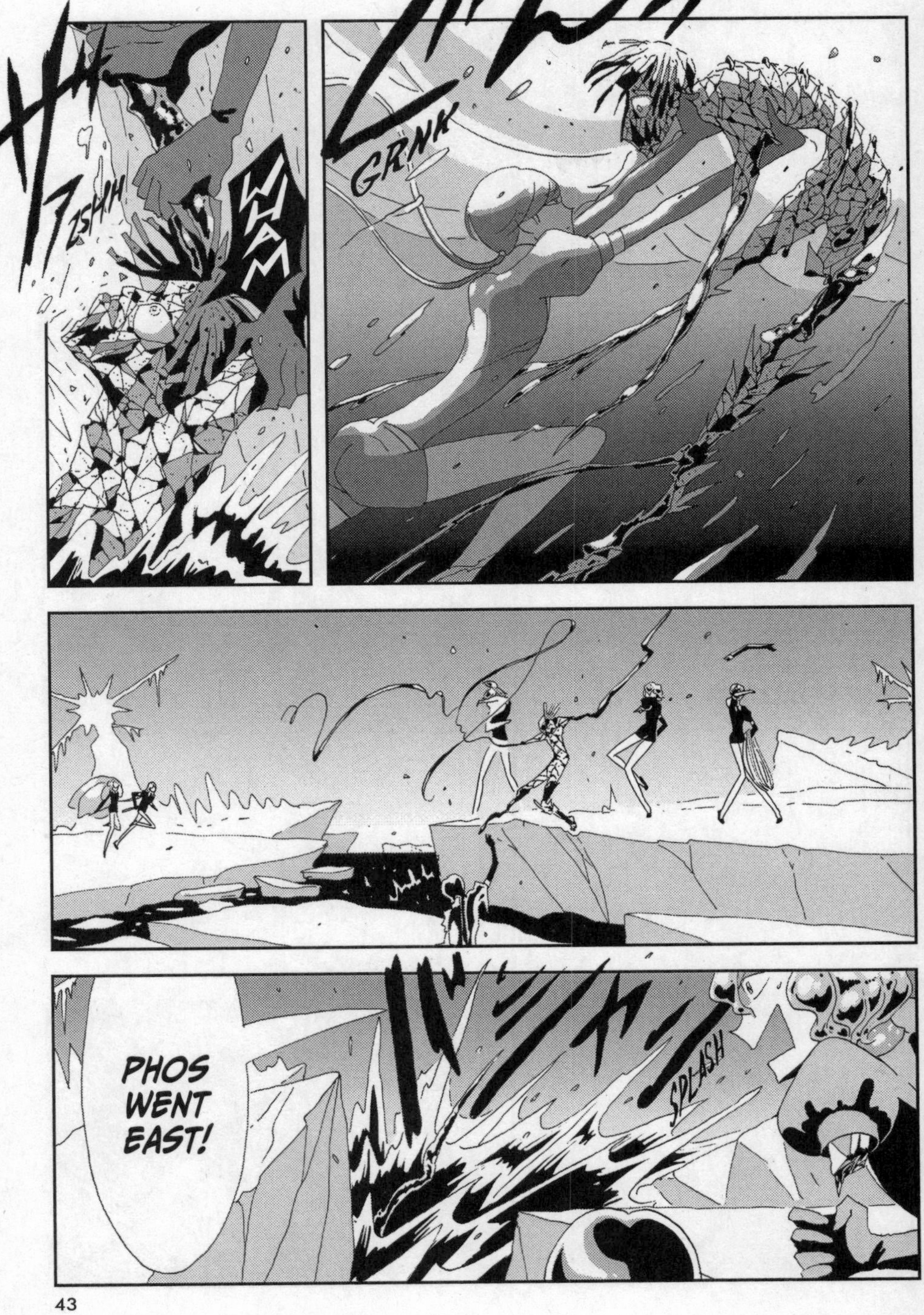
ZSHH
WHAM
GRNK
SPLASH
PHOS WENT EAST!

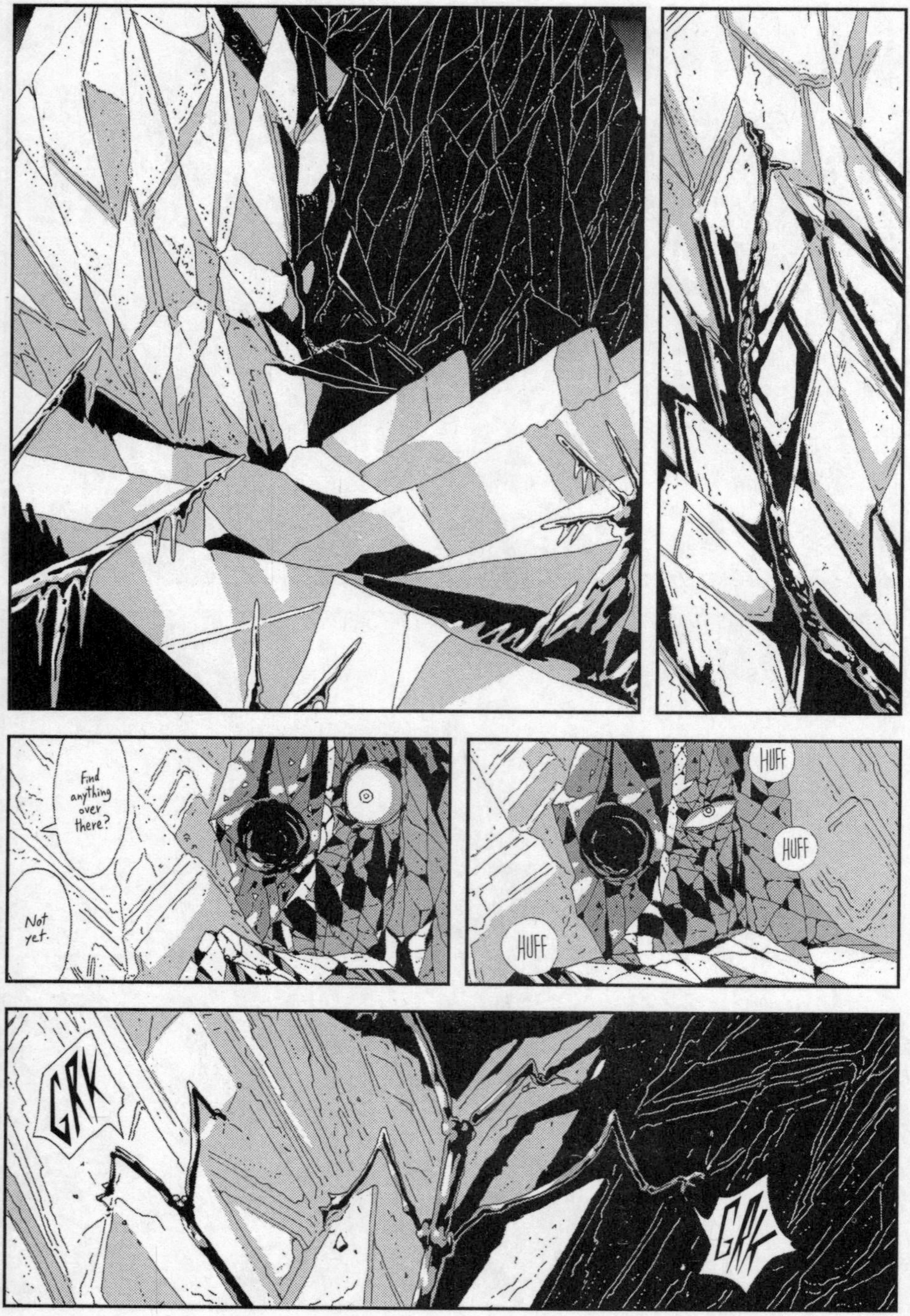

Find anything over there?
Not yet.
HUFF
HUFF
HUFF
GRK
GRK

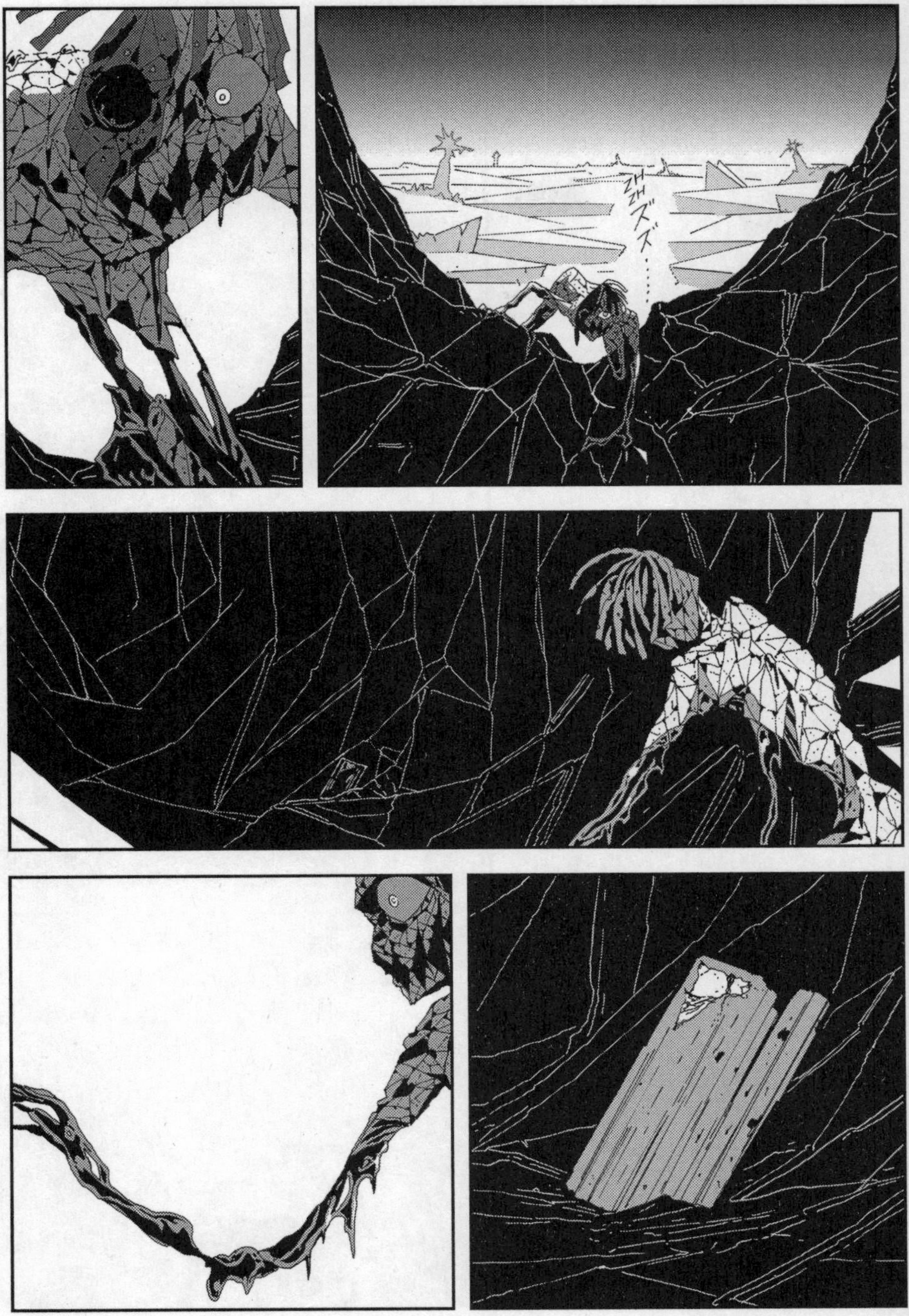
ズズ……

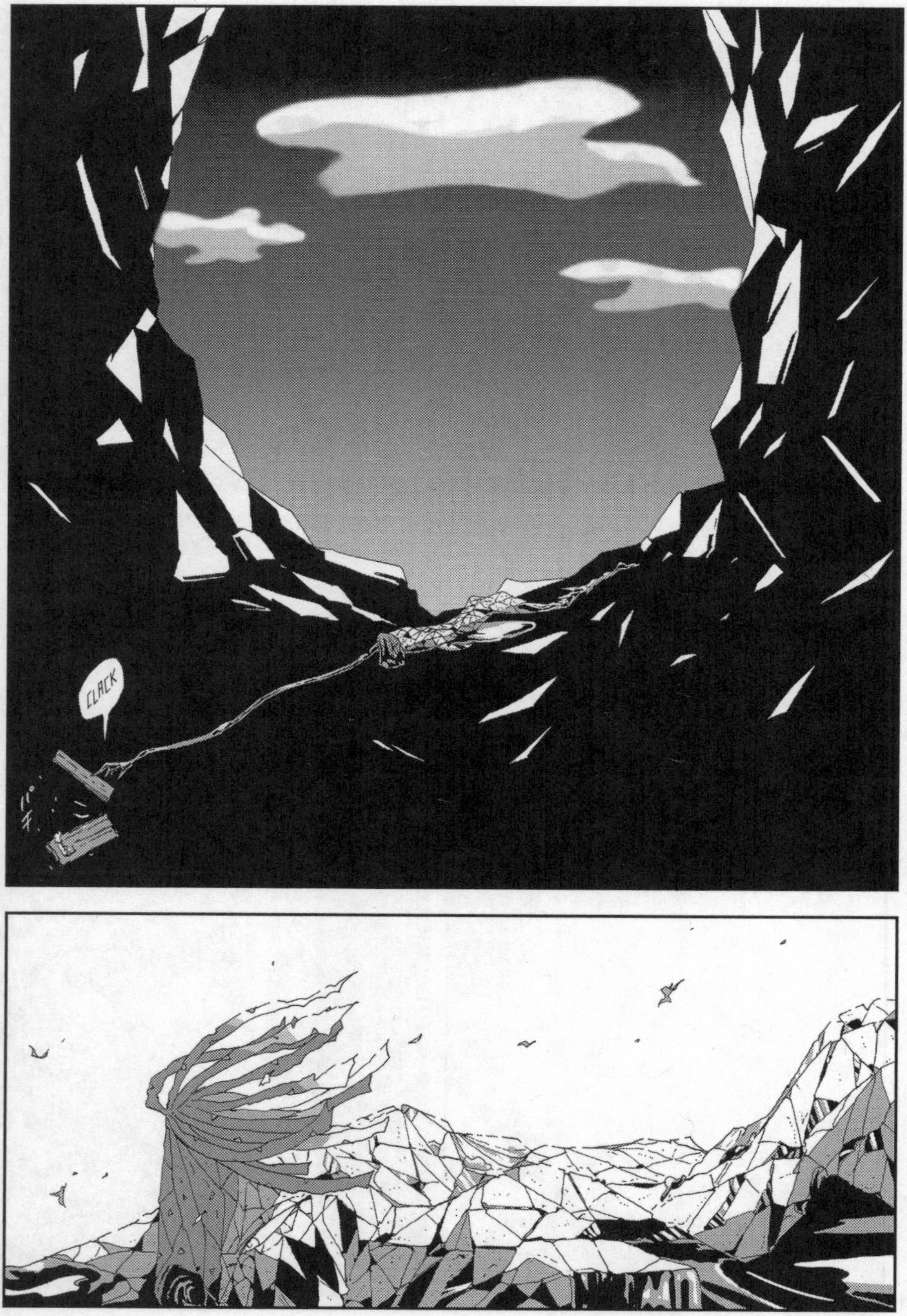
CLACK

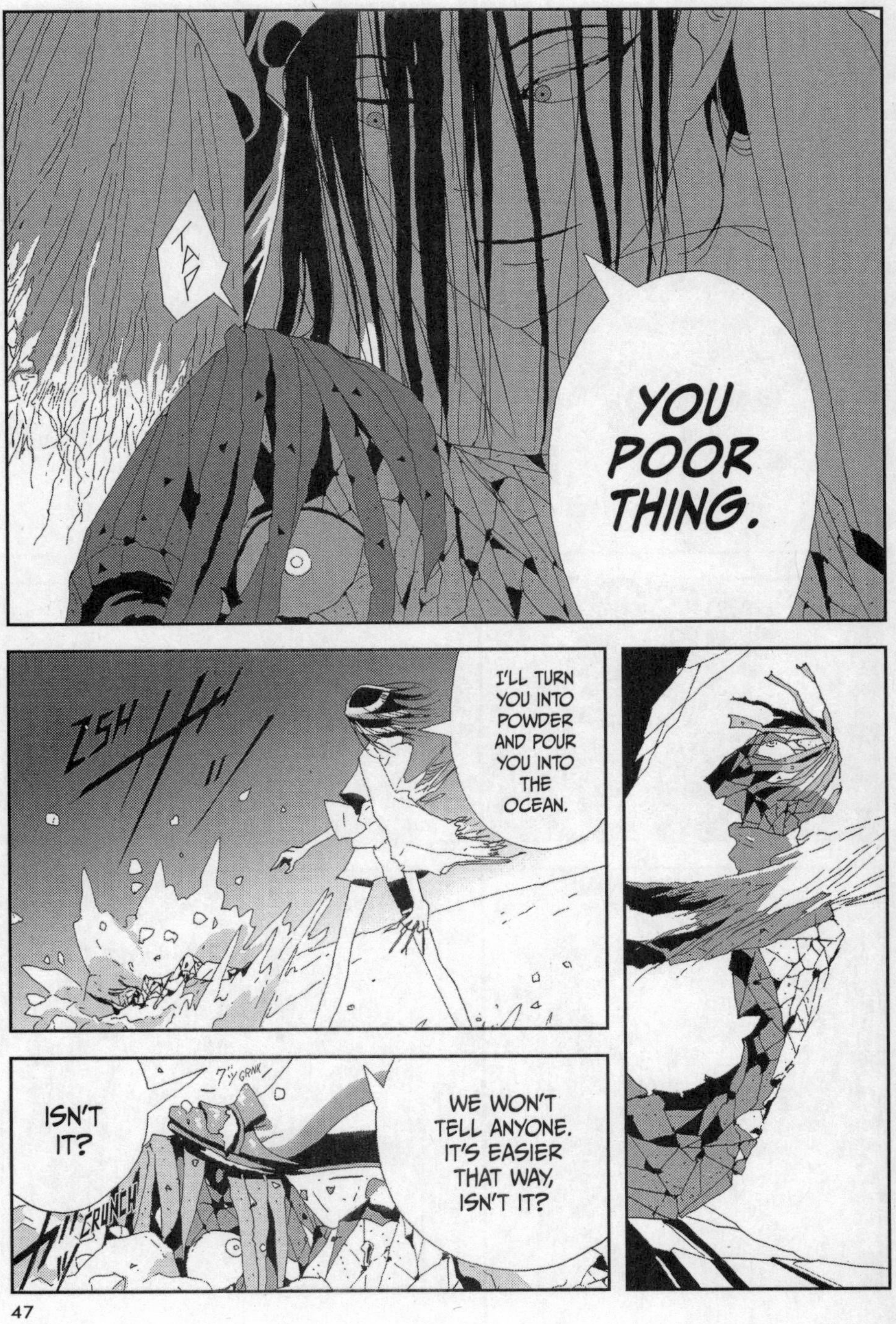
TAP
YOU POOR THING.
I'LL TURN YOU INTO POWDER AND POUR YOU INTO THE OCEAN.
ISH
WE WON'T TELL ANYONE. IT'S EASIER THAT WAY, ISN'T IT?
ISN'T IT?
GRNK
CRUNCH

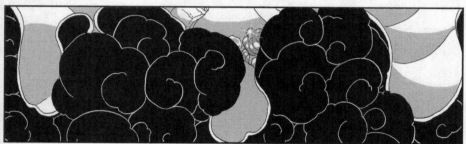

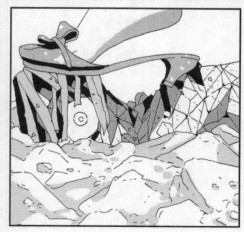

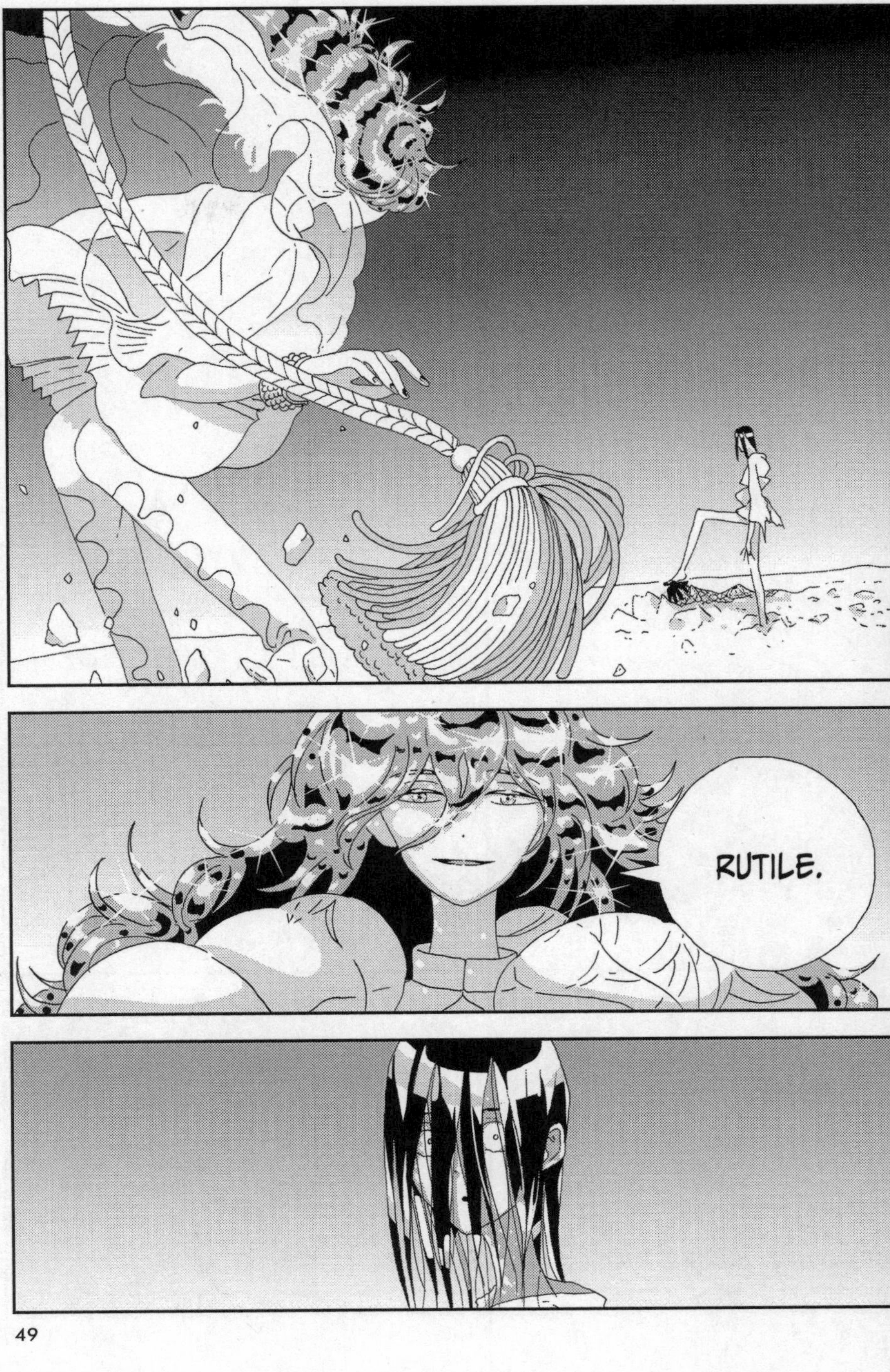
RUTILE.

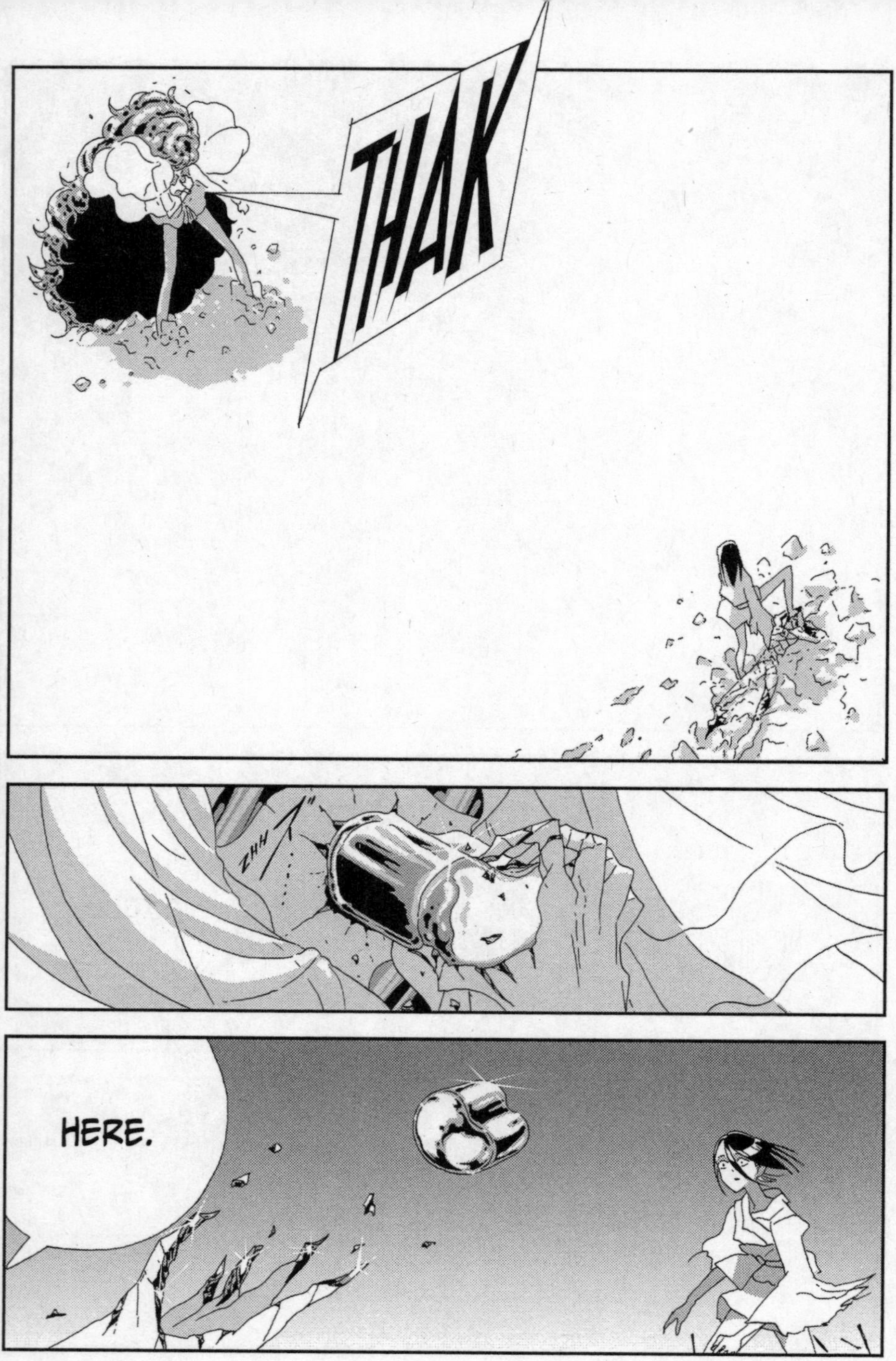
THAK
ZHH
HERE.

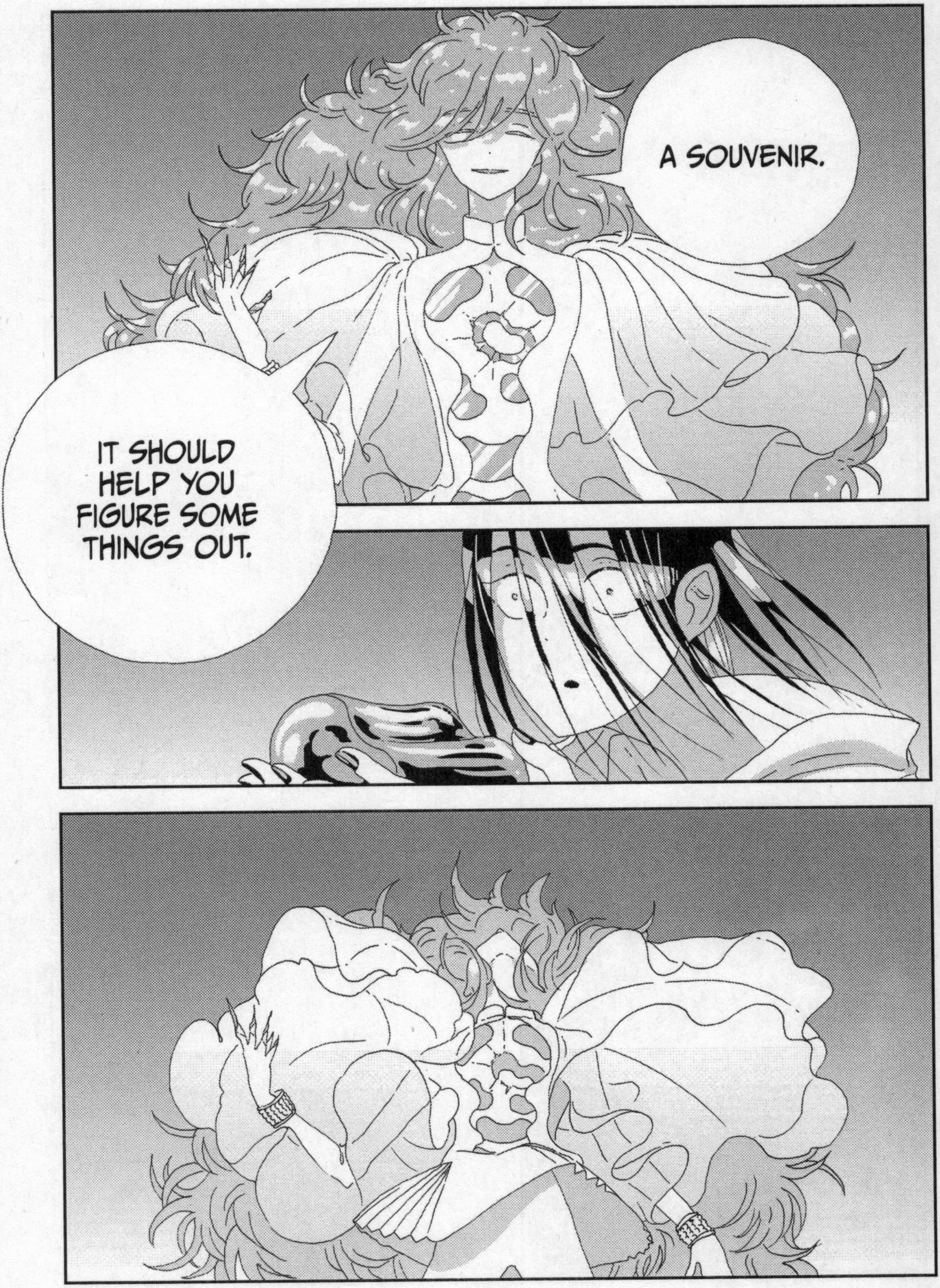
A SOUVENIR.
IT SHOULD HELP YOU FIGURE SOME THINGS OUT.

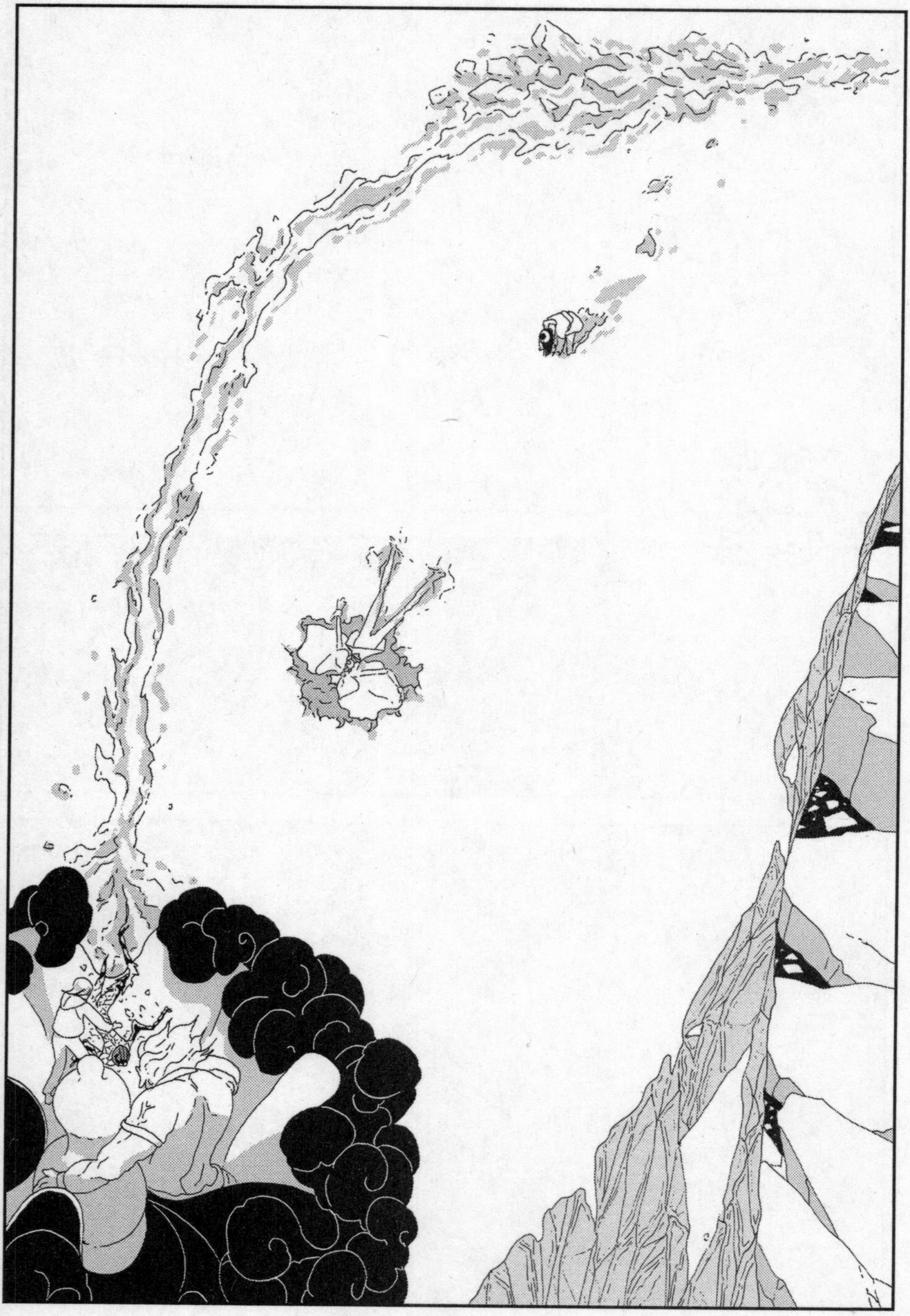

CHAPTER 82:

Outcome

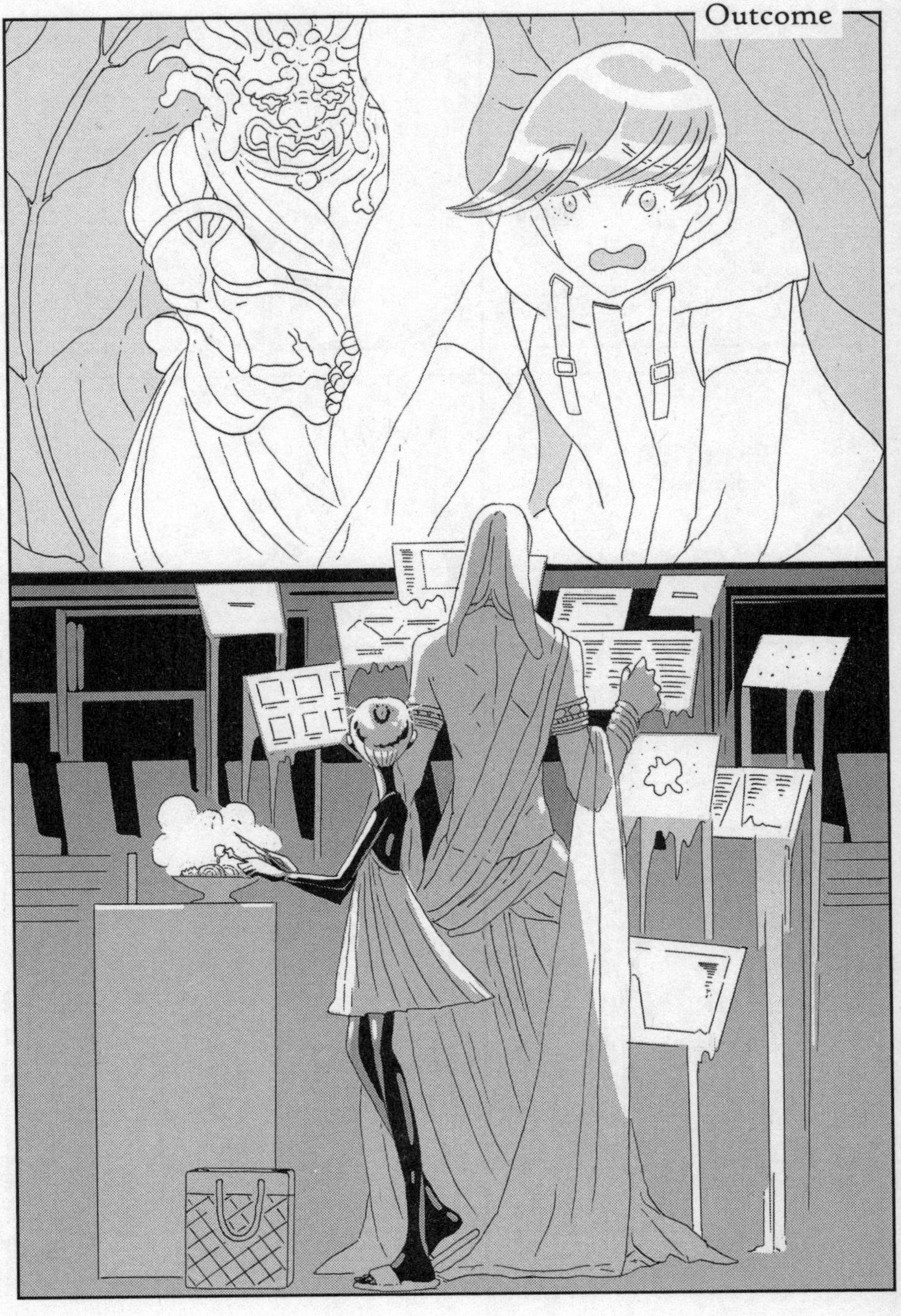

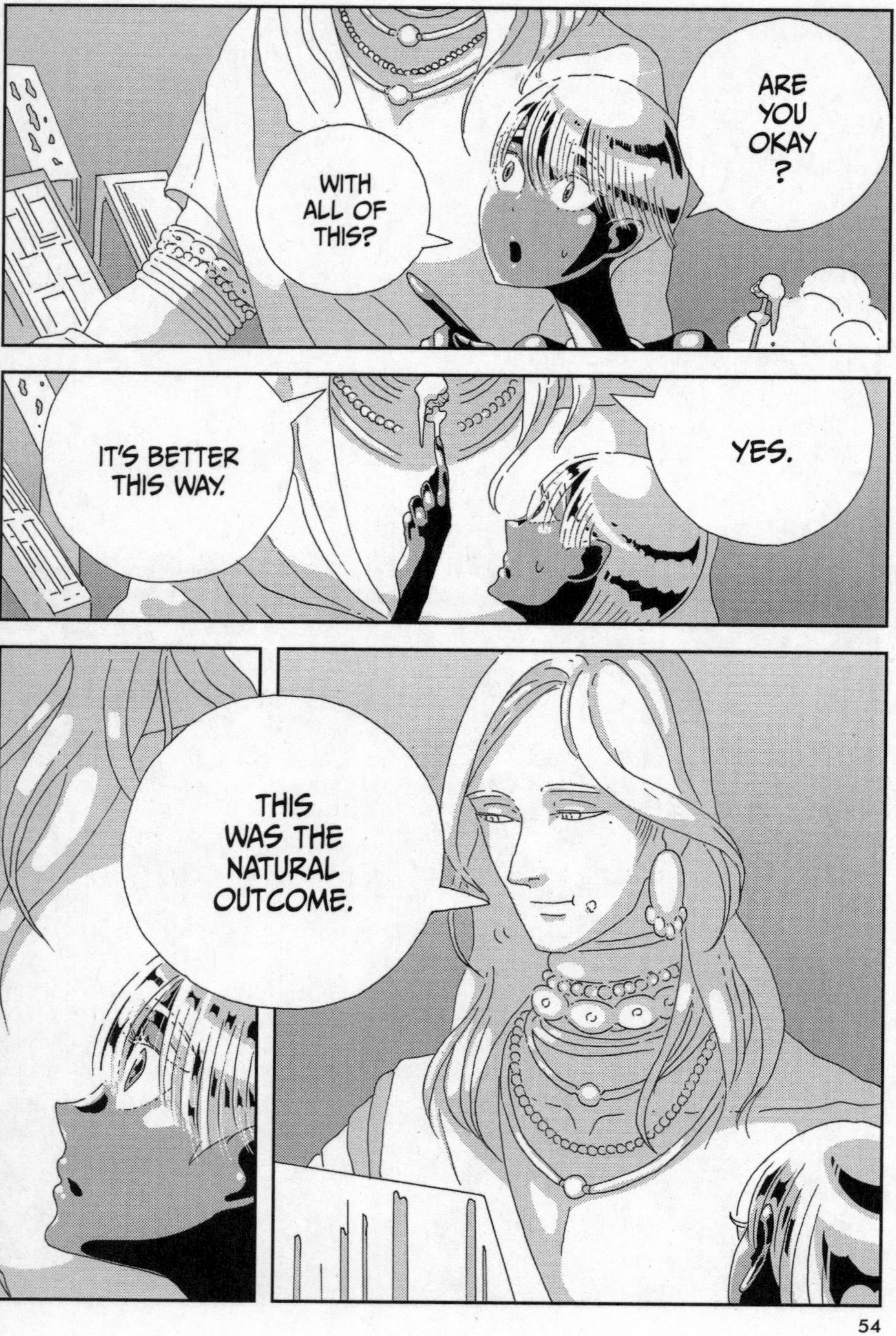
ARE YOU OKAY?
WITH ALL OF THIS?
YES.
IT'S BETTER THIS WAY.
THIS WAS THE NATURAL OUTCOME.

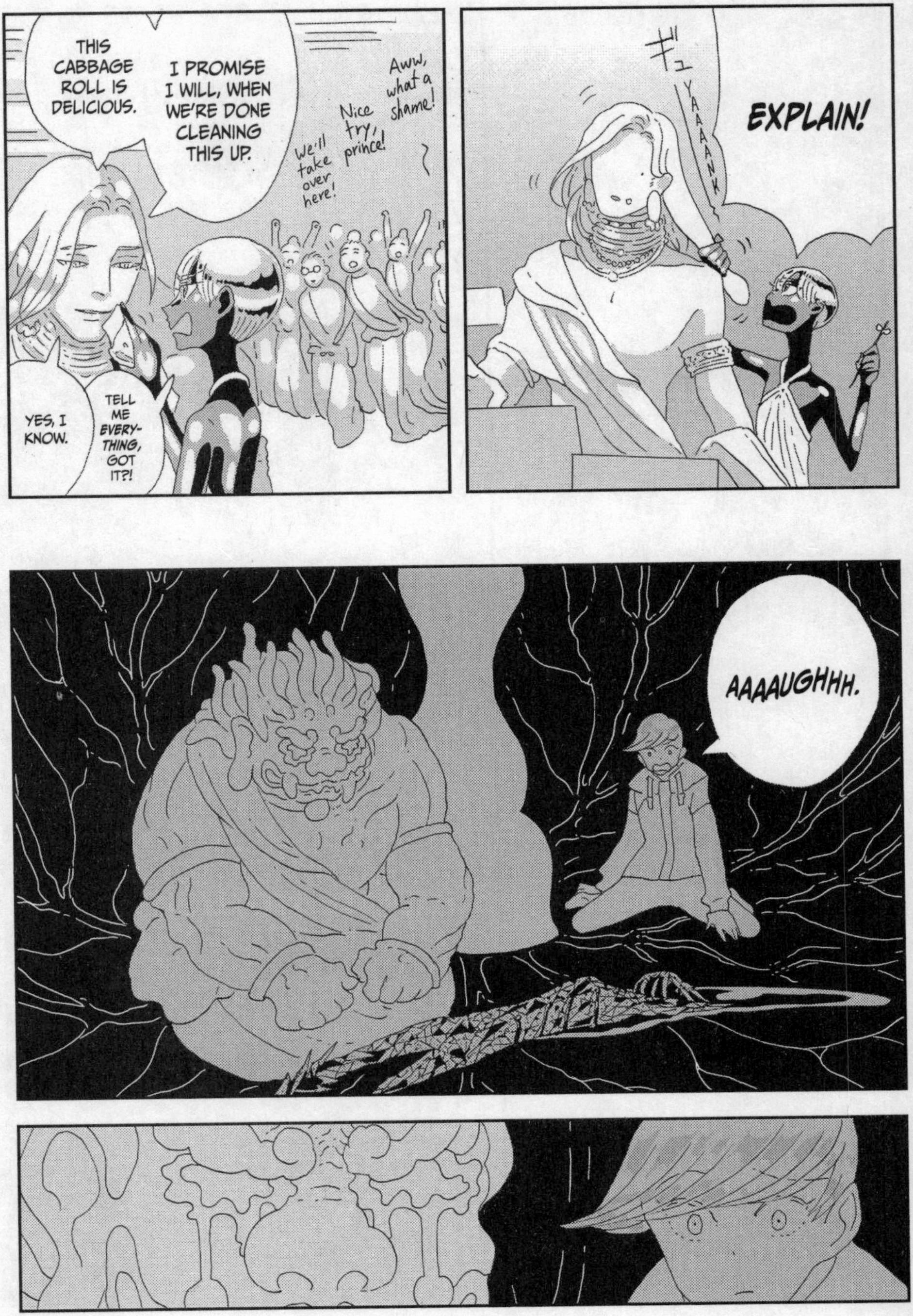
EXPLAIN!
ギュ
YAAAAANK
I PROMISE I WILL, WHEN WE'RE DONE CLEANING THIS UP.
THIS CABBAGE ROLL IS DELICIOUS.
Aww, what a shame!
Nice try, prince!
We'll take over here!
TELL ME EVERYTHING, GOT IT?!
YES, I KNOW.
AAAAUGHHH.

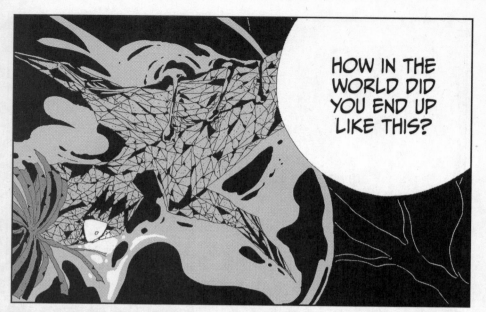

HOW IN THE WORLD DID YOU END UP LIKE THIS?

NOPE.

OH.

SENIOR PHOS? CAN YOU MOVE?

CLACK CLACK

POOF

IT'S SO GOOD TO SEE YOU!

NOBLE GOSHEN!

N—

N—

N—

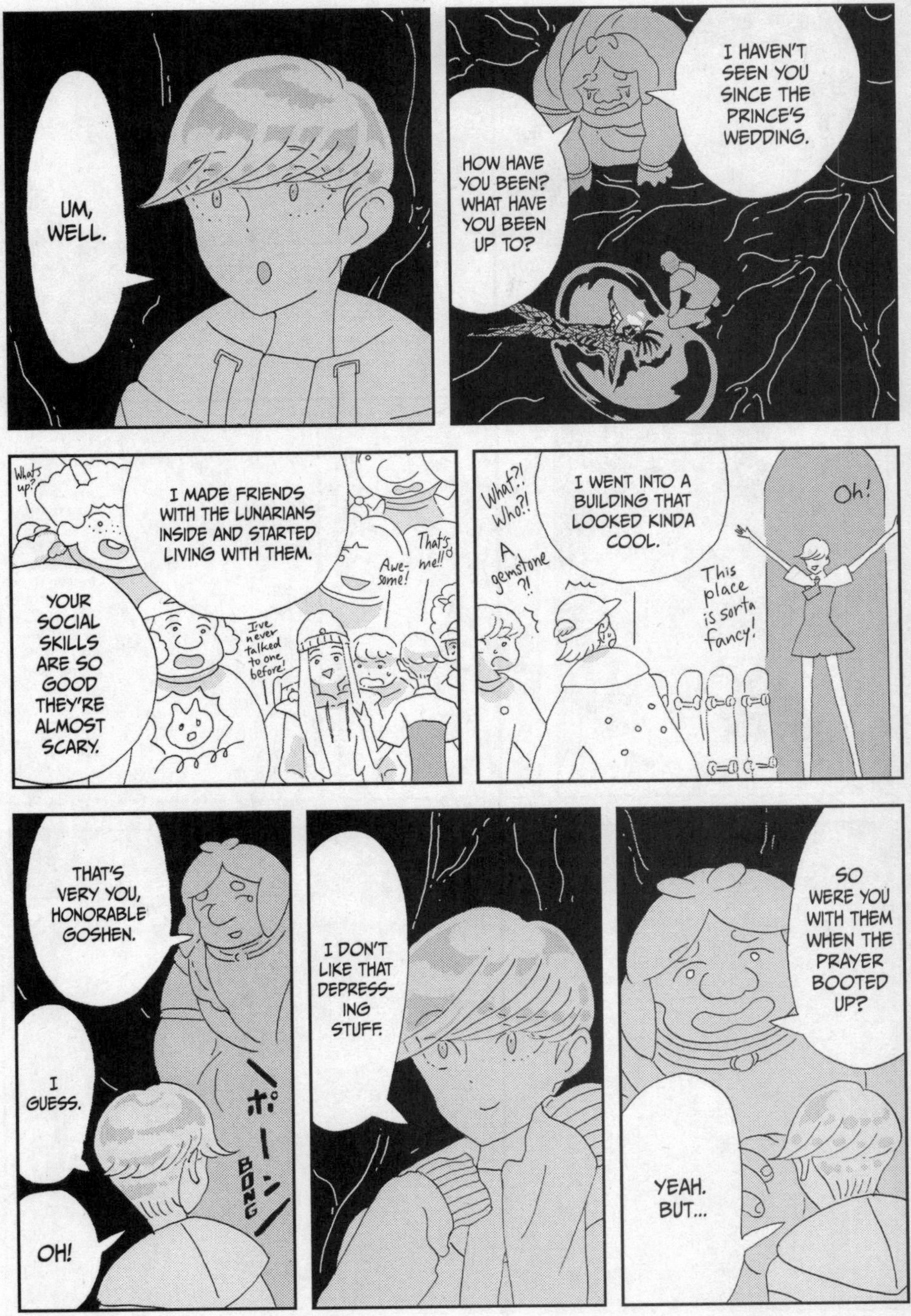
I HAVEN'T SEEN YOU SINCE THE PRINCE'S WEDDING.
HOW HAVE YOU BEEN? WHAT HAVE YOU BEEN UP TO?
UM, WELL.
I WENT INTO A BUILDING THAT LOOKED KINDA COOL.
Oh!
This place is sorta fancy!
What?! Who?!
A gemstone ?!
I MADE FRIENDS WITH THE LUNARIANS INSIDE AND STARTED LIVING WITH THEM.
That's me!!
Awe-some!
I've never talked to one before!
What's up?
YOUR SOCIAL SKILLS ARE SO GOOD THEY'RE ALMOST SCARY.
SO WERE YOU WITH THEM WHEN THE PRAYER BOOTED UP?
YEAH. BUT...
I DON'T LIKE THAT DEPRESS-ING STUFF.
THAT'S VERY YOU, HONORABLE GOSHEN.
I GUESS.
ポーン
BONG
OH!

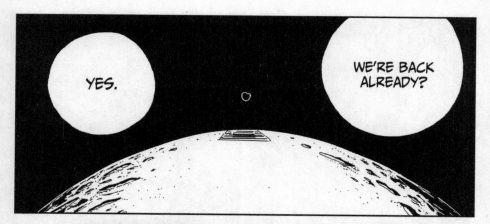

WE'RE BACK ALREADY?
YES.
I KNOW WE HAD TO RESCUE GREAT PHOS, BUT WE TOOK THE SHIP WITHOUT PERMISSION *AND* LEFT THE VENERABLE PADPARADSCHA ON EARTH.
WHAT WILL PRINCE AECHMEA SAY ...?
Yo, Cicada! Help us out here!
WHAT DO YOU *THINK* PRINCE AECHMEA WILL SAY?
I DON'T KNOW.

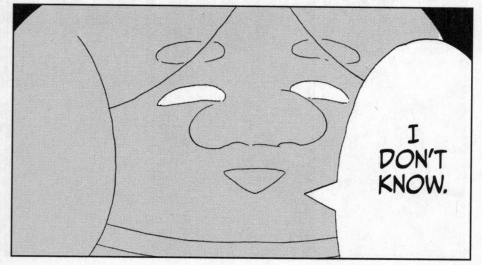

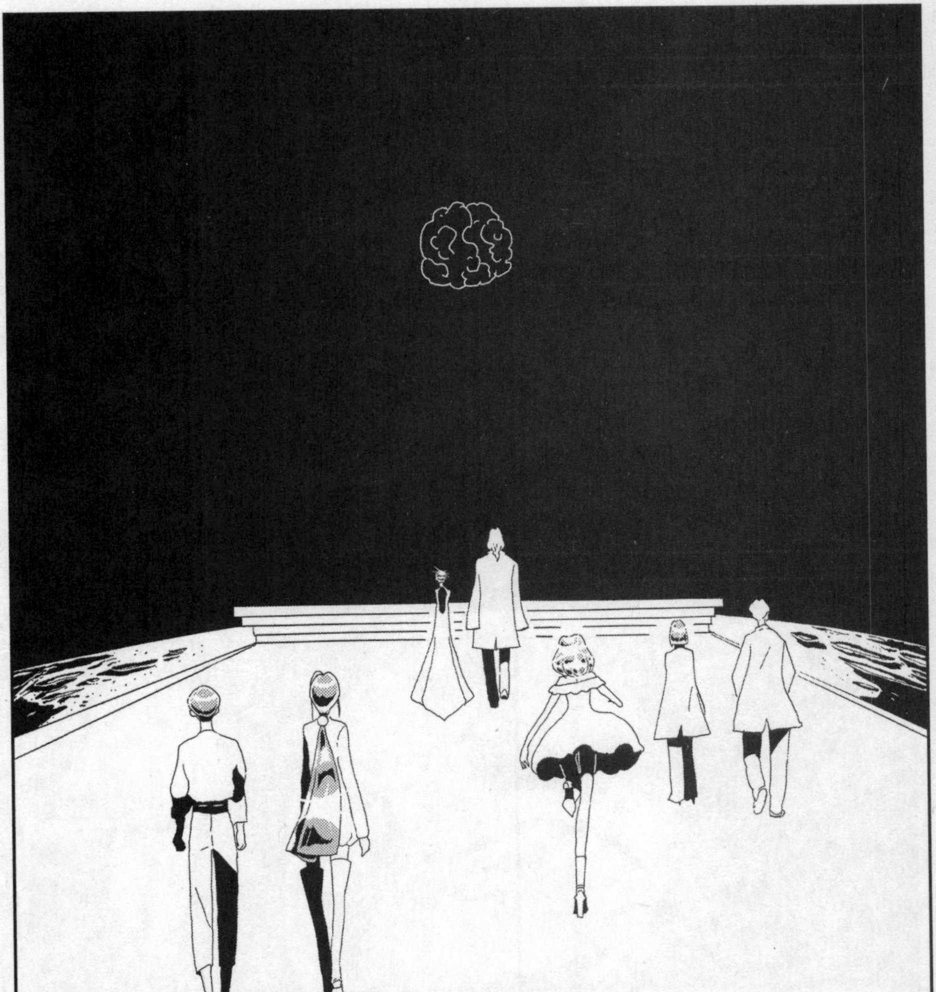

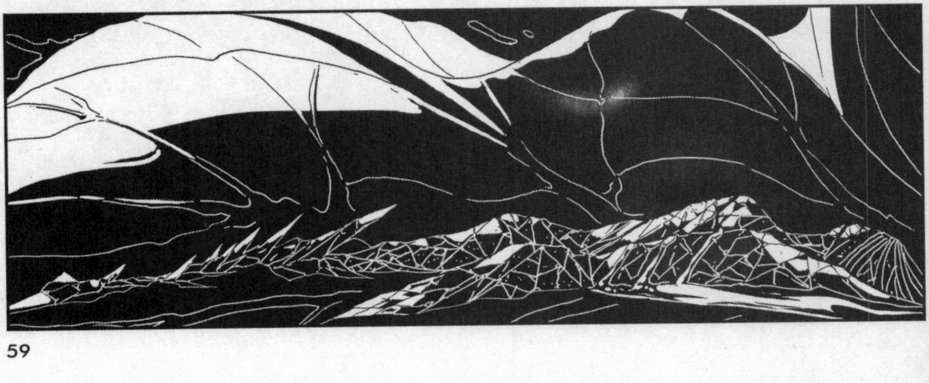

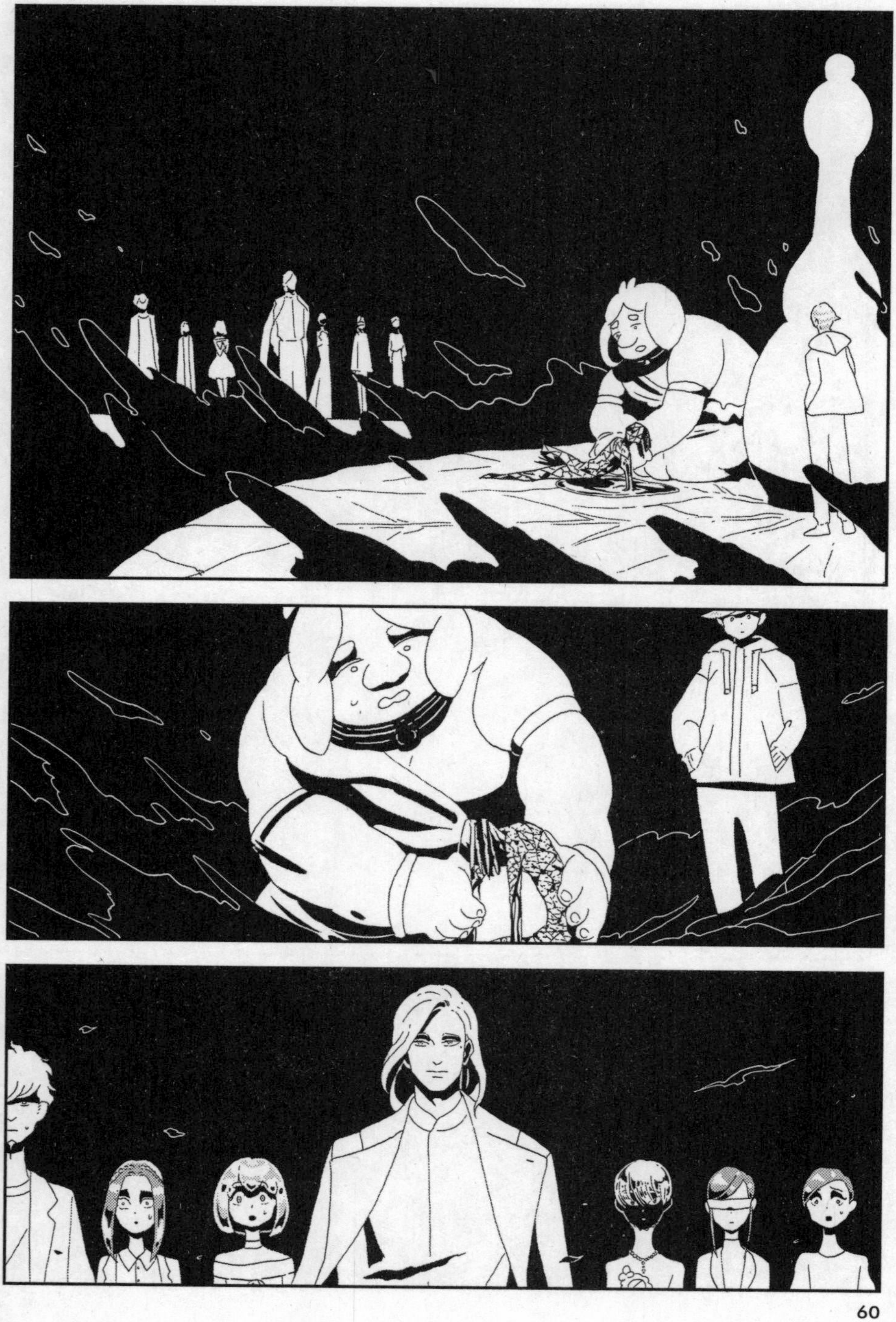

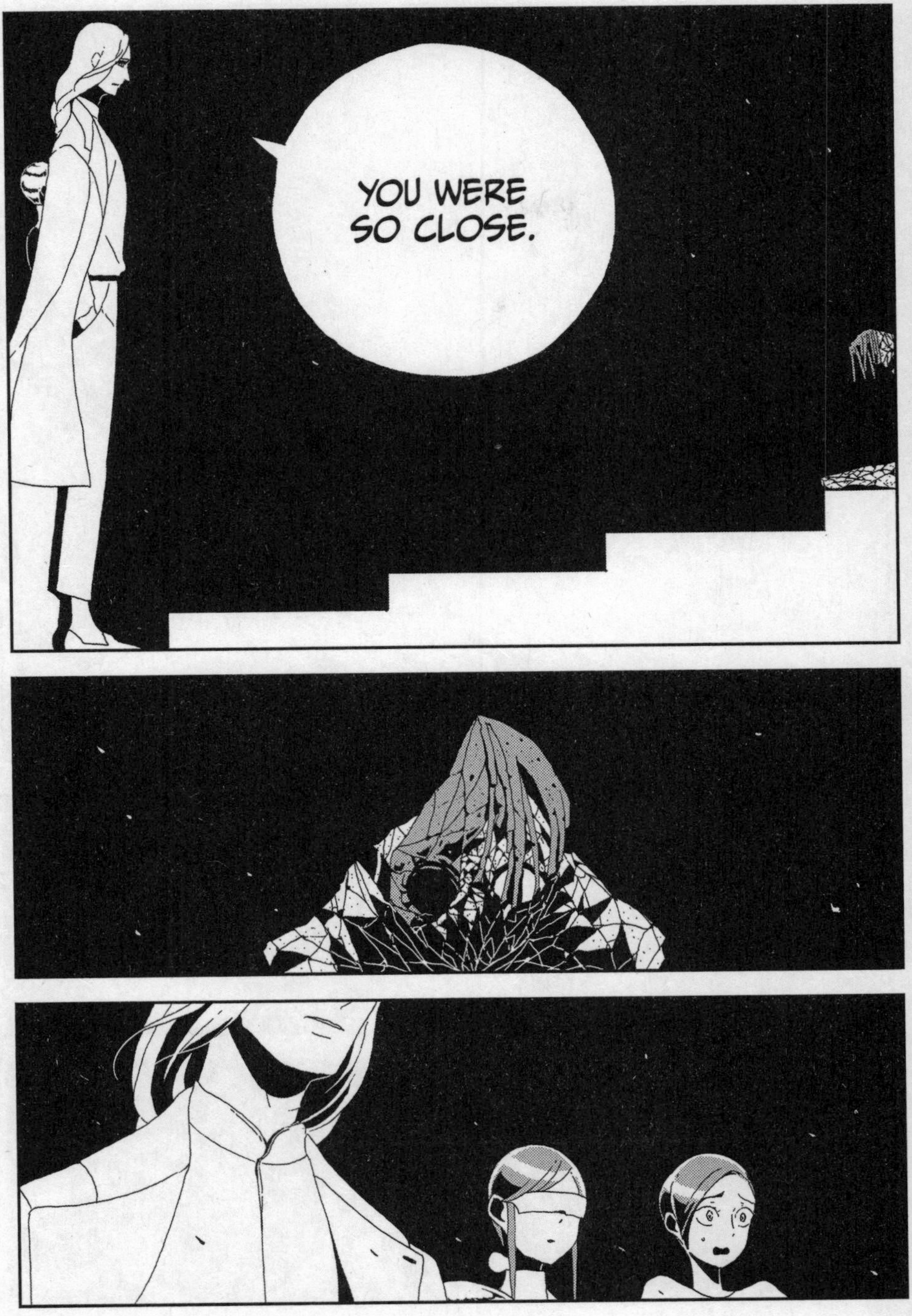
YOU WERE
SO CLOSE.

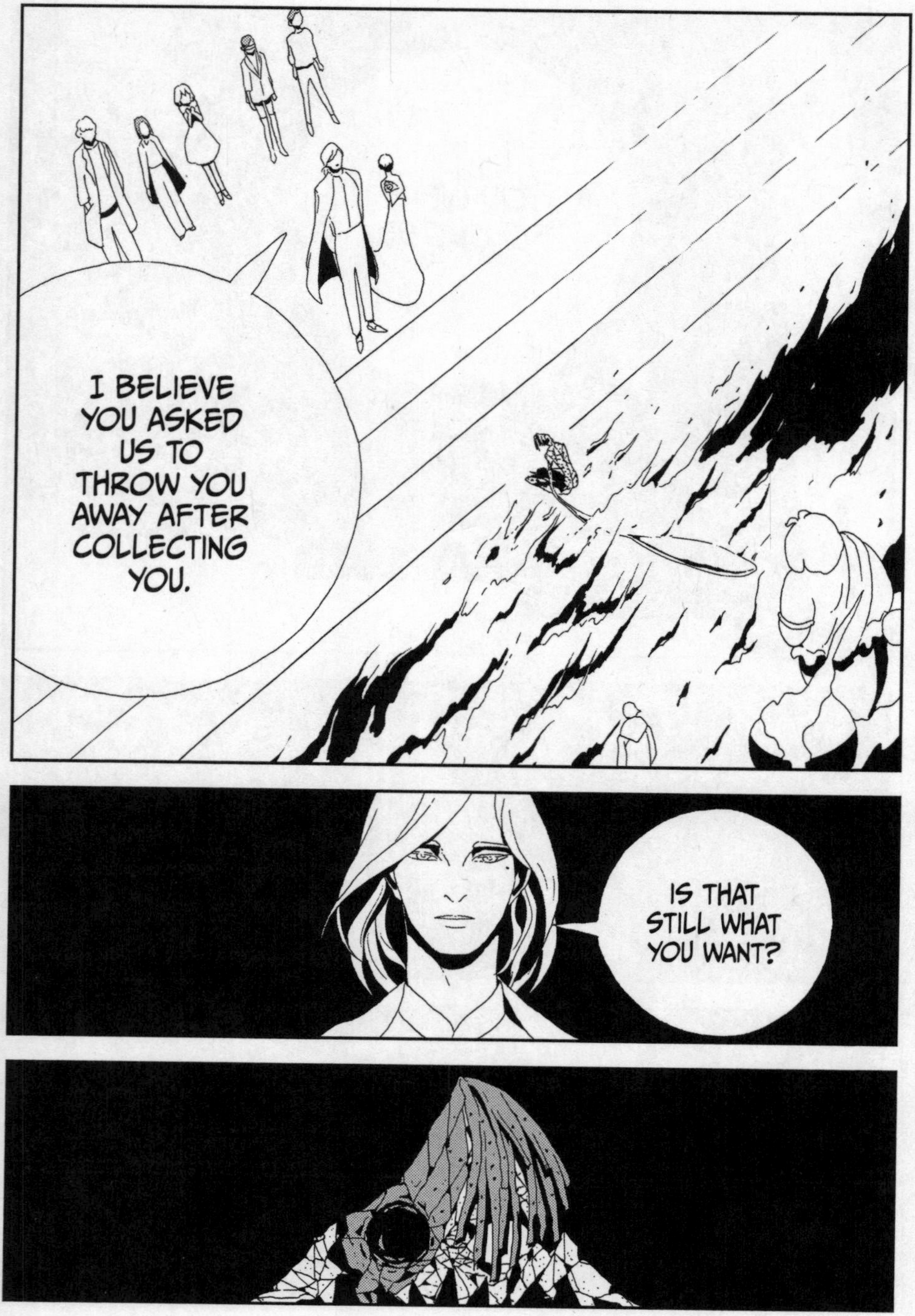
I BELIEVE YOU ASKED US TO THROW YOU AWAY AFTER COLLECTING YOU.
IS THAT STILL WHAT YOU WANT?

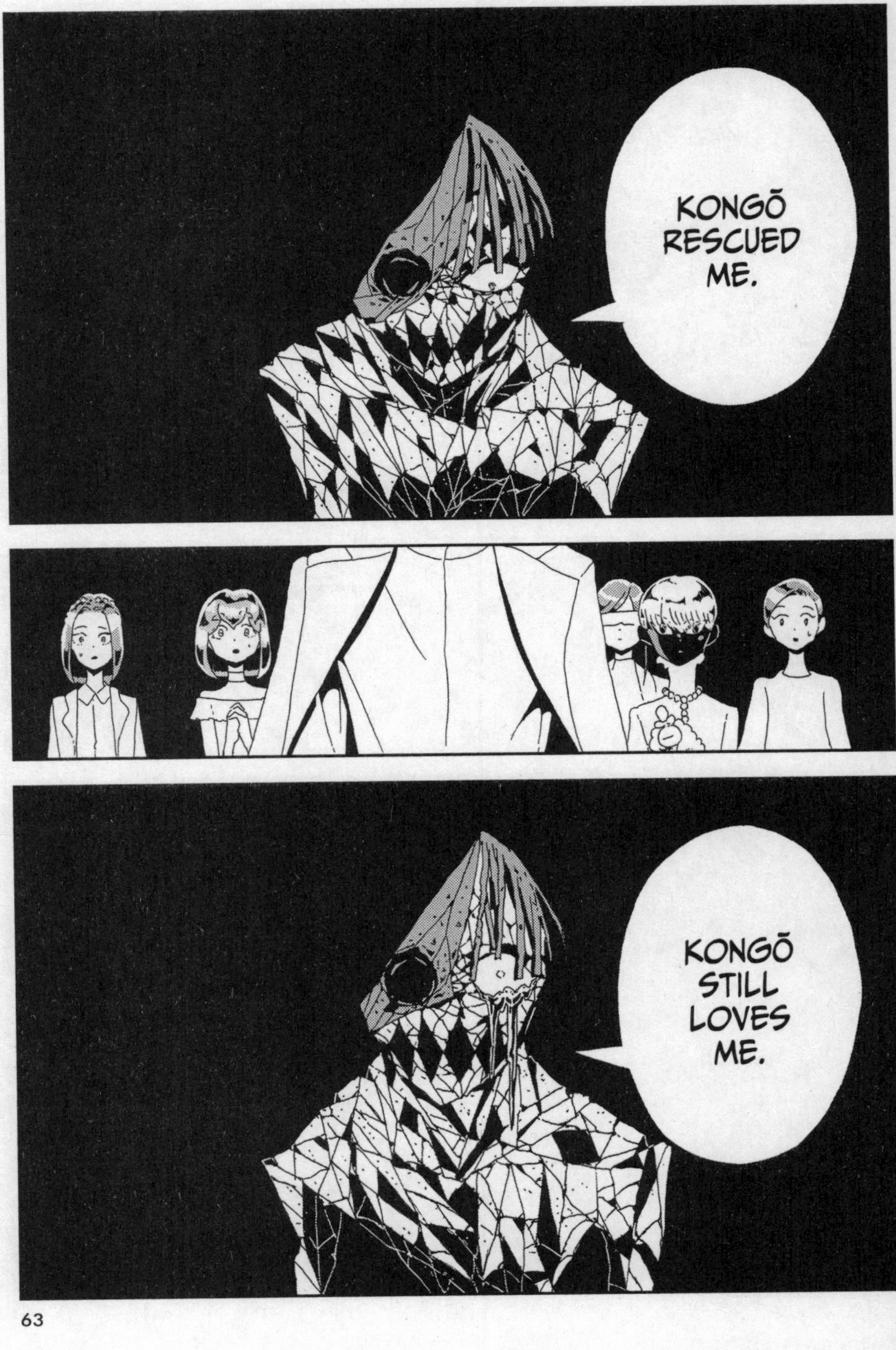
KONGŌ RESCUED ME.
KONGŌ STILL LOVES ME.

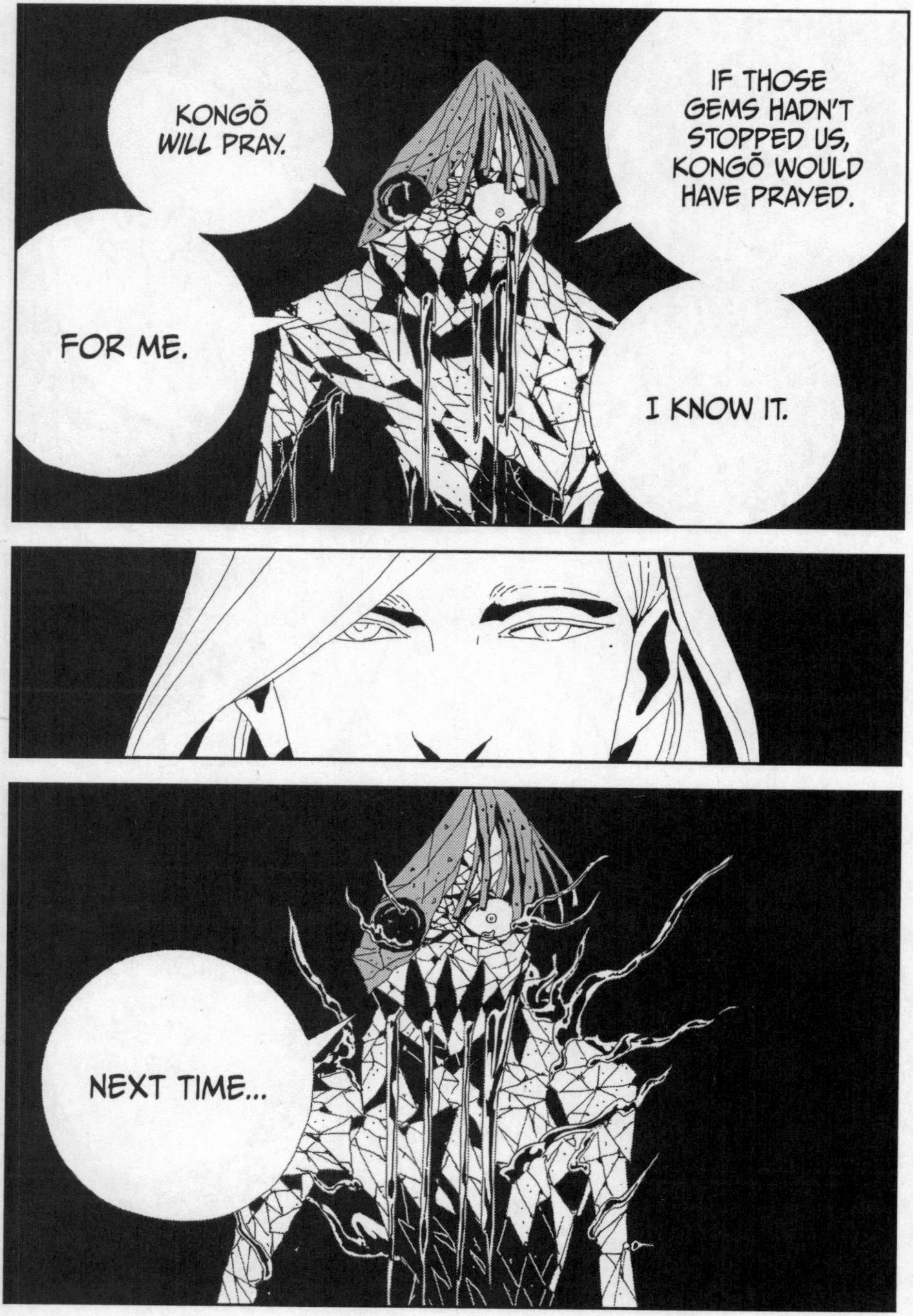
IF THOSE GEMS HADN'T STOPPED US, KONGŌ WOULD HAVE PRAYED.
I KNOW IT.
KONGŌ WILL PRAY.
FOR ME.
NEXT TIME...

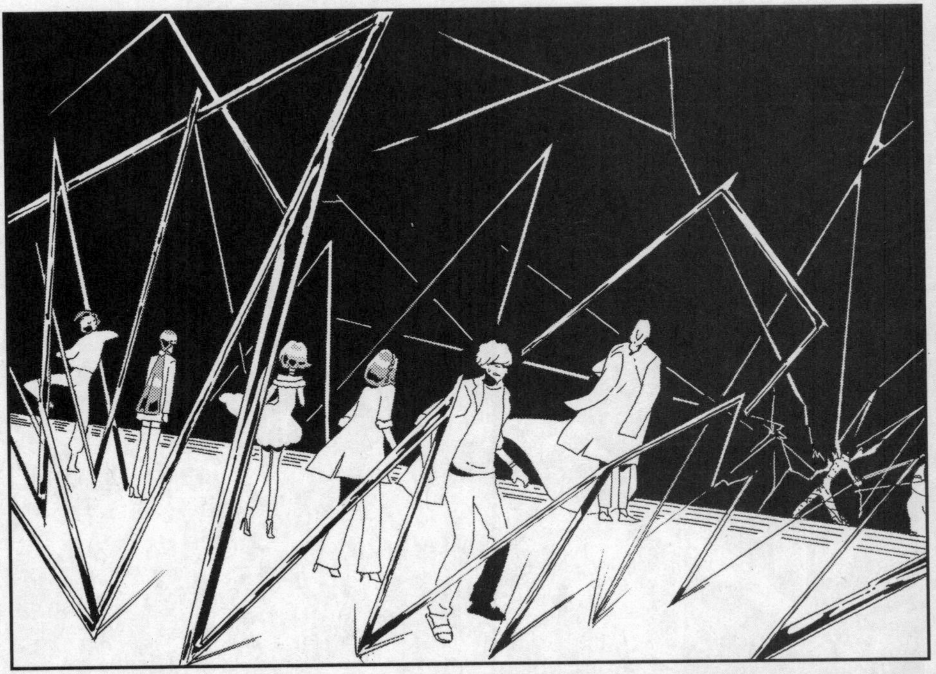

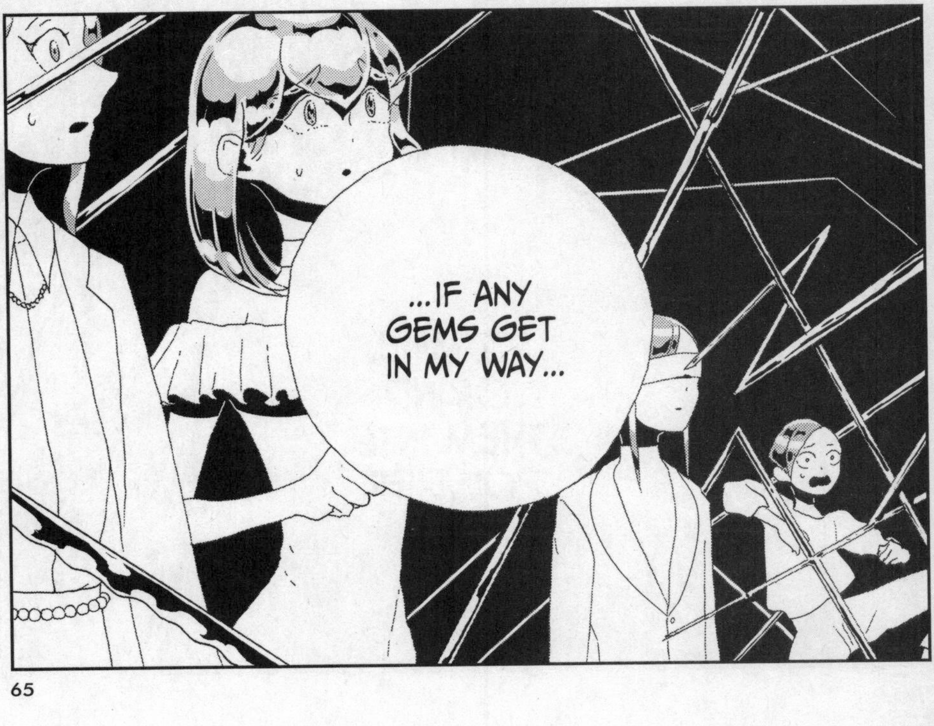
...IF ANY
GEMS GET
IN MY WAY...

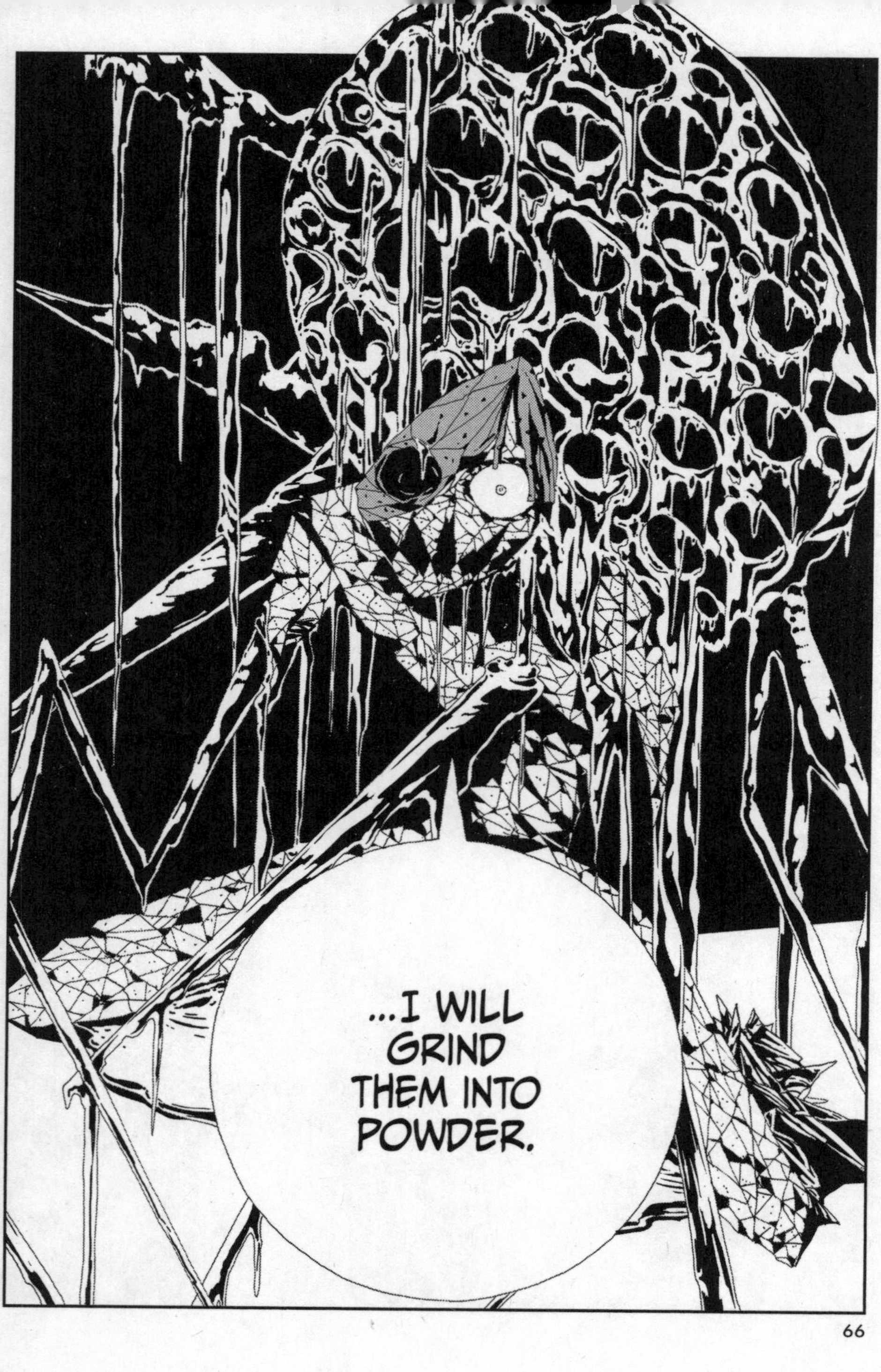
...I WILL GRIND THEM INTO POWDER.

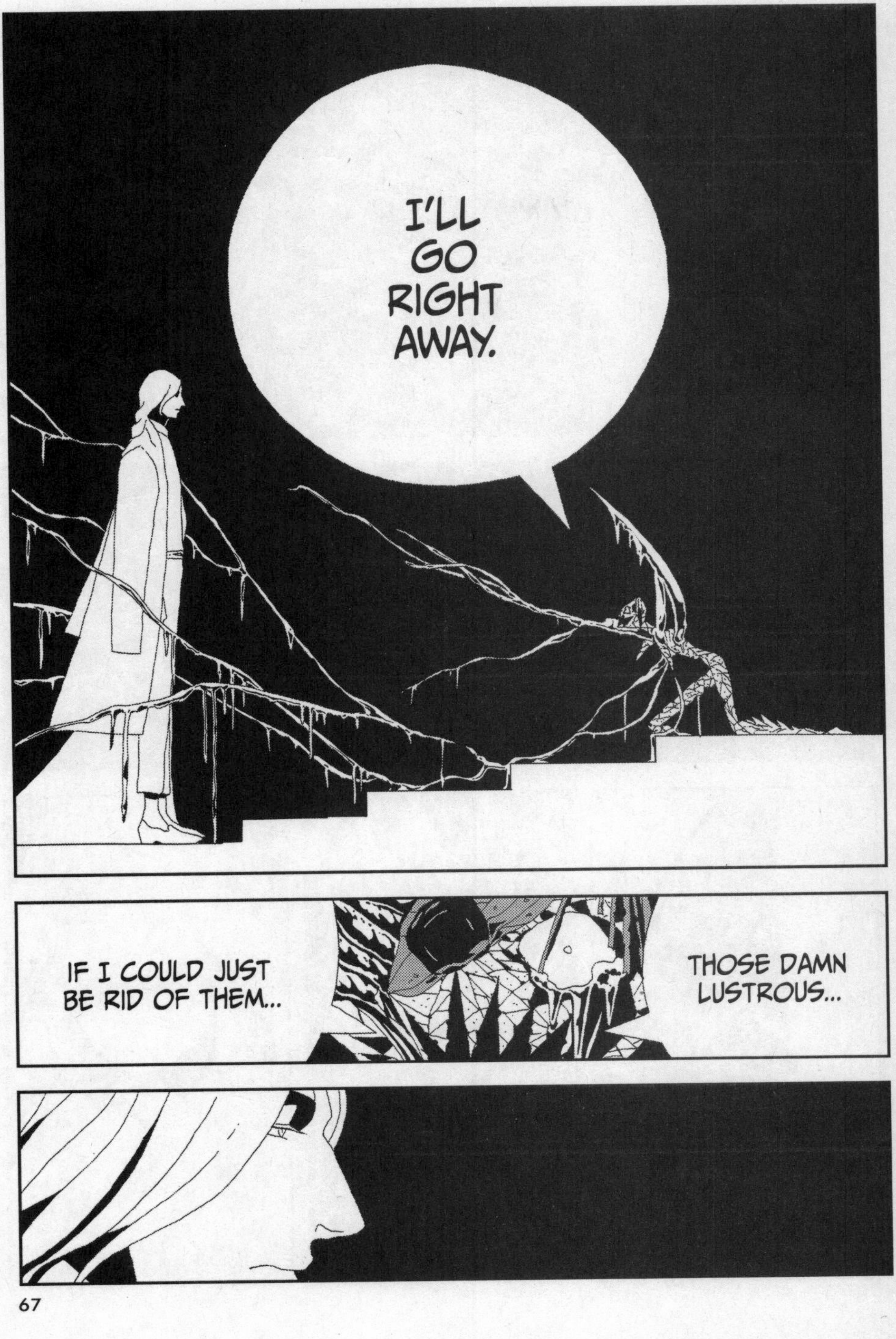
I'LL GO RIGHT AWAY.
THOSE DAMN LUSTROUS...
IF I COULD JUST BE RID OF THEM...

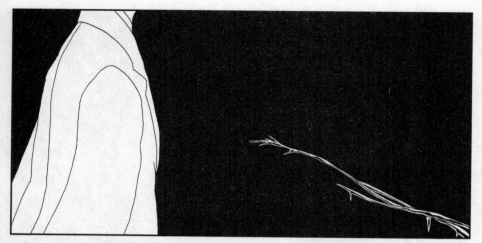

SPLURCH

HA
HA
HA
HA
HA.

VERY
WELL.

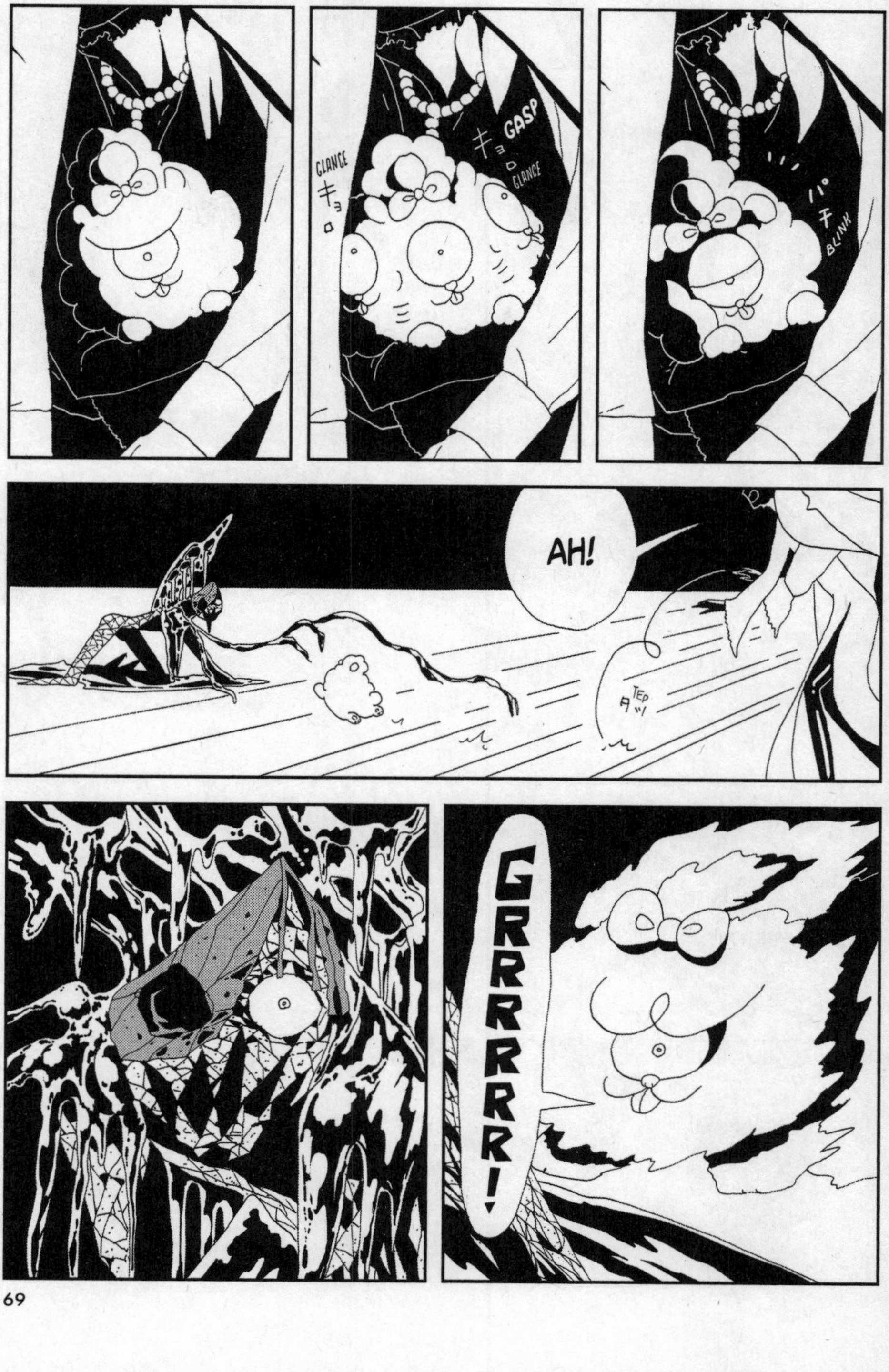

パチ
BLINK
キョロ
GASP
GLANCE
GLANCE
キョロ
AH!
TEP
タッ
GRRRRRR!

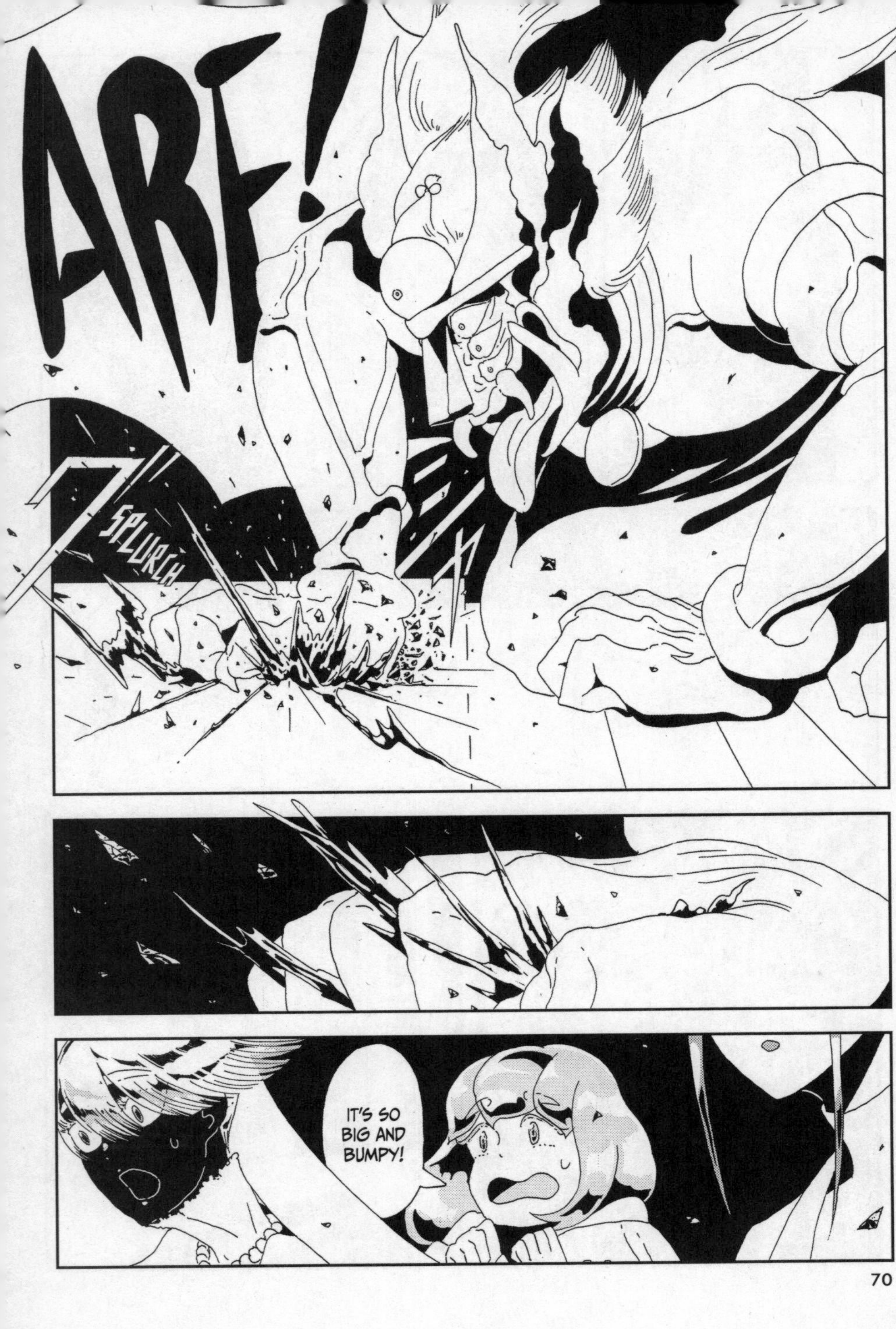
ABF!
SPLURCH
IT'S SO
BIG AND
BUMPY!

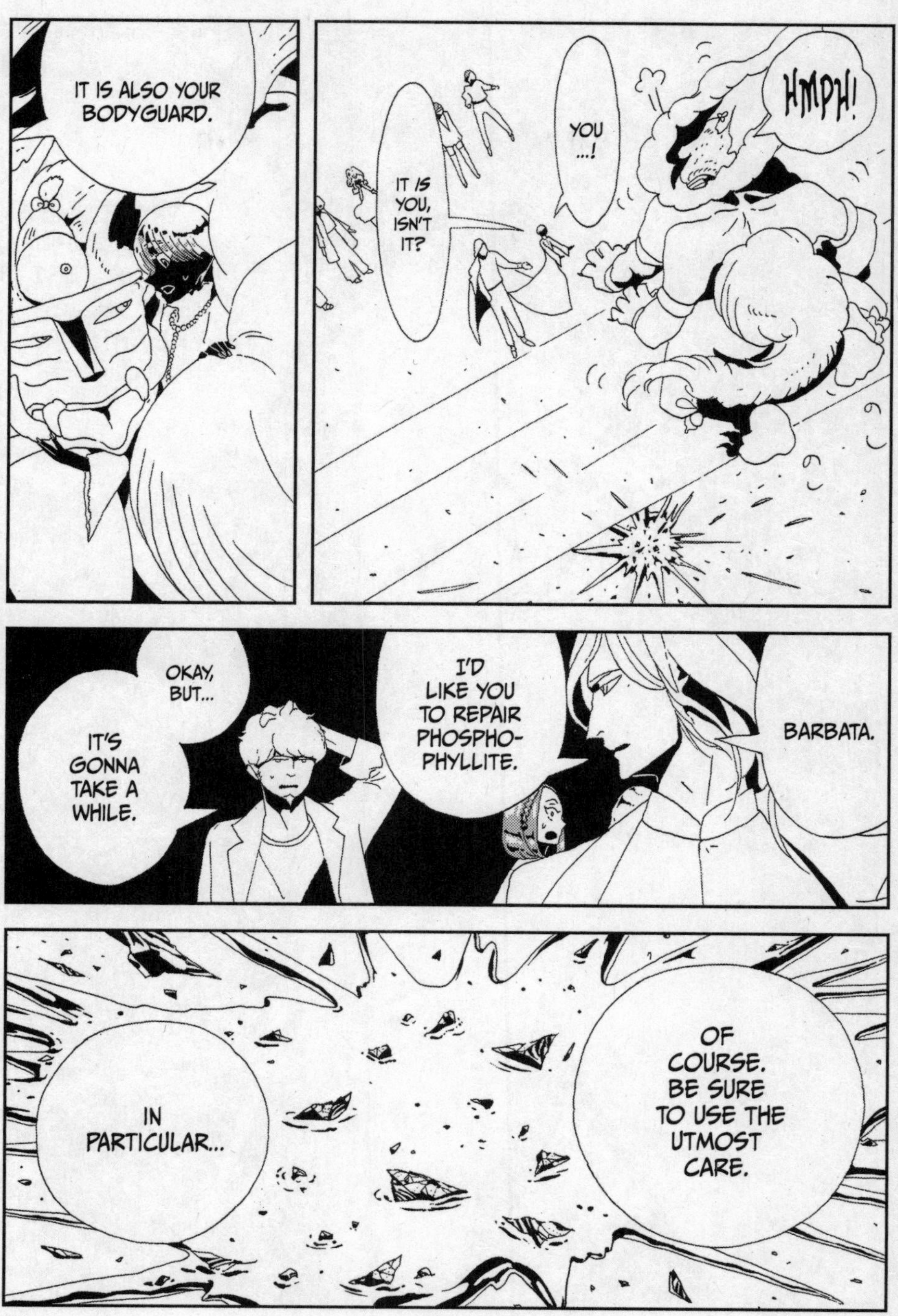
HMPH!
YOU ...!
IT IS YOU, ISN'T IT?
IT IS ALSO YOUR BODYGUARD.
BARBATA.
I'D LIKE YOU TO REPAIR PHOSPHOPHYLLITE.
OKAY, BUT...
IT'S GONNA TAKE A WHILE.
OF COURSE. BE SURE TO USE THE UTMOST CARE.
IN PARTICULAR...

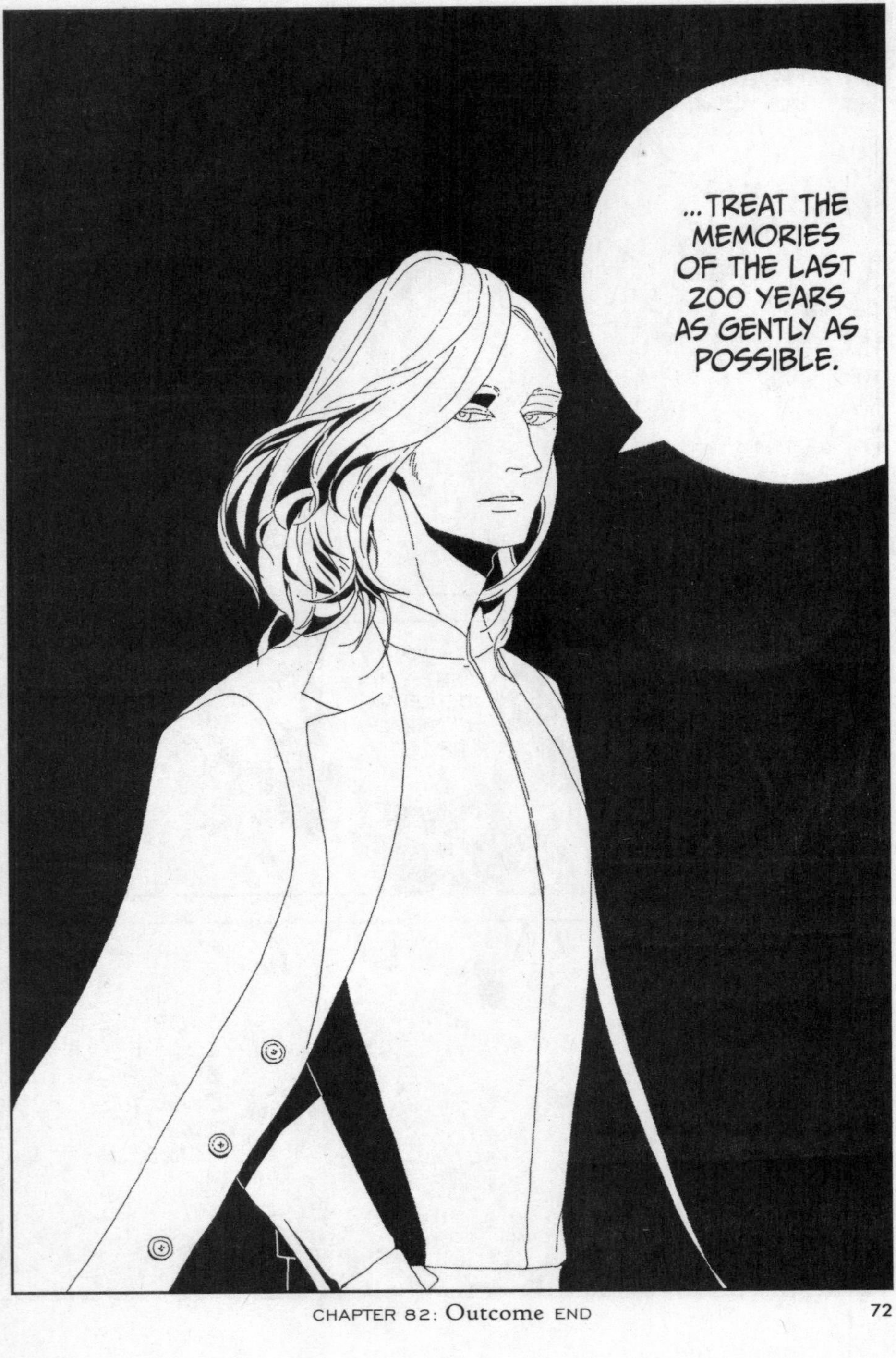
...TREAT THE MEMORIES OF THE LAST 200 YEARS AS GENTLY AS POSSIBLE.

CHAPTER 82: Outcome END

CHAPTER 83:

Reflection

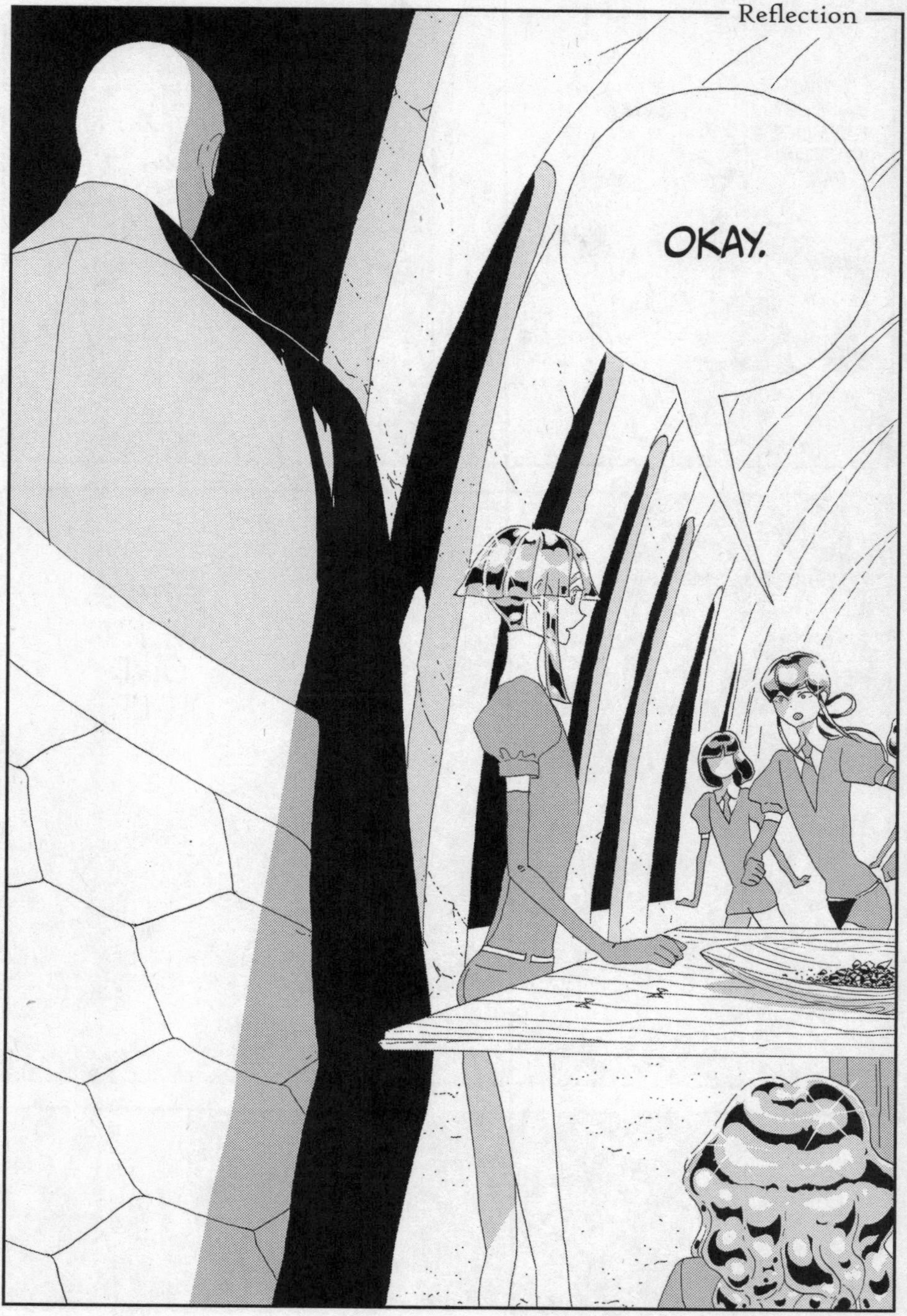
OKAY.

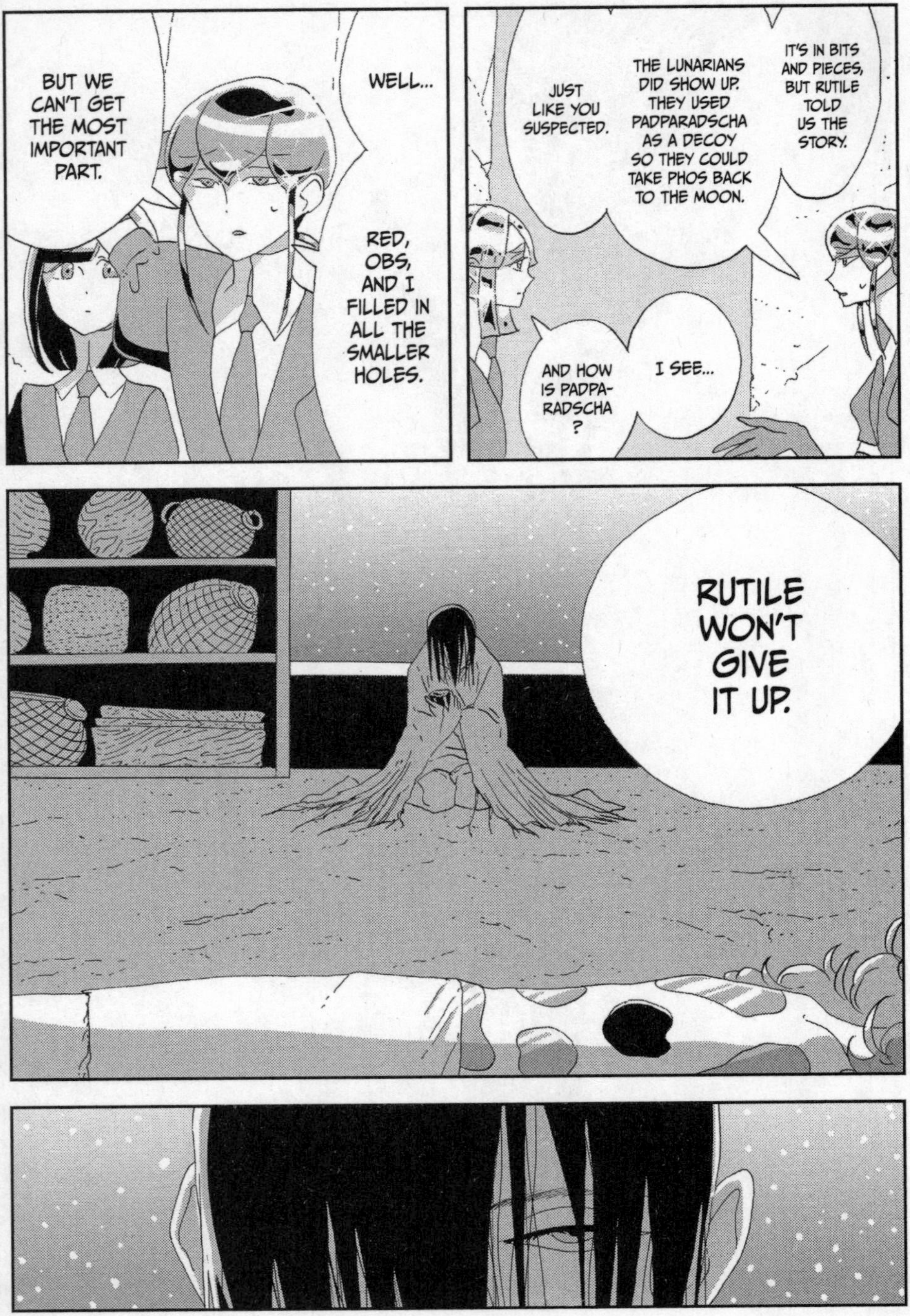

IT'S IN BITS AND PIECES, BUT RUTILE TOLD US THE STORY.
THE LUNARIANS DID SHOW UP. THEY USED PADPARADSCHA AS A DECOY SO THEY COULD TAKE PHOS BACK TO THE MOON.
JUST LIKE YOU SUSPECTED.
I SEE...
AND HOW IS PADPARADSCHA?
WELL...
RED, OBS, AND I FILLED IN ALL THE SMALLER HOLES.
BUT WE CAN'T GET THE MOST IMPORTANT PART.
RUTILE WON'T GIVE IT UP.

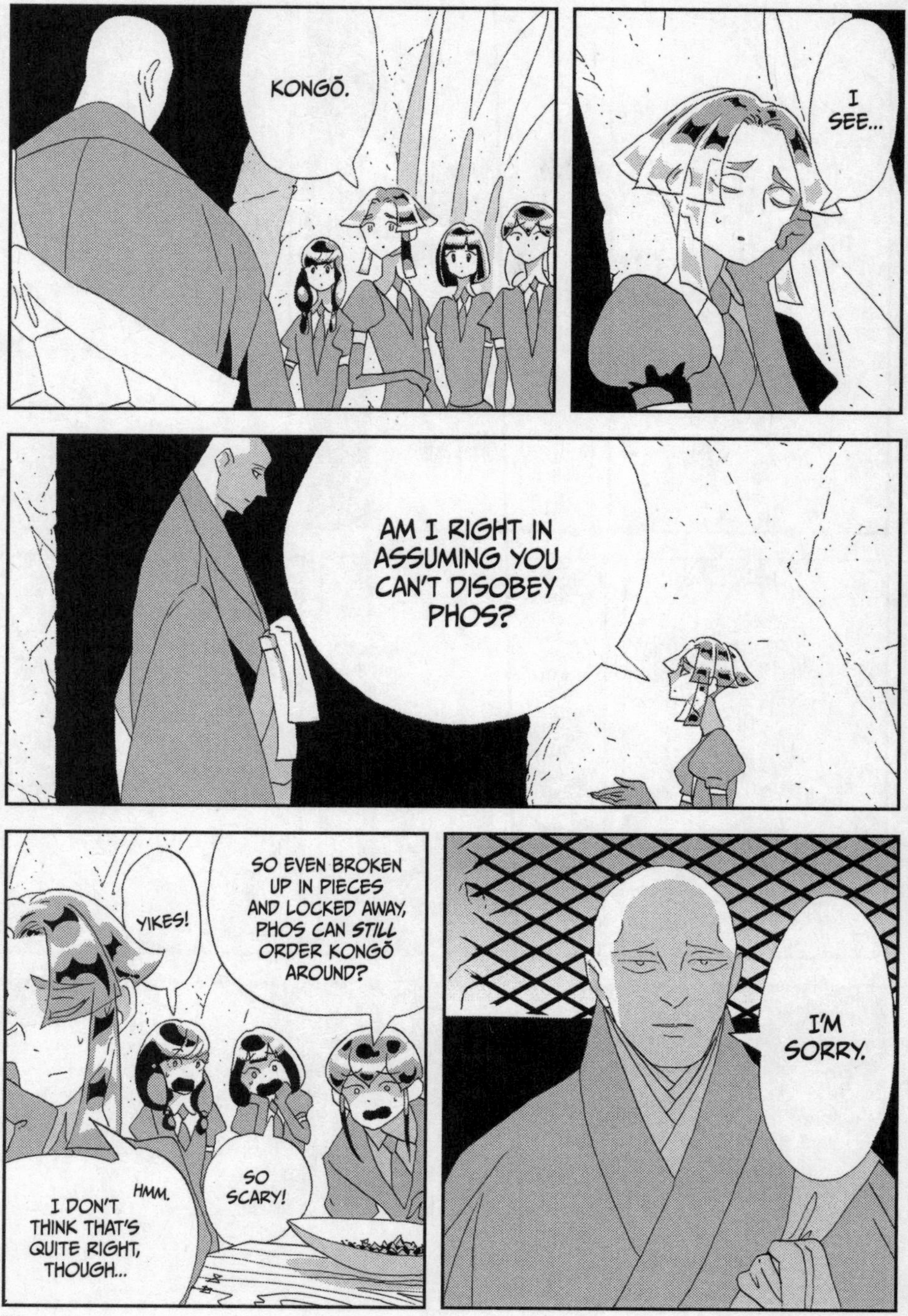
I SEE...
KONGŌ.
AM I RIGHT IN ASSUMING YOU CAN'T DISOBEY PHOS?
I'M SORRY.
SO EVEN BROKEN UP IN PIECES AND LOCKED AWAY, PHOS CAN *STILL* ORDER KONGŌ AROUND?
YIKES!
SO SCARY!
HMM.
I DON'T THINK THAT'S QUITE RIGHT, THOUGH...

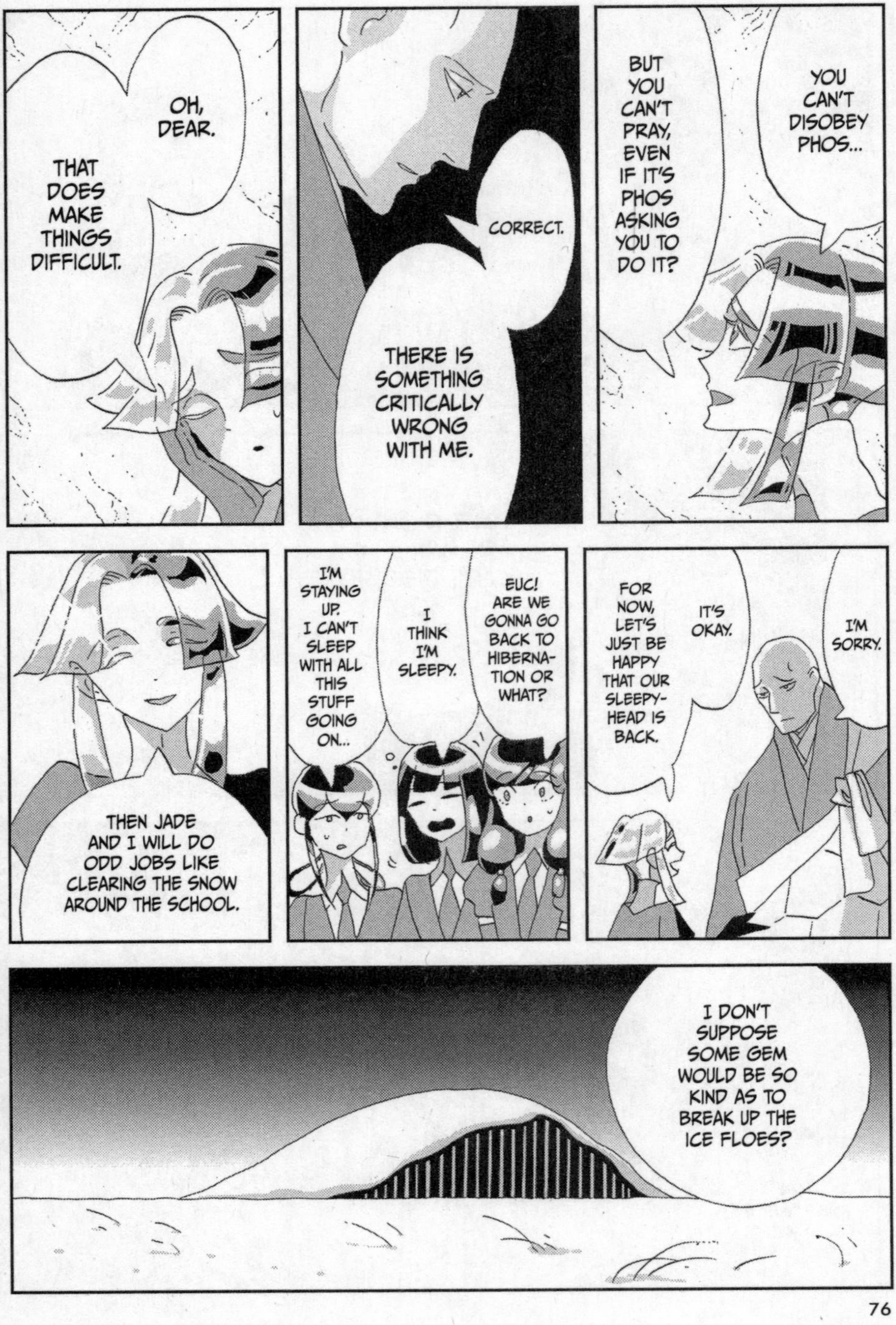
YOU CAN'T DISOBEY PHOS...
BUT YOU CAN'T PRAY, EVEN IF IT'S PHOS ASKING YOU TO DO IT?
CORRECT.
THERE IS SOMETHING CRITICALLY WRONG WITH ME.
OH, DEAR.
THAT DOES MAKE THINGS DIFFICULT.
I'M SORRY.
IT'S OKAY.
FOR NOW, LET'S JUST BE HAPPY THAT OUR SLEEPY-HEAD IS BACK.
EUC! ARE WE GONNA GO BACK TO HIBERNATION OR WHAT?
I THINK I'M SLEEPY.
I'M STAYING UP. I CAN'T SLEEP WITH ALL THIS STUFF GOING ON...
THEN JADE AND I WILL DO ODD JOBS LIKE CLEARING THE SNOW AROUND THE SCHOOL.
I DON'T SUPPOSE SOME GEM WOULD BE SO KIND AS TO BREAK UP THE ICE FLOES?

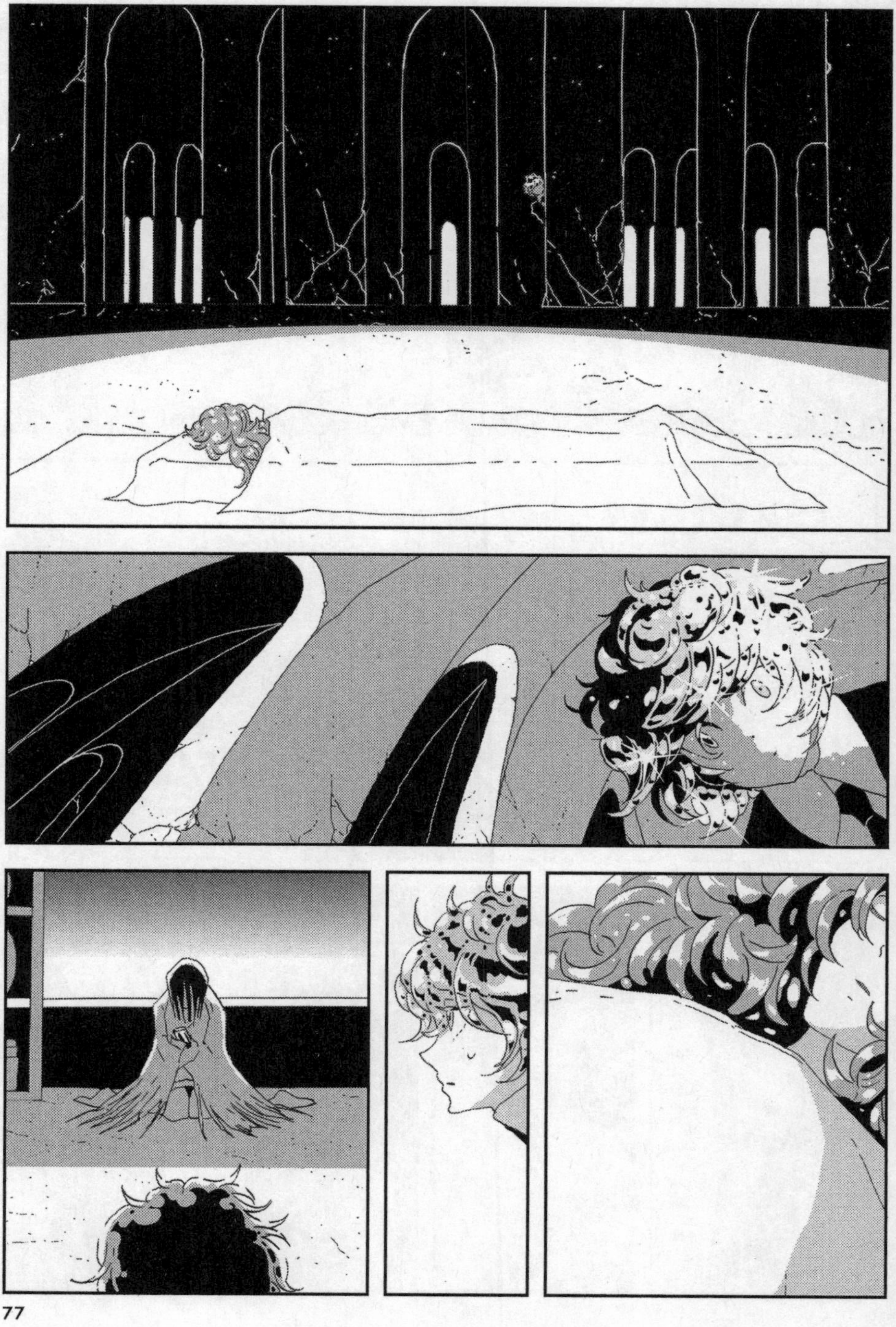

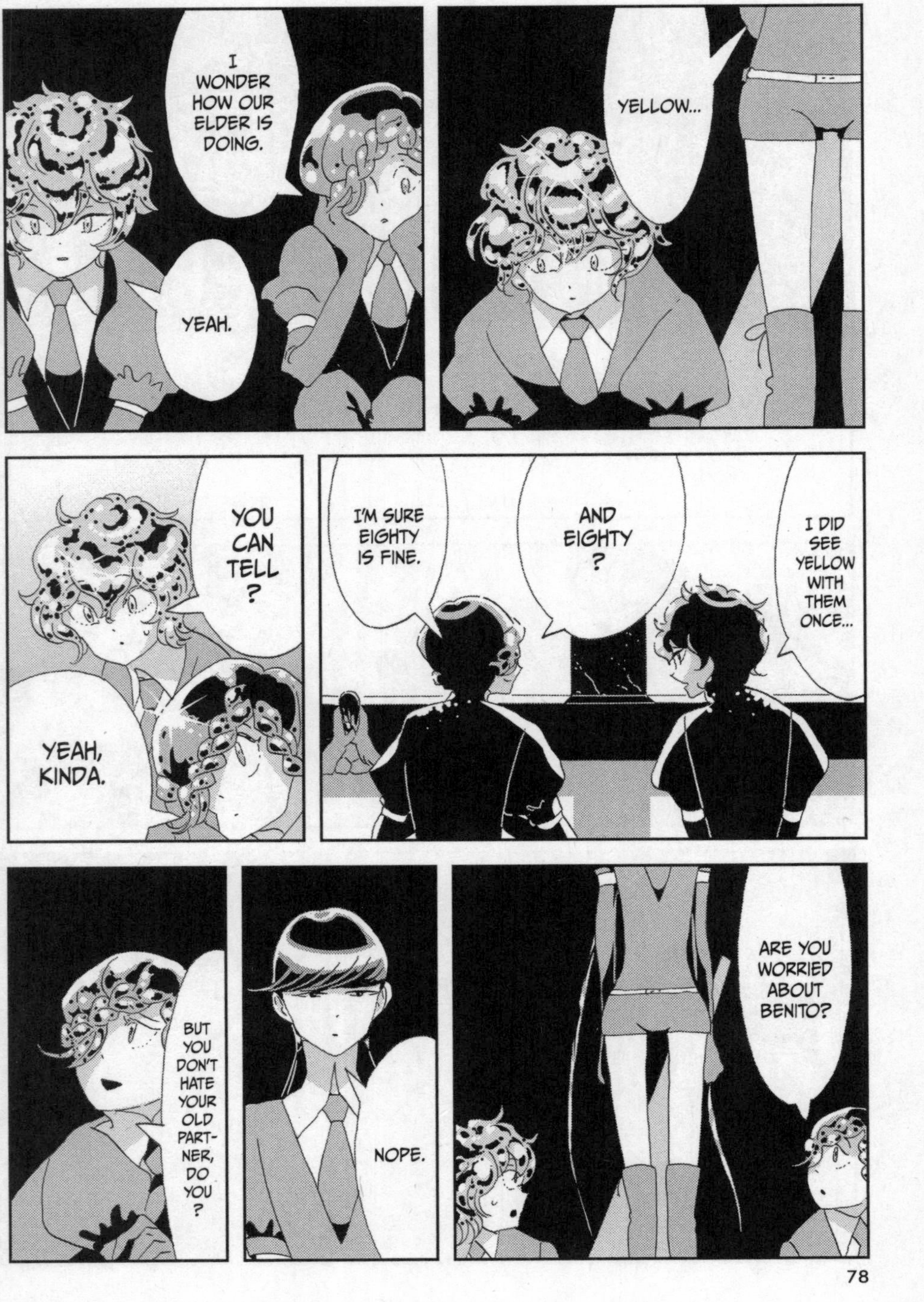
YELLOW...
I WONDER HOW OUR ELDER IS DOING.
YEAH.
I DID SEE YELLOW WITH THEM ONCE...
AND EIGHTY?
I'M SURE EIGHTY IS FINE.
YOU CAN TELL?
YEAH, KINDA.
ARE YOU WORRIED ABOUT BENITO?
NOPE.
BUT YOU DON'T HATE YOUR OLD PARTNER, DO YOU?

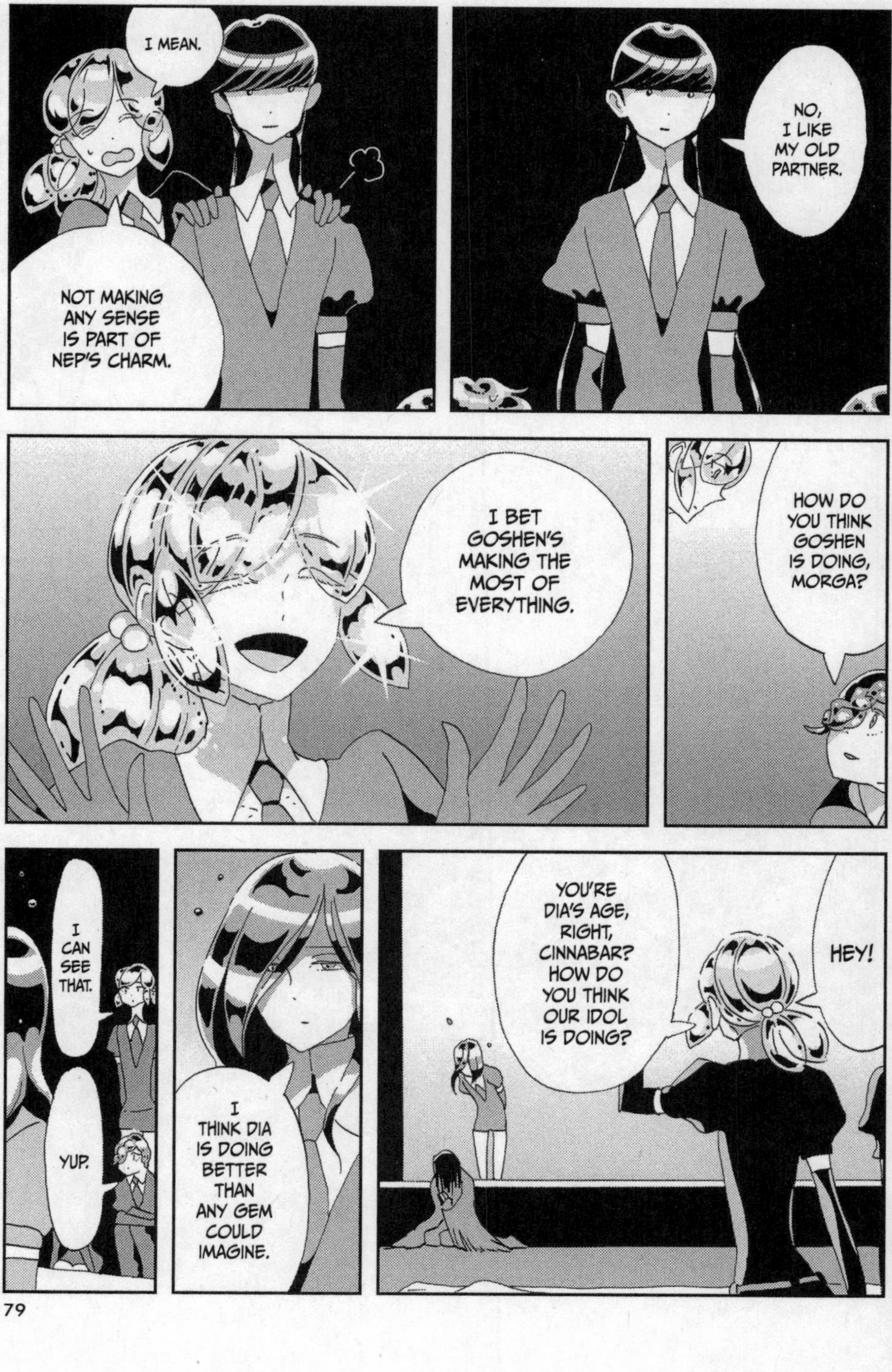
NO, I LIKE MY OLD PARTNER.
I MEAN.
NOT MAKING ANY SENSE IS PART OF NEP'S CHARM.
HOW DO YOU THINK GOSHEN IS DOING, MORGA?
I BET GOSHEN'S MAKING THE MOST OF EVERYTHING.
HEY!
YOU'RE DIA'S AGE, RIGHT, CINNABAR? HOW DO YOU THINK OUR IDOL IS DOING?
I THINK DIA IS DOING BETTER THAN ANY GEM COULD IMAGINE.
I CAN SEE THAT.
YUP.

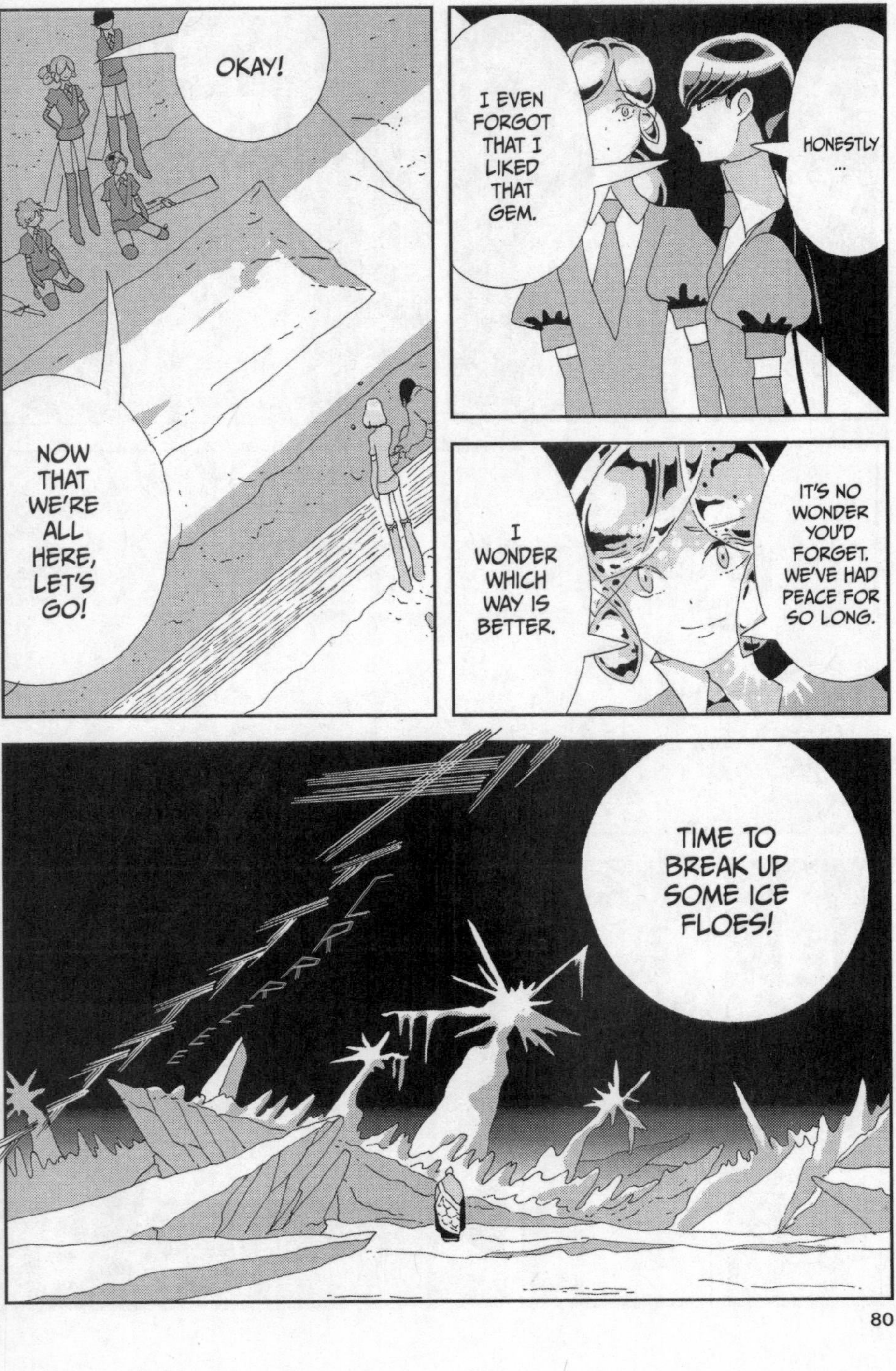

HONESTLY ...
I EVEN FORGOT THAT I LIKED THAT GEM.
IT'S NO WONDER YOU'D FORGET. WE'VE HAD PEACE FOR SO LONG.
I WONDER WHICH WAY IS BETTER.
OKAY!
NOW THAT WE'RE ALL HERE, LET'S GO!
TIME TO BREAK UP SOME ICE FLOES!

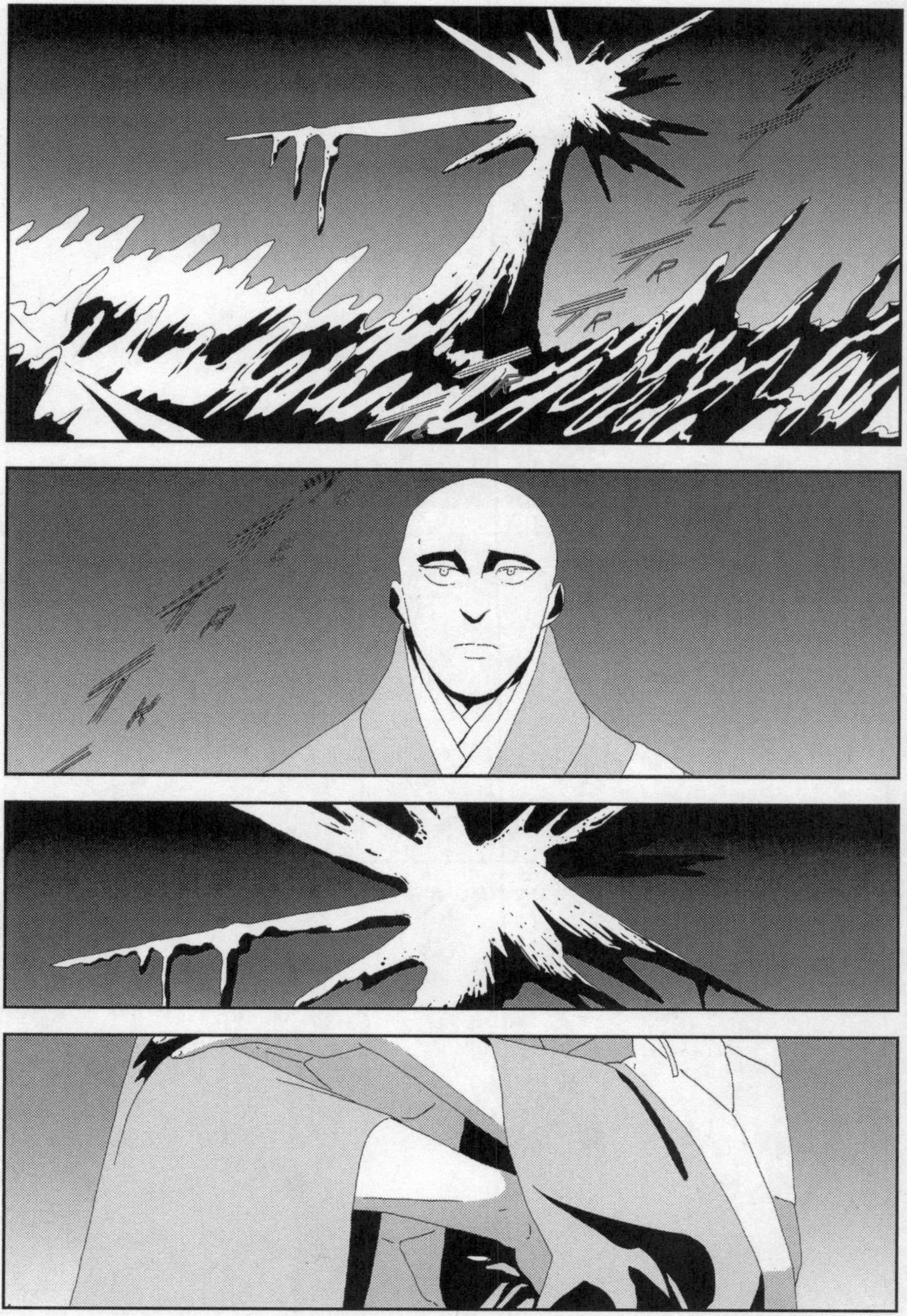

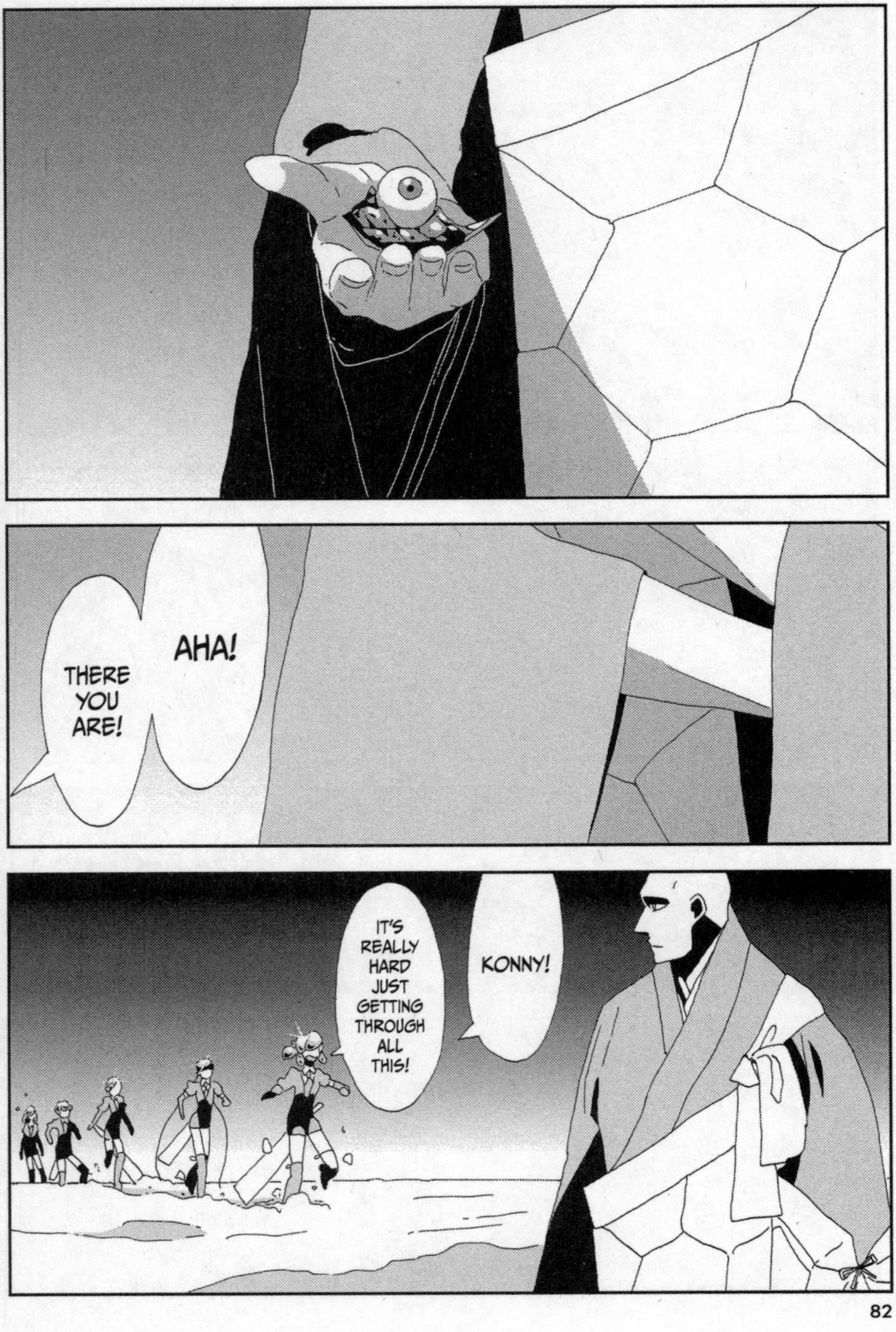
AHA!
THERE YOU ARE!
KONNY!
IT'S REALLY HARD JUST GETTING THROUGH ALL THIS!

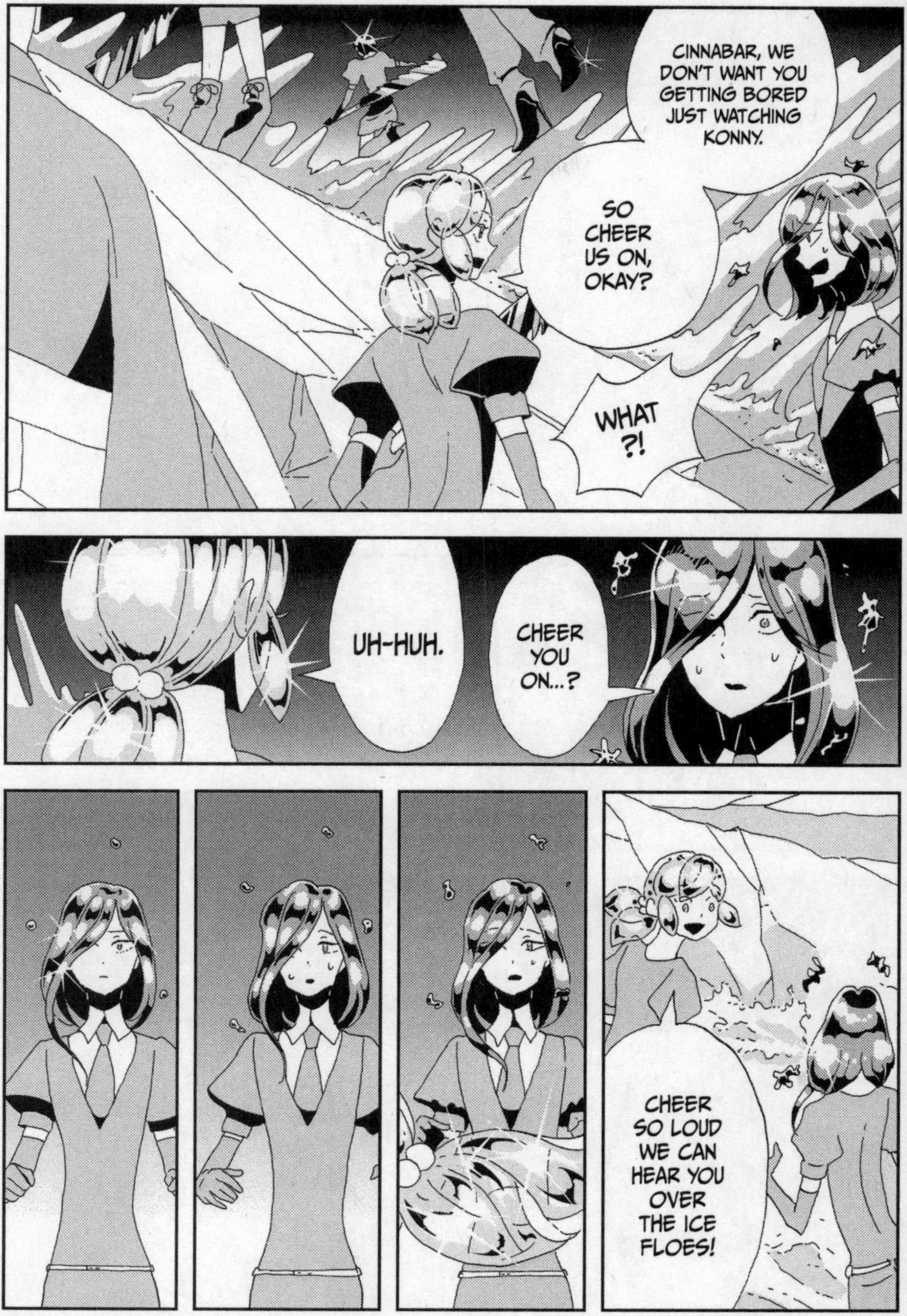
CINNABAR, WE DON'T WANT YOU GETTING BORED JUST WATCHING KONNY.
SO CHEER US ON, OKAY?
WHAT?!
CHEER YOU ON...?
UH-HUH.
CHEER SO LOUD WE CAN HEAR YOU OVER THE ICE FLOES!

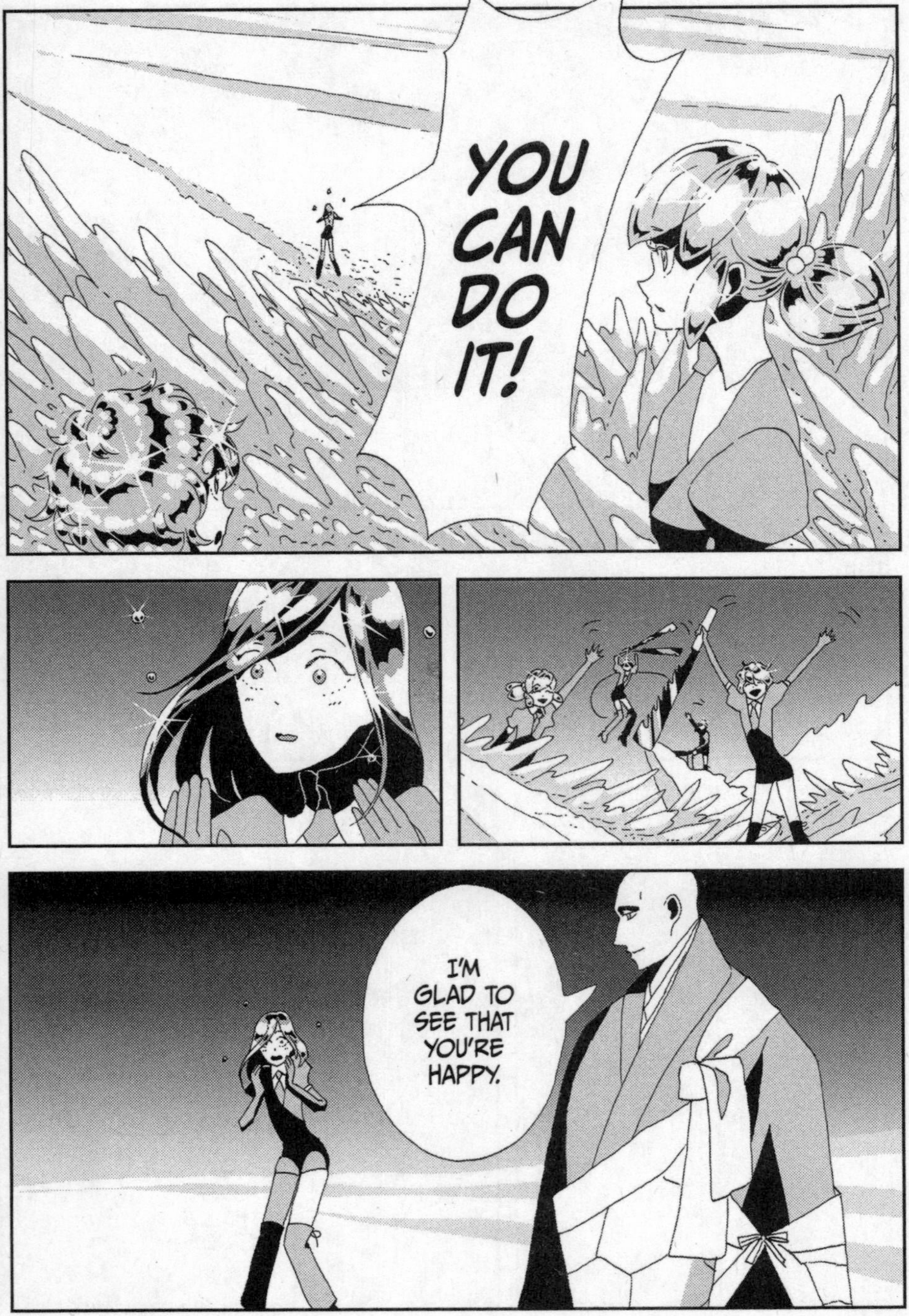
YOU CAN DO IT!
I'M GLAD TO SEE THAT YOU'RE HAPPY.

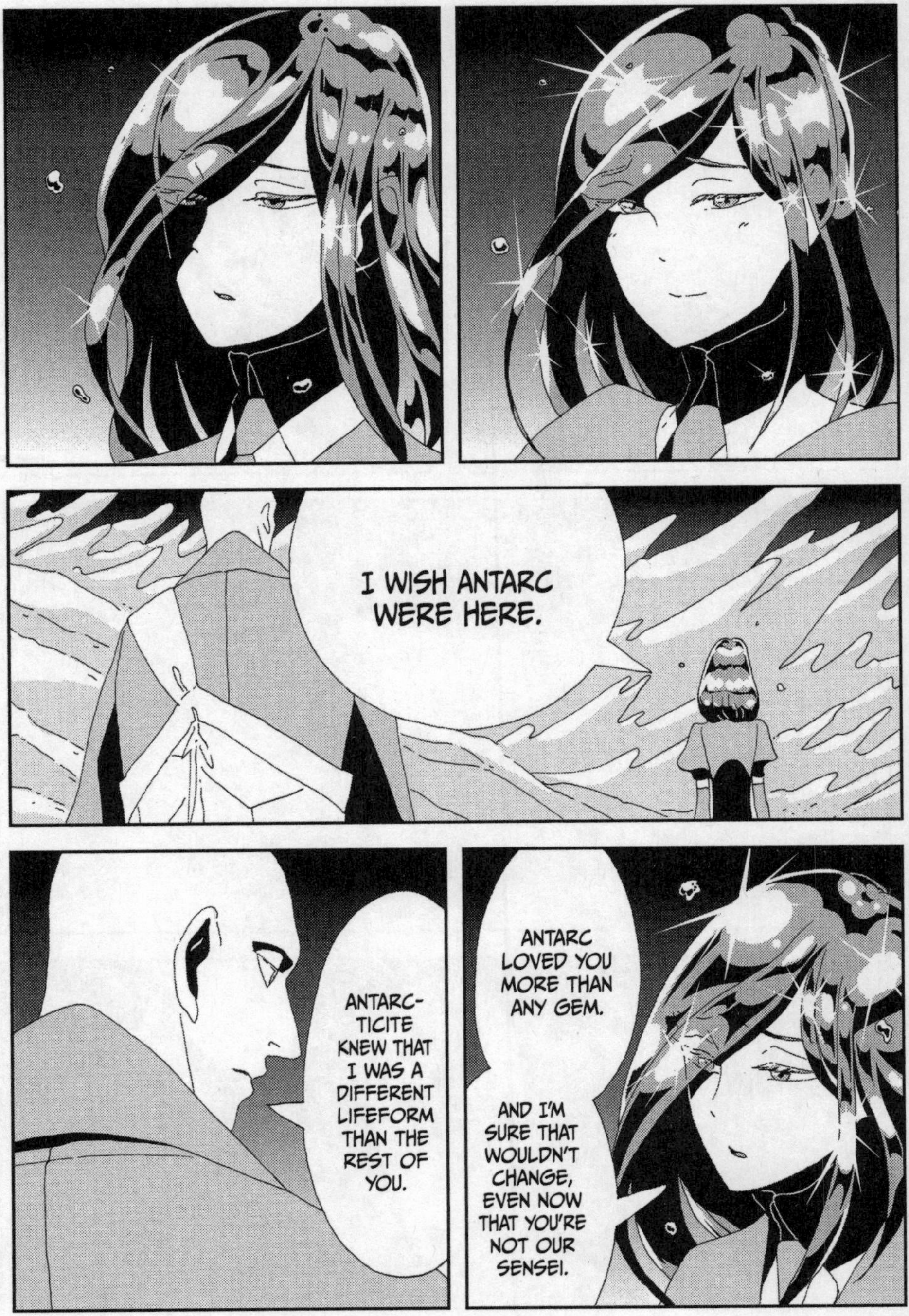
I WISH ANTARC WERE HERE.
ANTARC LOVED YOU MORE THAN ANY GEM.
AND I'M SURE THAT WOULDN'T CHANGE, EVEN NOW THAT YOU'RE NOT OUR SENSEI.
ANTARCTICITE KNEW THAT I WAS A DIFFERENT LIFEFORM THAN THE REST OF YOU.

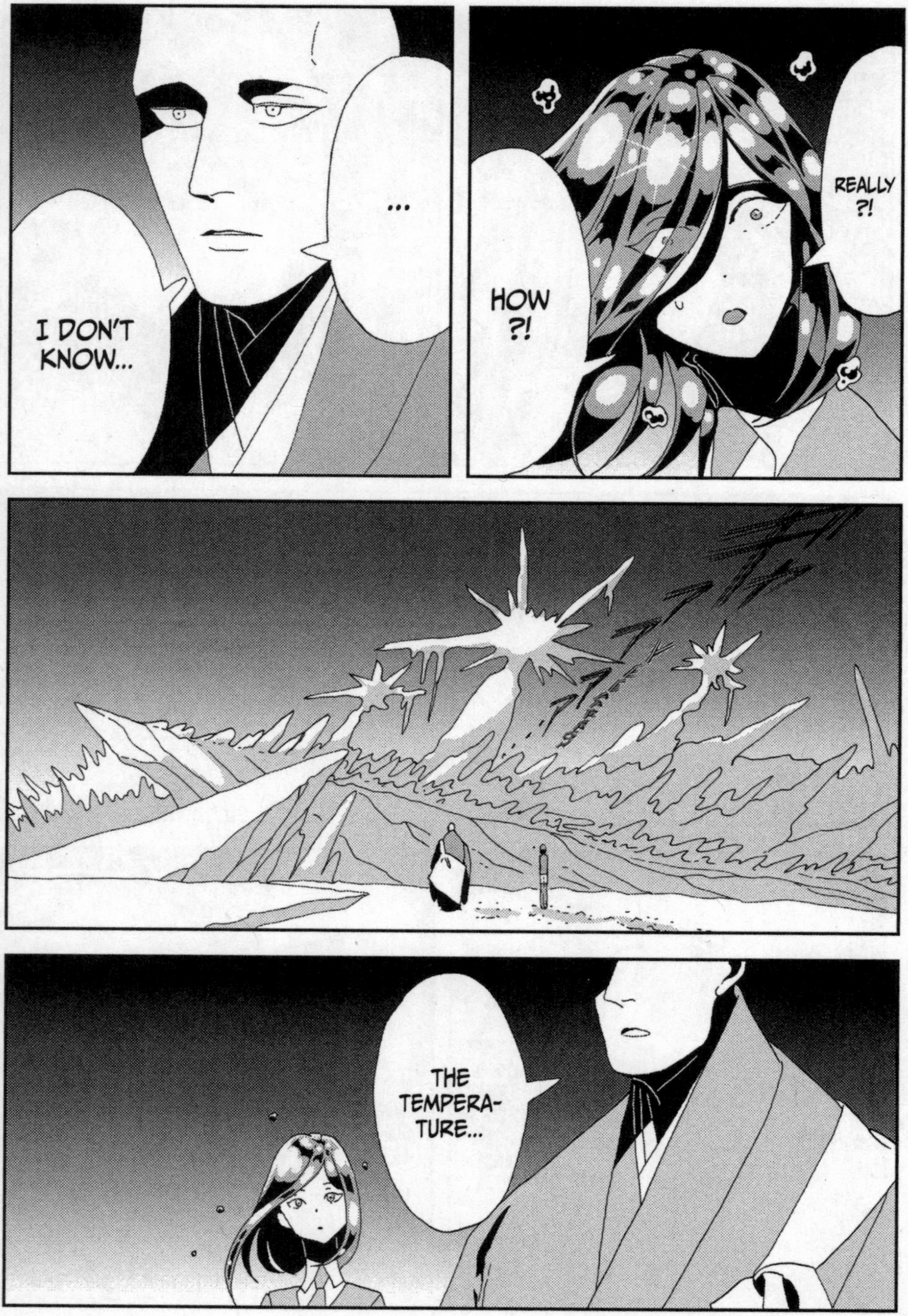
REALLY ?!
HOW ?!
...
I DON'T KNOW...
THE TEMPERA-TURE...

...IS
STEADILY
RISING.

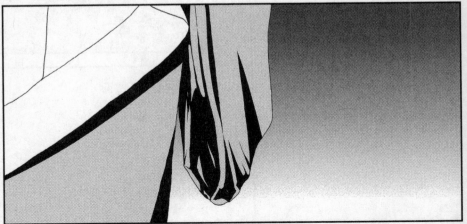

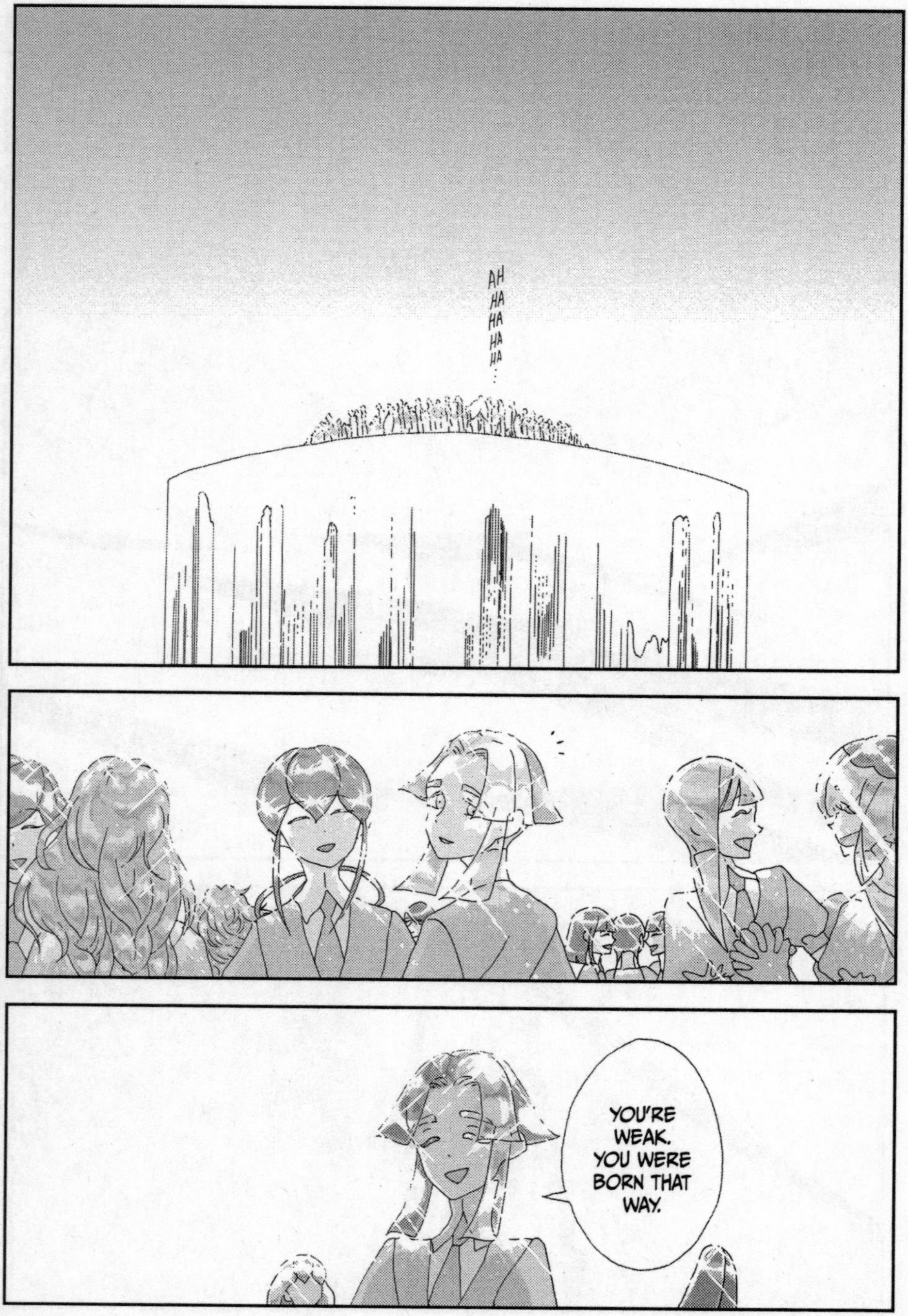
AH HA HA HA HA...
YOU'RE WEAK. YOU WERE BORN THAT WAY.

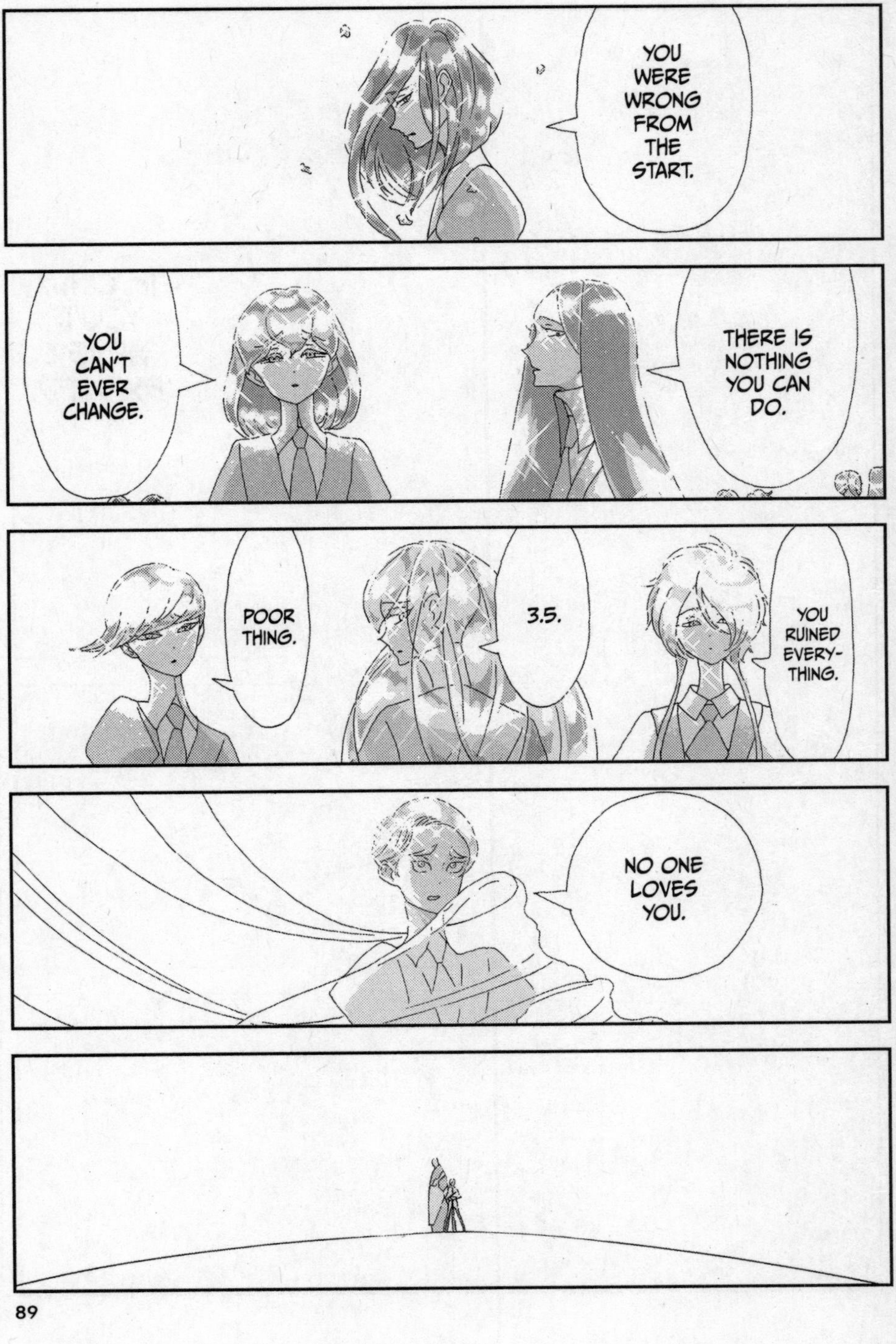
YOU WERE WRONG FROM THE START.
THERE IS NOTHING YOU CAN DO.
YOU CAN'T EVER CHANGE.
YOU RUINED EVERY-THING.
3.5.
POOR THING.
NO ONE LOVES YOU.

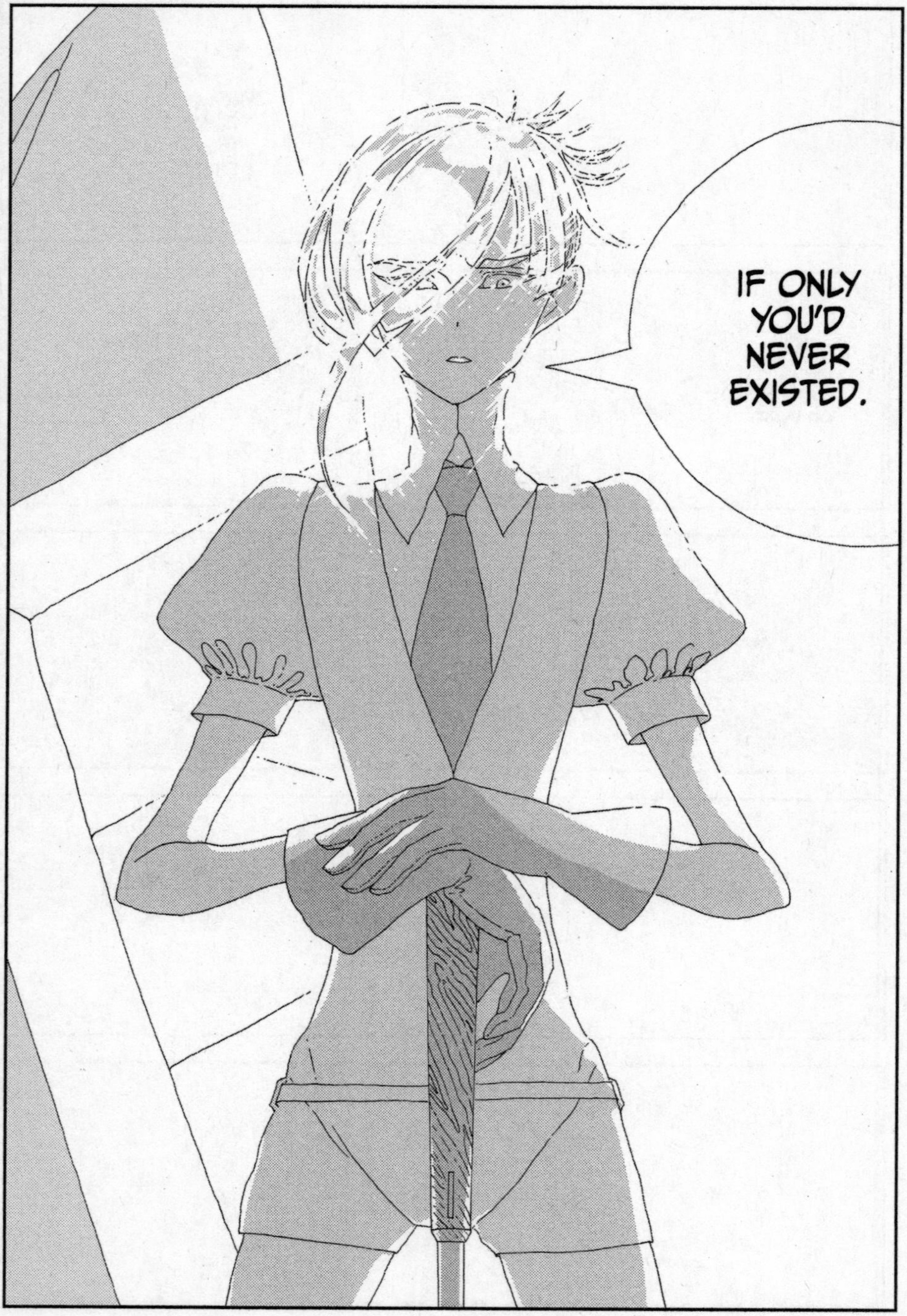
IF ONLY YOU'D NEVER EXISTED.

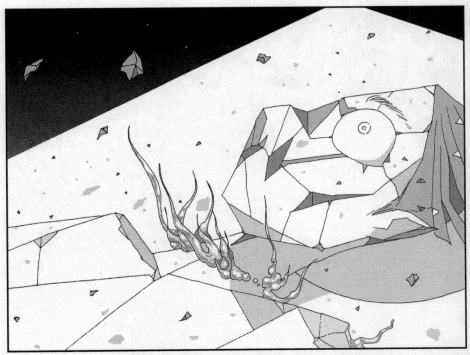

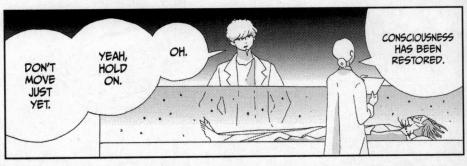

CONSCIOUSNESS HAS BEEN RESTORED.
OH.
YEAH, HOLD ON.
DON'T MOVE JUST YET.
YOUR PHYSICAL COMPOSITION IS PRETTY COMPLEX. WE'RE BEING VERY PARTICULAR ABOUT SYNTHESIZING GEMSTONES TO FILL IN THE MISSING PIECES.
IT'S STILL GOING TO TAKE TIME.

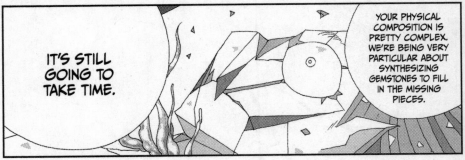

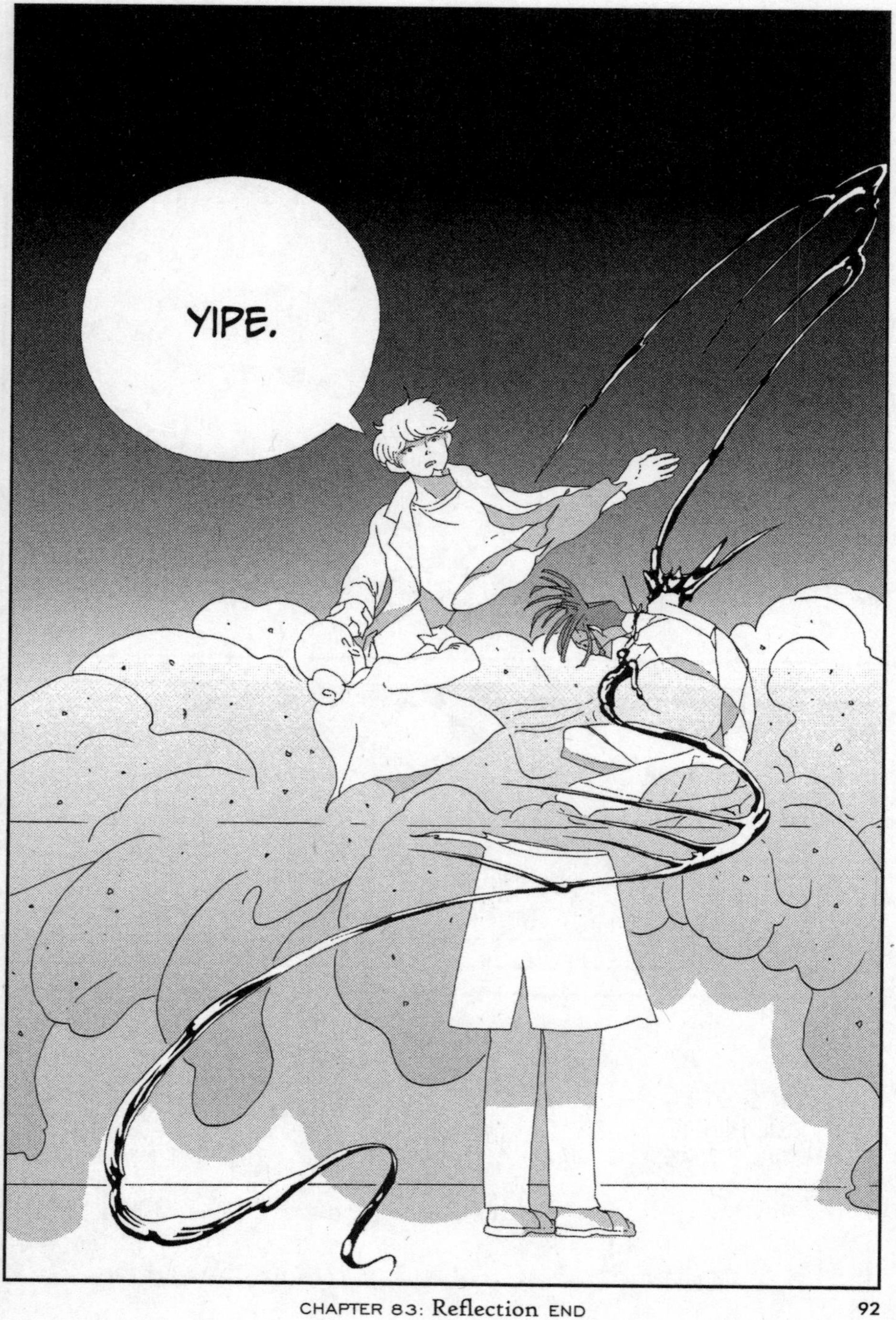
YIPE.

CHAPTER 84:

The Eve

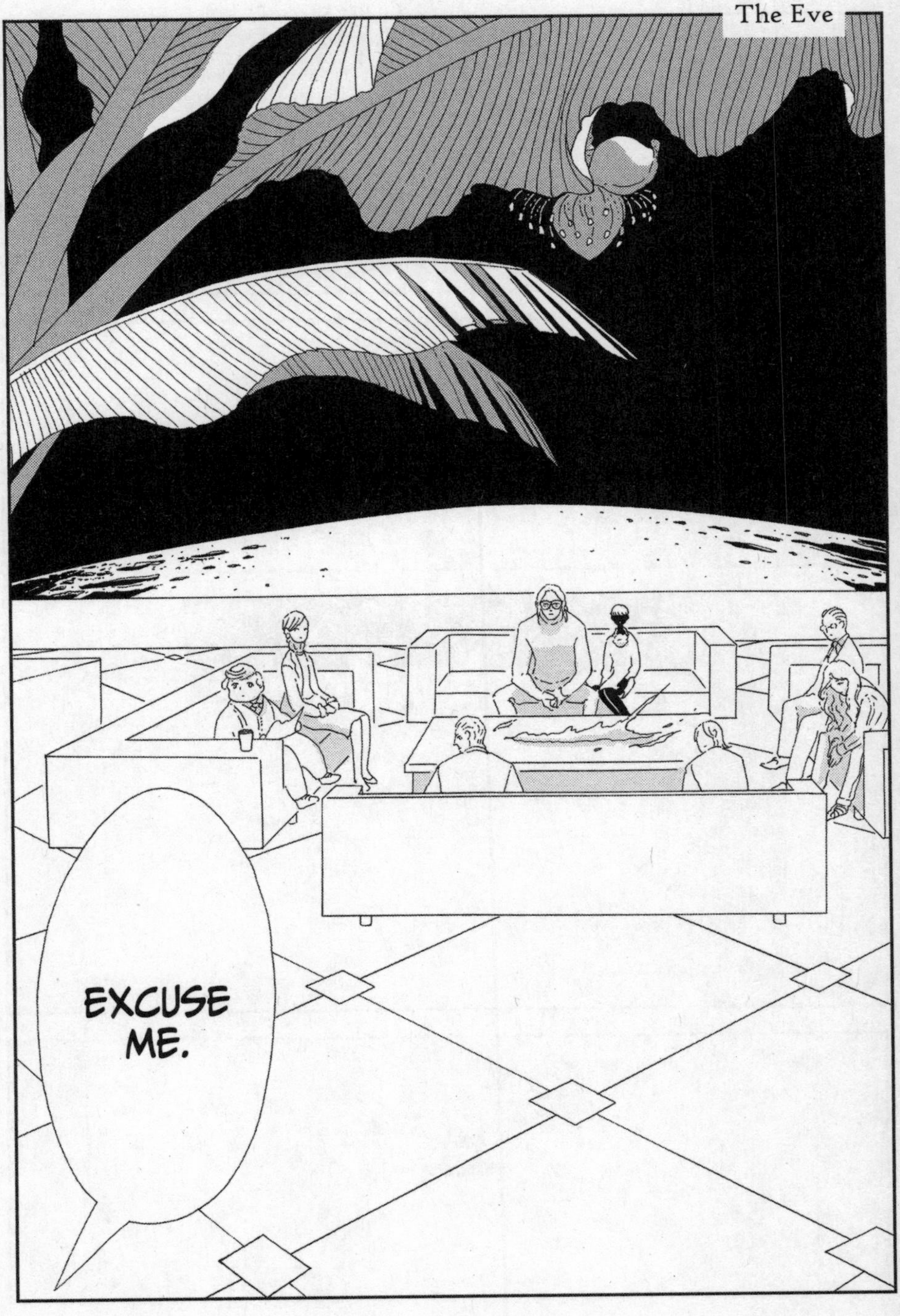
EXCUSE ME.

WE WERE
REPAIRING—

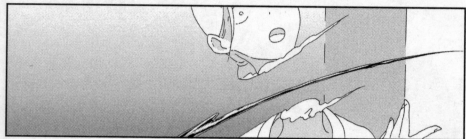

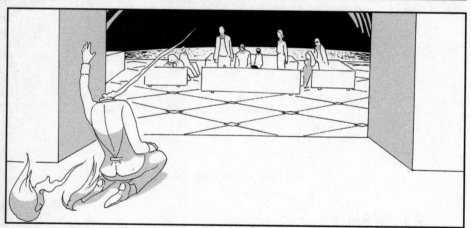

COME
IN.

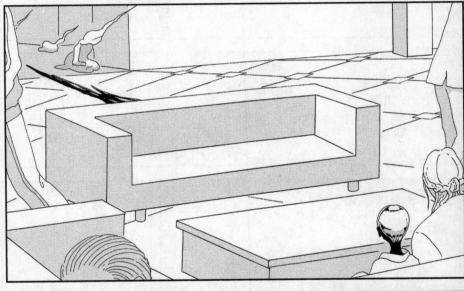

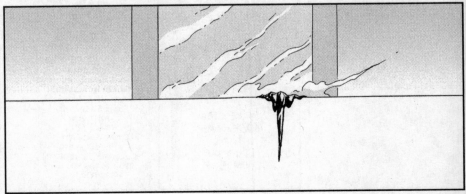

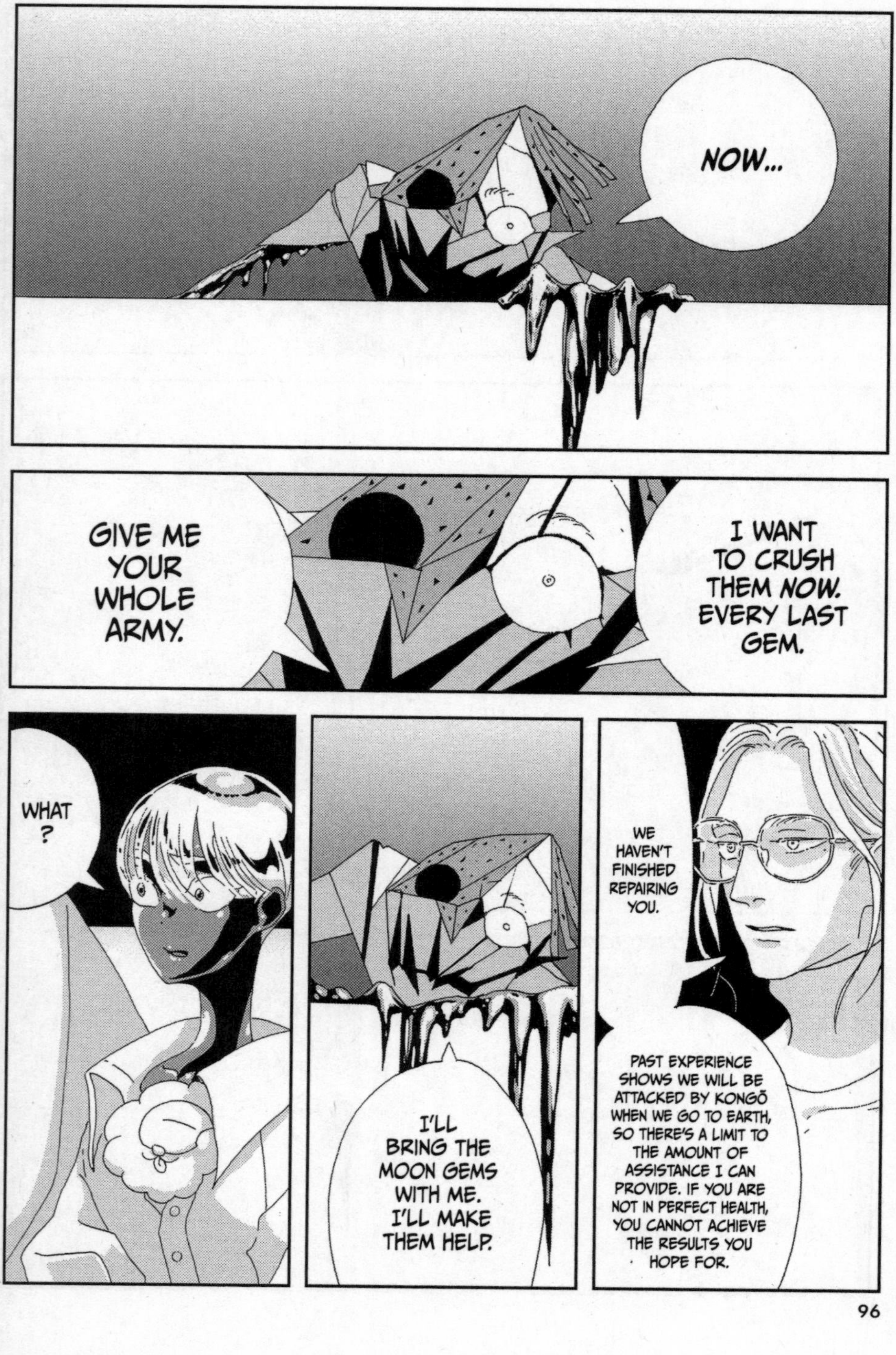
NOW...
I WANT TO CRUSH THEM NOW. EVERY LAST GEM.
GIVE ME YOUR WHOLE ARMY.
WE HAVEN'T FINISHED REPAIRING YOU.
PAST EXPERIENCE SHOWS WE WILL BE ATTACKED BY KONGŌ WHEN WE GO TO EARTH, SO THERE'S A LIMIT TO THE AMOUNT OF ASSISTANCE I CAN PROVIDE. IF YOU ARE NOT IN PERFECT HEALTH, YOU CANNOT ACHIEVE THE RESULTS YOU HOPE FOR.
I'LL BRING THE MOON GEMS WITH ME. I'LL MAKE THEM HELP.
WHAT?

YOU'RE STILL TALKING ABOUT THAT?

YOU NEVER CHANGE.

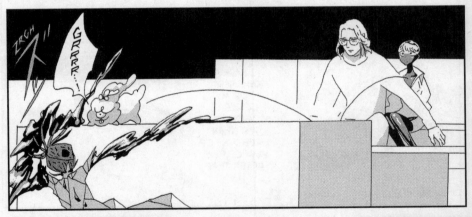

WOULD YOU LIKE TO ASK THE OTHER GEMS?

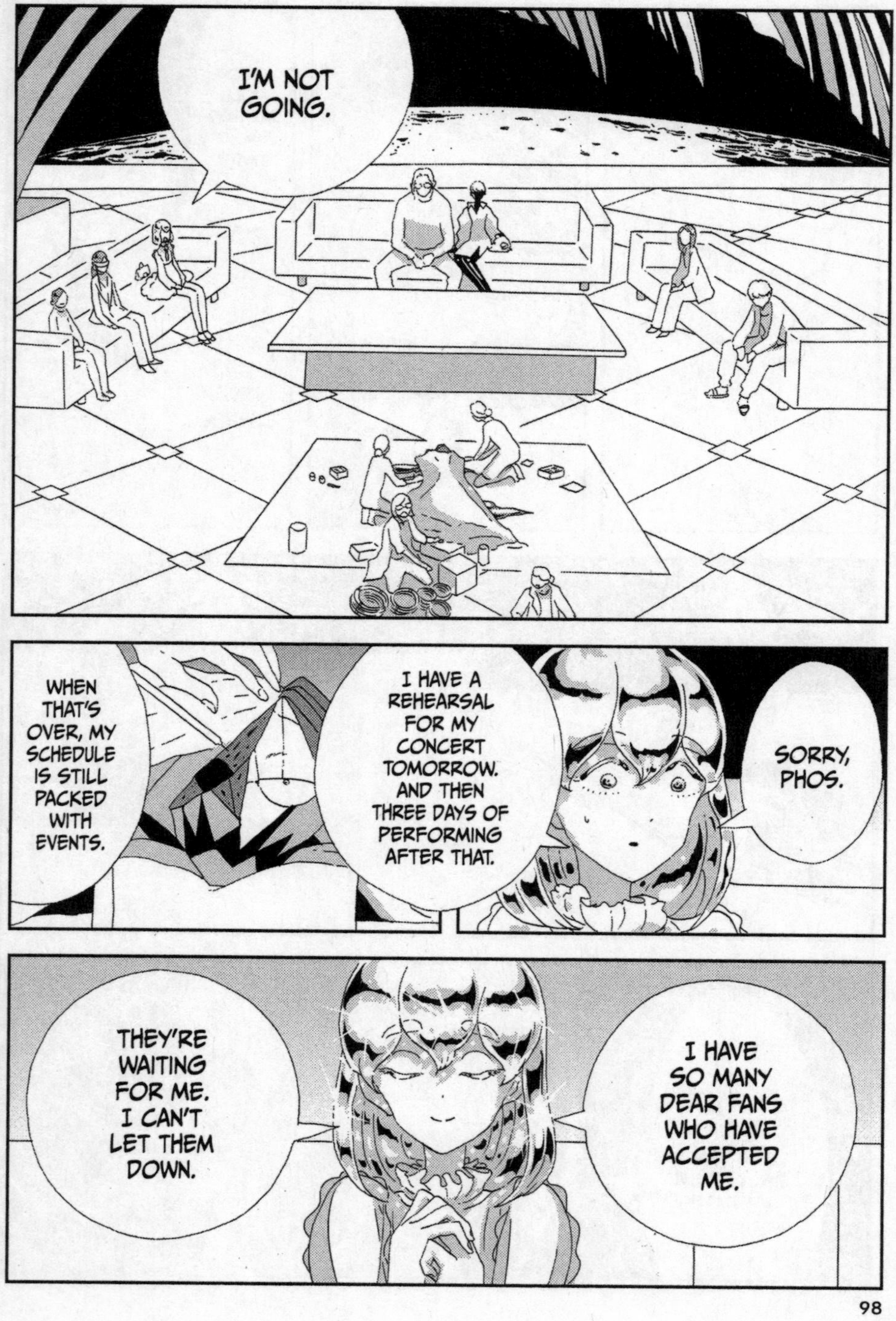
I'M NOT GOING.
SORRY, PHOS.
I HAVE A REHEARSAL FOR MY CONCERT TOMORROW. AND THEN THREE DAYS OF PERFORMING AFTER THAT.
WHEN THAT'S OVER, MY SCHEDULE IS STILL PACKED WITH EVENTS.
I HAVE SO MANY DEAR FANS WHO HAVE ACCEPTED ME.
THEY'RE WAITING FOR ME. I CAN'T LET THEM DOWN.

THEN I'LL BRING BORT HERE.

AND EVERYTHING THAT MAKES YOU HAPPY WILL DISAPPEAR.

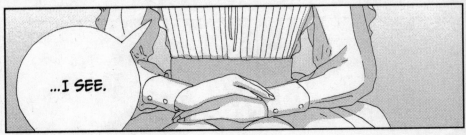

...I SEE.

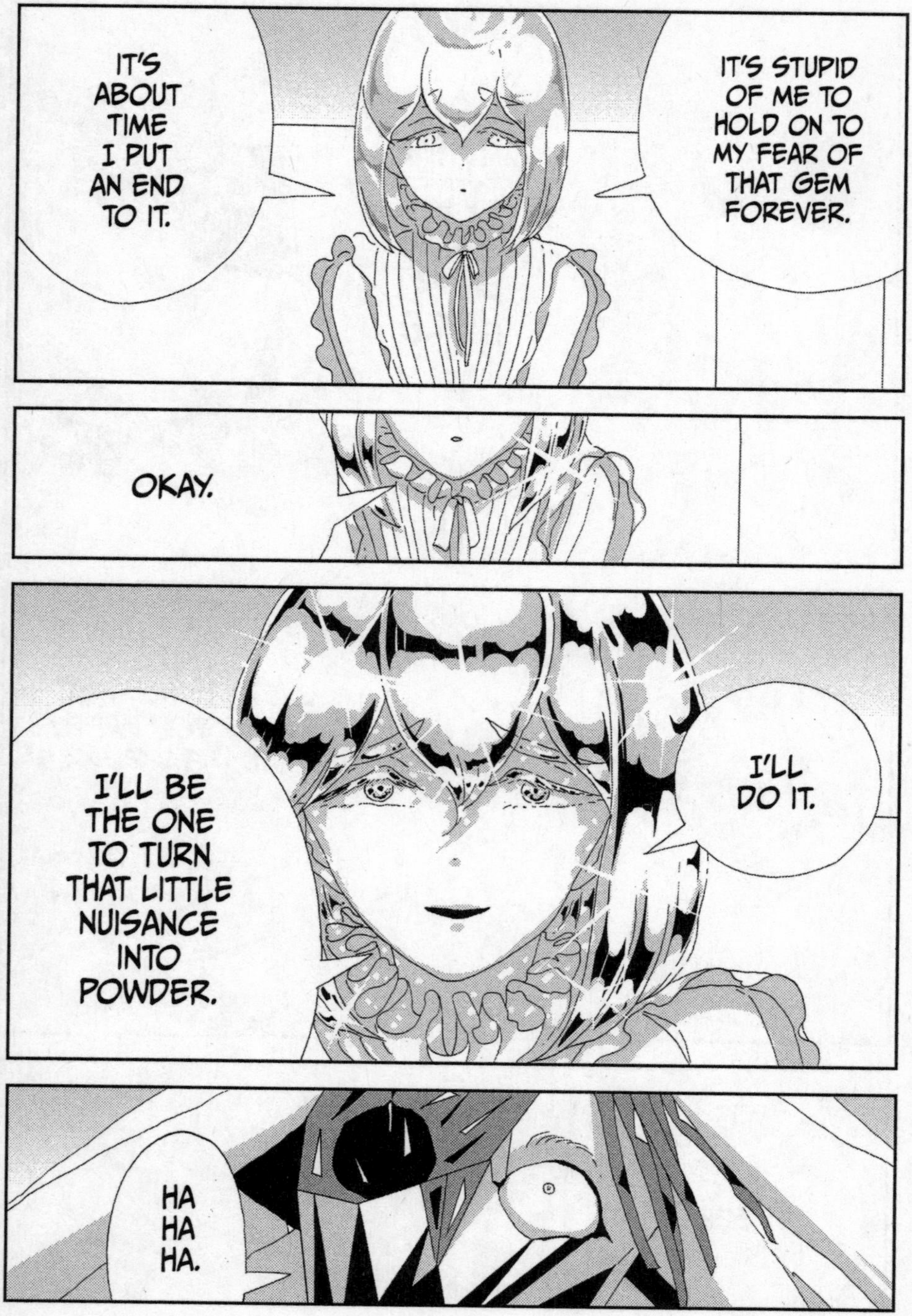
IT'S STUPID OF ME TO HOLD ON TO MY FEAR OF THAT GEM FOREVER.
IT'S ABOUT TIME I PUT AN END TO IT.
OKAY.
I'LL DO IT.
I'LL BE THE ONE TO TURN THAT LITTLE NUISANCE INTO POWDER.
HA HA HA.

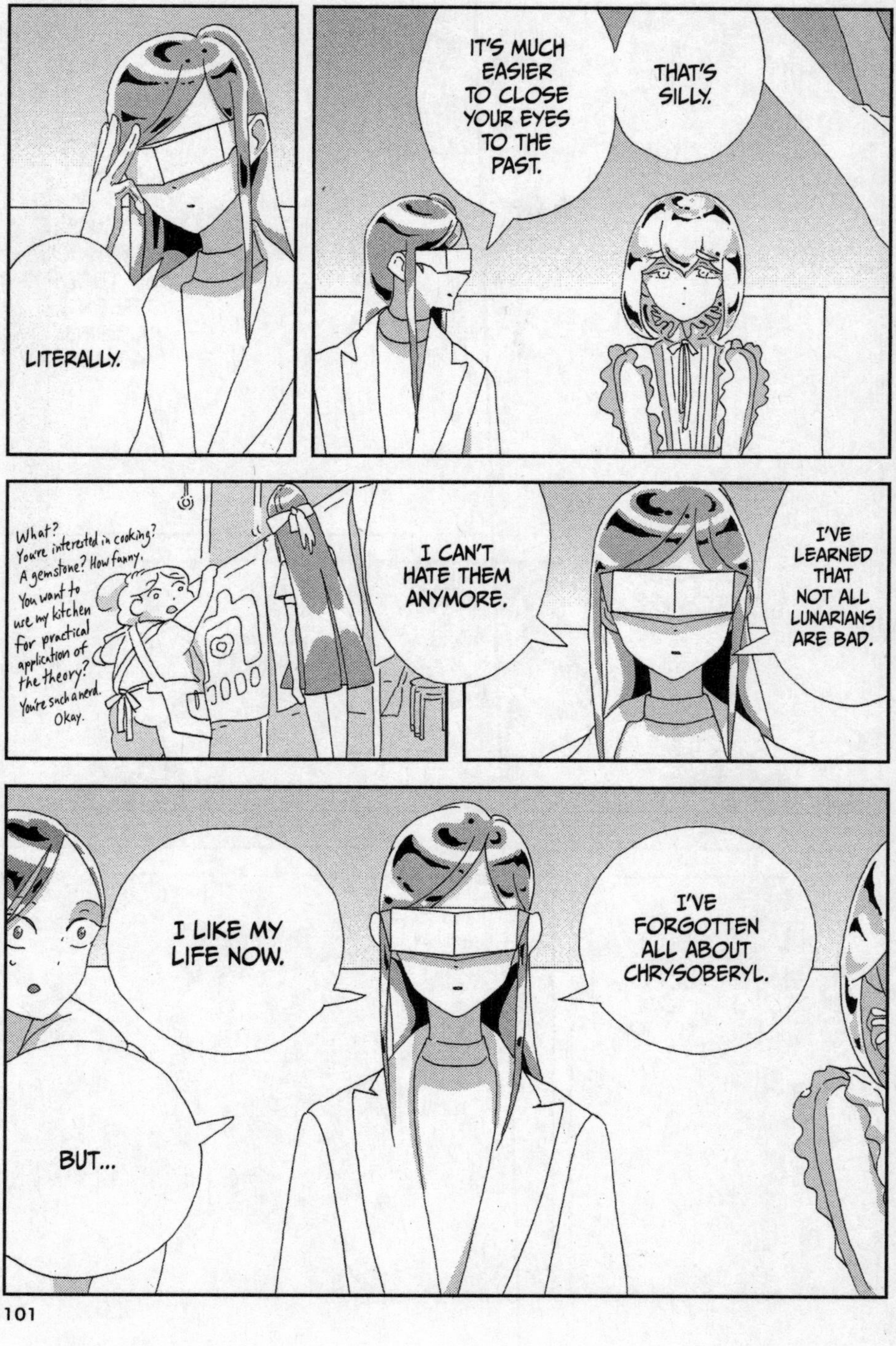
THAT'S SILLY.
IT'S MUCH EASIER TO CLOSE YOUR EYES TO THE PAST.
LITERALLY.
I'VE LEARNED THAT NOT ALL LUNARIANS ARE BAD.
I CAN'T HATE THEM ANYMORE.
What? You're interested in cooking? A gemstone? How funny. You want to use my kitchen for practical application of the theory? You're such a nerd. Okay.
I'VE FORGOTTEN ALL ABOUT CHRYSOBERYL.
I LIKE MY LIFE NOW.
BUT...

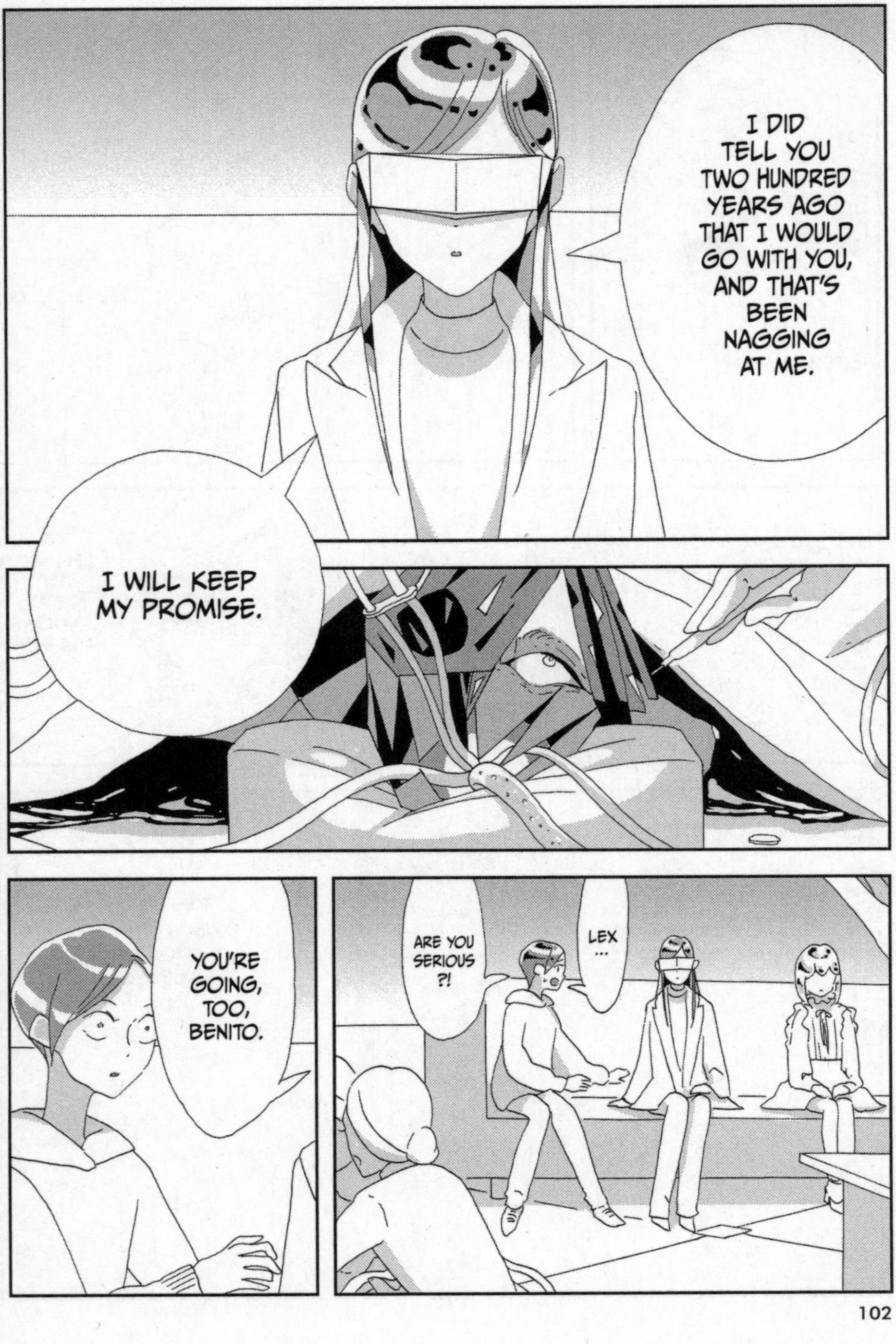
I DID TELL YOU TWO HUNDRED YEARS AGO THAT I WOULD GO WITH YOU, AND THAT'S BEEN NAGGING AT ME.
I WILL KEEP MY PROMISE.
LEX ...
ARE YOU SERIOUS ?!
YOU'RE GOING, TOO, BENITO.

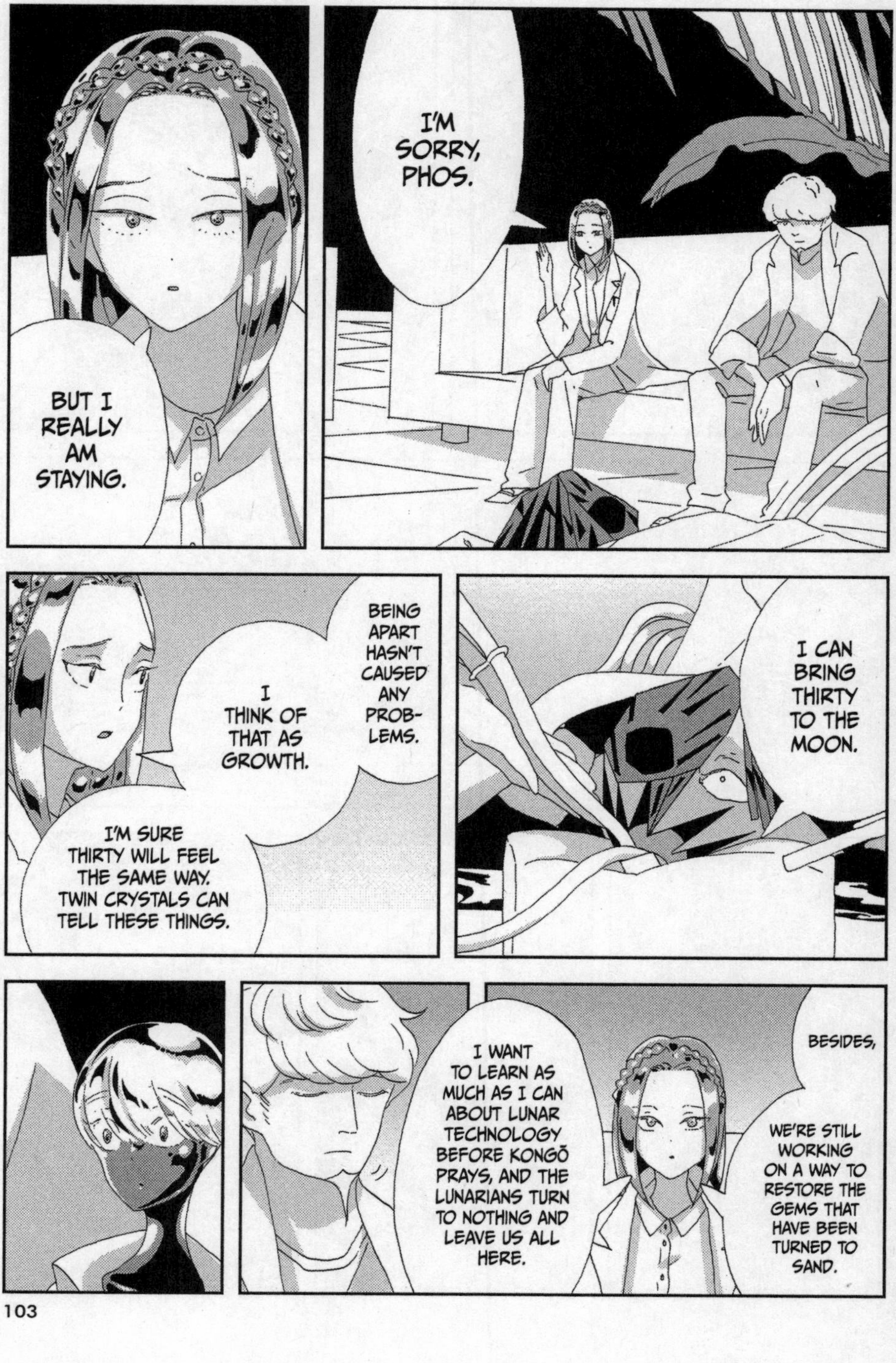
I'M SORRY, PHOS.
BUT I REALLY AM STAYING.
I CAN BRING THIRTY TO THE MOON.
BEING APART HASN'T CAUSED ANY PROB-LEMS.
I THINK OF THAT AS GROWTH.
I'M SURE THIRTY WILL FEEL THE SAME WAY. TWIN CRYSTALS CAN TELL THESE THINGS.
BESIDES,
WE'RE STILL WORKING ON A WAY TO RESTORE THE GEMS THAT HAVE BEEN TURNED TO SAND.
I WANT TO LEARN AS MUCH AS I CAN ABOUT LUNAR TECHNOLOGY BEFORE KONGŌ PRAYS, AND THE LUNARIANS TURN TO NOTHING AND LEAVE US ALL HERE.

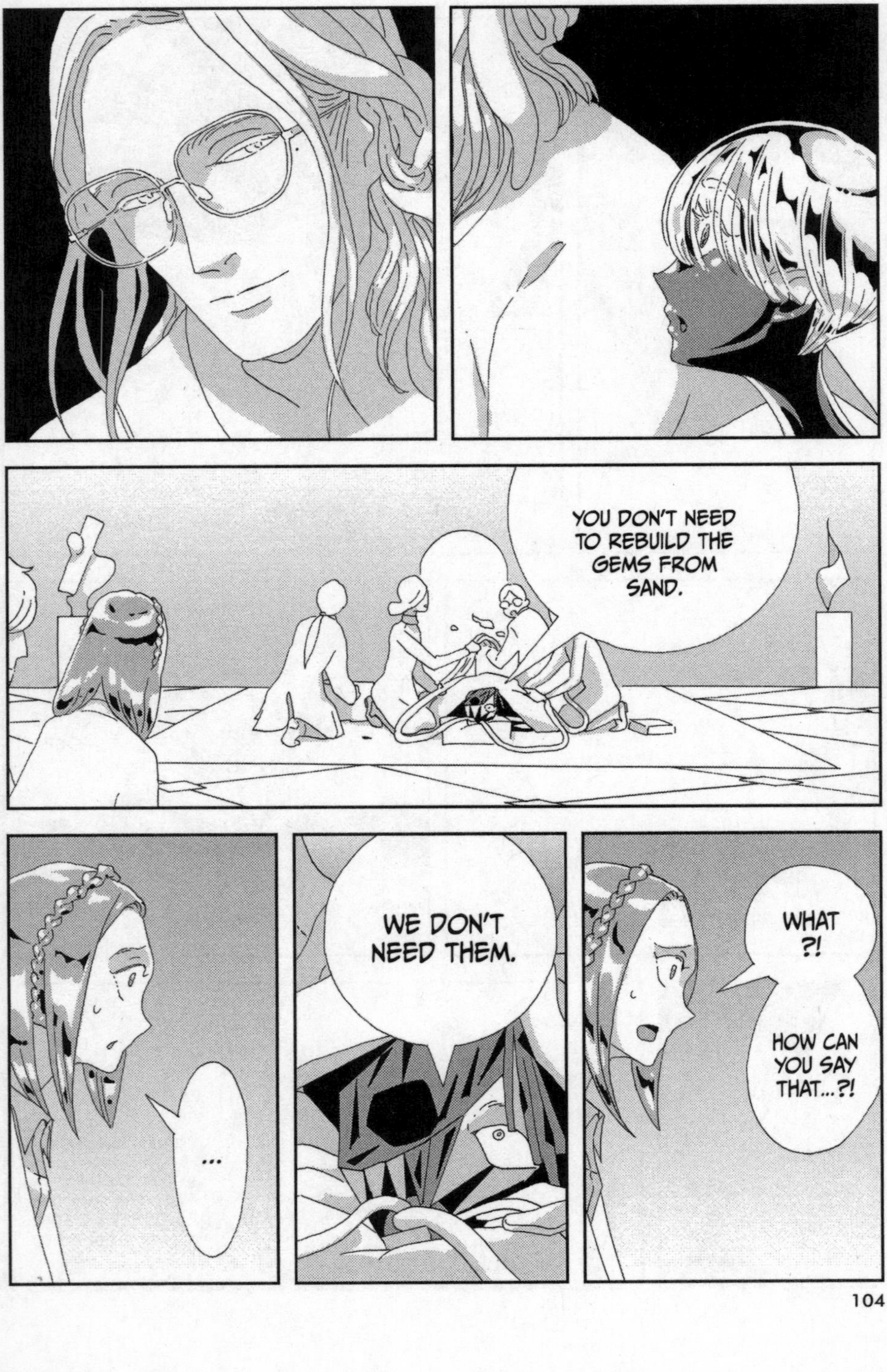
YOU DON'T NEED TO REBUILD THE GEMS FROM SAND.
WHAT ?!
HOW CAN YOU SAY THAT...?!
WE DON'T NEED THEM.
...

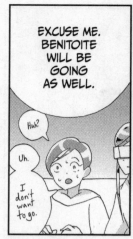

WELL THEN.
DIAMOND AND ALEXANDRITE WILL ACCOMPANY PHOSPHOPHYLLITE. IS THAT CORRECT?
EXCUSE ME. BENITOITE WILL BE GOING AS WELL.
Huh?
Uh.
I don't want to go.
OH, AND...
YOUR RIGHT EYE. KONGŌ HAS IT.
WE CAN MAKE YOU A NEW ONE.
WHAT WOULD YOU PREFER?

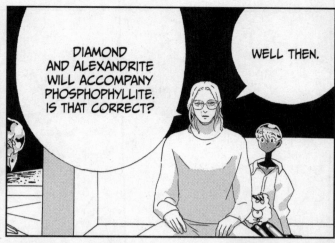

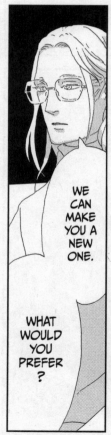

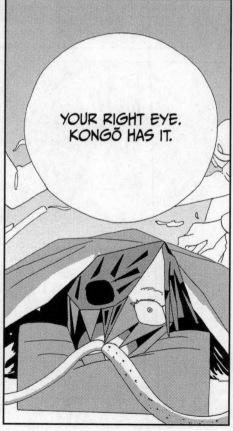

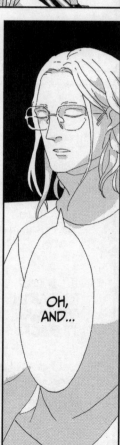

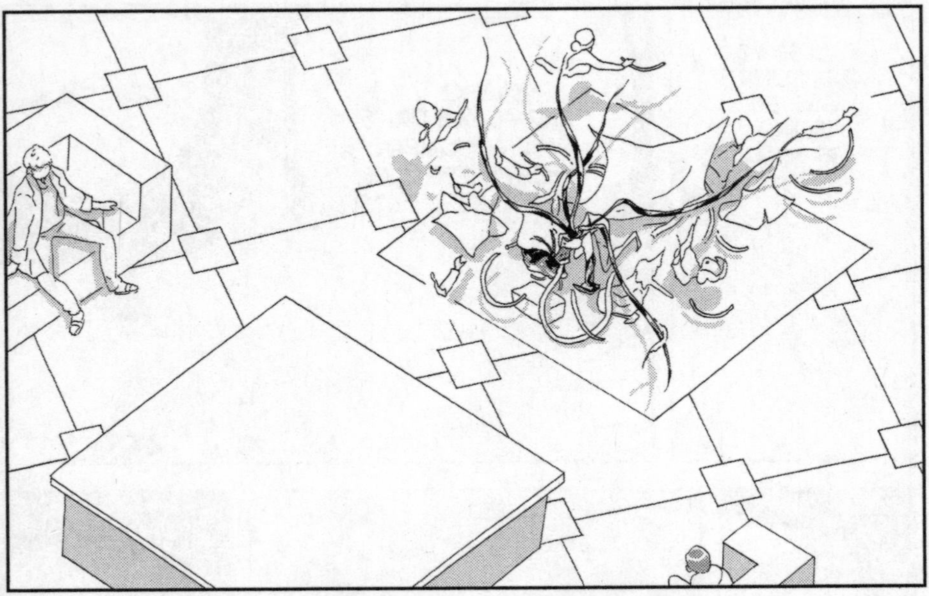

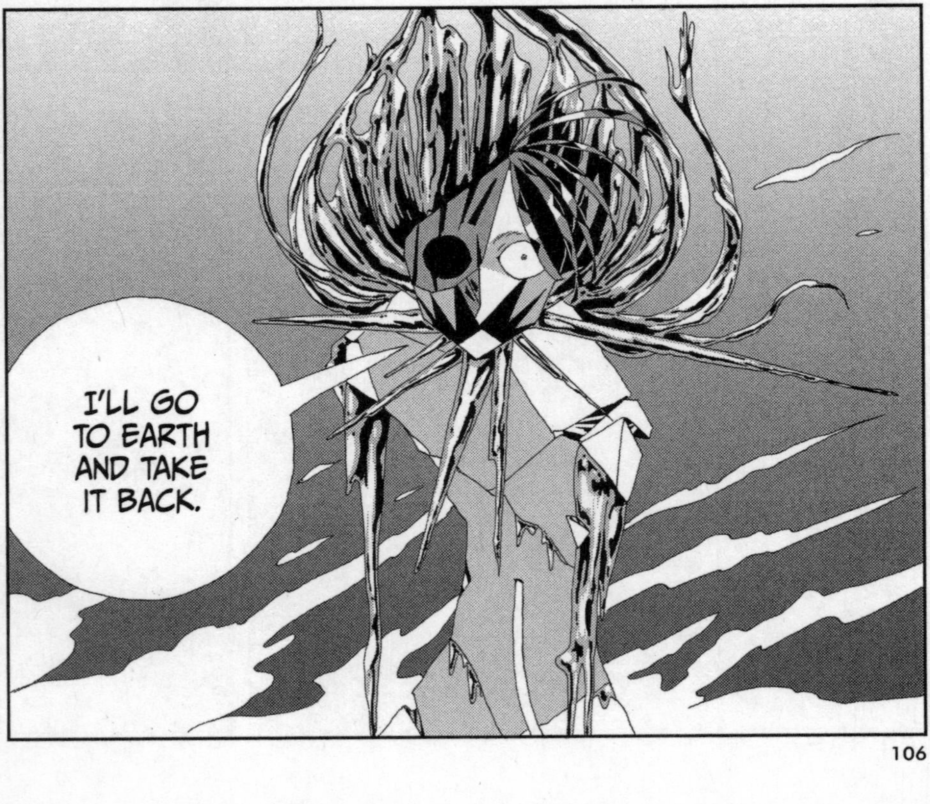
I'LL GO
TO EARTH
AND TAKE
IT BACK.

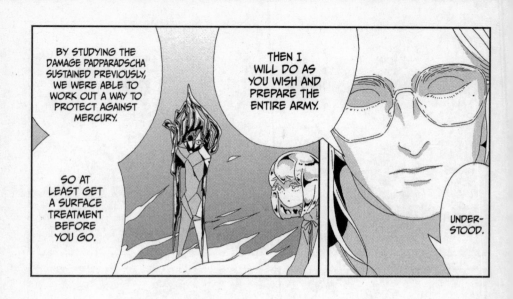

UNDER-
STOOD.
THEN I WILL DO AS YOU WISH AND PREPARE THE ENTIRE ARMY.
BY STUDYING THE DAMAGE PADPARADSCHA SUSTAINED PREVIOUSLY, WE WERE ABLE TO WORK OUT A WAY TO PROTECT AGAINST MERCURY.
SO AT LEAST GET A SURFACE TREATMENT BEFORE YOU GO.
IT WON'T CLOSE.

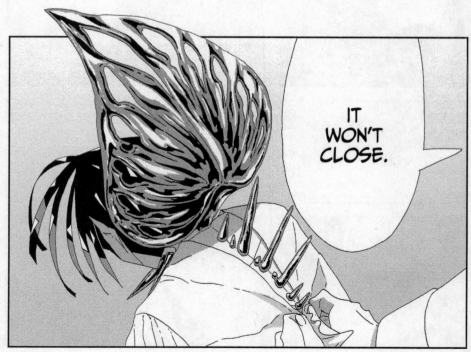

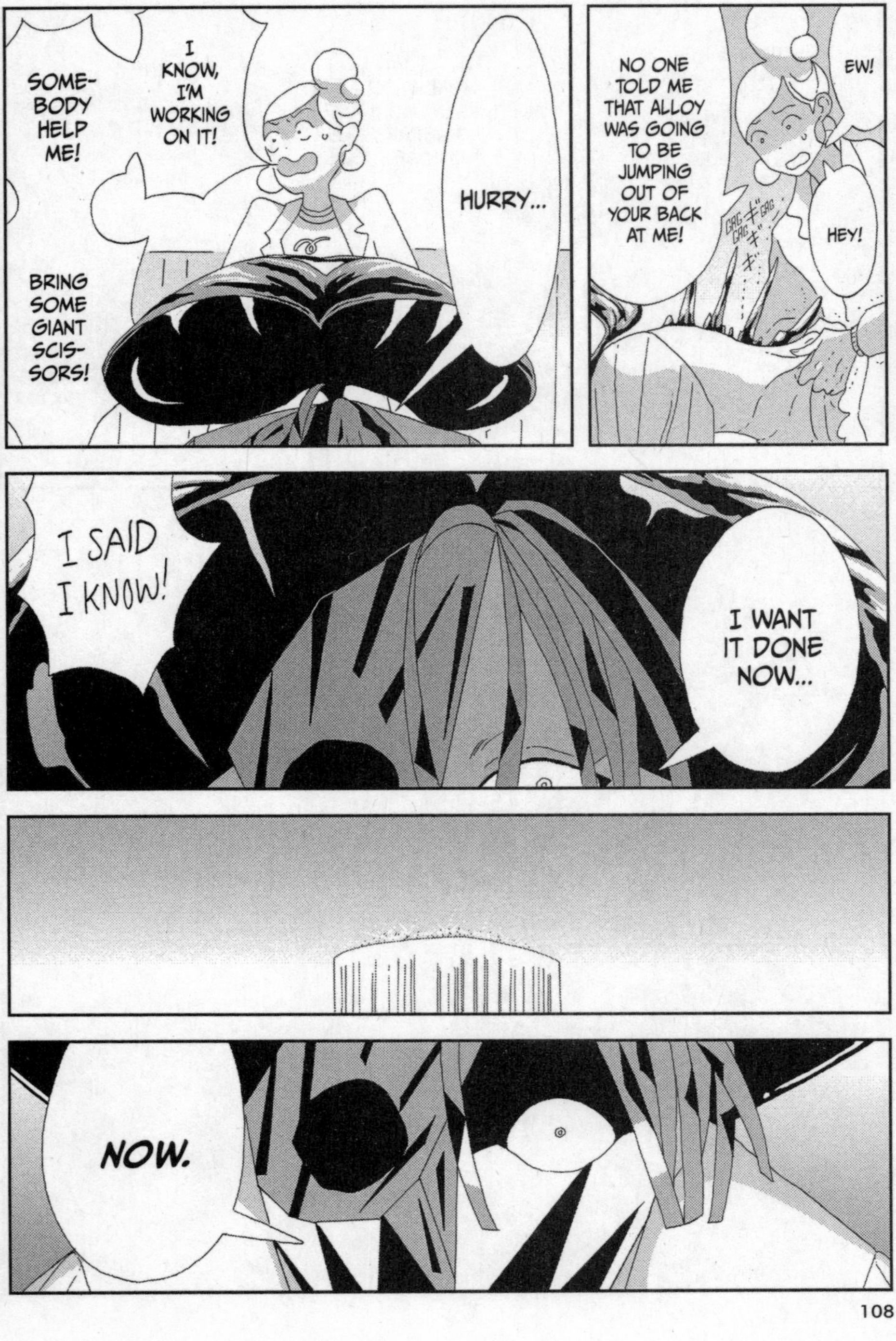

EW!
NO ONE TOLD ME THAT ALLOY WAS GOING TO BE JUMPING OUT OF YOUR BACK AT ME!
GAG GAG GAG
HEY!
HURRY...
I KNOW, I'M WORKING ON IT!
SOME-BODY HELP ME!
BRING SOME GIANT SCIS-SORS!
I WANT IT DONE NOW...
I SAID I KNOW!
NOW.

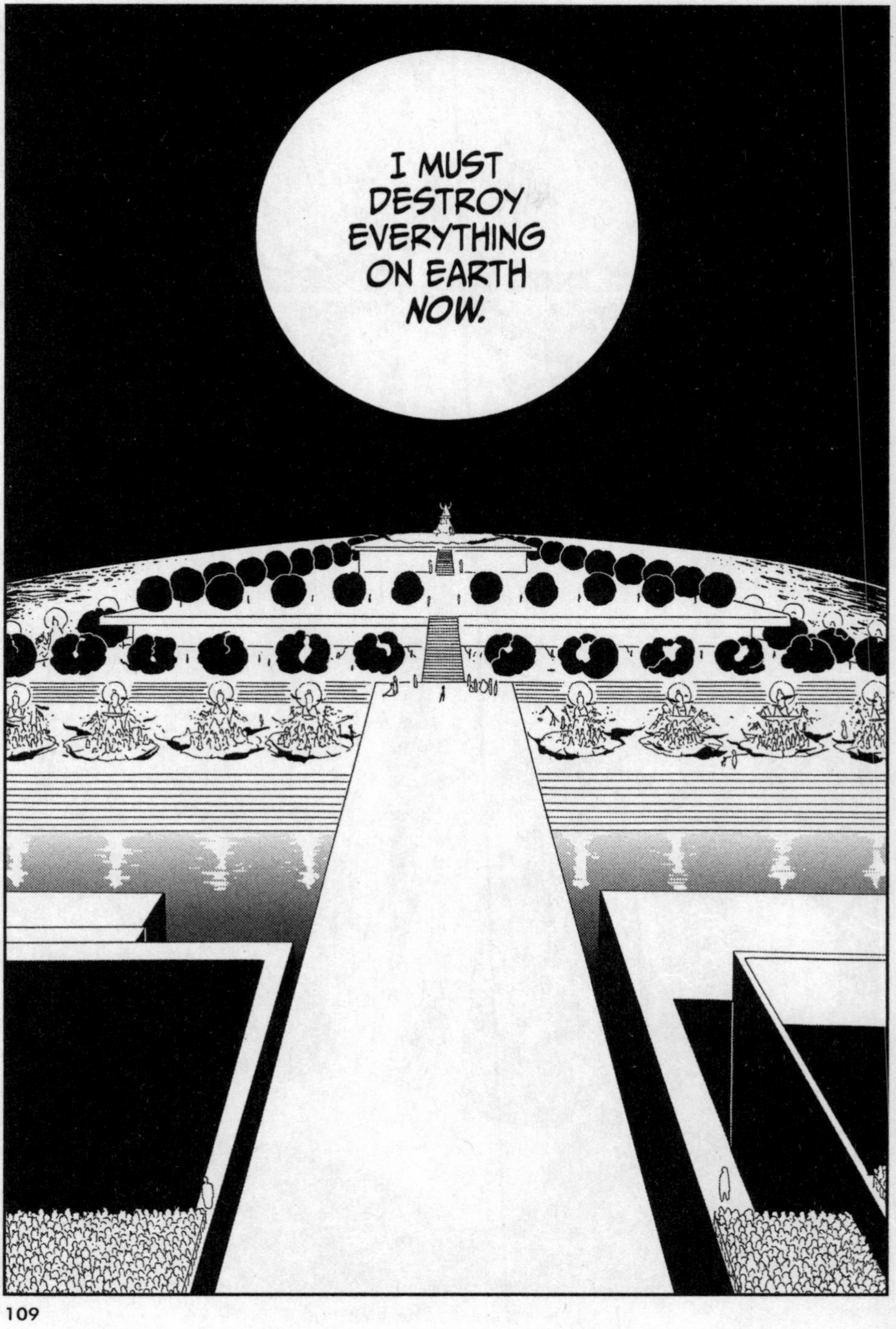
I MUST DESTROY EVERYTHING ON EARTH NOW.

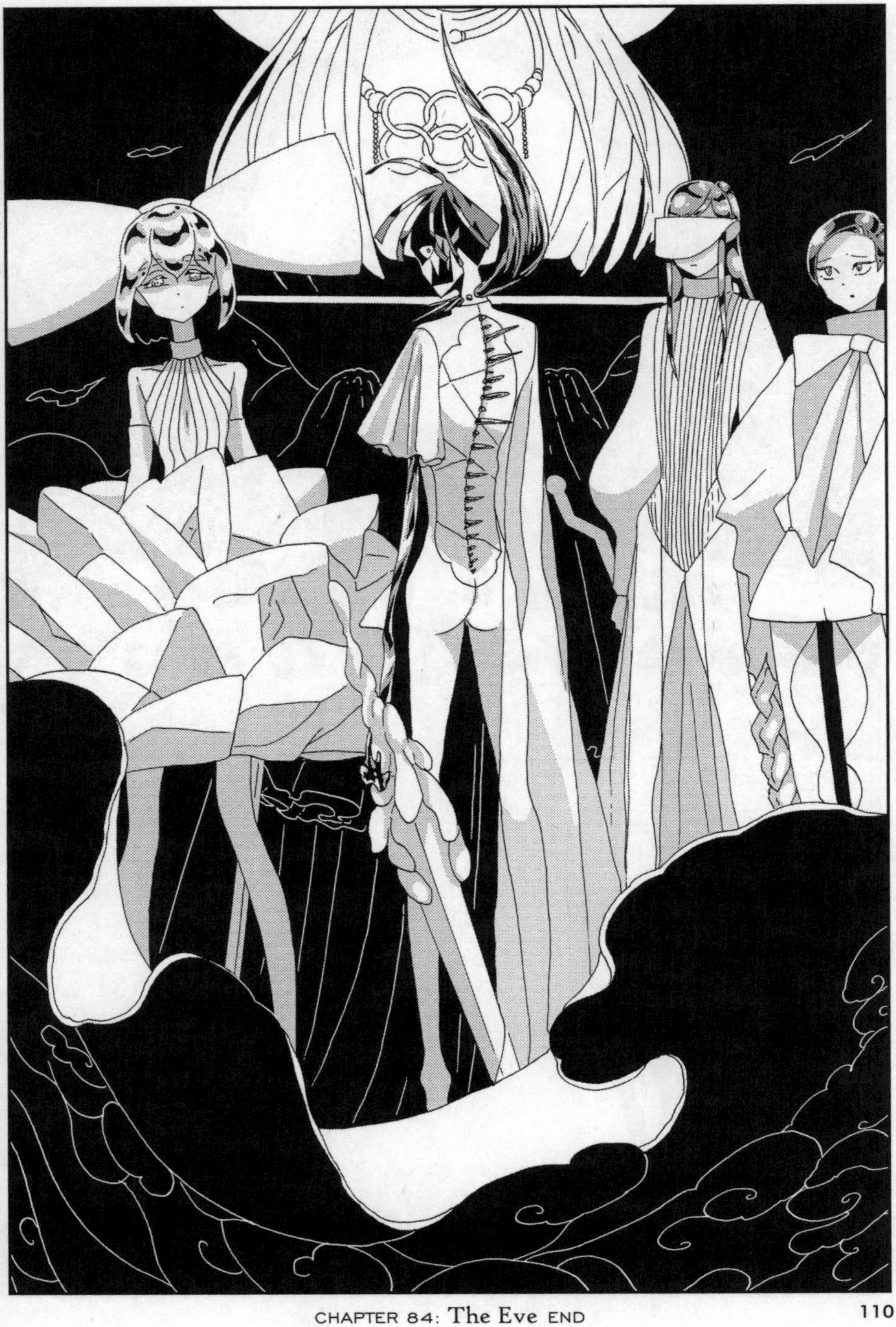

CHAPTER 84: The Eve END

CHAPTER 85:

Birthday

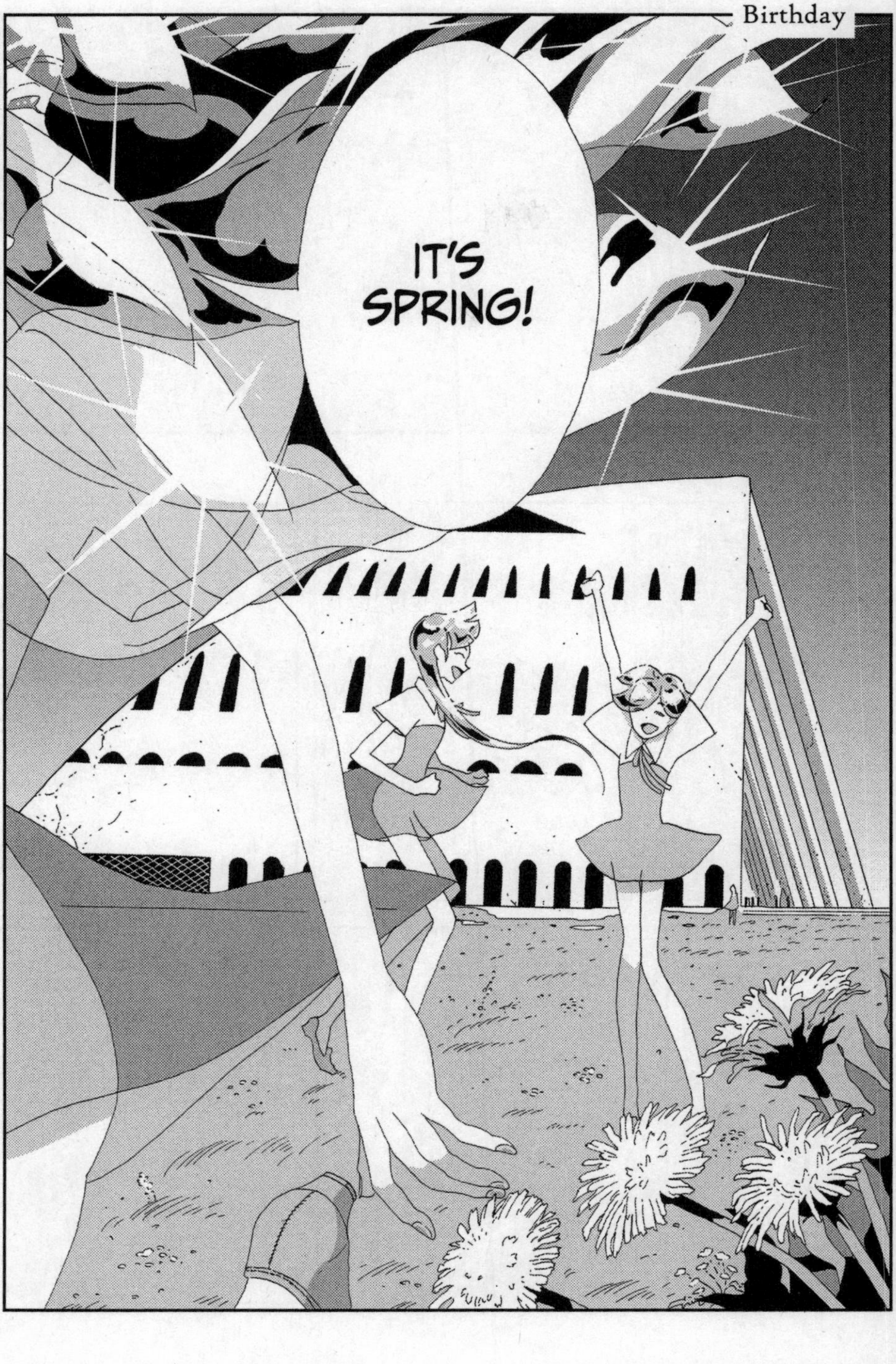
IT'S SPRING!

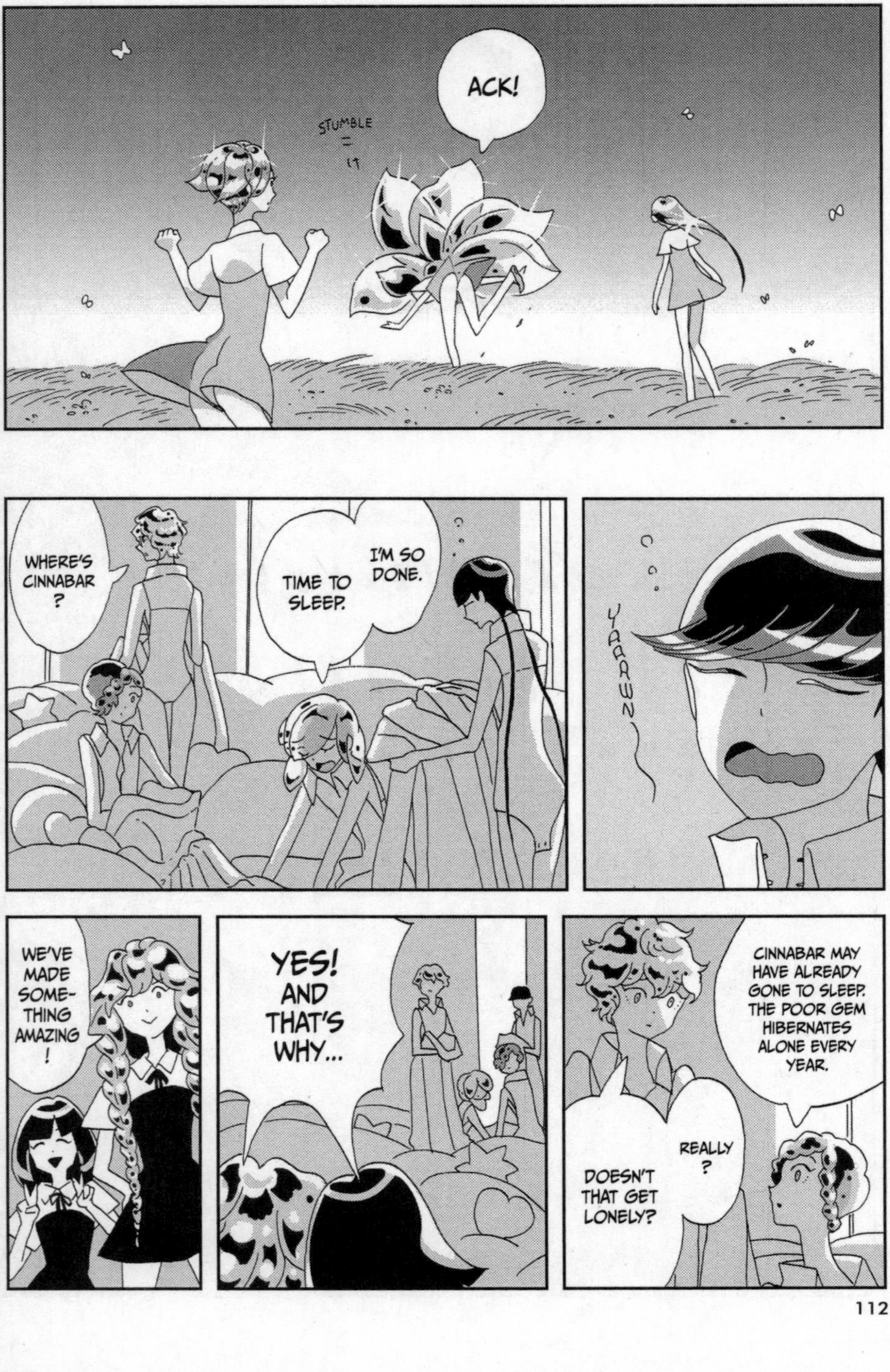
STUMBLE
ACK!
YAAAWN
I'M SO DONE.
TIME TO SLEEP.
WHERE'S CINNABAR?
CINNABAR MAY HAVE ALREADY GONE TO SLEEP. THE POOR GEM HIBERNATES ALONE EVERY YEAR.
REALLY?
DOESN'T THAT GET LONELY?
YES! AND THAT'S WHY...
WE'VE MADE SOMETHING AMAZING!

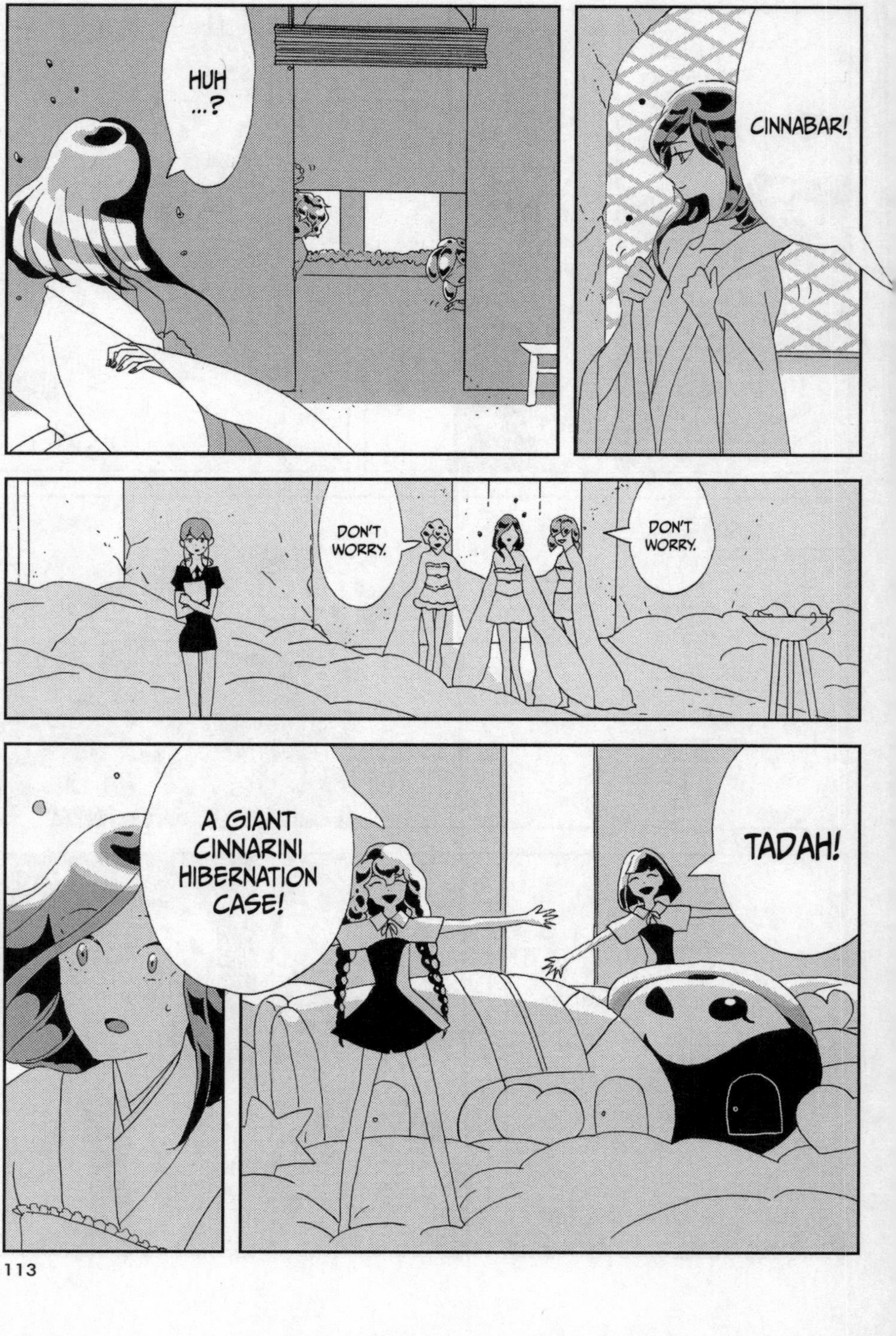
CINNABAR!
HUH ...?
DON'T WORRY.
DON'T WORRY.
TADAH!
A GIANT CINNARINI HIBERNATION CASE!

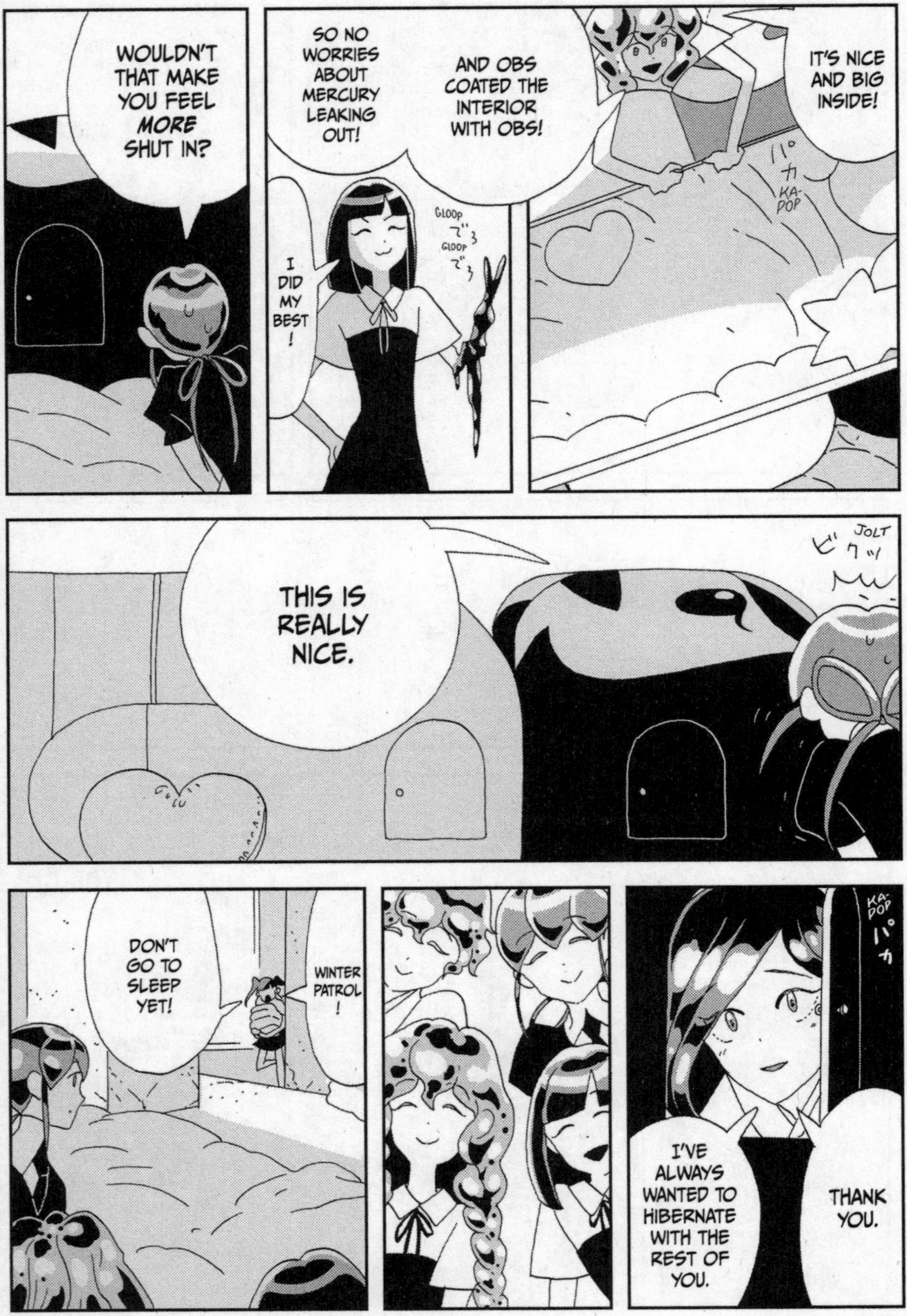
IT'S NICE AND BIG INSIDE!
パカ
KA-POP
AND OBS COATED THE INTERIOR WITH OBS!
SO NO WORRIES ABOUT MERCURY LEAKING OUT!
GLOOP
GLOOP
I DID MY BEST!
WOULDN'T THAT MAKE YOU FEEL *MORE* SHUT IN?
JOLT
ビクッ
THIS IS REALLY NICE.
KA-POP
パカ
THANK YOU.
I'VE ALWAYS WANTED TO HIBERNATE WITH THE REST OF YOU.
WINTER PATROL!
DON'T GO TO SLEEP YET!

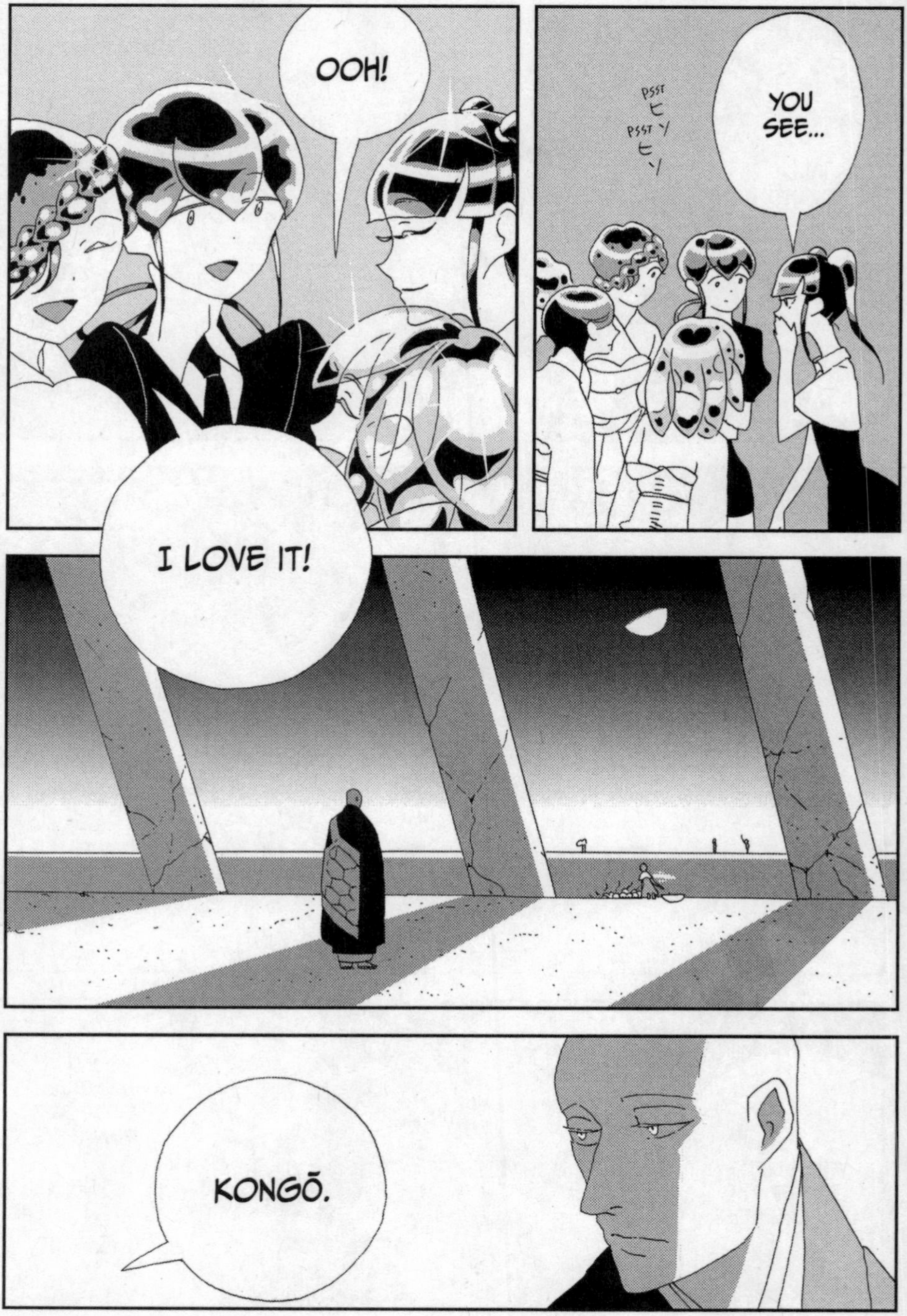
PSST ヒソ
PSST ヒソ
YOU SEE...
OOH!
I LOVE IT!
KONGŌ.

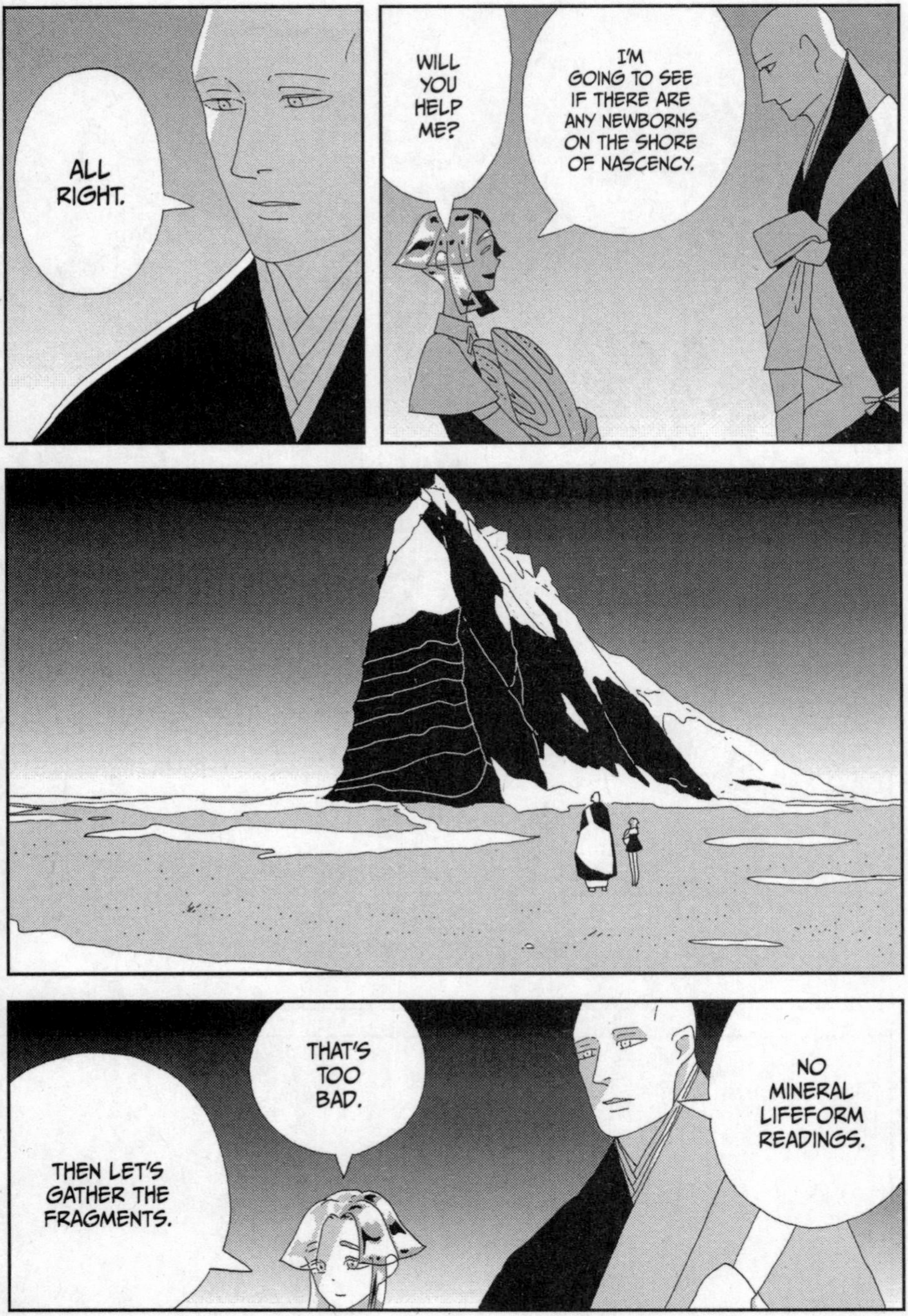
I'M GOING TO SEE IF THERE ARE ANY NEWBORNS ON THE SHORE OF NASCENCY.
WILL YOU HELP ME?
ALL RIGHT.
NO MINERAL LIFEFORM READINGS.
THAT'S TOO BAD.
THEN LET'S GATHER THE FRAGMENTS.

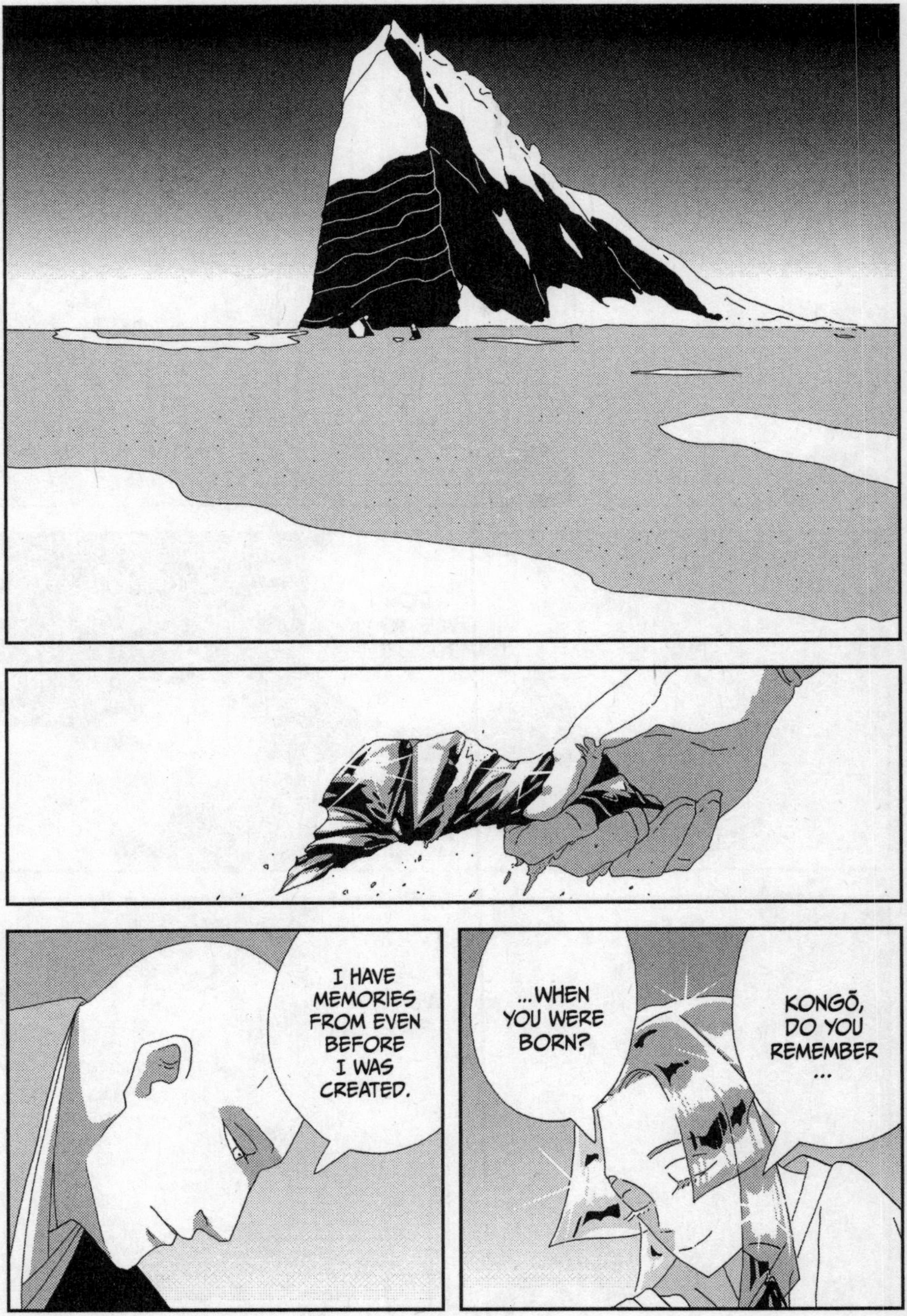
KONGŌ, DO YOU REMEMBER ...
...WHEN YOU WERE BORN?
I HAVE MEMORIES FROM EVEN BEFORE I WAS CREATED.

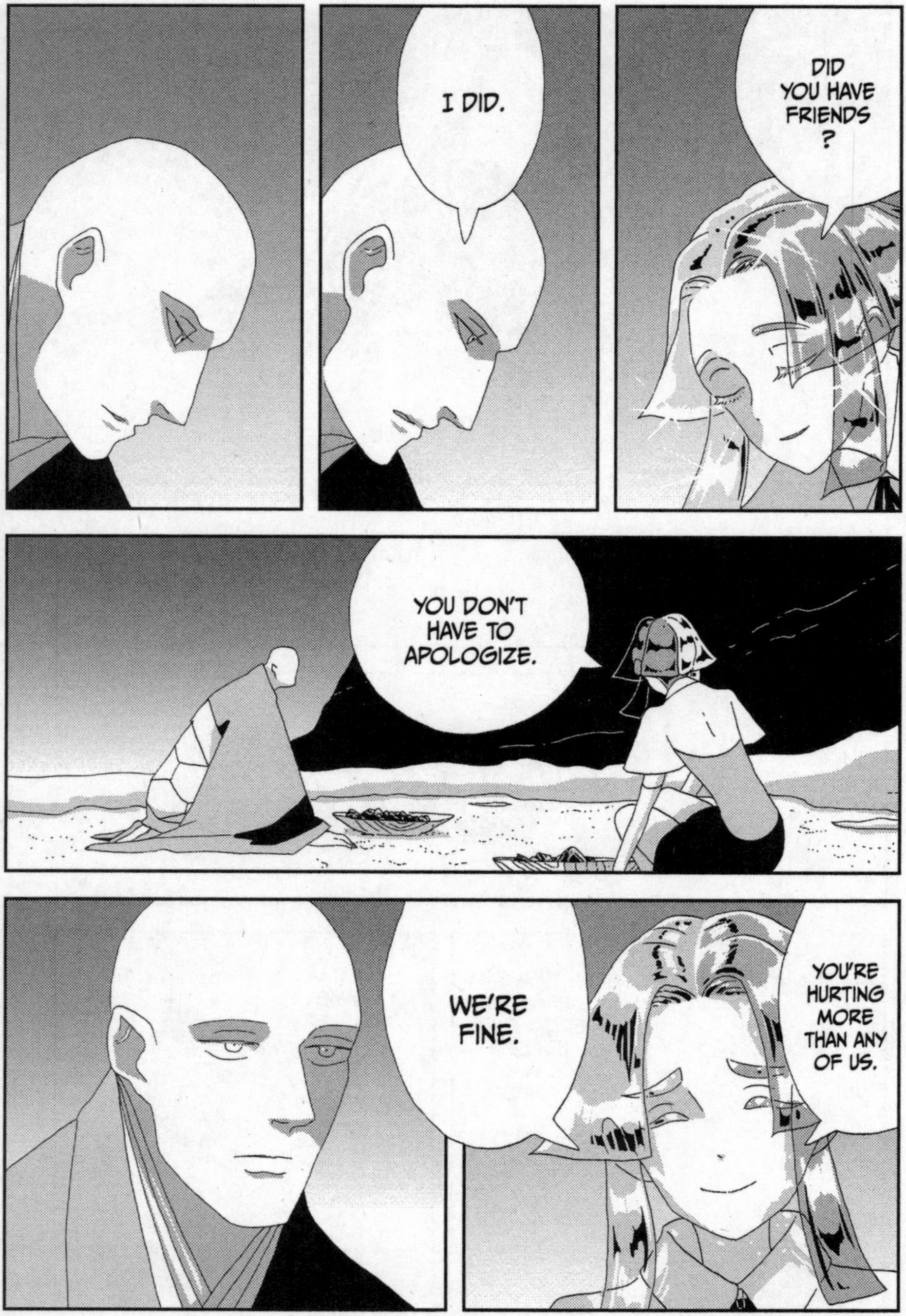
DID YOU HAVE FRIENDS ?
I DID.
YOU DON'T HAVE TO APOLOGIZE.
YOU'RE HURTING MORE THAN ANY OF US.
WE'RE FINE.

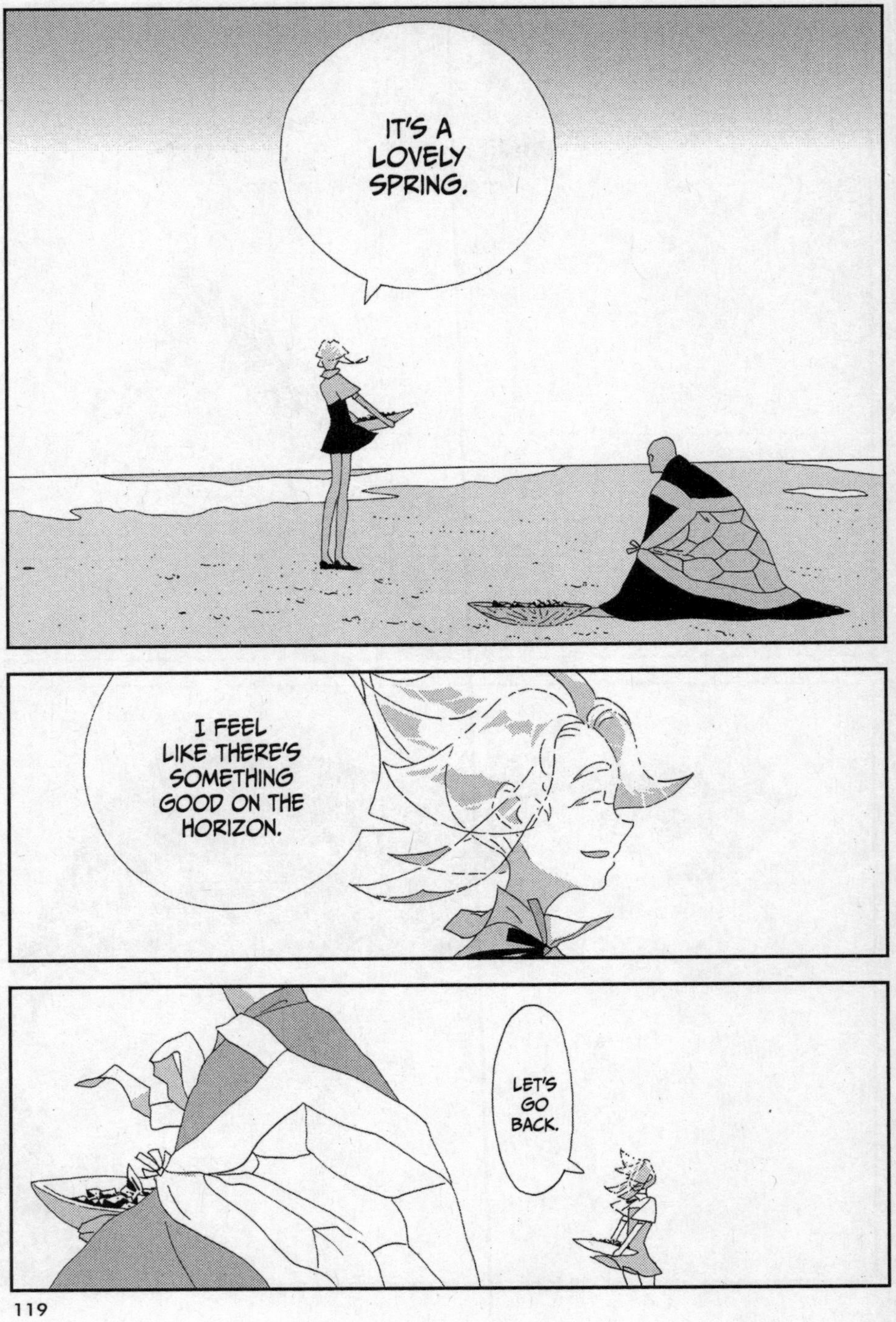
IT'S A LOVELY SPRING.
I FEEL LIKE THERE'S SOMETHING GOOD ON THE HORIZON.
LET'S GO BACK.

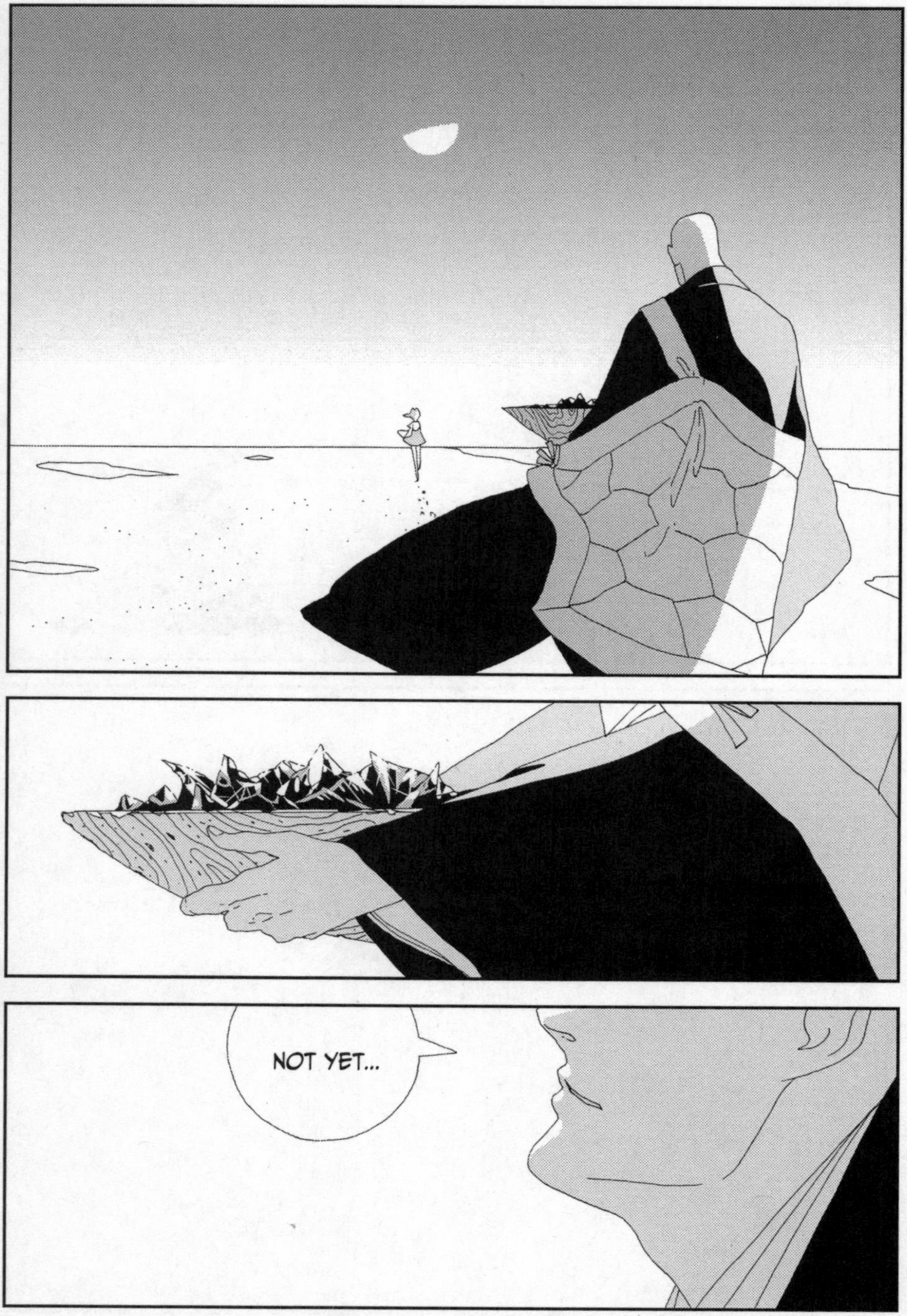
NOT YET...

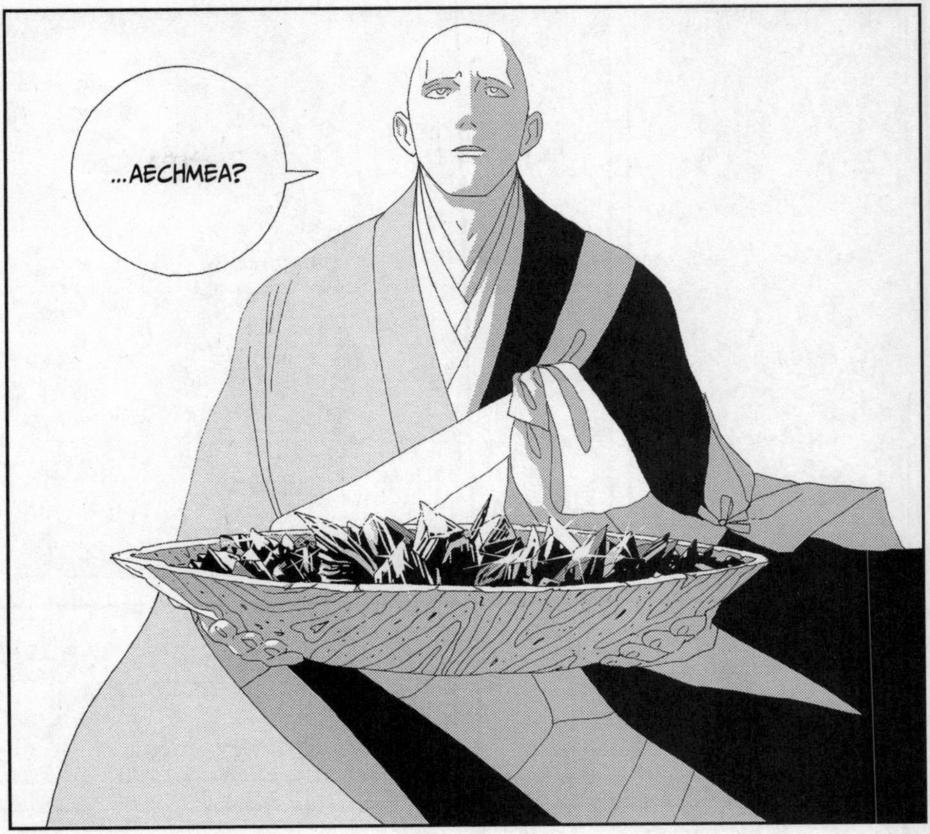
...AECHMEA?

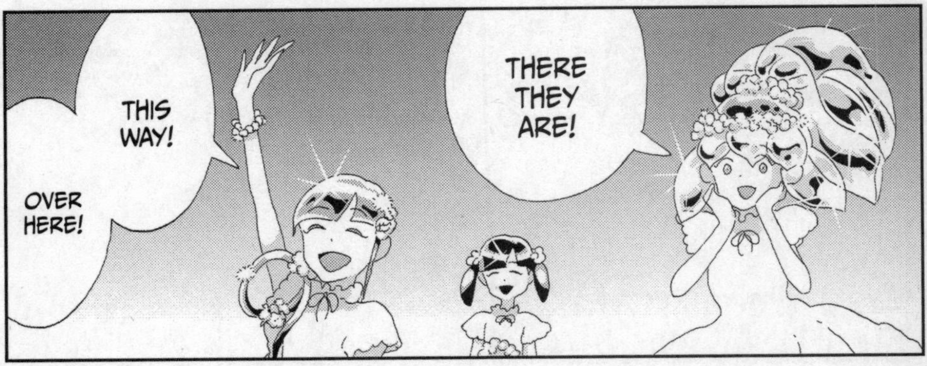
THERE THEY ARE!
THIS WAY!
OVER HERE!

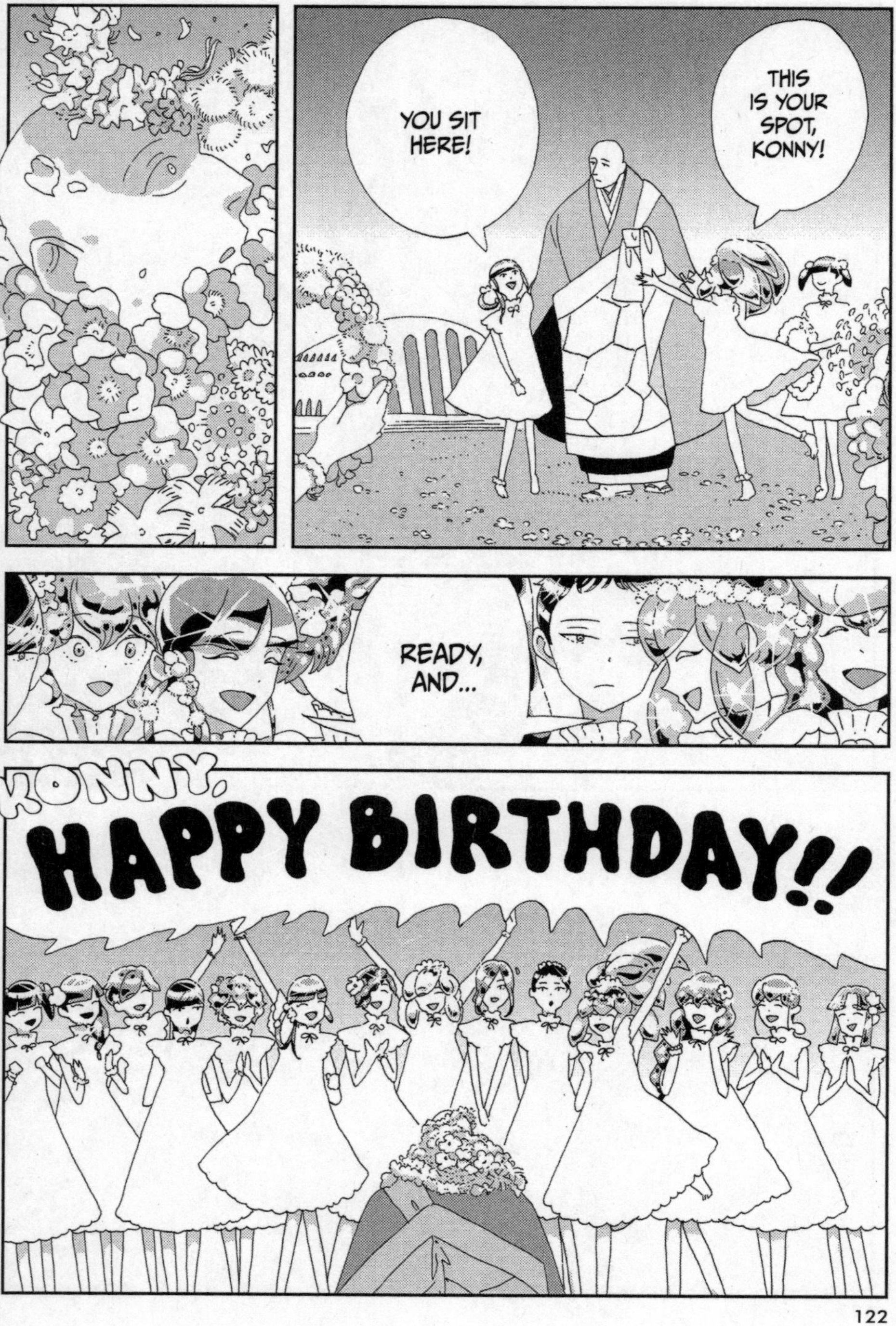
THIS IS YOUR SPOT, KONNY!
YOU SIT HERE!
READY, AND...
KONNY, HAPPY BIRTHDAY!!

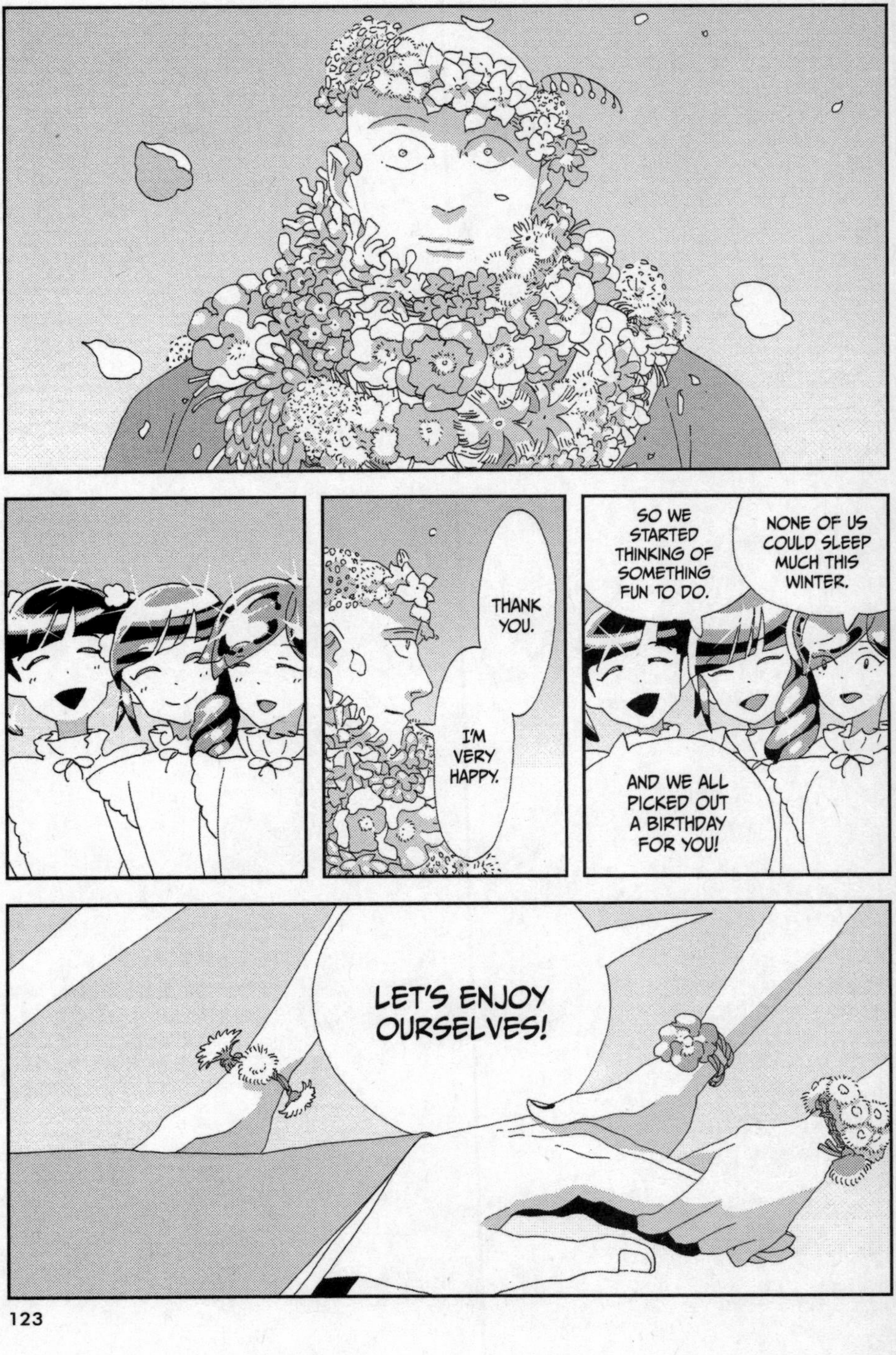
NONE OF US COULD SLEEP MUCH THIS WINTER.
SO WE STARTED THINKING OF SOMETHING FUN TO DO.
AND WE ALL PICKED OUT A BIRTHDAY FOR YOU!
THANK YOU.
I'M VERY HAPPY.
LET'S ENJOY OURSELVES!

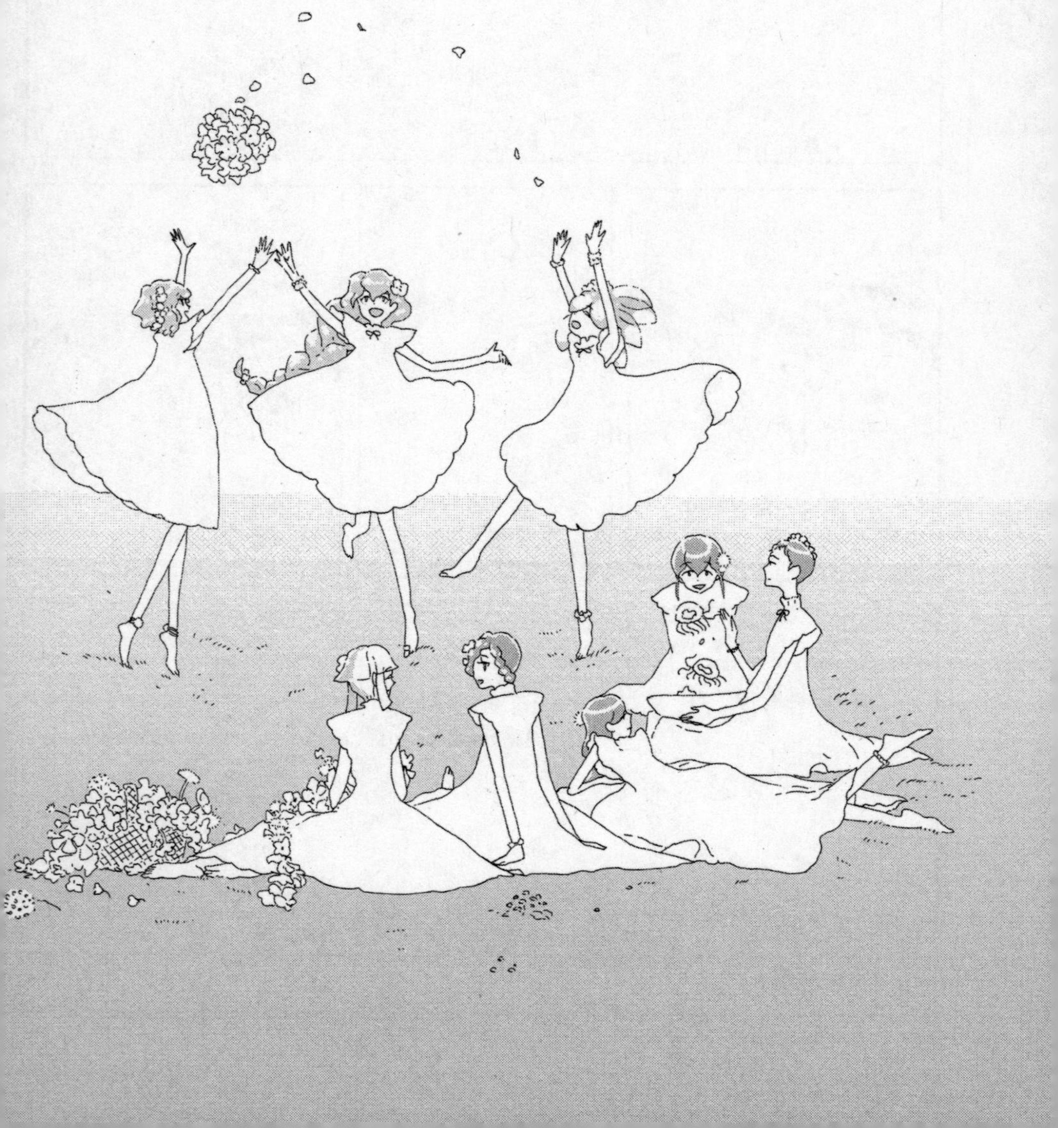

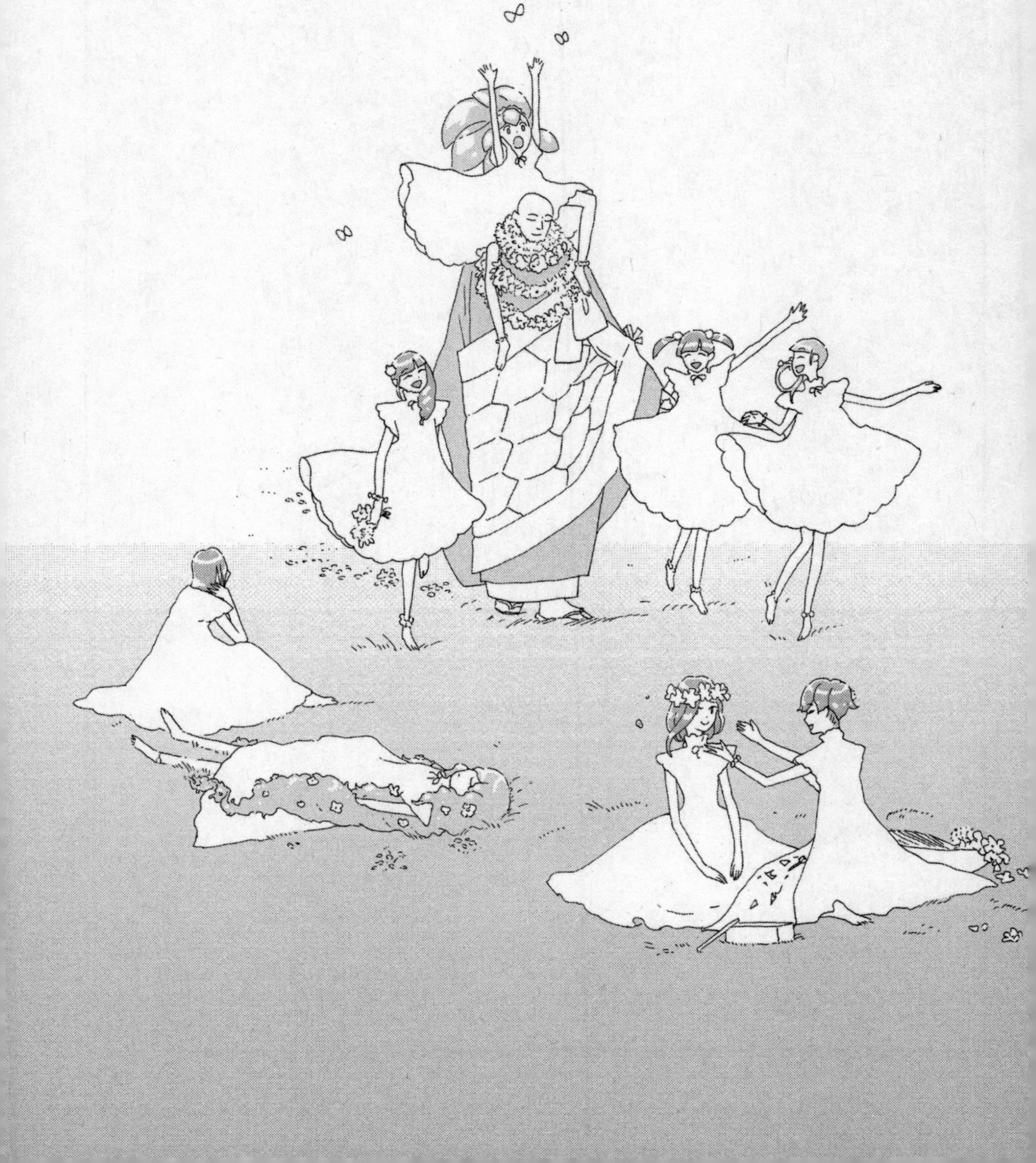

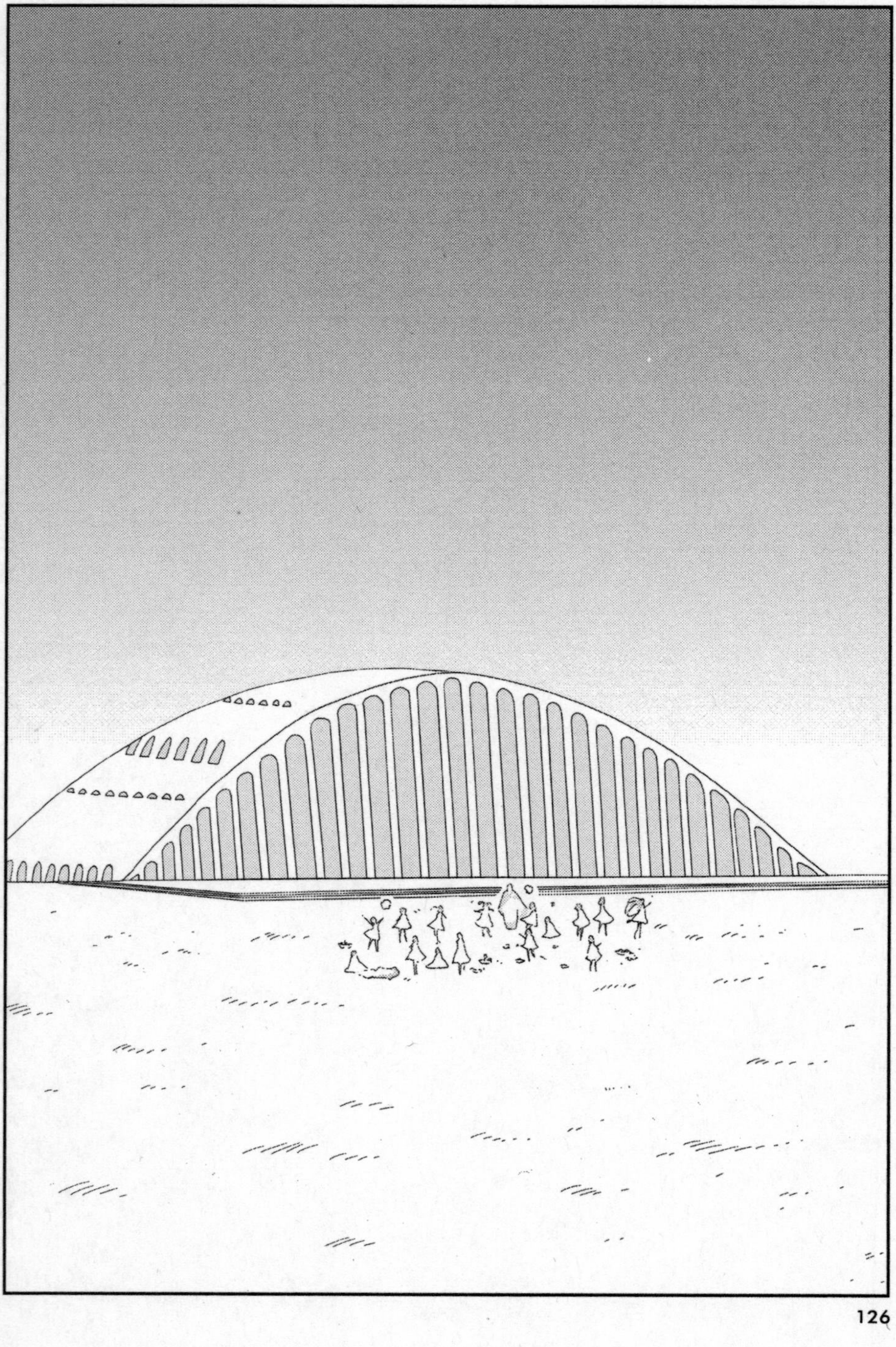

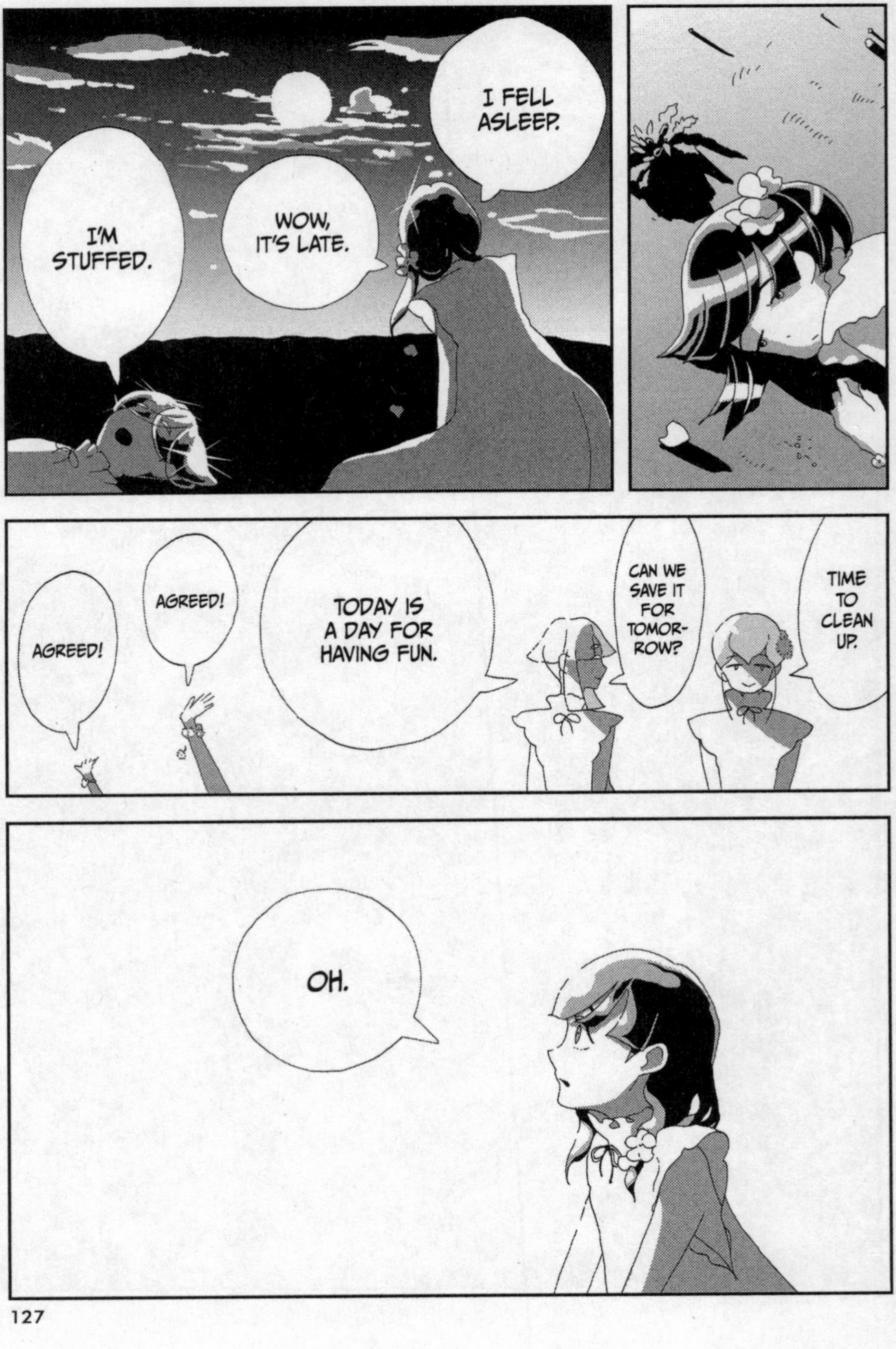
I FELL ASLEEP.
WOW, IT'S LATE.
I'M STUFFED.
TIME TO CLEAN UP.
CAN WE SAVE IT FOR TOMOR-ROW?
TODAY IS A DAY FOR HAVING FUN.
AGREED!
AGREED!
OH.

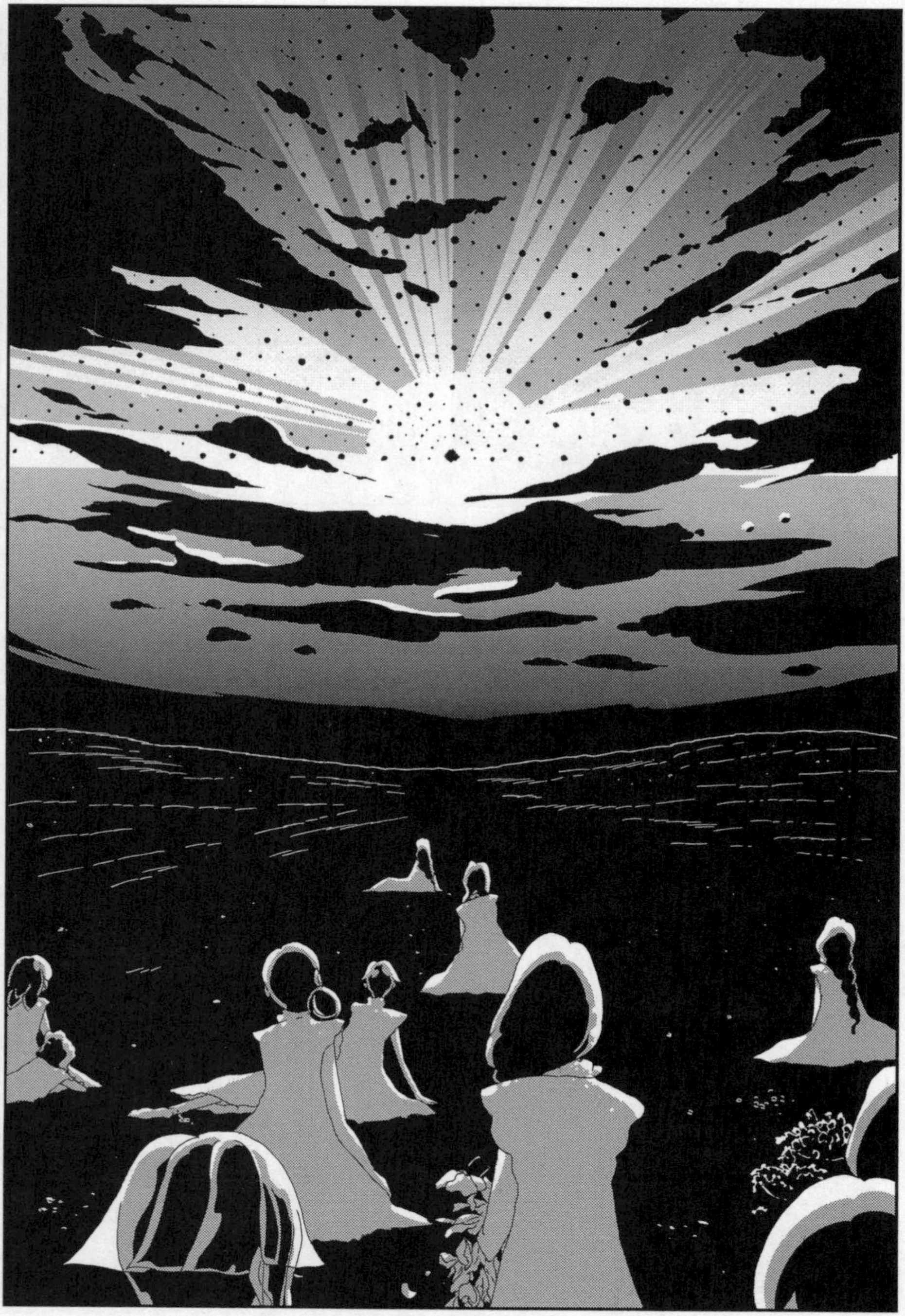

CHAPTER 85: Birthday END

CHAPTER 86:

War

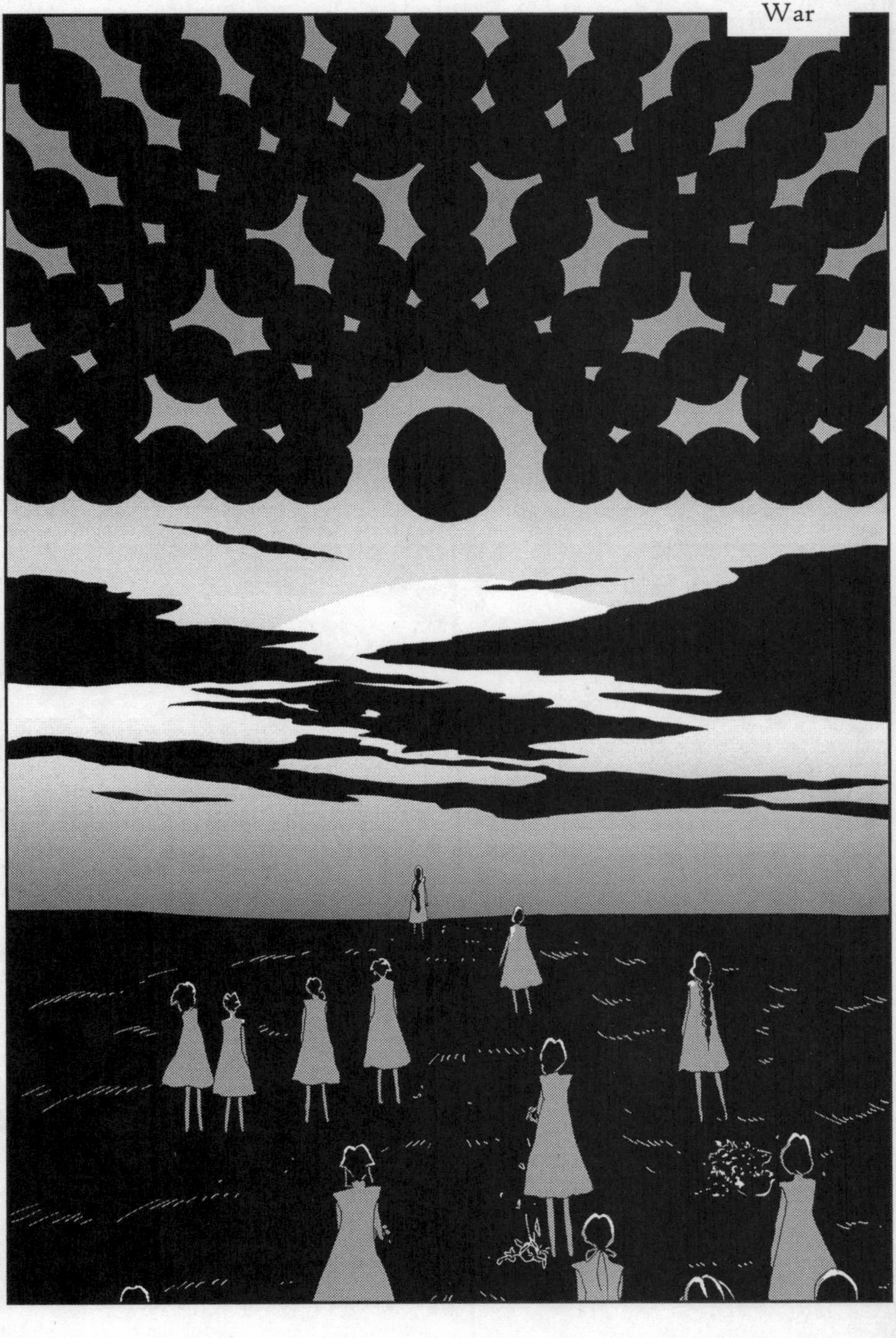

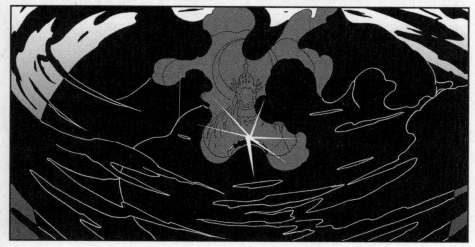

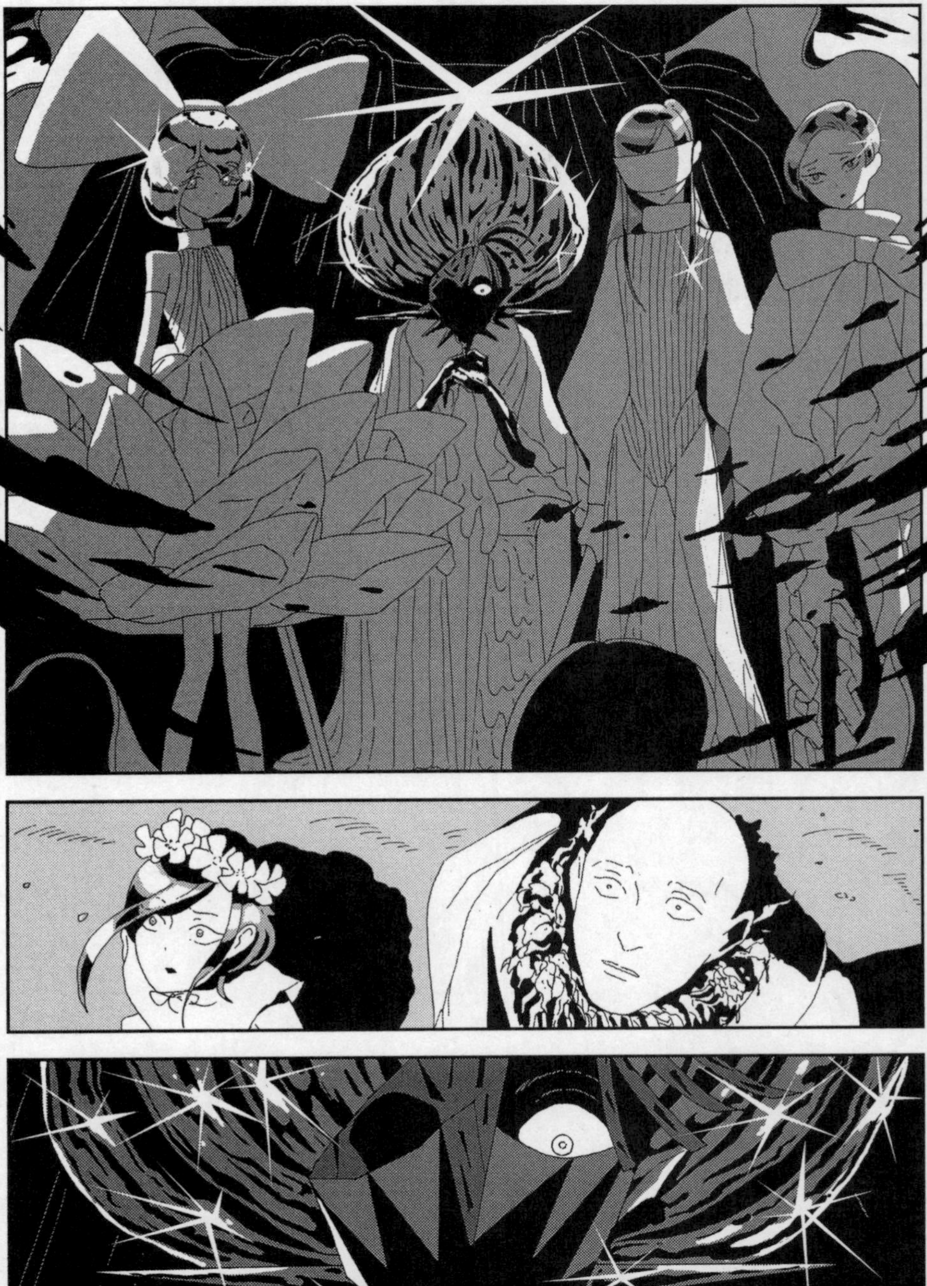

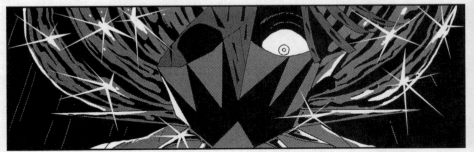

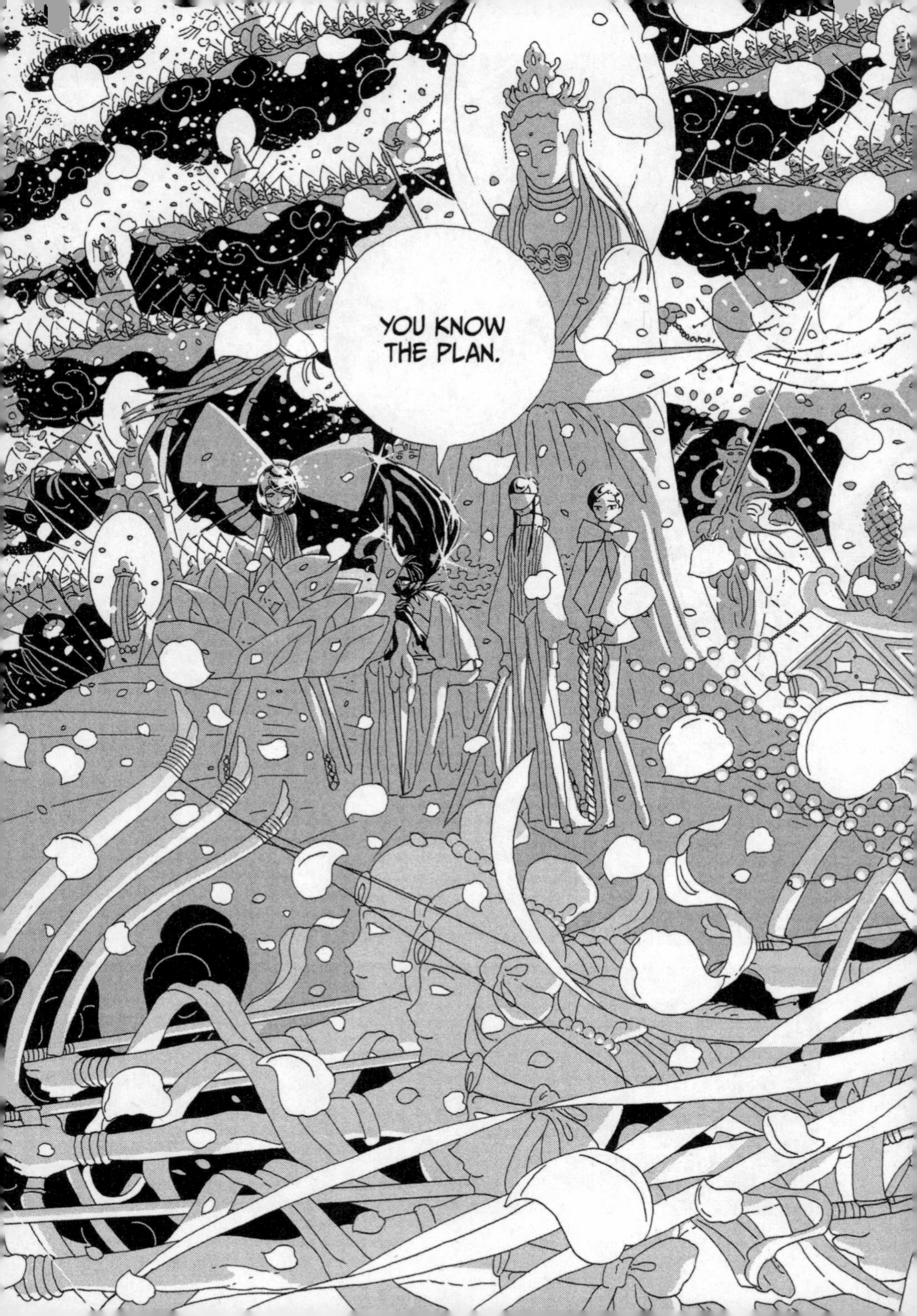
YOU KNOW THE PLAN.

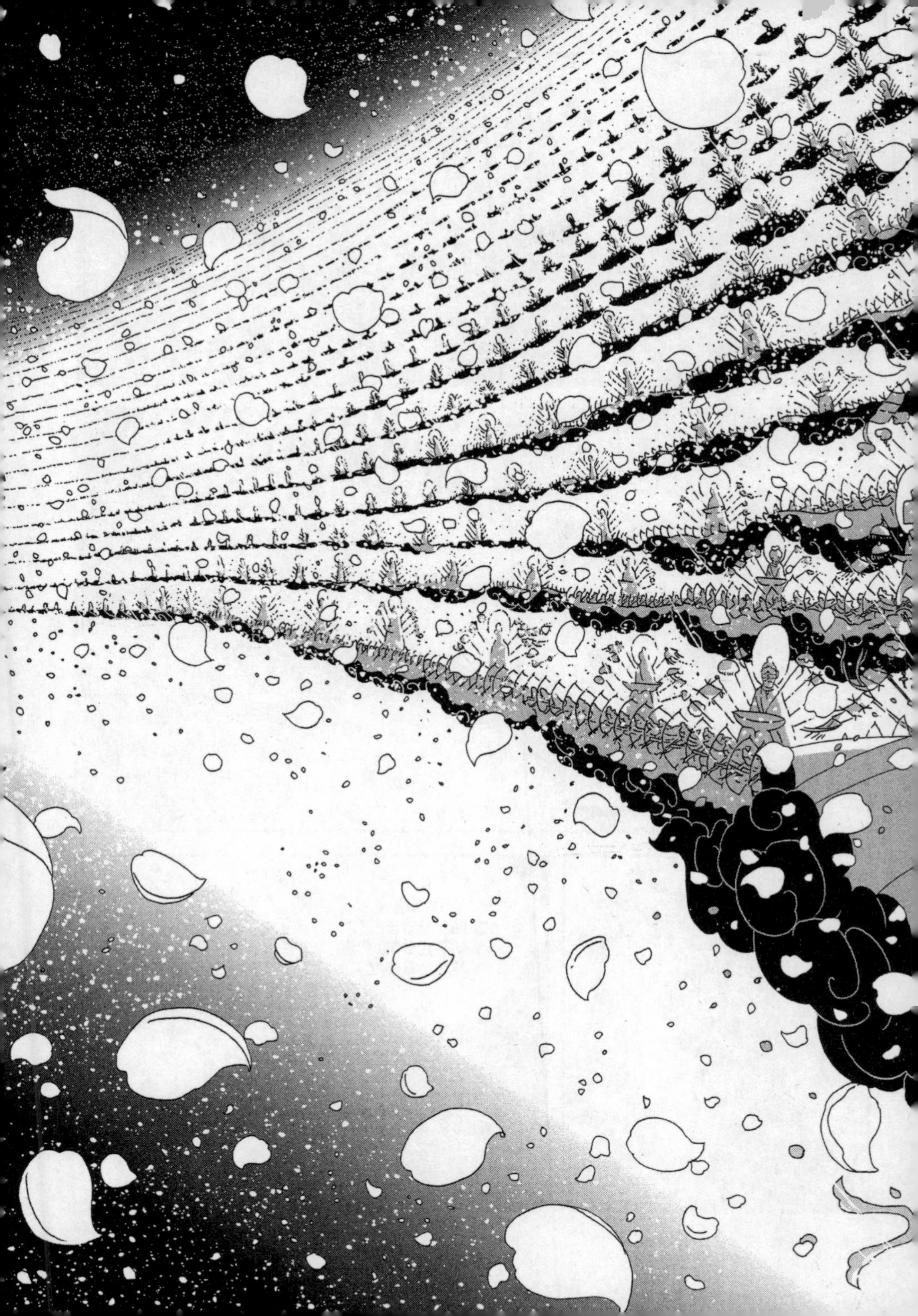

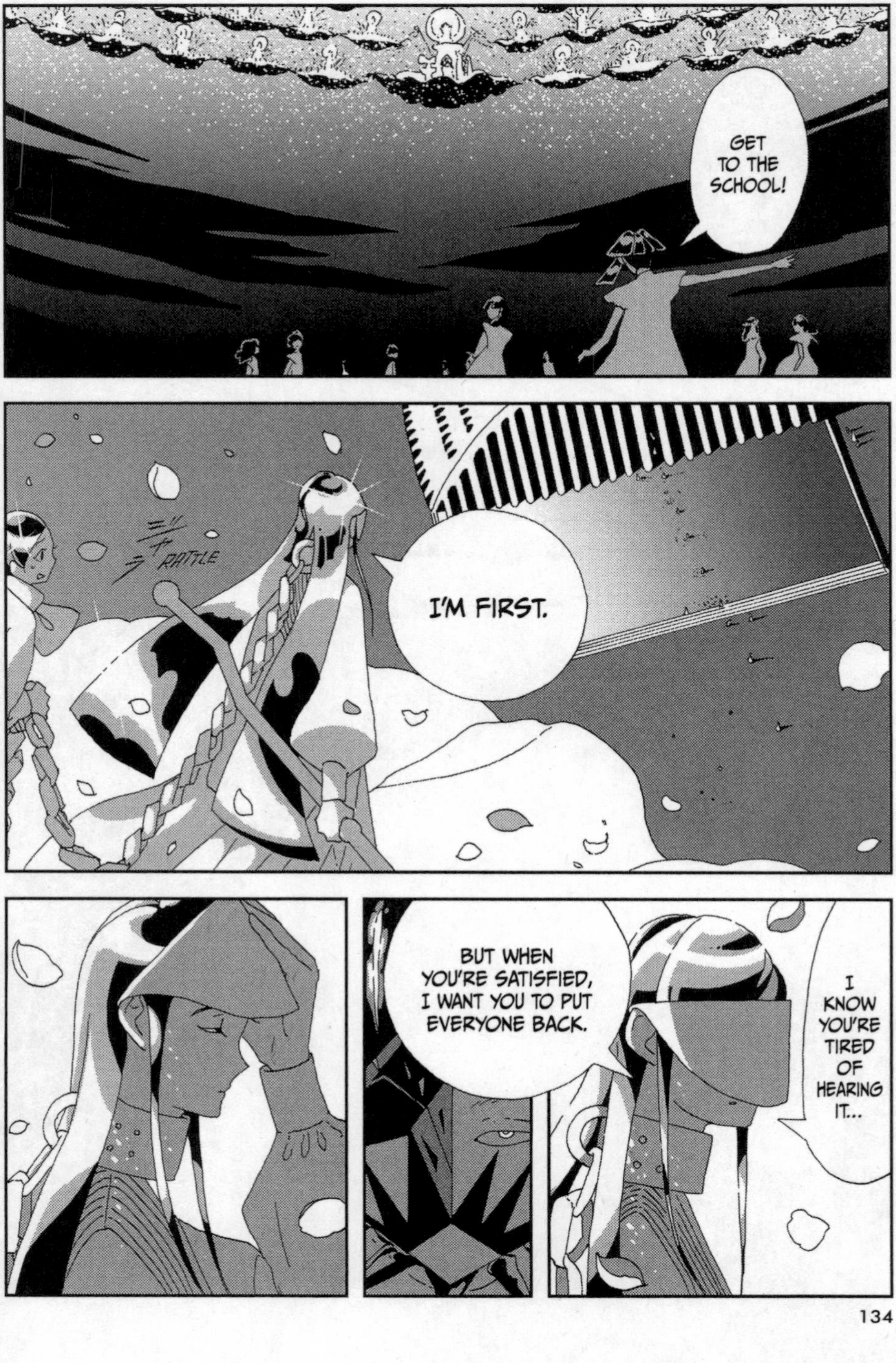
GET TO THE SCHOOL!
ジャラ
RATTLE
I'M FIRST.
I KNOW YOU'RE TIRED OF HEARING IT...
BUT WHEN YOU'RE SATISFIED, I WANT YOU TO PUT EVERYONE BACK.

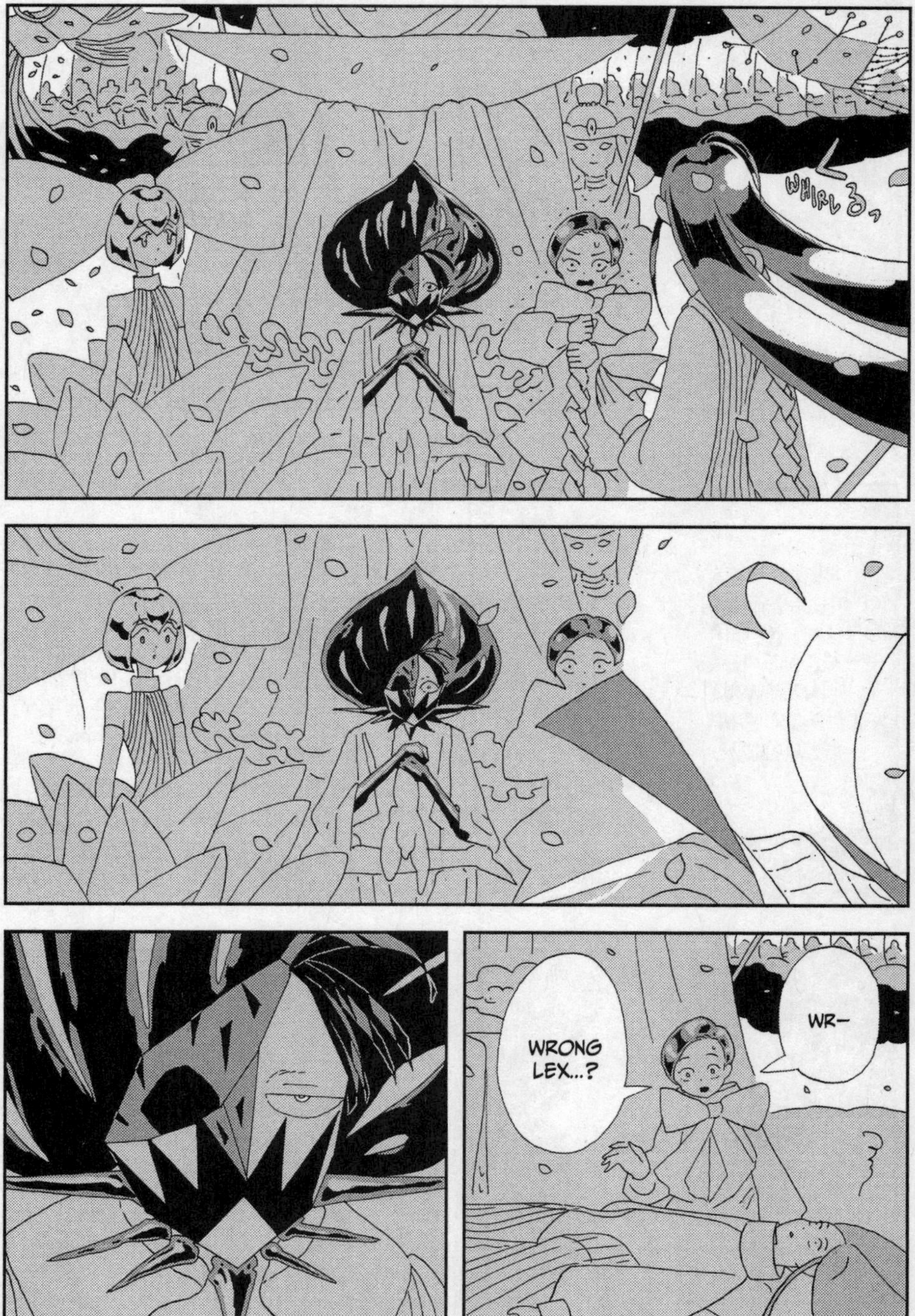
WHIRL
WR–
WRONG LEX...?

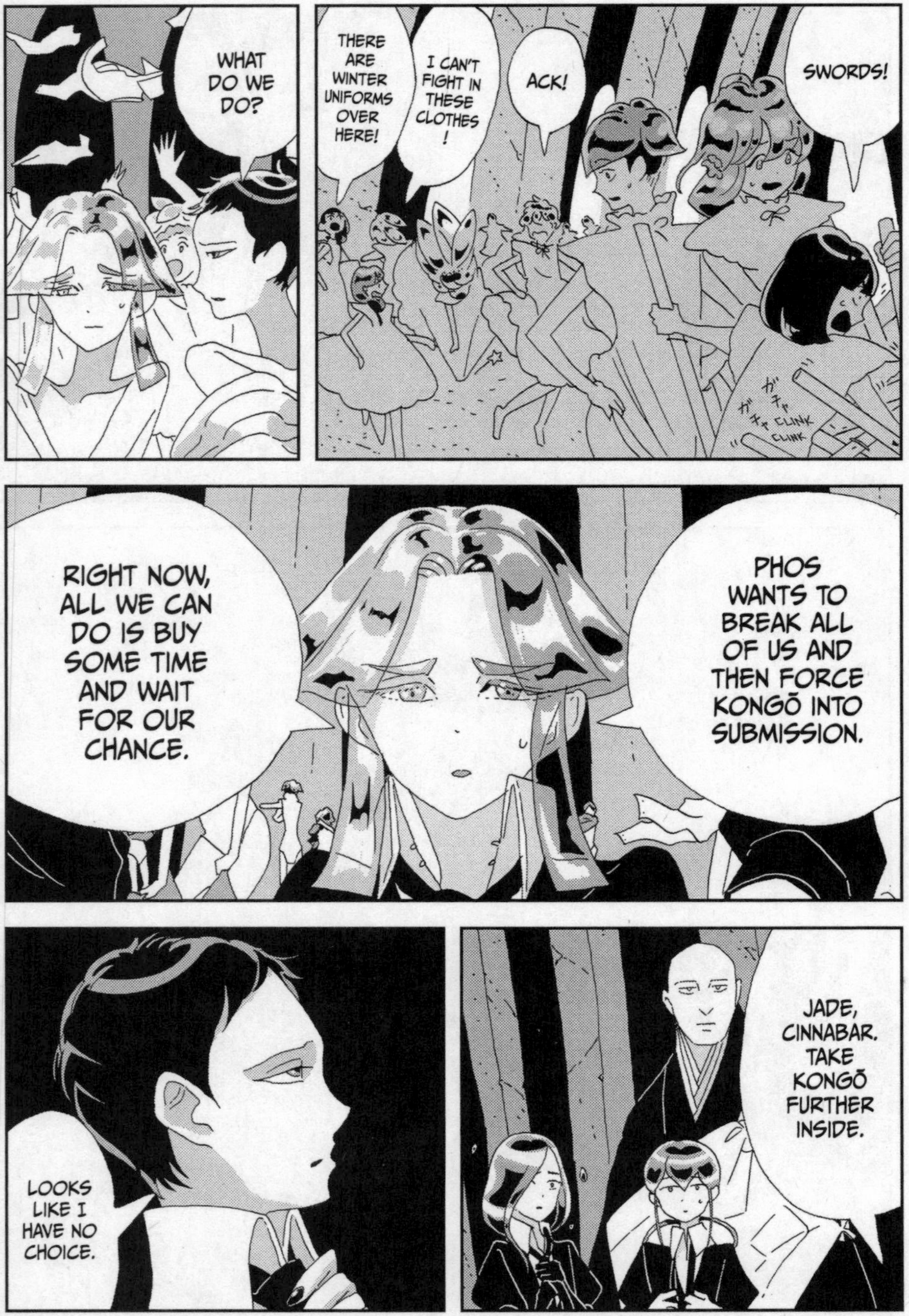
SWORDS!
ACK!
I CAN'T FIGHT IN THESE CLOTHES!
THERE ARE WINTER UNIFORMS OVER HERE!
ガチャ ガチャ CLINK CLINK
WHAT DO WE DO?
PHOS WANTS TO BREAK ALL OF US AND THEN FORCE KONGŌ INTO SUBMISSION.
RIGHT NOW, ALL WE CAN DO IS BUY SOME TIME AND WAIT FOR OUR CHANCE.
JADE, CINNABAR. TAKE KONGŌ FURTHER INSIDE.
LOOKS LIKE I HAVE NO CHOICE.

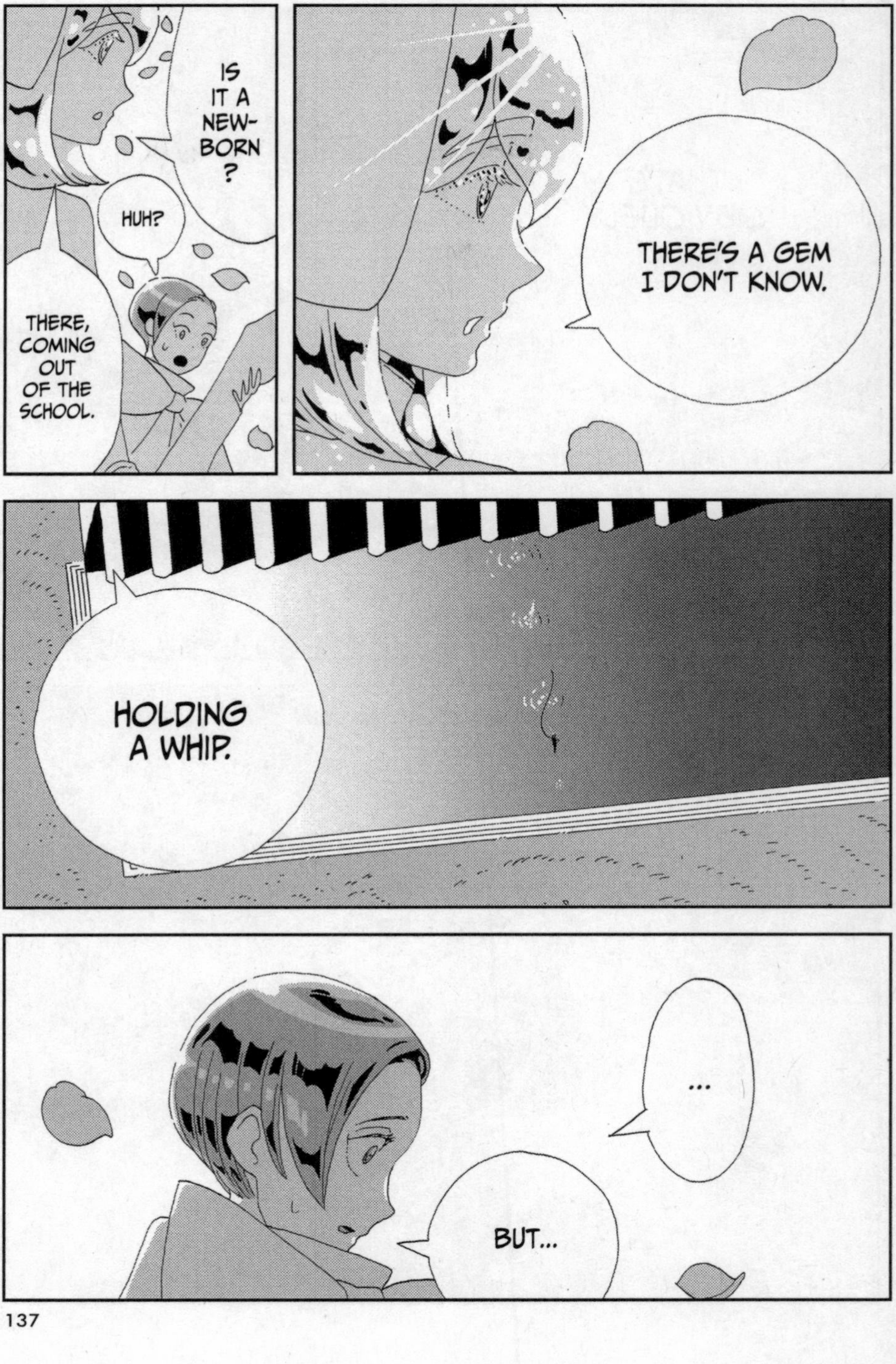
THERE'S A GEM I DON'T KNOW.
IS IT A NEW-BORN?
HUH?
THERE, COMING OUT OF THE SCHOOL.
HOLDING A WHIP.
...
BUT...

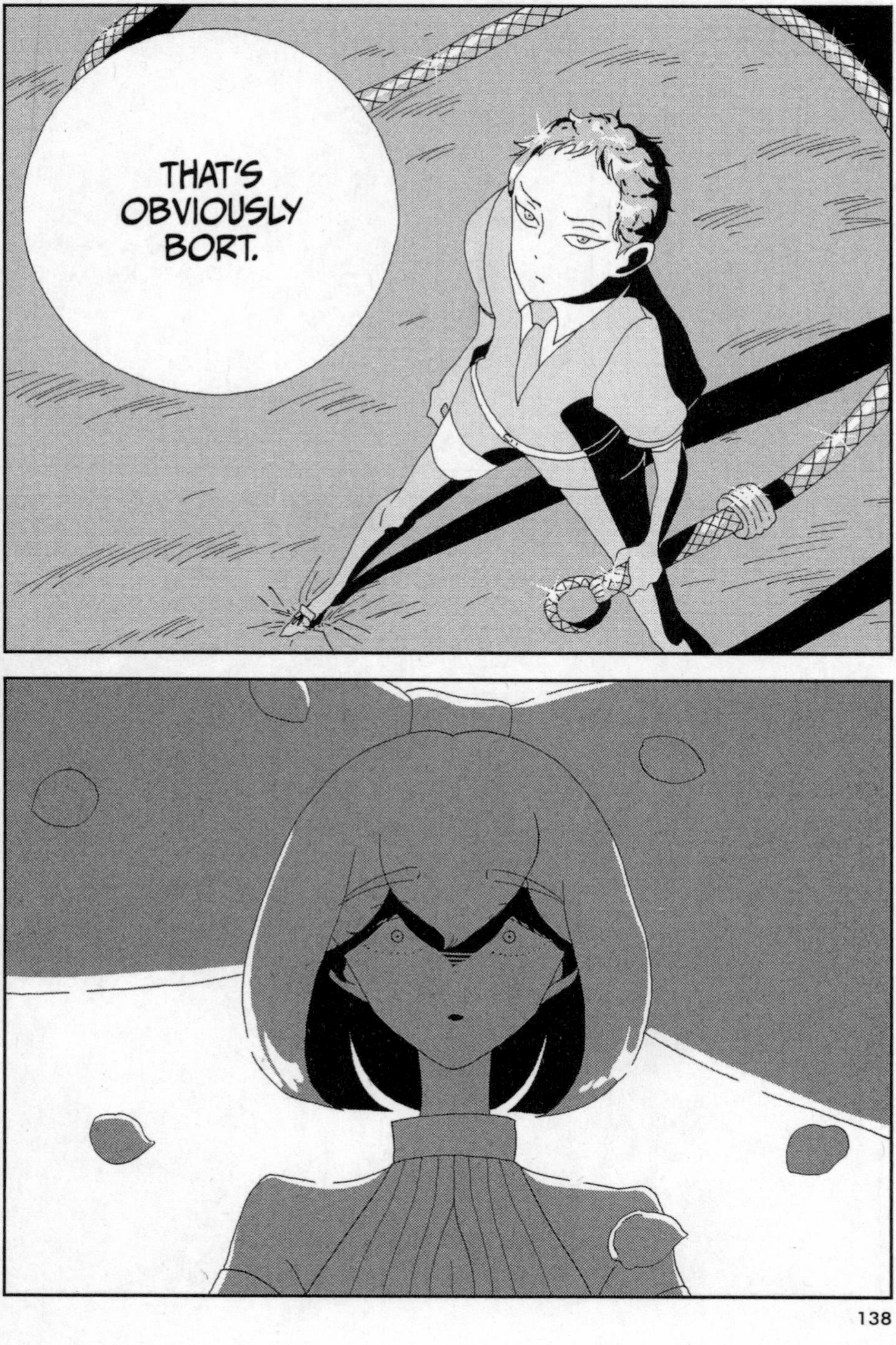
THAT'S OBVIOUSLY BORT.

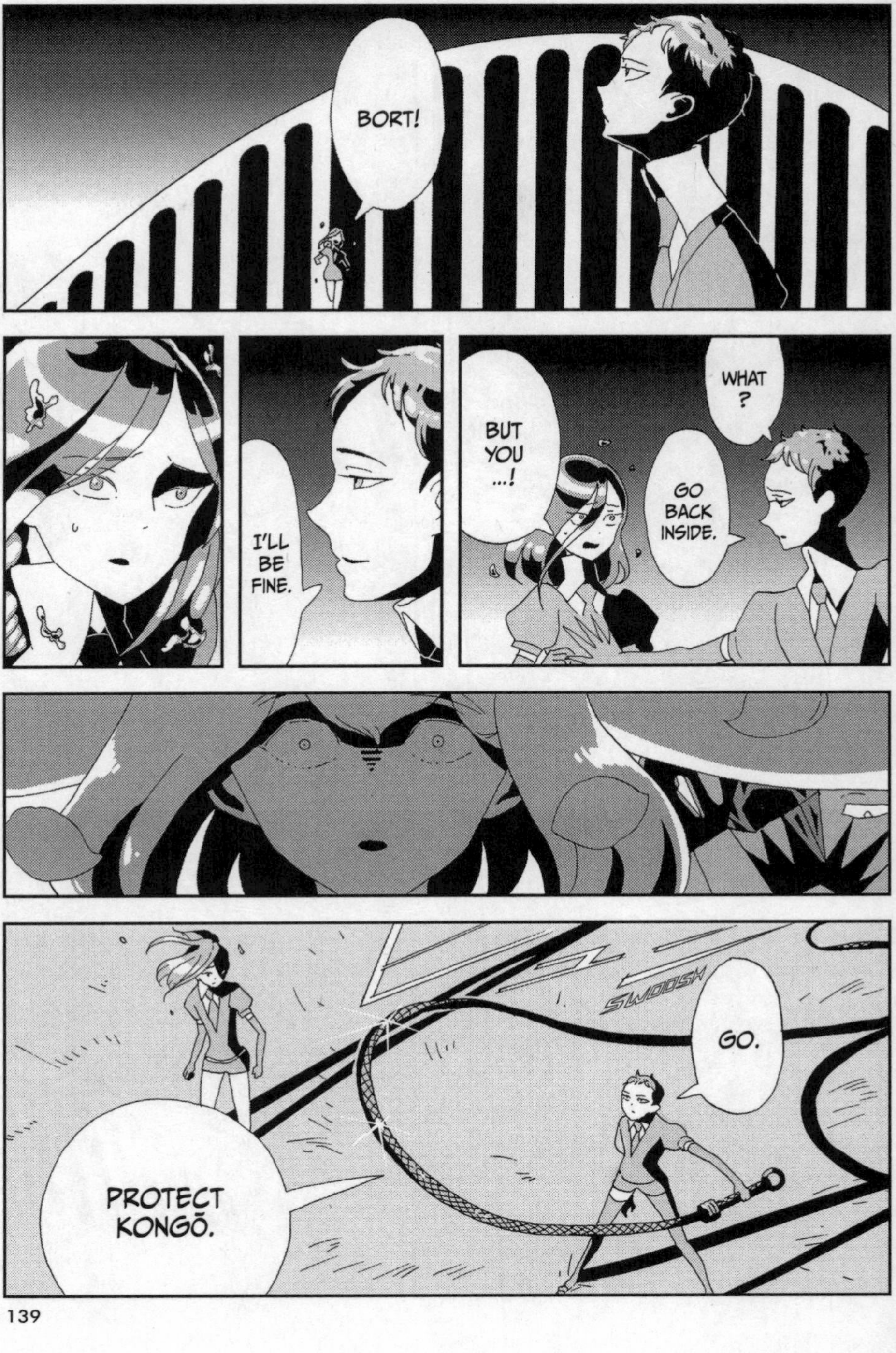
BORT!
WHAT?
GO BACK INSIDE.
BUT YOU...!
I'LL BE FINE.
SWOOSH
GO.
PROTECT KONGŌ.

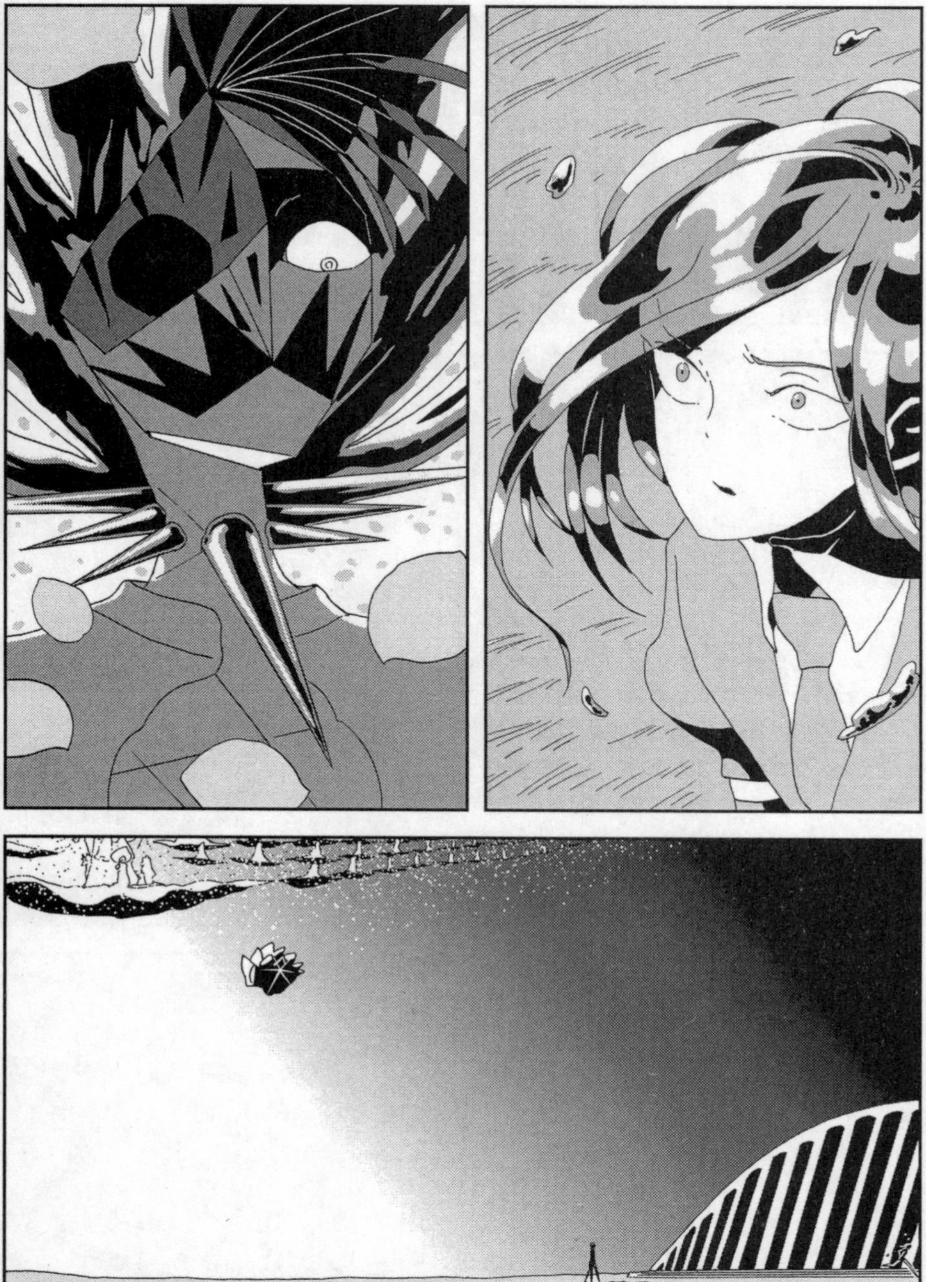

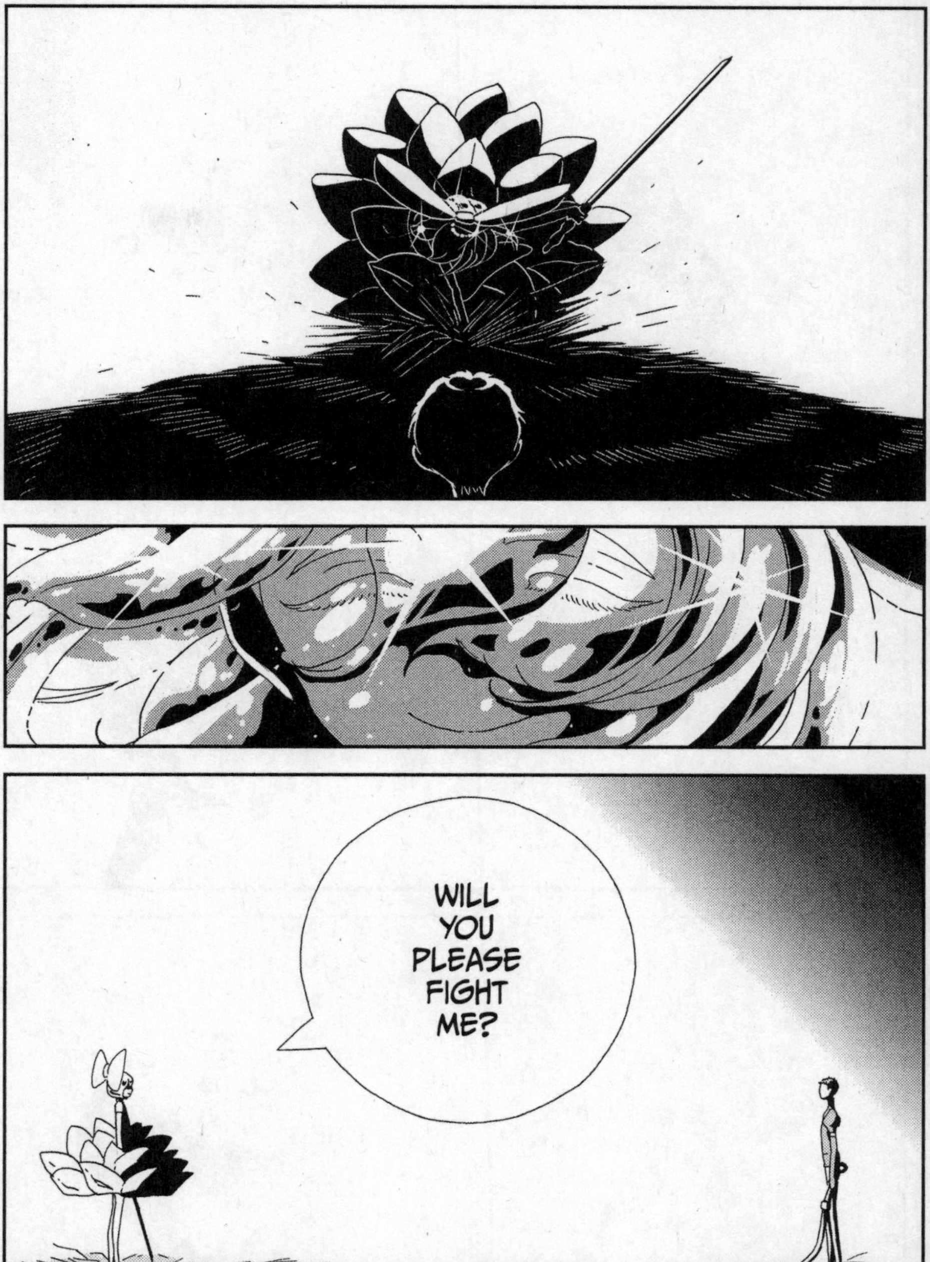
WILL YOU PLEASE FIGHT ME?

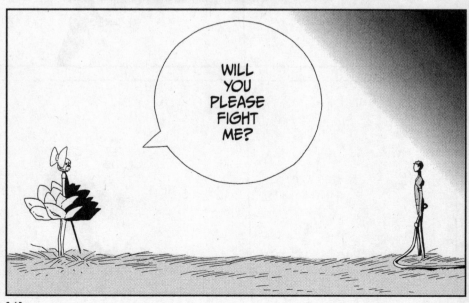

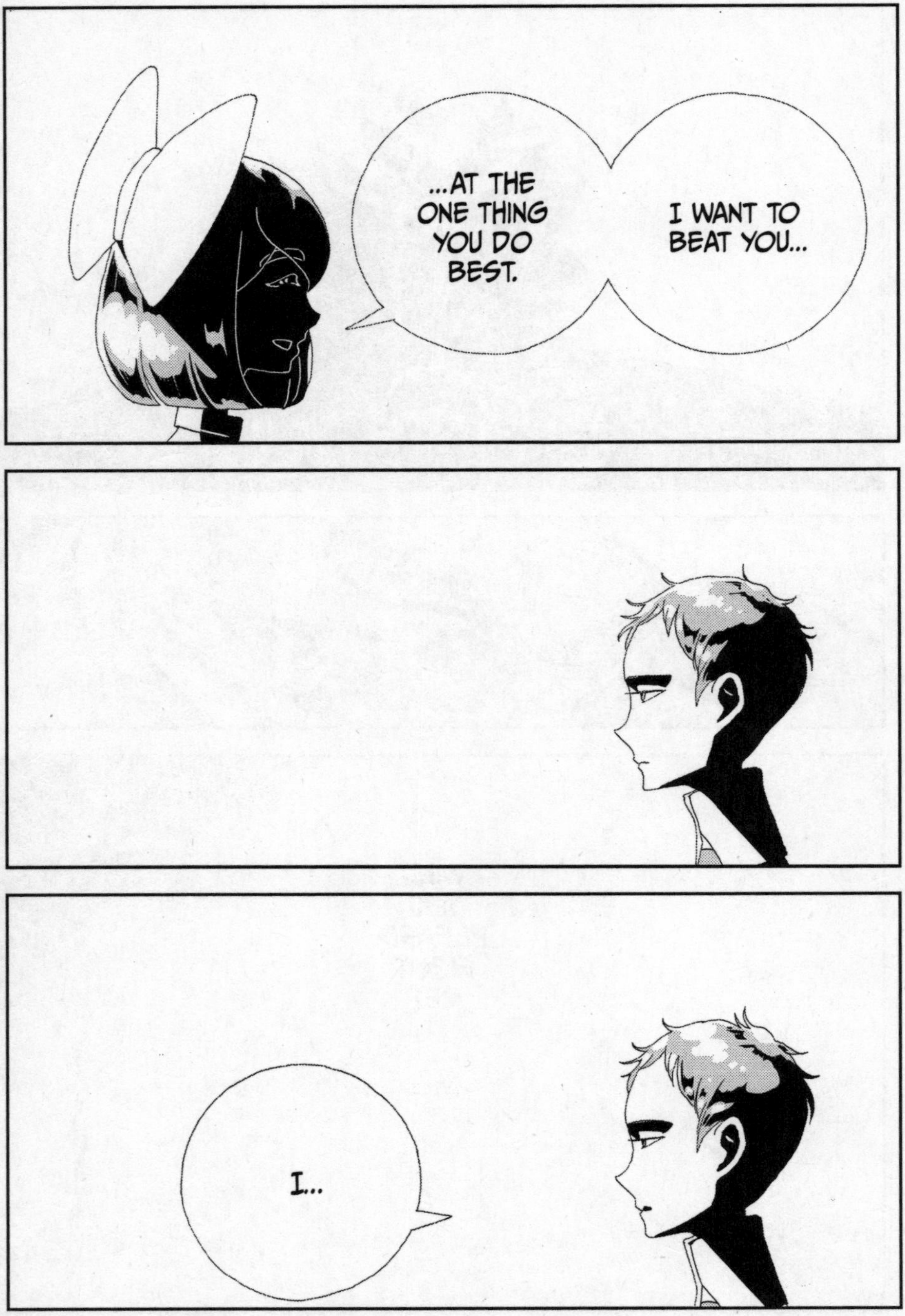
I WANT TO BEAT YOU...
...AT THE ONE THING YOU DO BEST.
I...

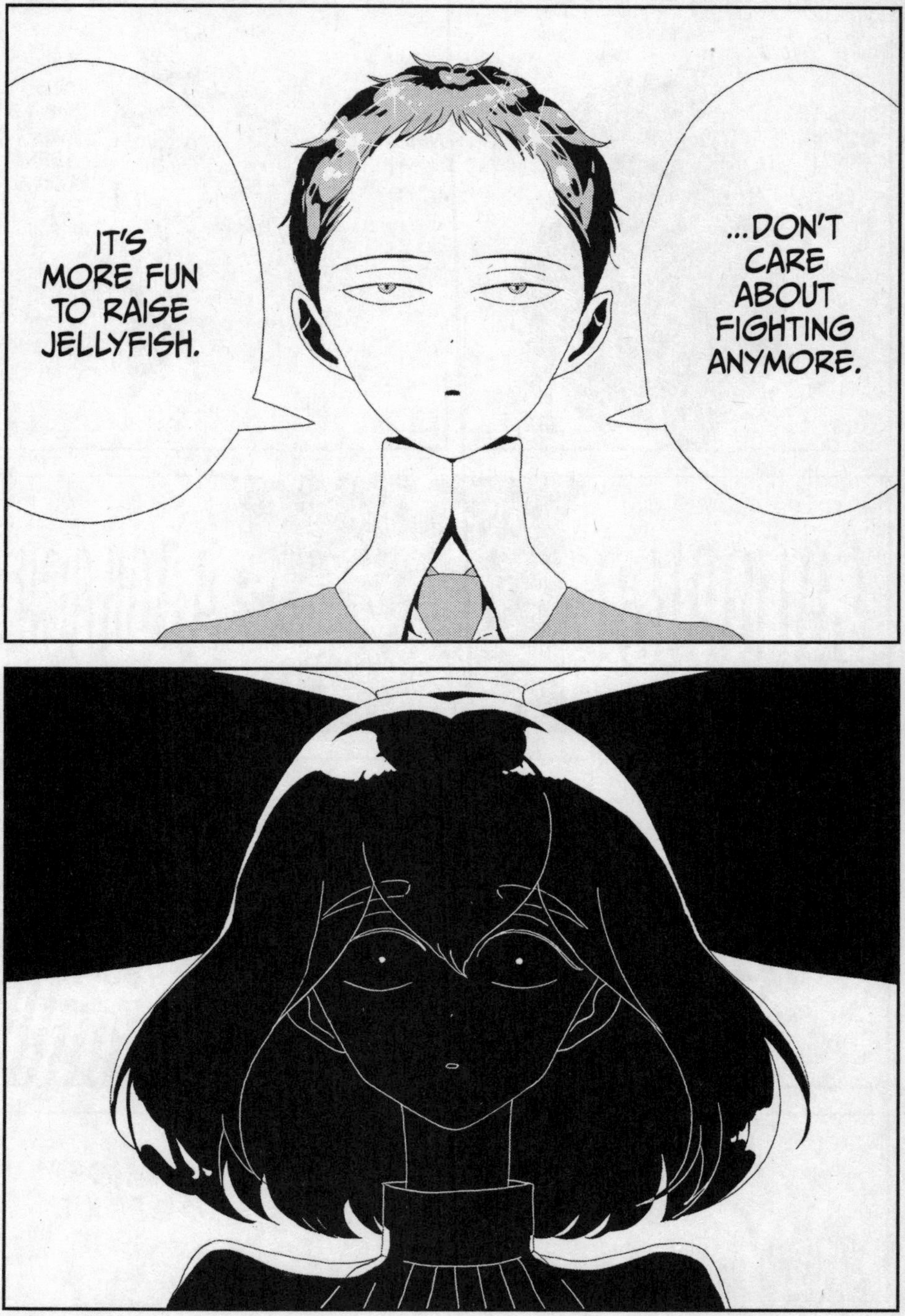
...DON'T CARE ABOUT FIGHTING ANYMORE.
IT'S MORE FUN TO RAISE JELLYFISH.

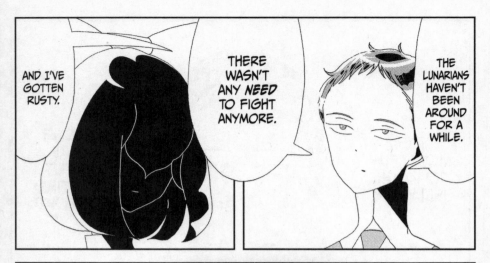

THE LUNARIANS HAVEN'T BEEN AROUND FOR A WHILE.
THERE WASN'T ANY *NEED* TO FIGHT ANYMORE.
AND I'VE GOTTEN RUSTY.
AAAAAGH.
GAAAAHH!
WHOOSH
WHOSE FAULT IS IT...

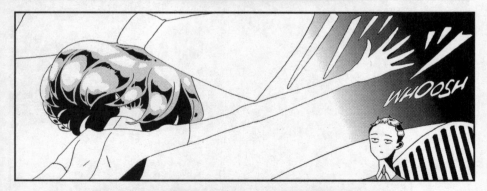

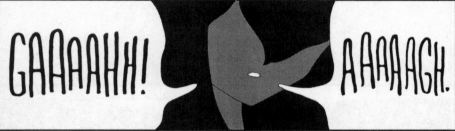

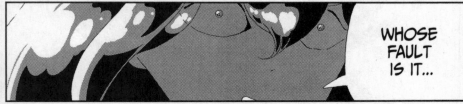

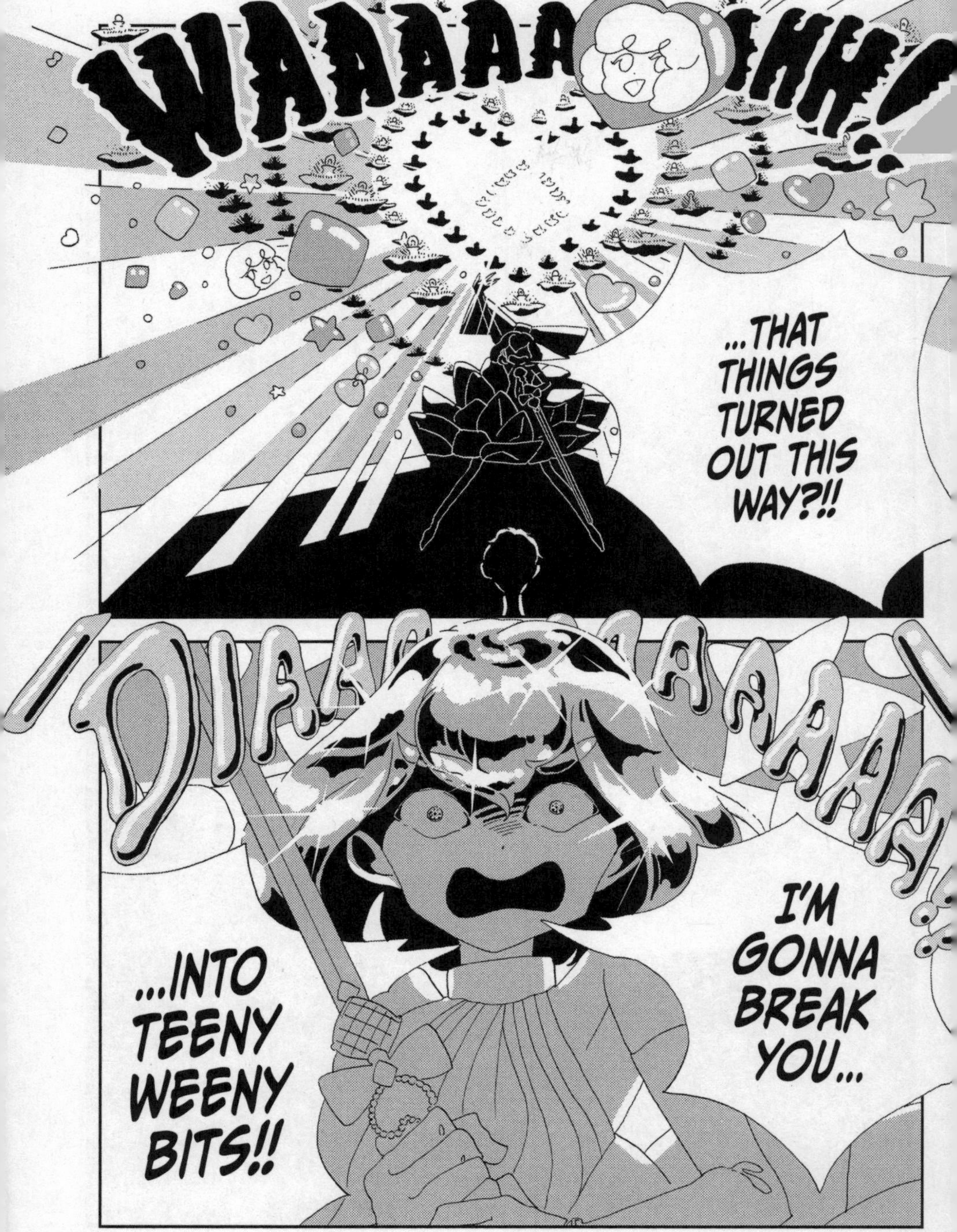
...THAT THINGS TURNED OUT THIS WAY?!!
I'M GONNA BREAK YOU...
...INTO TEENY WEENY BITS!!

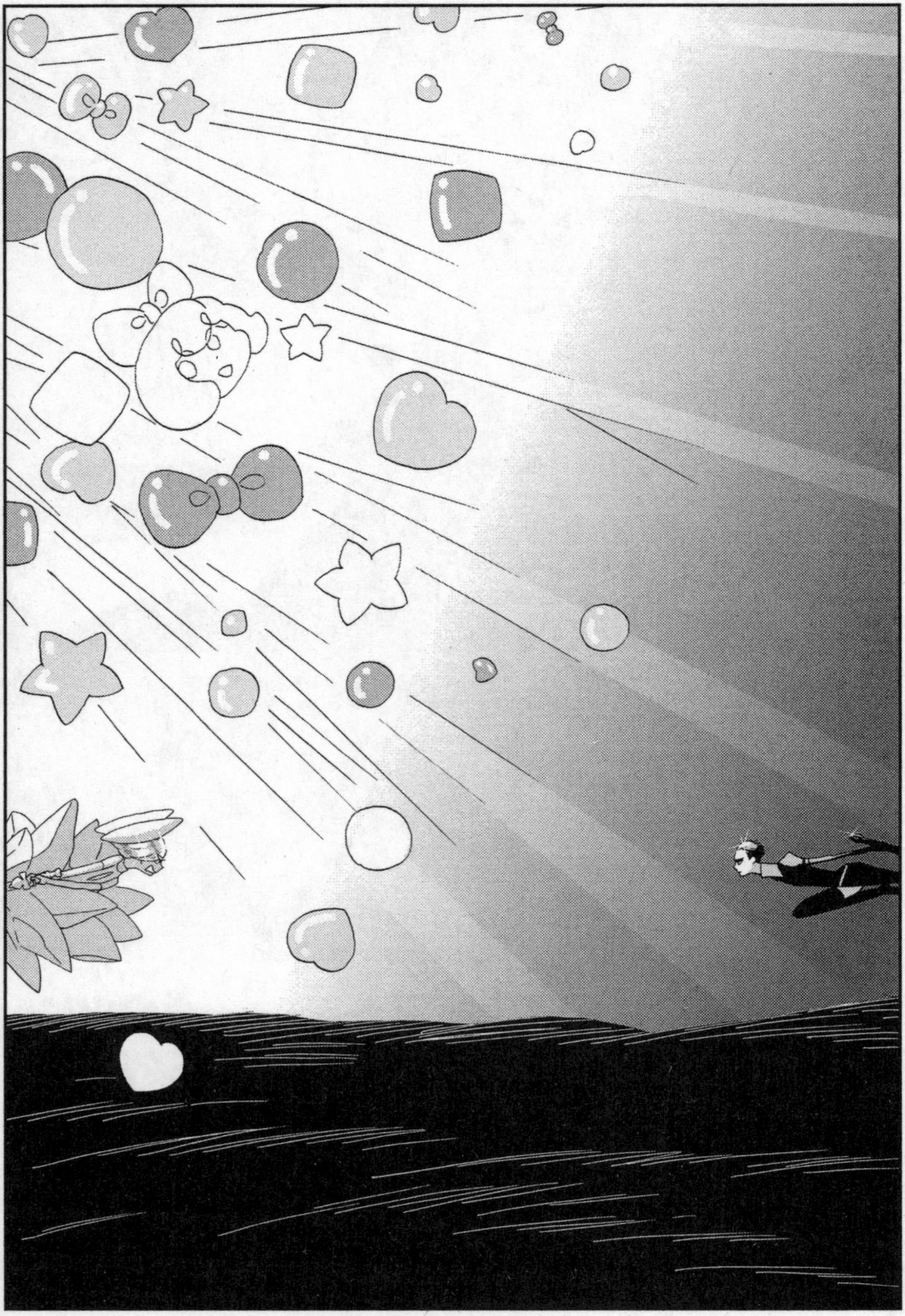

CHAPTER 87:

Silence

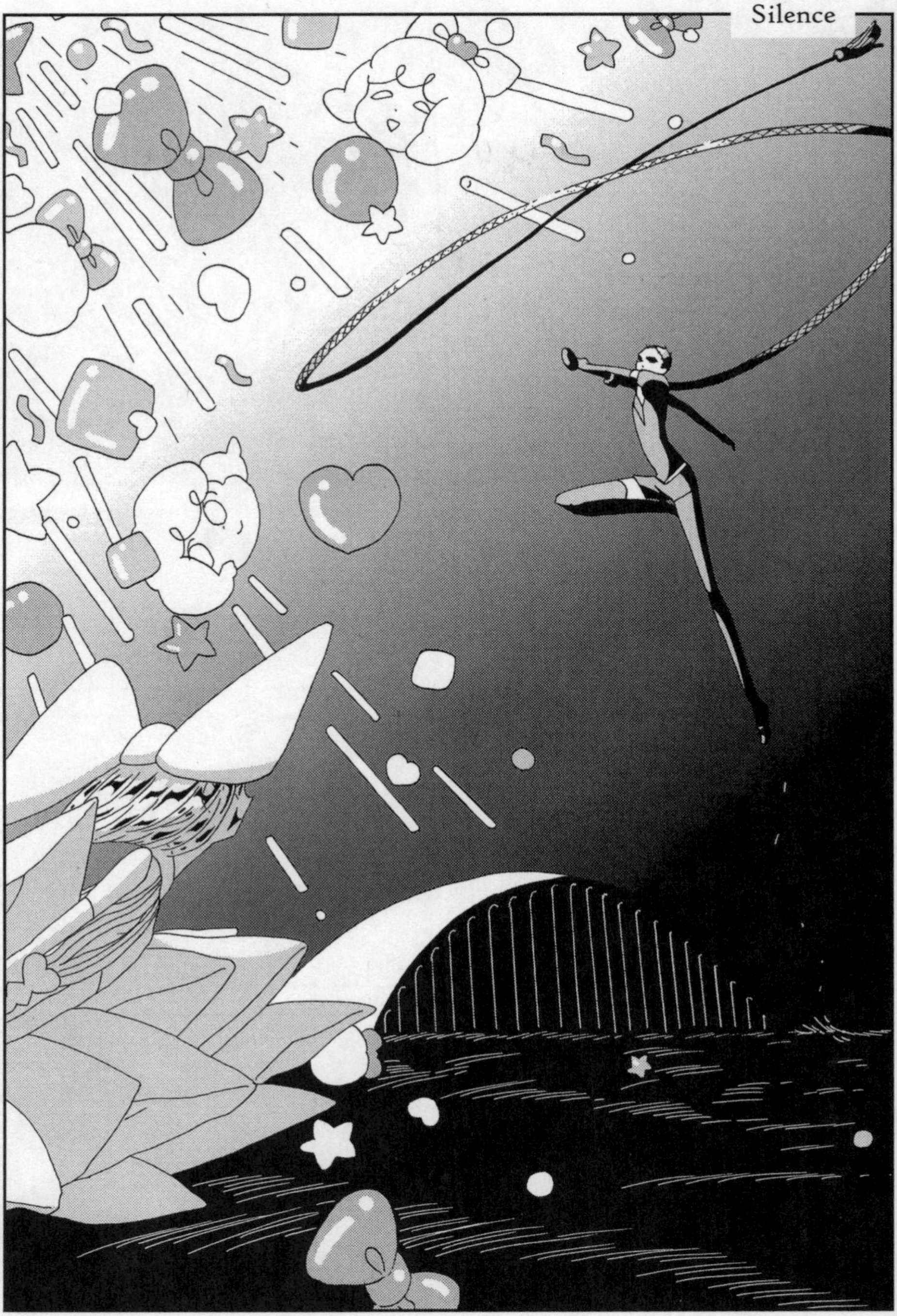

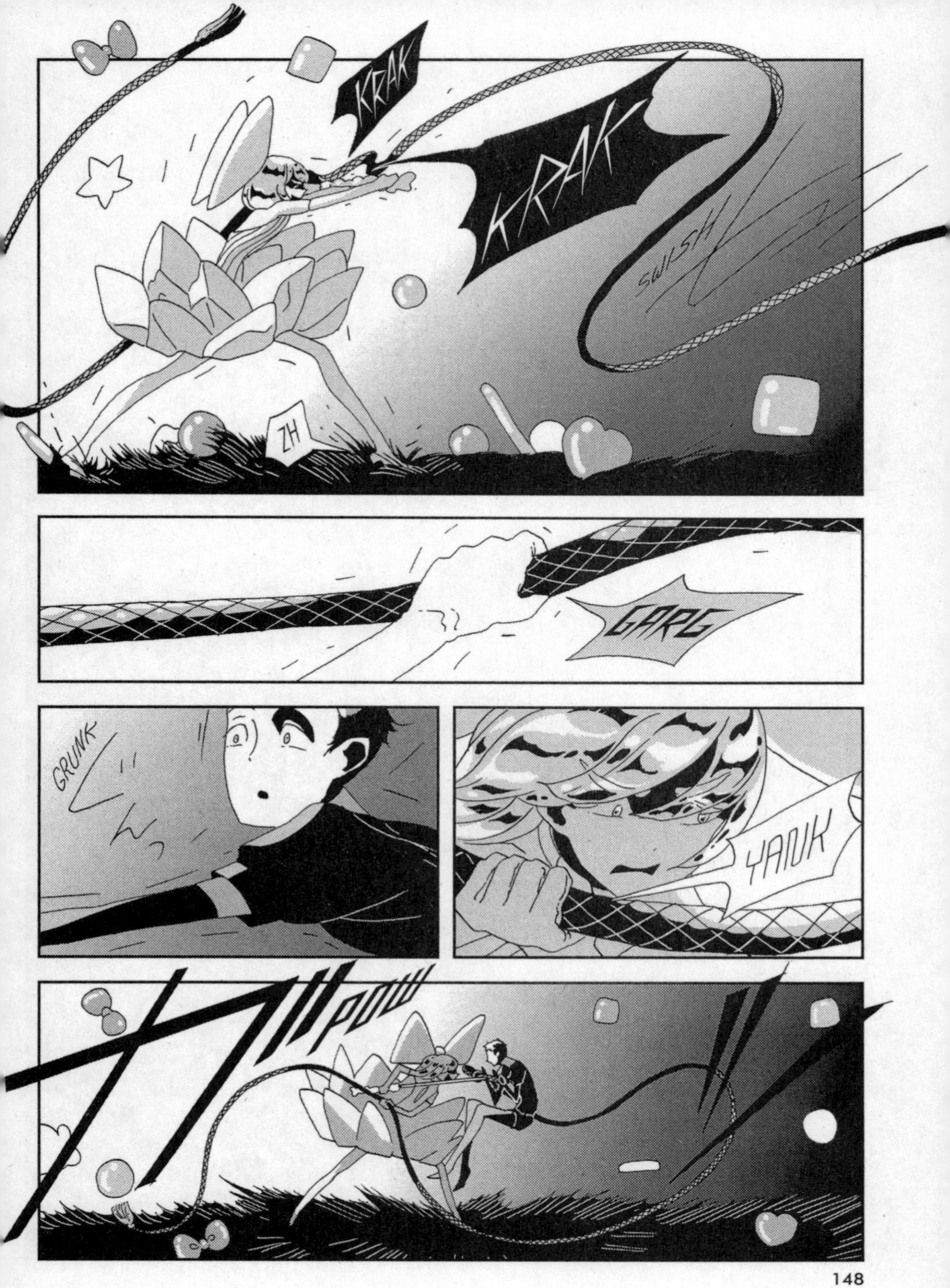
KRAK
KRAK
SWISH
ZH
GARG
GRUNK
YANK
POW

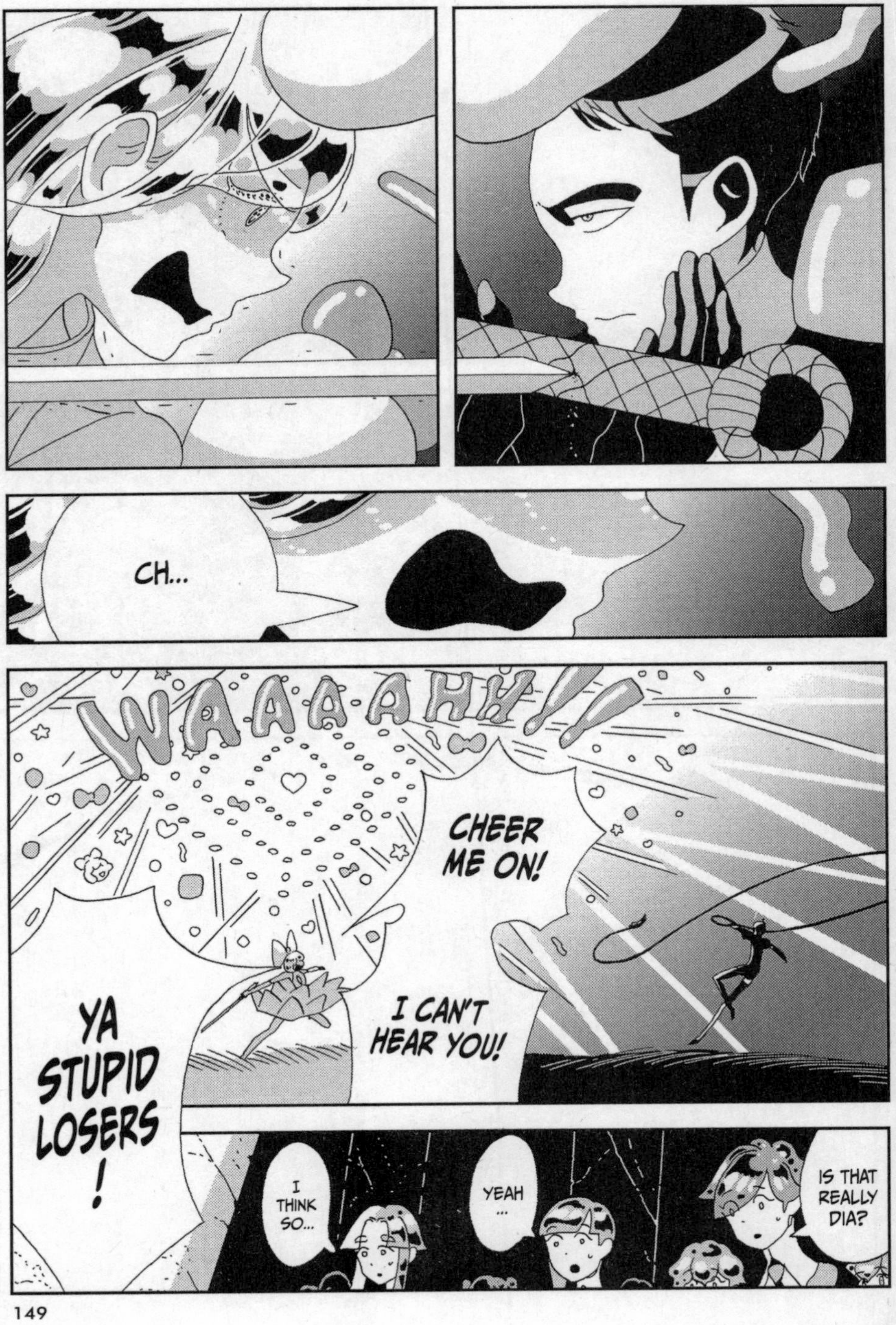
CH...
WAAAAHH!!
CHEER ME ON!
I CAN'T HEAR YOU!
YA STUPID LOSERS!
IS THAT REALLY DIA?
YEAH...
I THINK SO...

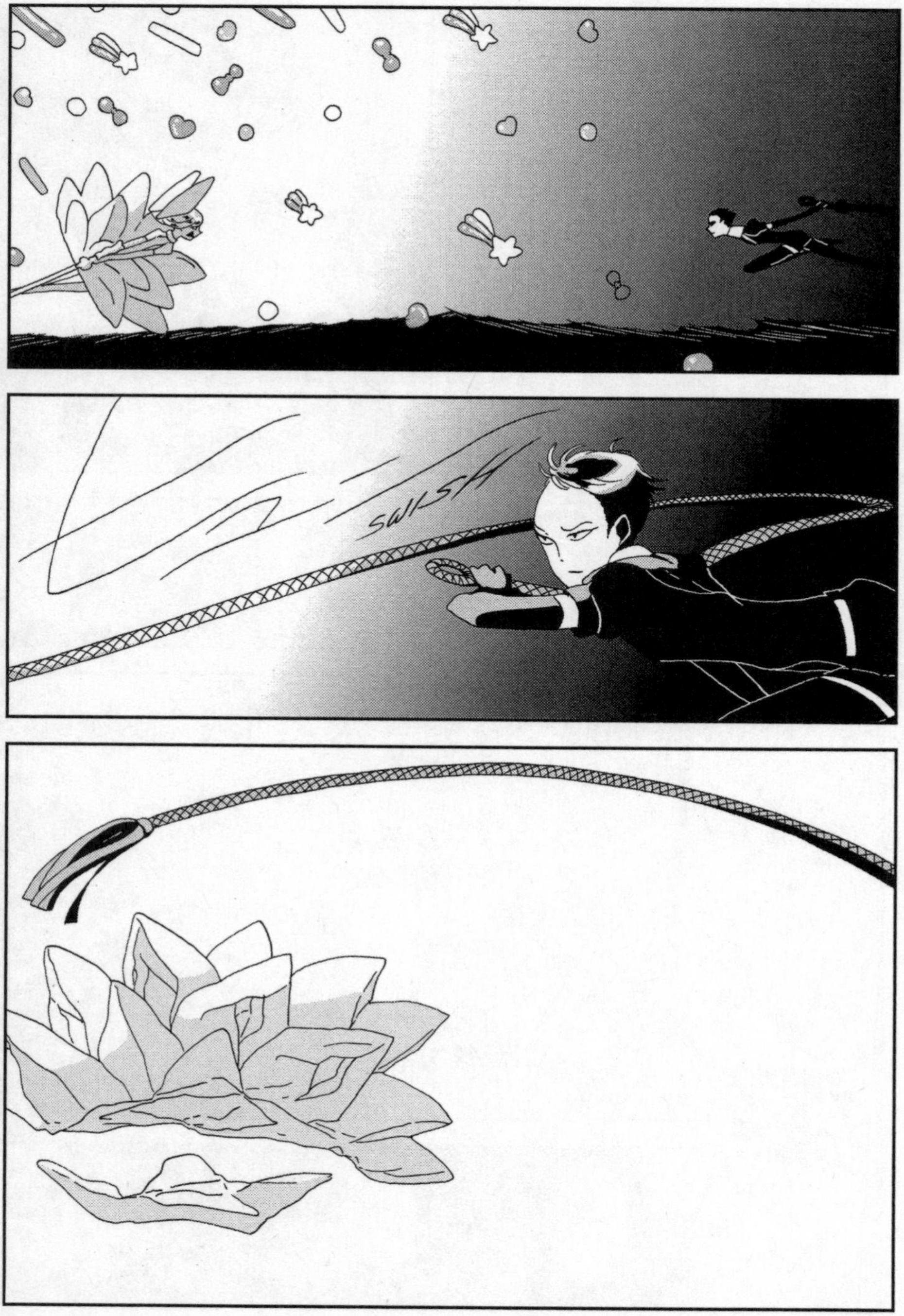
SWISH

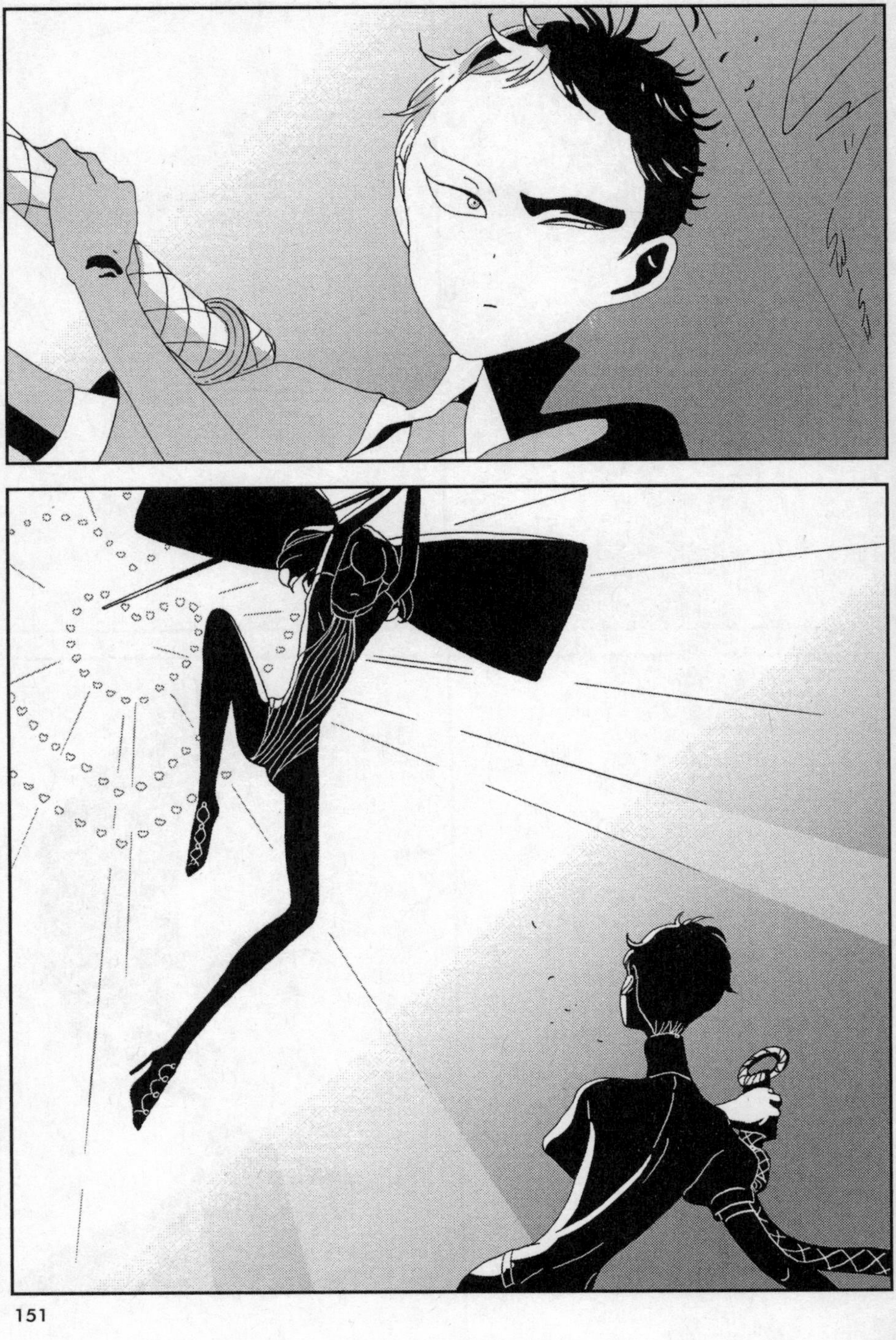

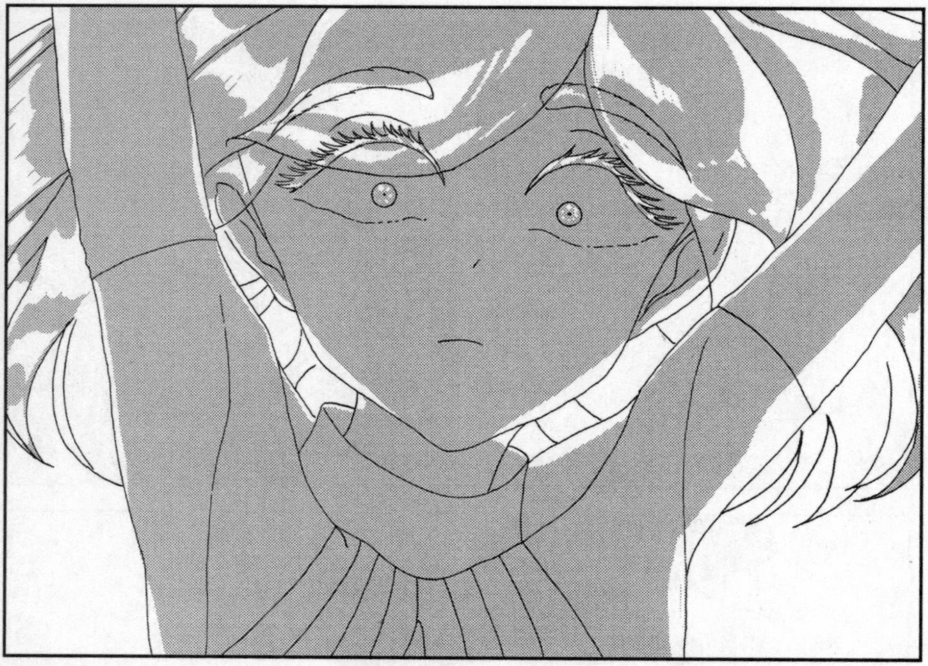

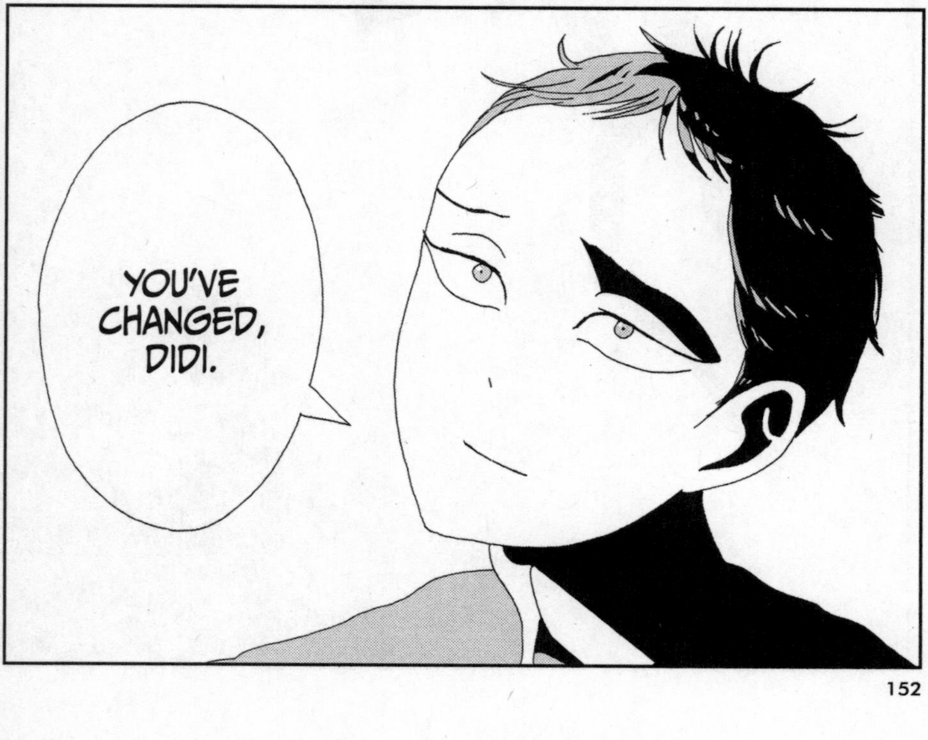
YOU'VE CHANGED, DIDI.

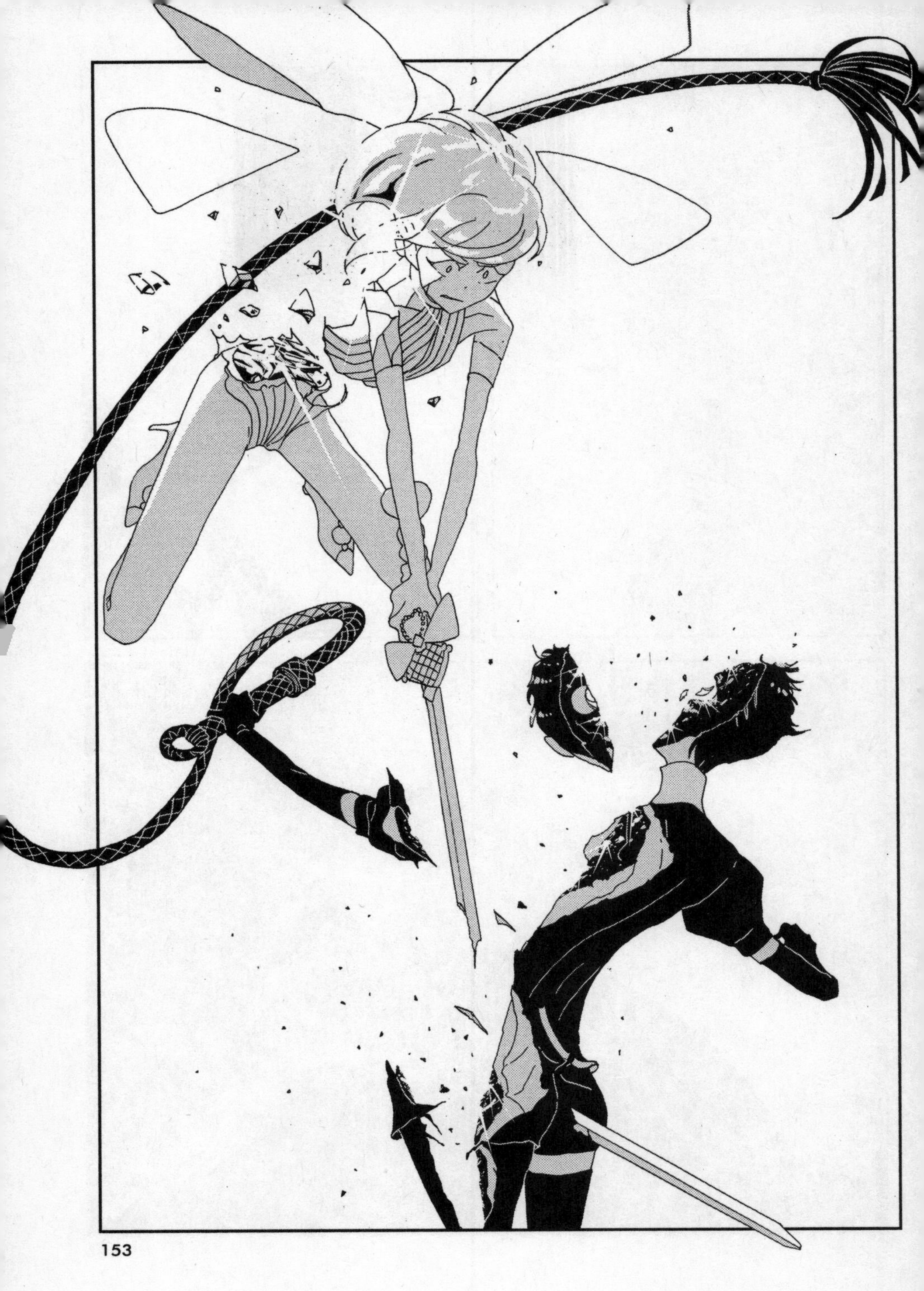

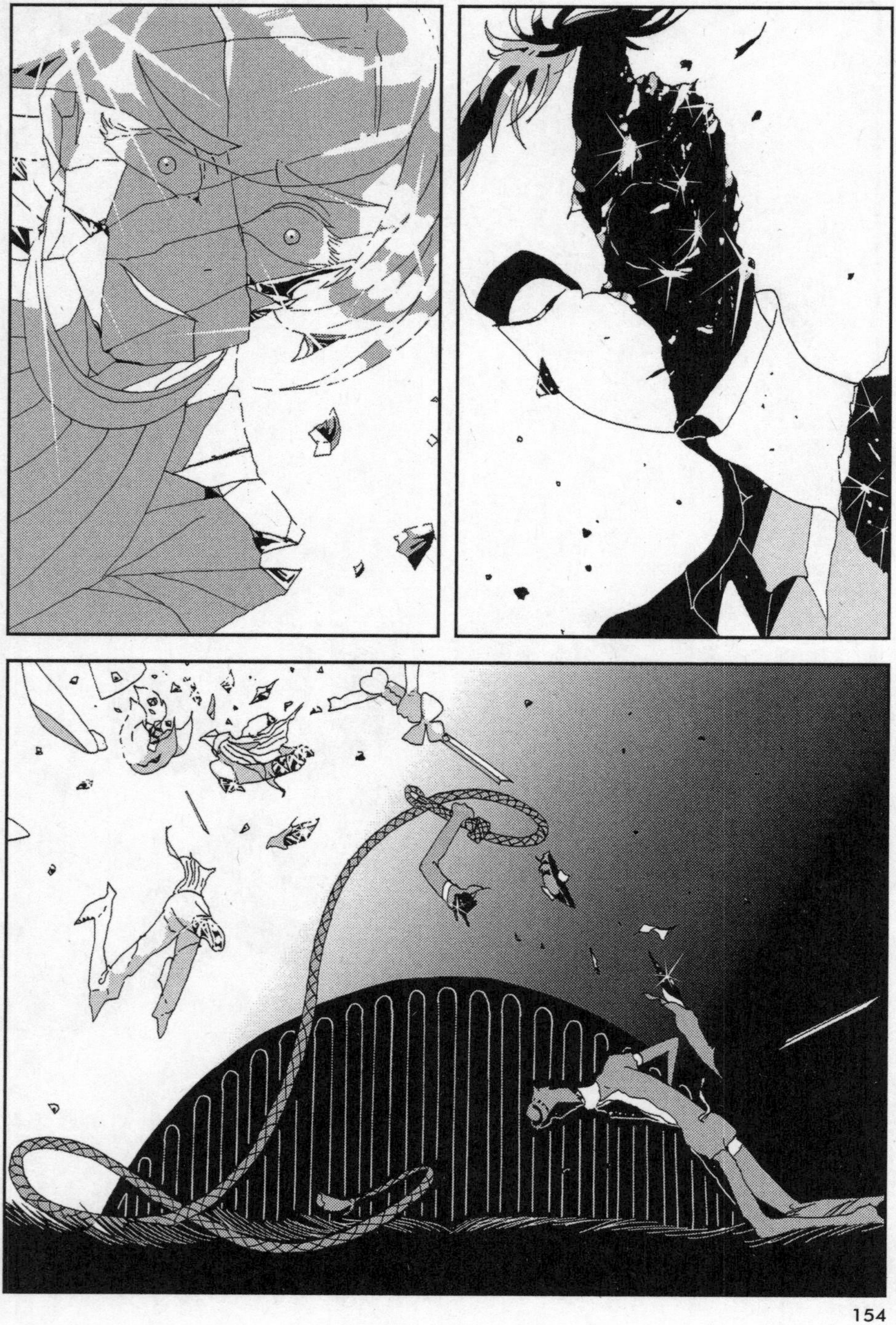

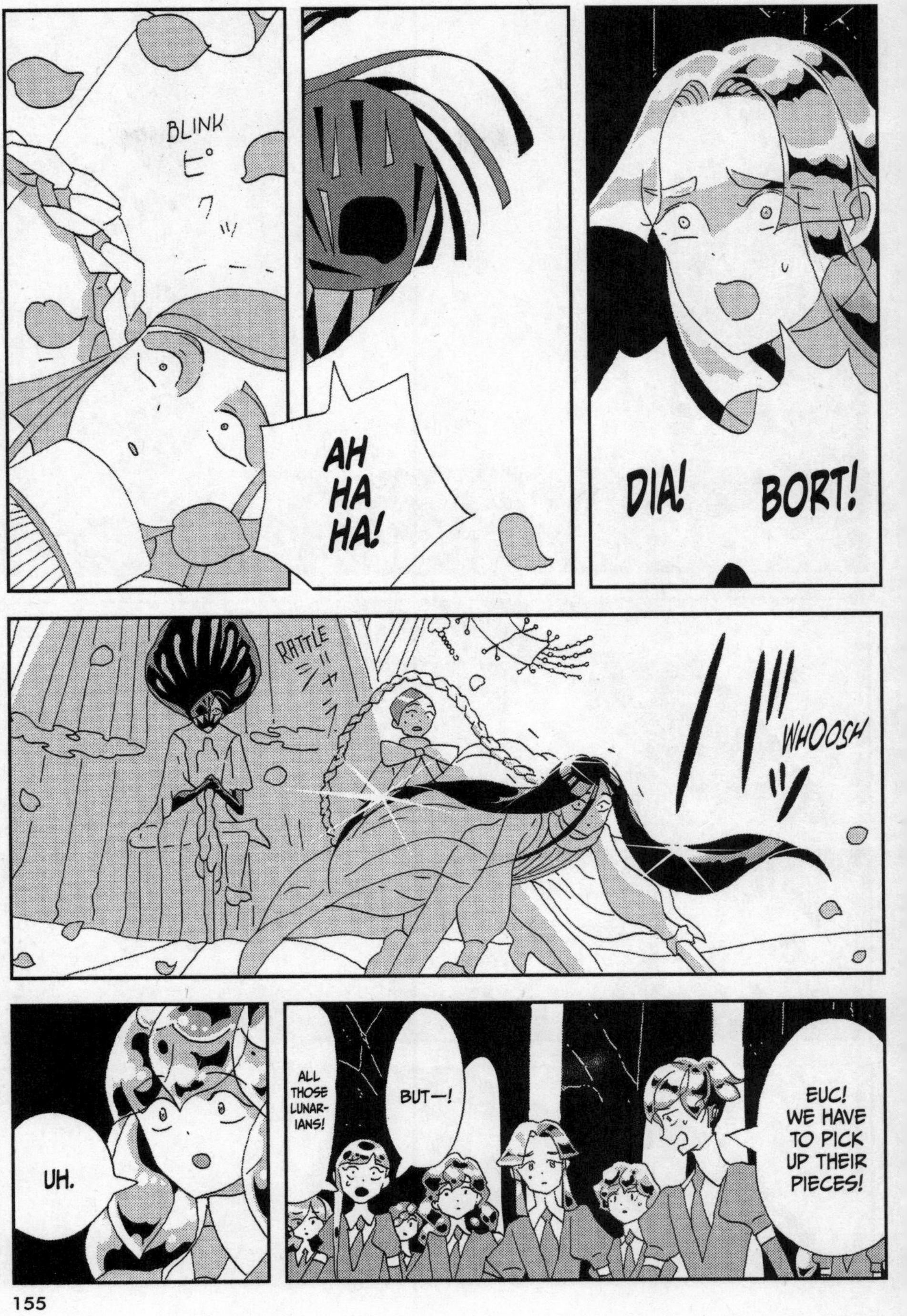
DIA!
BORT!
AH HA HA!
BLINK
ピクッ
WHOOSH
RATTLE
EUC! WE HAVE TO PICK UP THEIR PIECES!
BUT—!
ALL THOSE LUNAR-IANS!
UH.

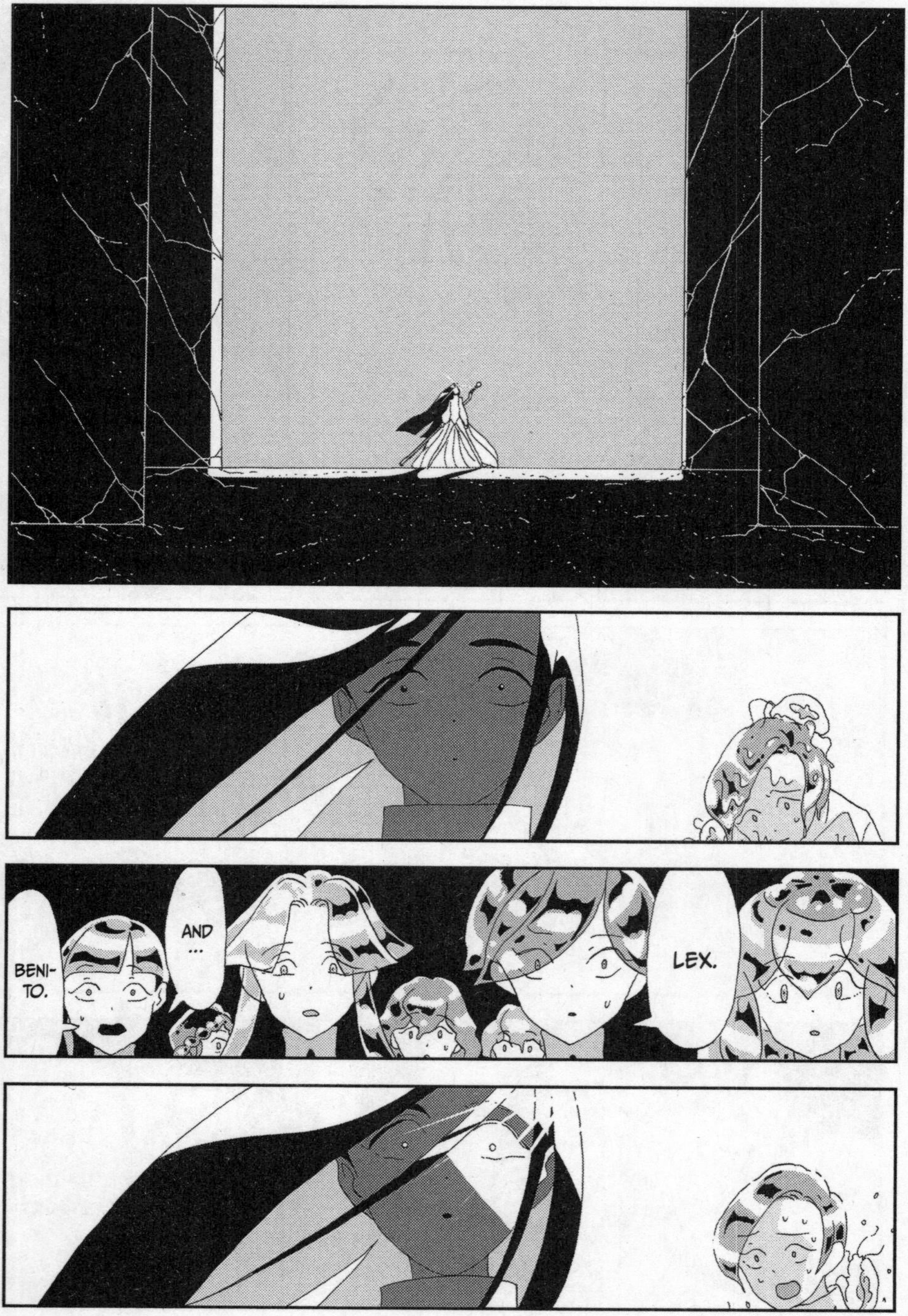
LEX.
AND ...
BENI-TO.

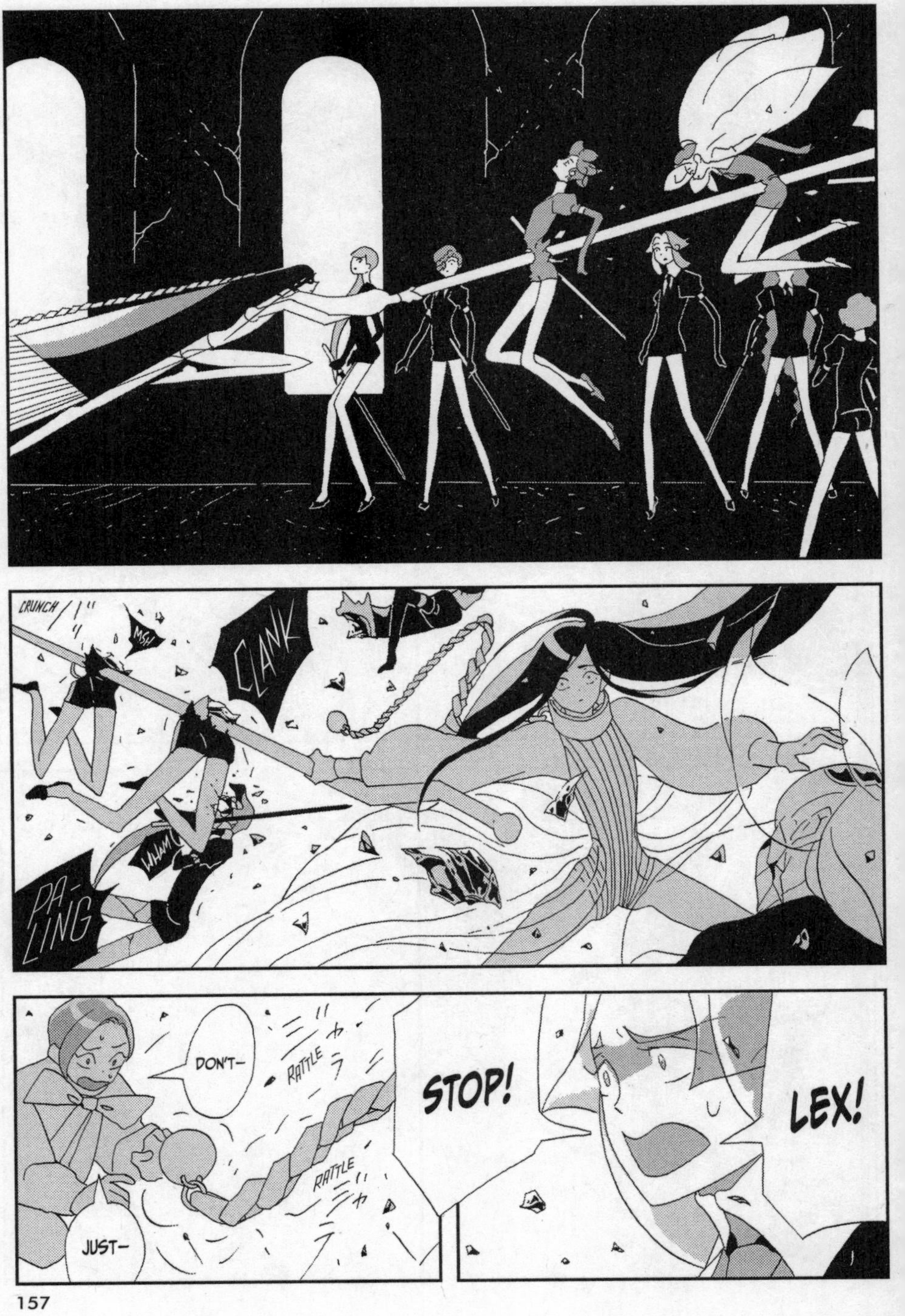
CRUNCH
MSH
CLANK
WHAM
PA-LING
LEX!
STOP!
DON'T-
RATTLE
RATTLE
JUST-

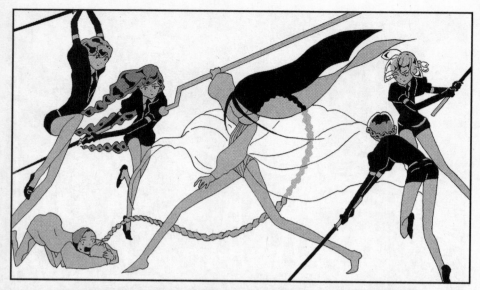

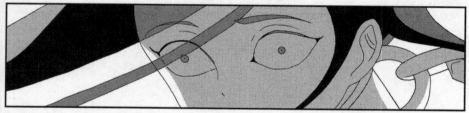

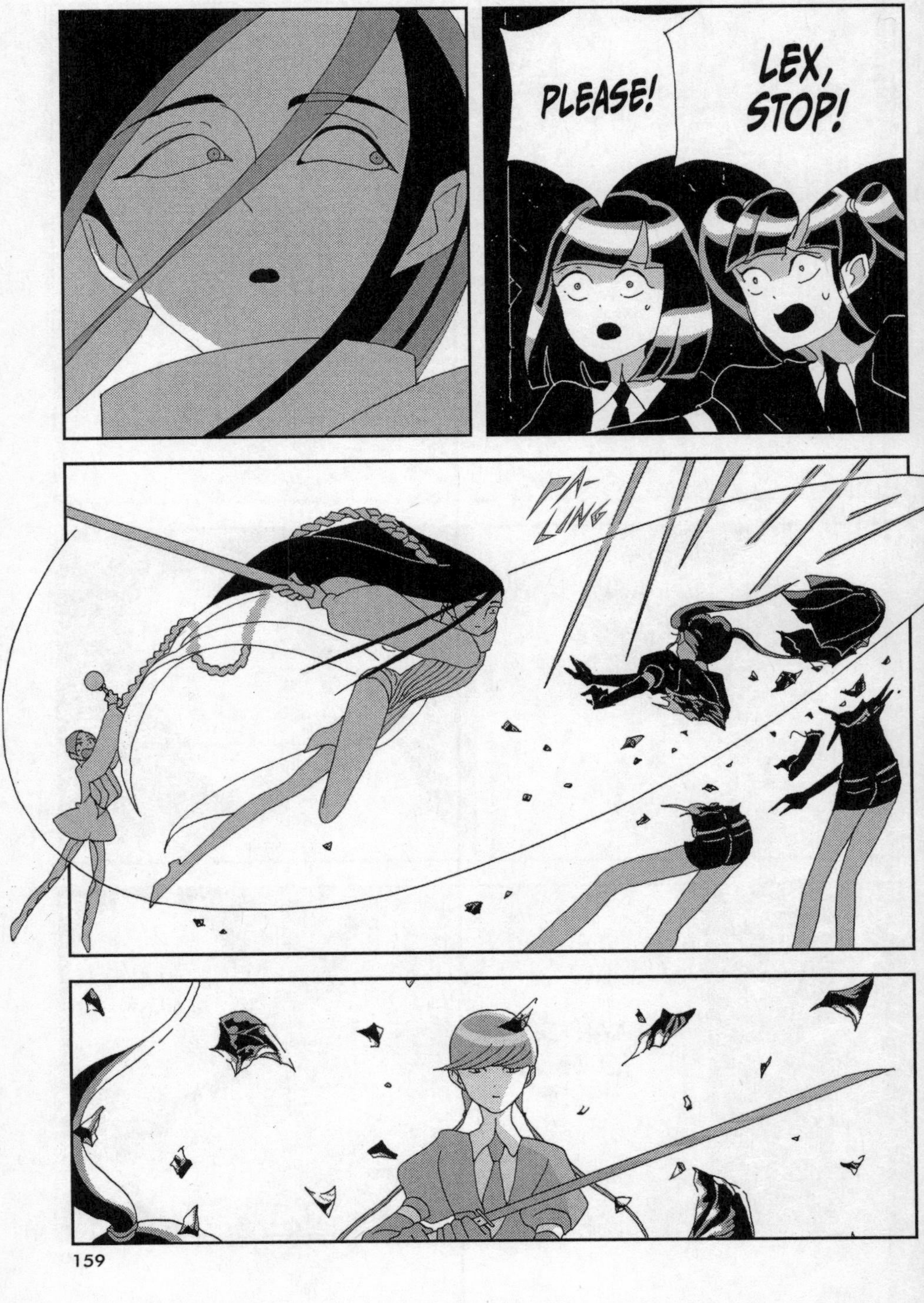
LEX, STOP!
PLEASE!
PA-LING

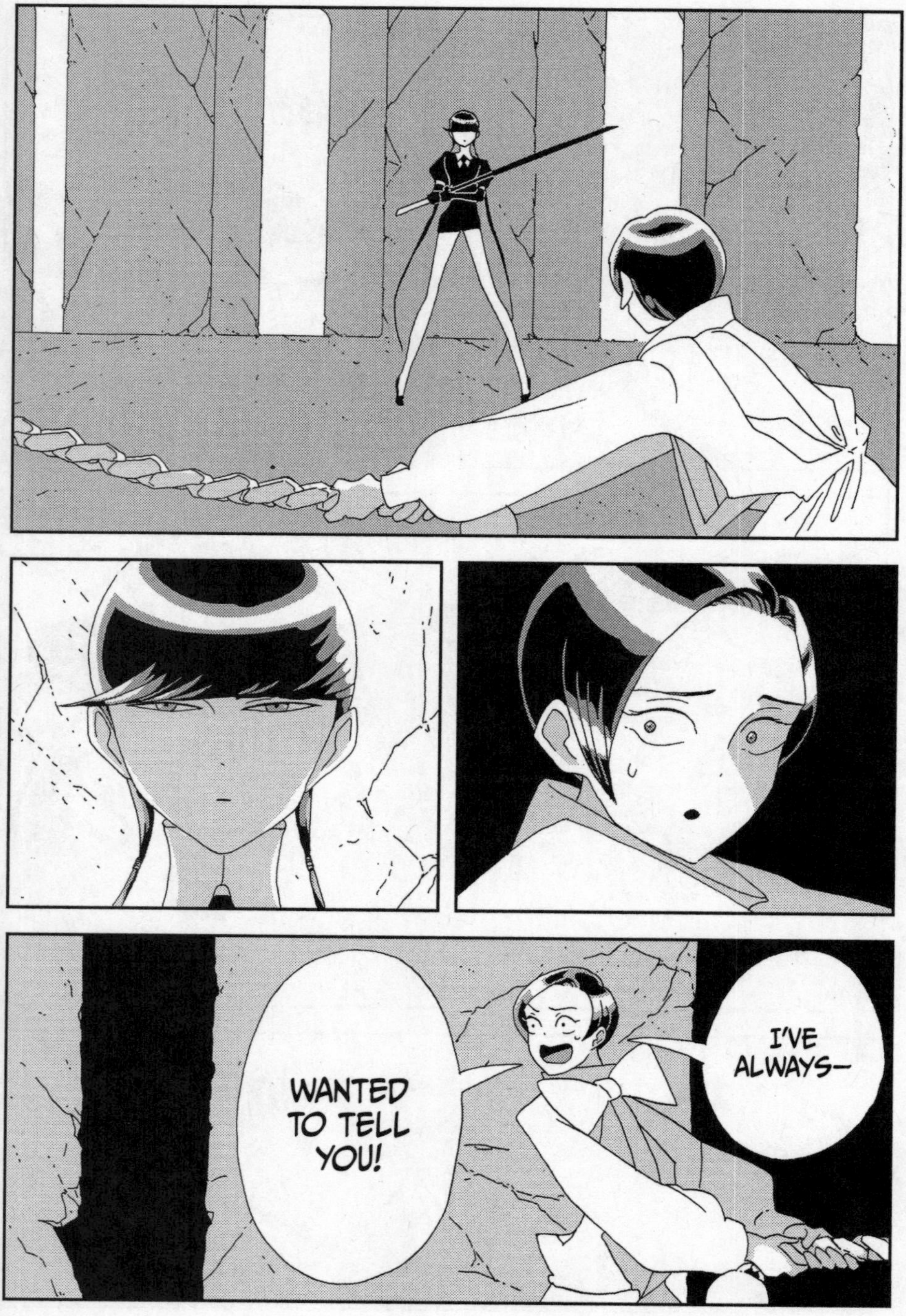
I'VE ALWAYS—
WANTED TO TELL YOU!

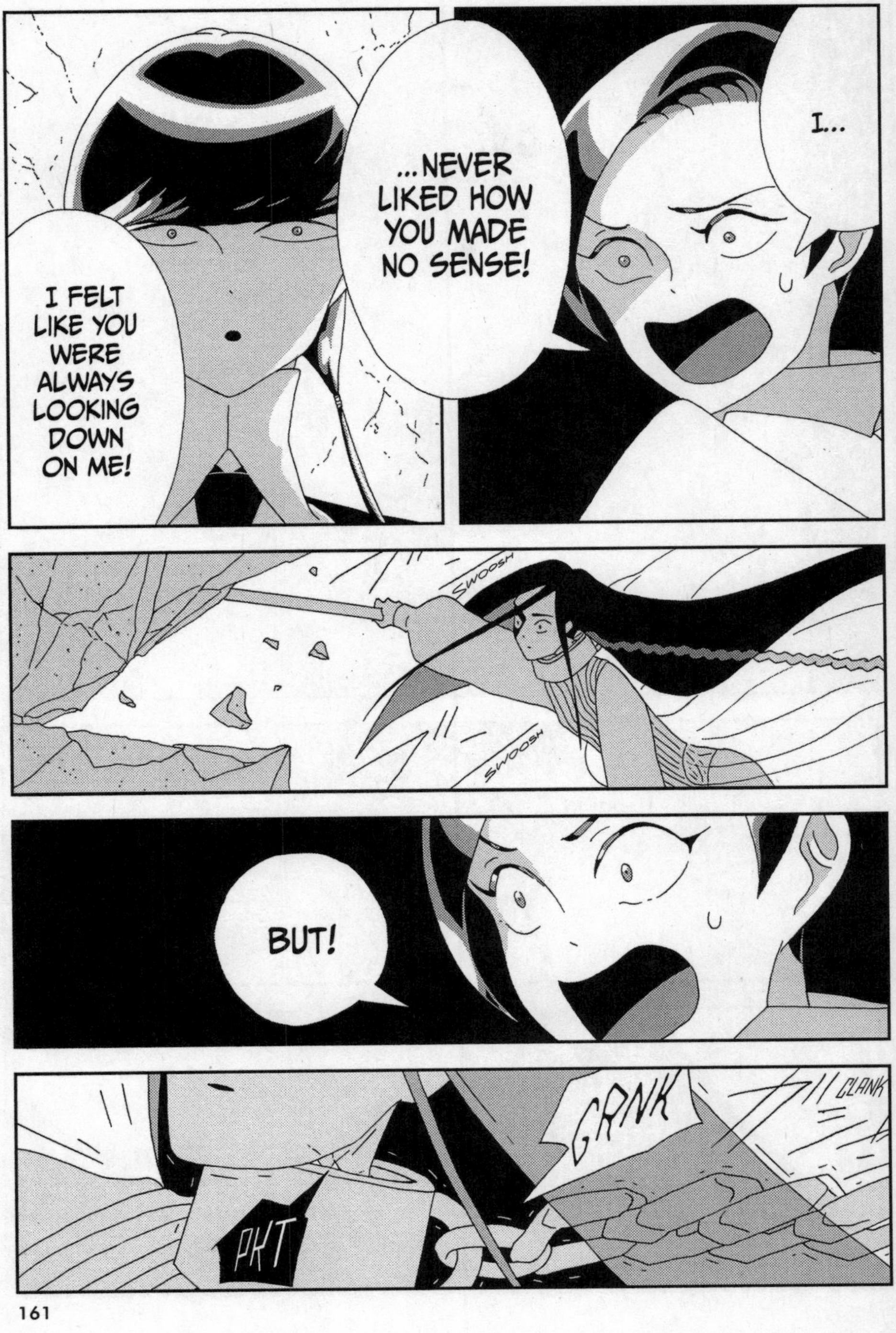

I...
...NEVER LIKED HOW YOU MADE NO SENSE!
I FELT LIKE YOU WERE ALWAYS LOOKING DOWN ON ME!
SWOOSH
SWOOSH
BUT!
CLANK
GRNK
PKT

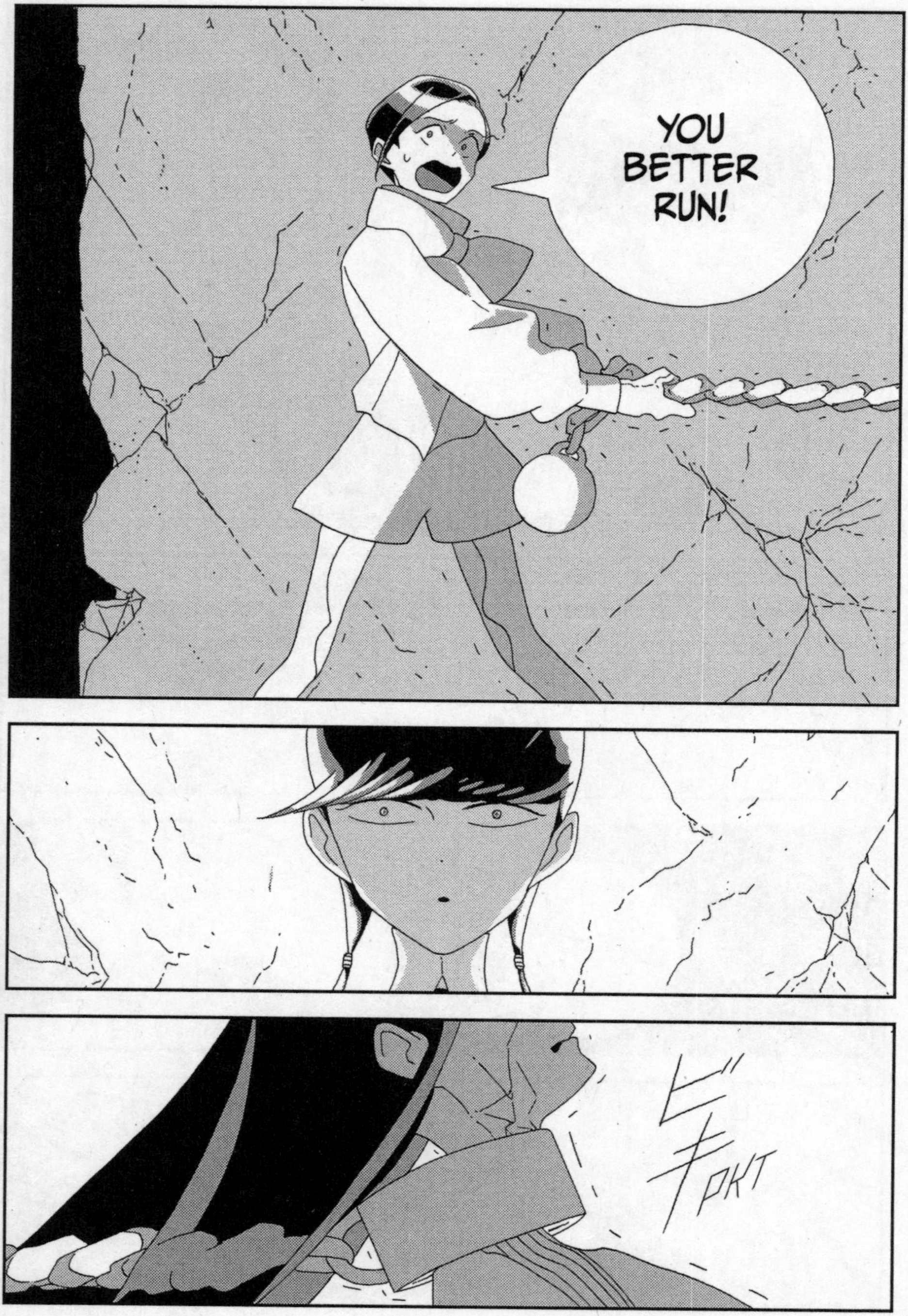
YOU BETTER RUN!
ビキ
PKT

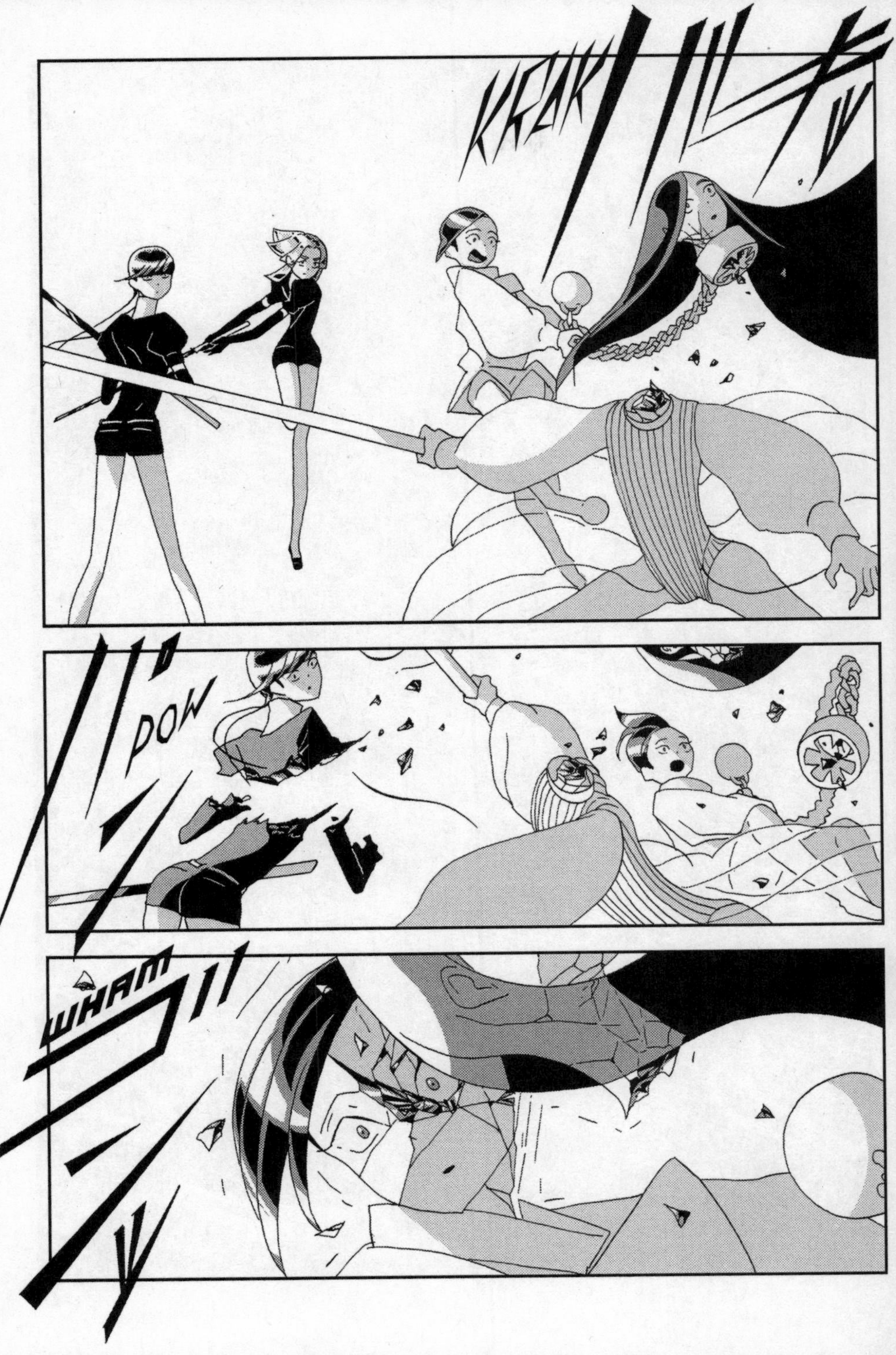
KRZAK
POW
WHAM

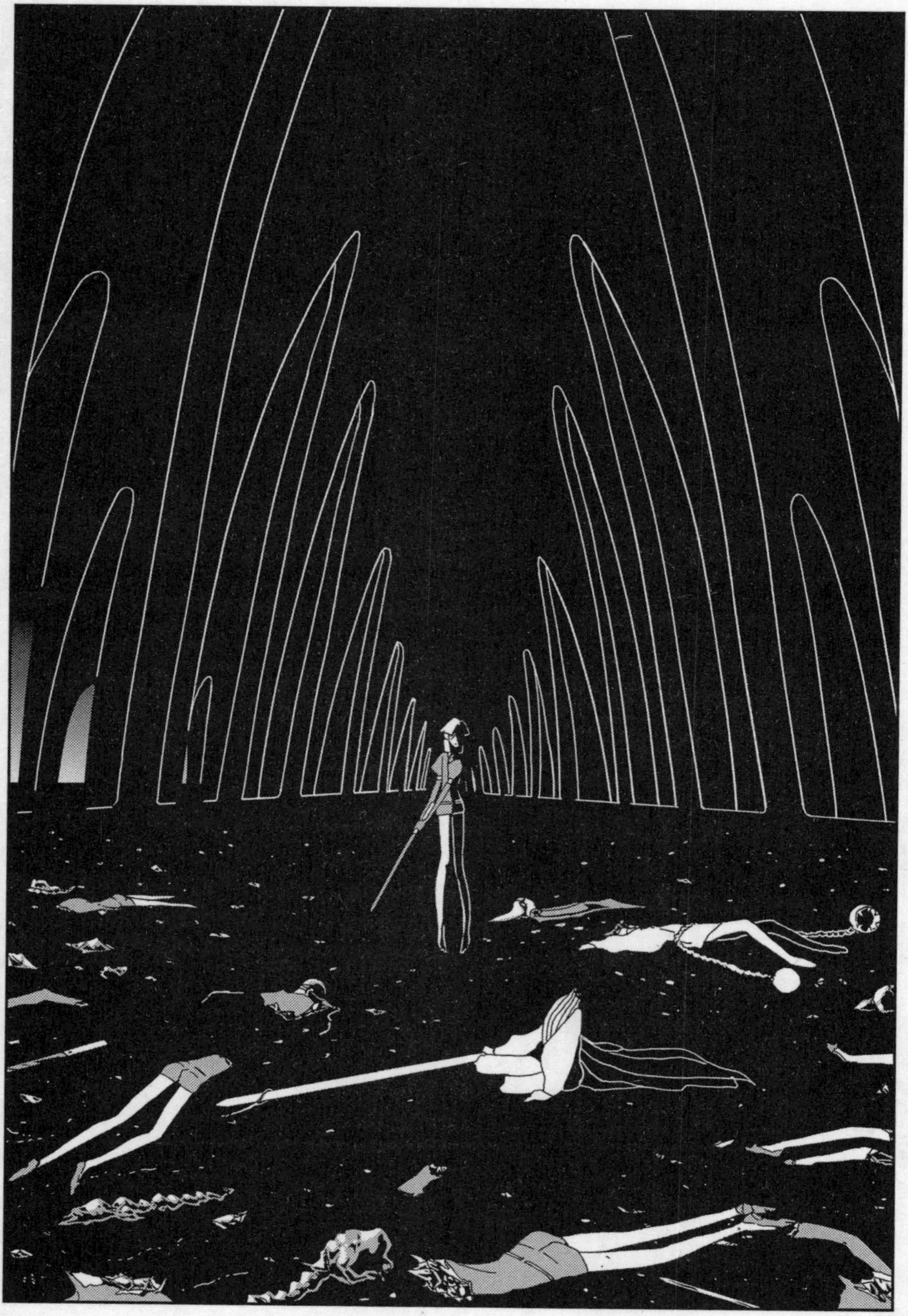

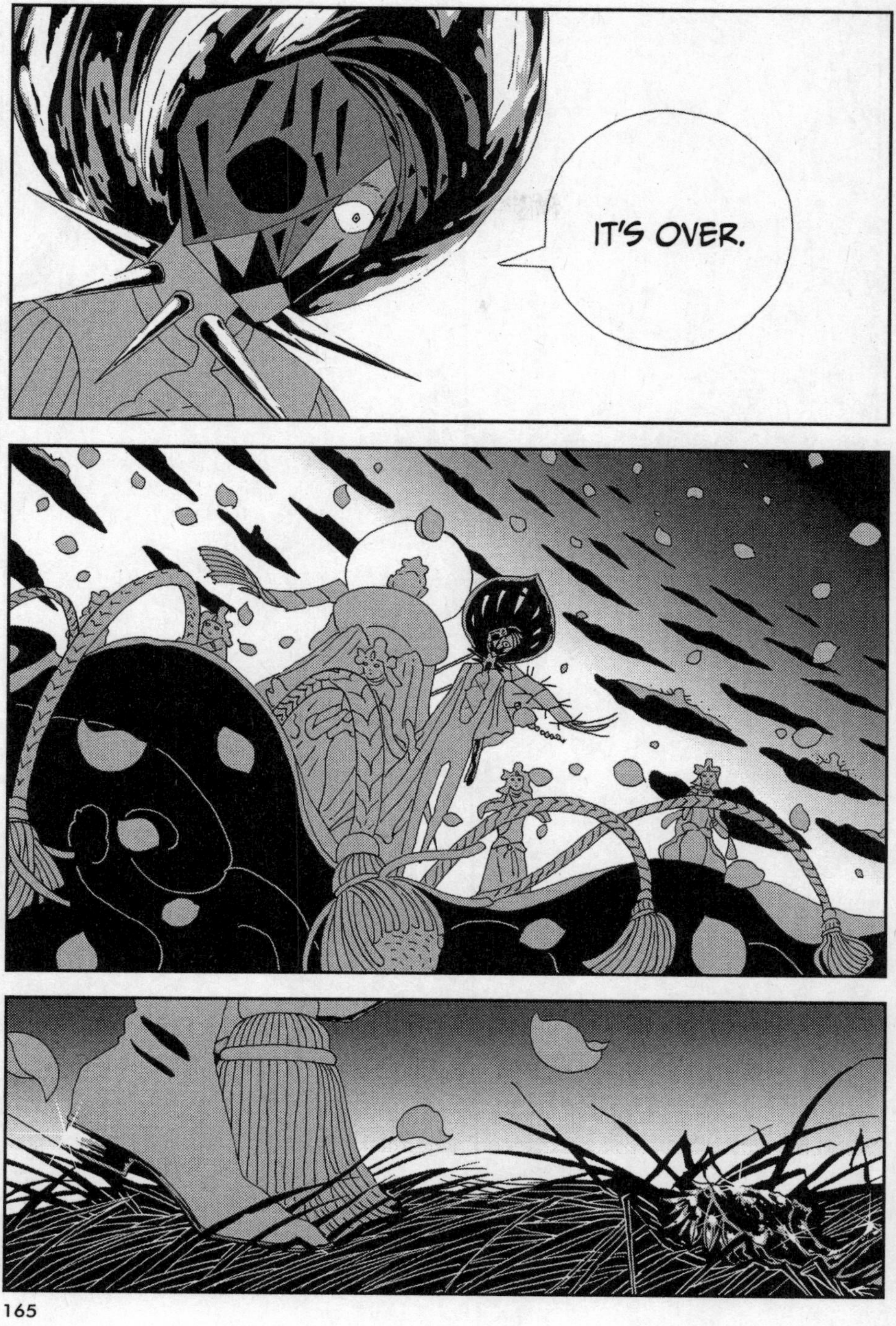
IT'S OVER.

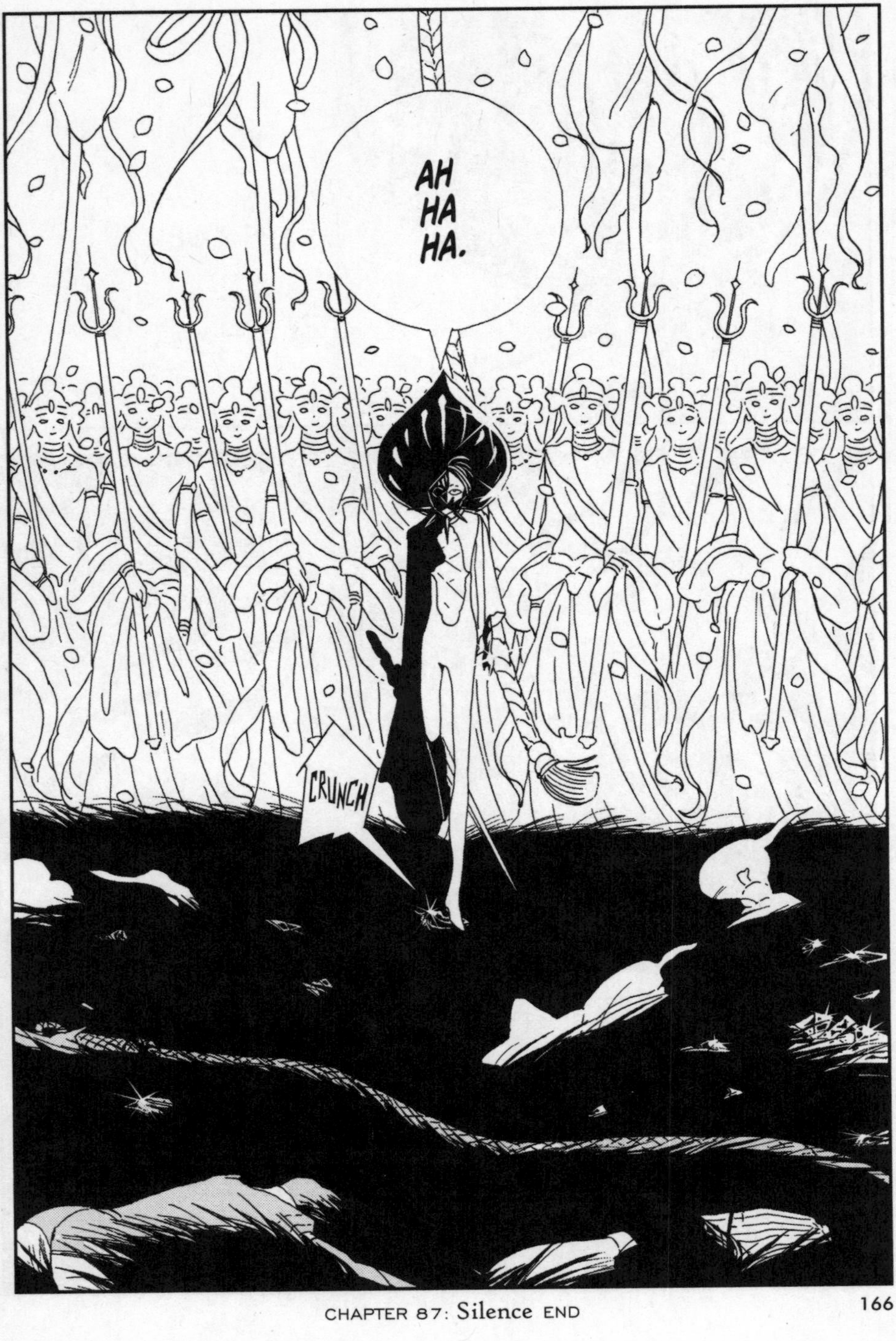
AH
HA
HA.
CRUNCH

CHAPTER 87: Silence END

CHAPTER 88:

Nature, Experiments, Future

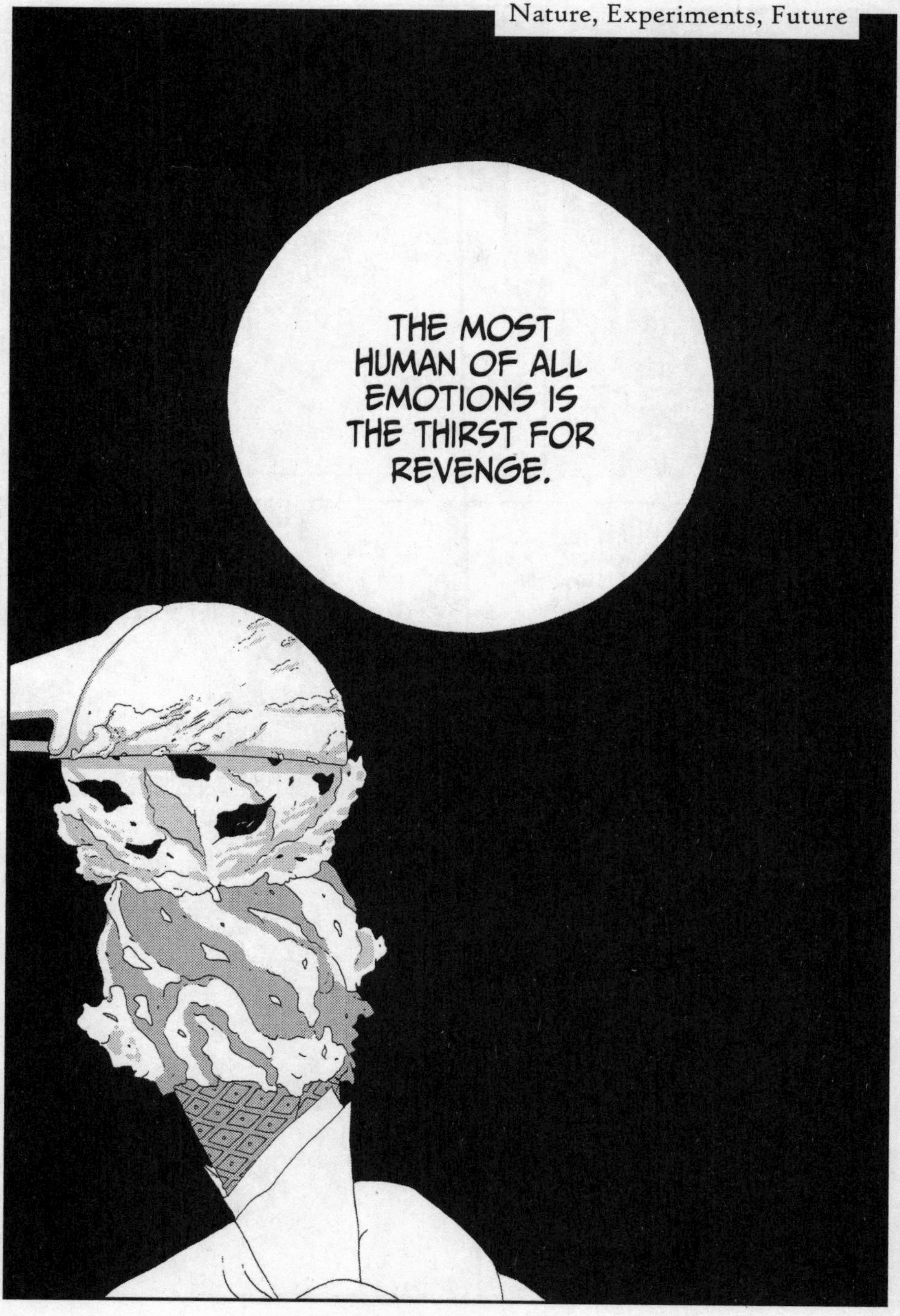
THE MOST HUMAN OF ALL EMOTIONS IS THE THIRST FOR REVENGE.

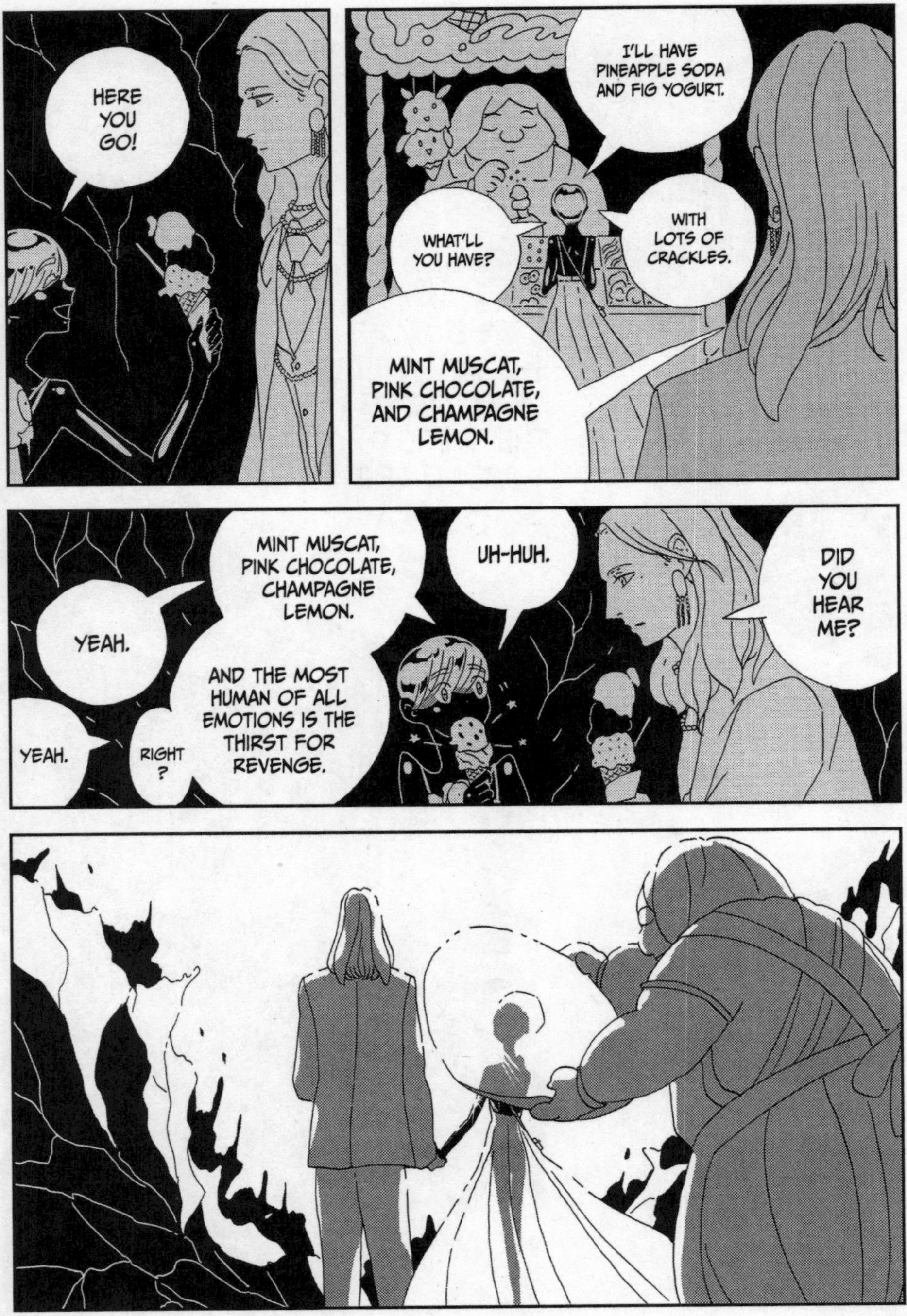
I'LL HAVE PINEAPPLE SODA AND FIG YOGURT.
WITH LOTS OF CRACKLES.
WHAT'LL YOU HAVE?
MINT MUSCAT, PINK CHOCOLATE, AND CHAMPAGNE LEMON.
HERE YOU GO!
DID YOU HEAR ME?
UH-HUH.
MINT MUSCAT, PINK CHOCOLATE, CHAMPAGNE LEMON.
YEAH.
AND THE MOST HUMAN OF ALL EMOTIONS IS THE THIRST FOR REVENGE.
RIGHT?
YEAH.

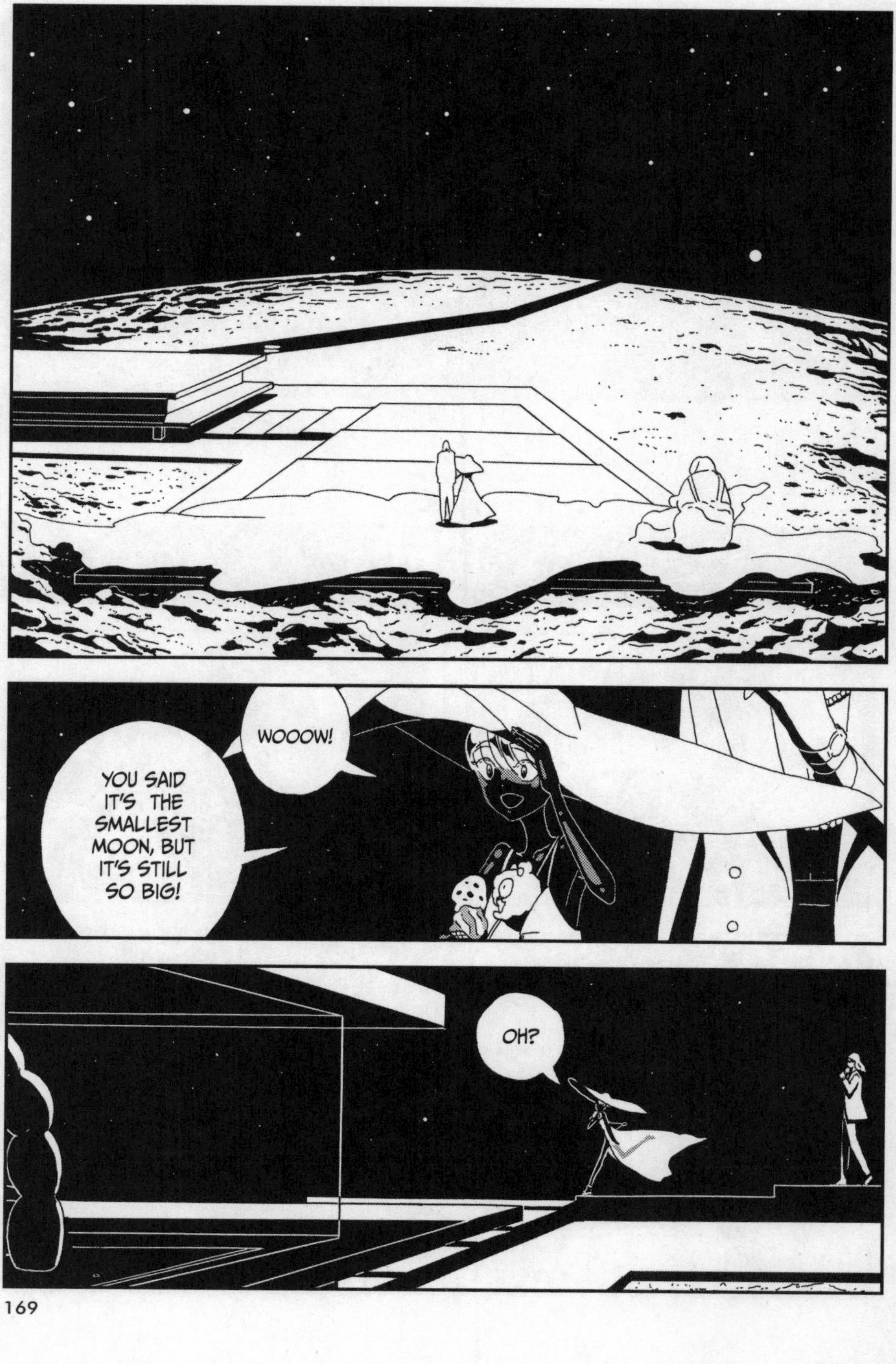
WOOOW!
YOU SAID IT'S THE SMALLEST MOON, BUT IT'S STILL SO BIG!
OH?

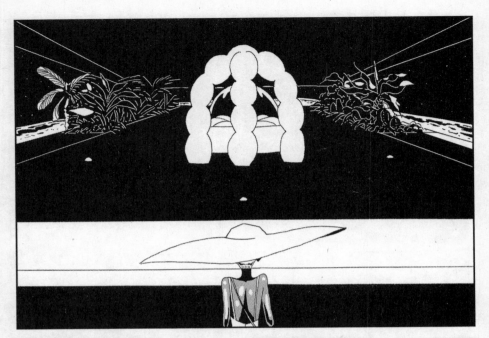

IS THIS ...
THE "ESTATE" ...
...YOU WANTED TO LOCK ME UP IN...?
WANT TO GO INSIDE ?
NOT A CHANCE.
HMMM.

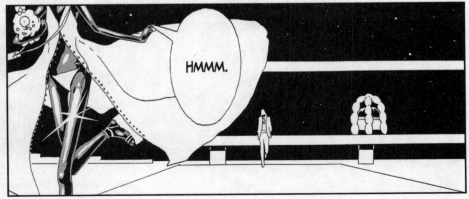

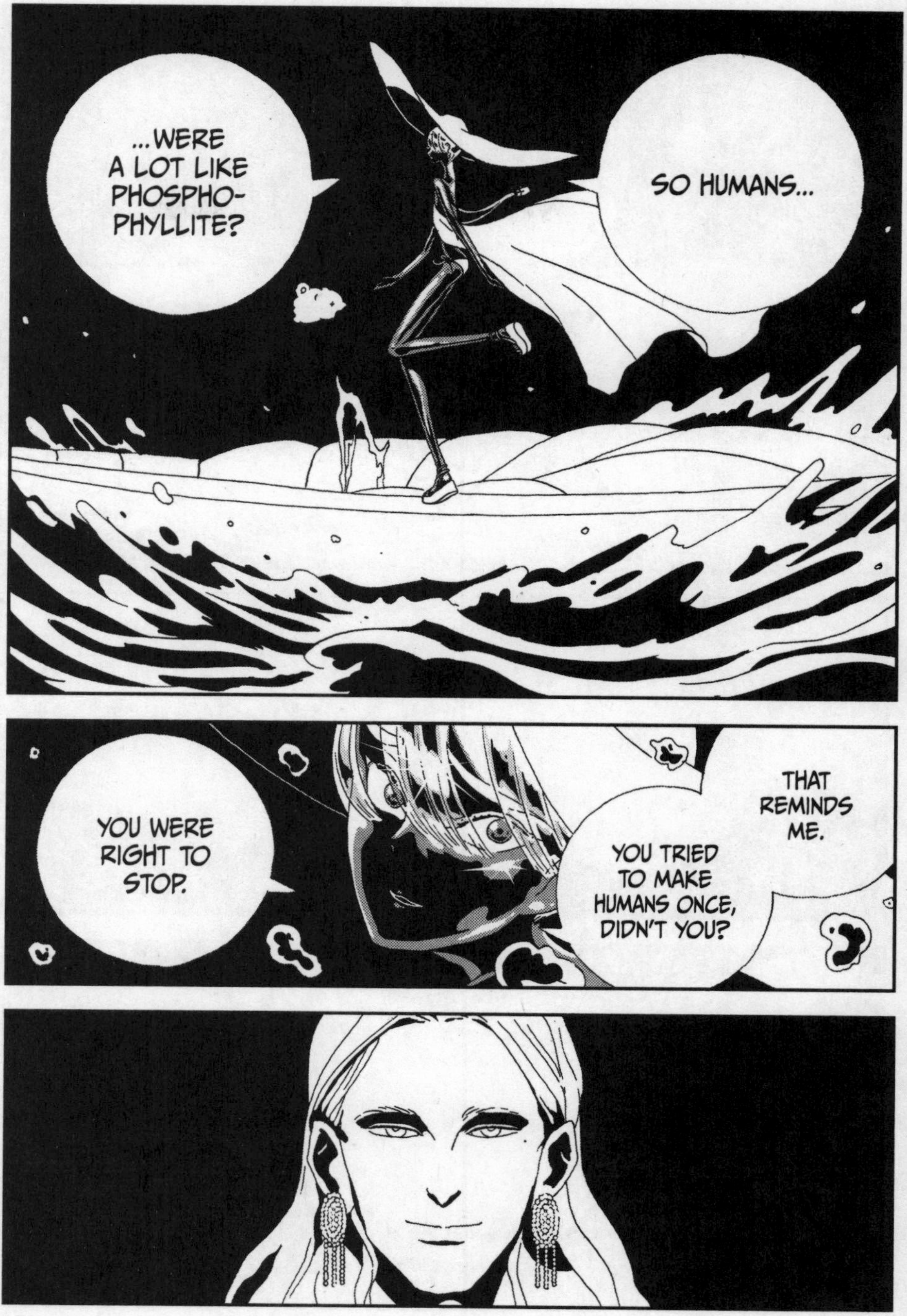
SO HUMANS...
...WERE A LOT LIKE PHOSPHO-PHYLLITE?
THAT REMINDS ME.
YOU TRIED TO MAKE HUMANS ONCE, DIDN'T YOU?
YOU WERE RIGHT TO STOP.

IN AN EMERGENCY...

...THERE ARE TWO CONDITIONS THAT WOULD ACTIVATE KONGŌ'S PRAYER.

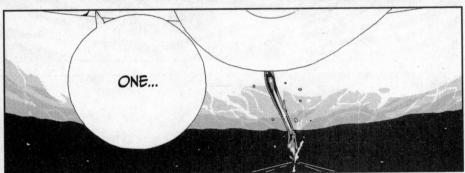

ONE...

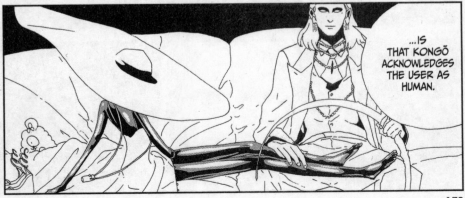

...IS THAT KONGŌ ACKNOWLEDGES THE USER AS HUMAN.

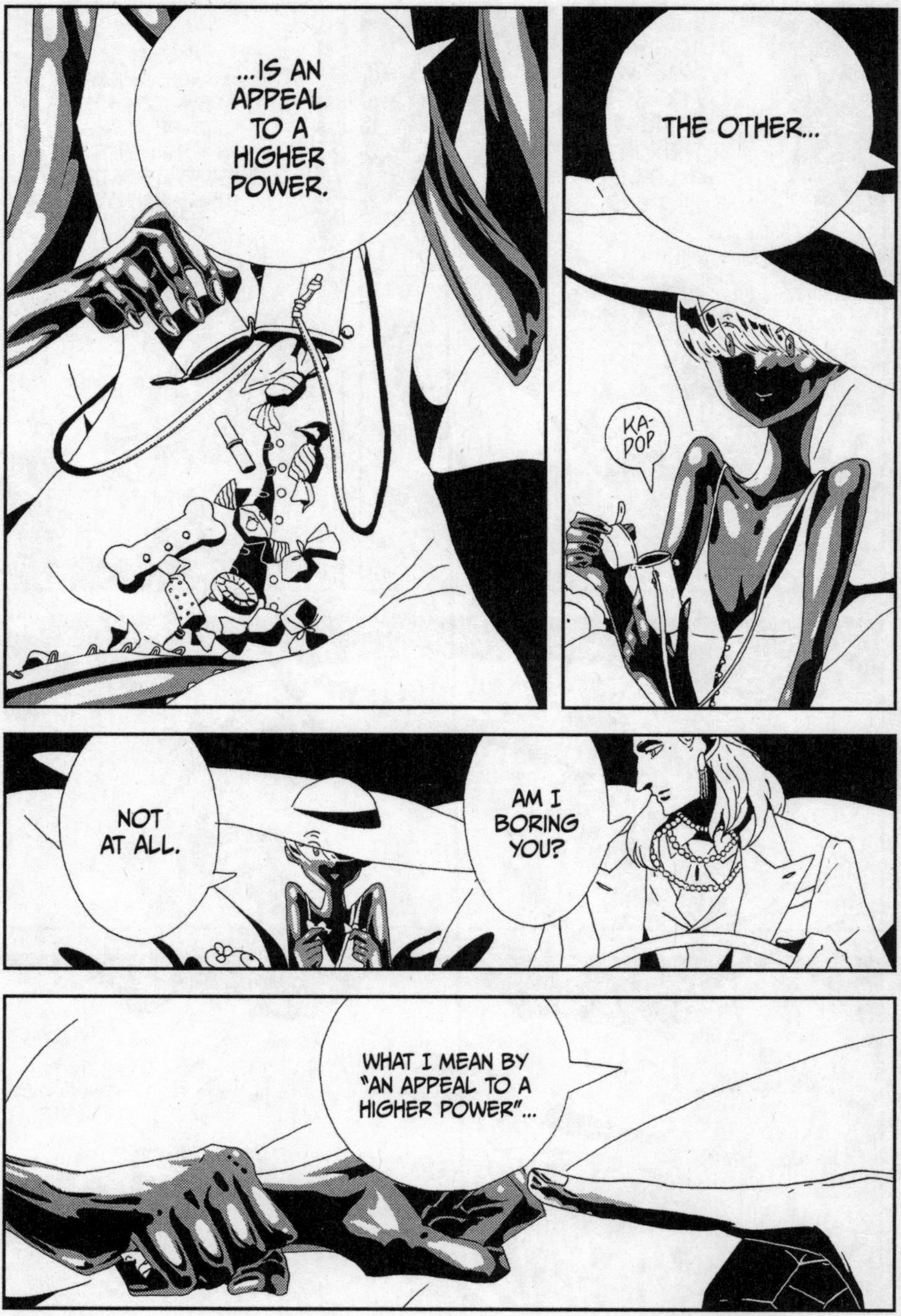
THE OTHER...
KA-POP
...IS AN APPEAL TO A HIGHER POWER.
AM I BORING YOU?
NOT AT ALL.
WHAT I MEAN BY "AN APPEAL TO A HIGHER POWER"...

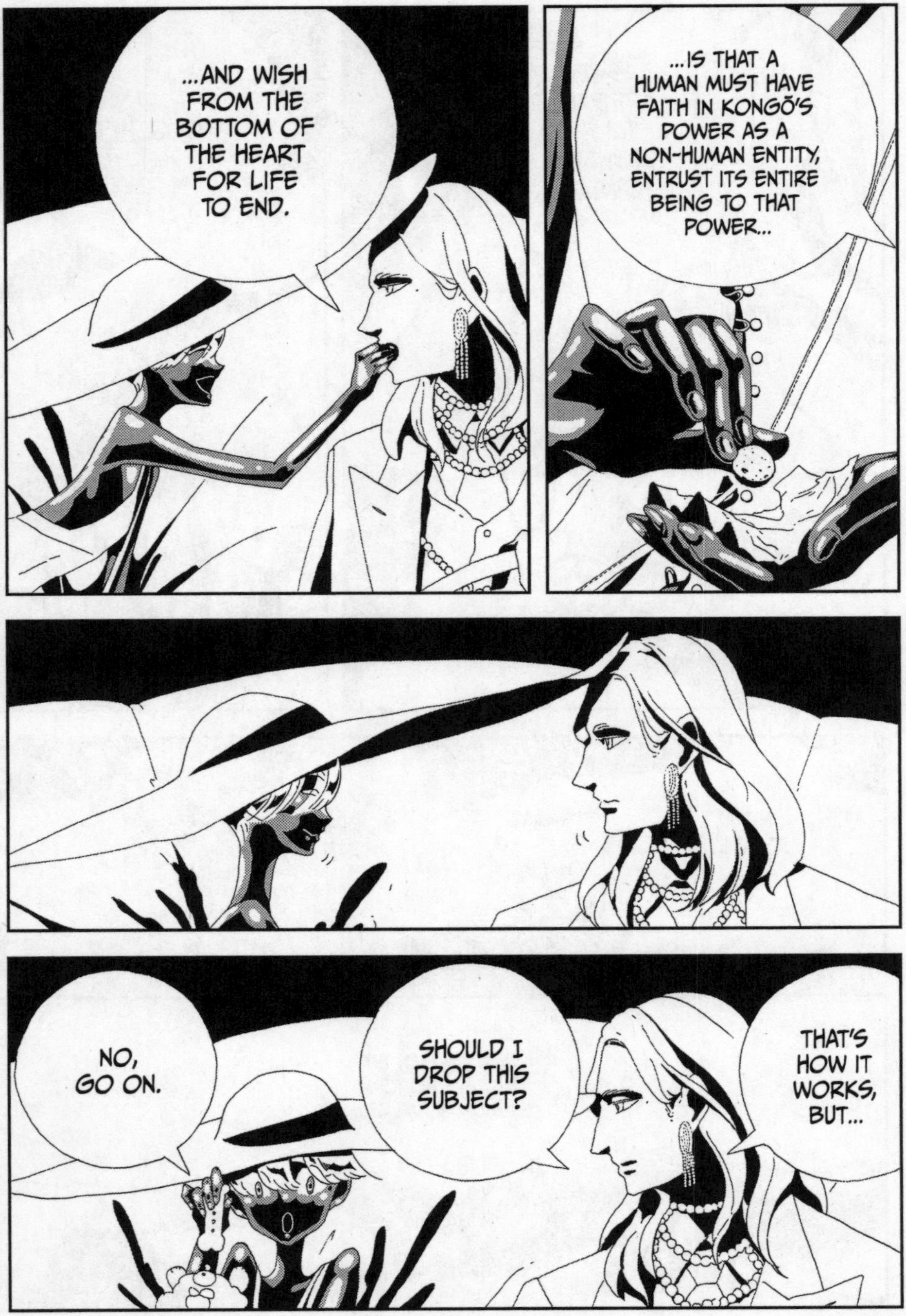
...IS THAT A HUMAN MUST HAVE FAITH IN KONGŌ'S POWER AS A NON-HUMAN ENTITY, ENTRUST ITS ENTIRE BEING TO THAT POWER...
...AND WISH FROM THE BOTTOM OF THE HEART FOR LIFE TO END.
THAT'S HOW IT WORKS, BUT...
SHOULD I DROP THIS SUBJECT?
NO, GO ON.

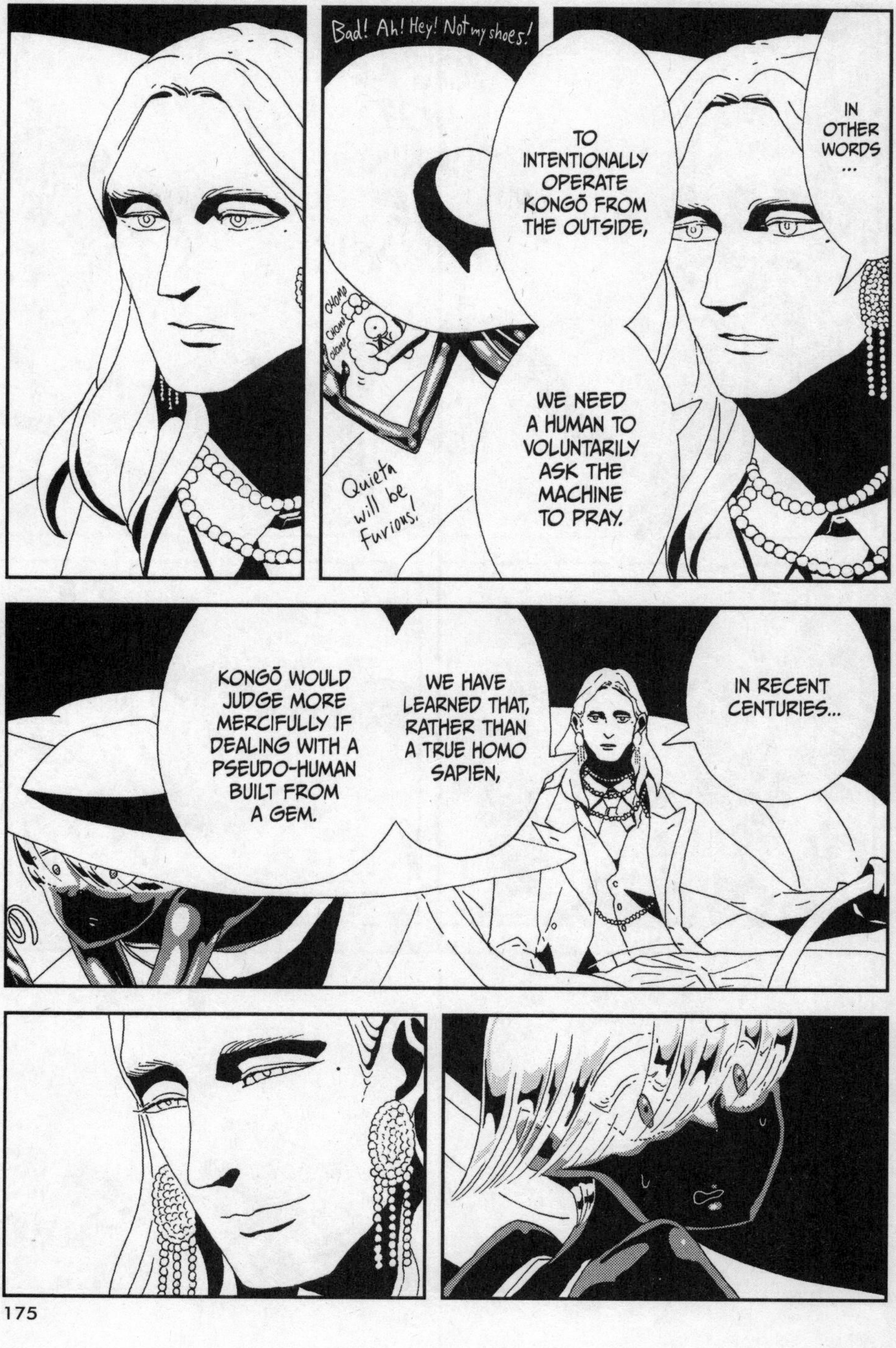
IN OTHER WORDS ...
TO INTENTIONALLY OPERATE KONGŌ FROM THE OUTSIDE,
WE NEED A HUMAN TO VOLUNTARILY ASK THE MACHINE TO PRAY.
Bad! Ah! Hey! Not my shoes!
Quieta will be Furious!
IN RECENT CENTURIES...
WE HAVE LEARNED THAT, RATHER THAN A TRUE HOMO SAPIEN,
KONGŌ WOULD JUDGE MORE MERCIFULLY IF DEALING WITH A PSEUDO-HUMAN BUILT FROM A GEM.

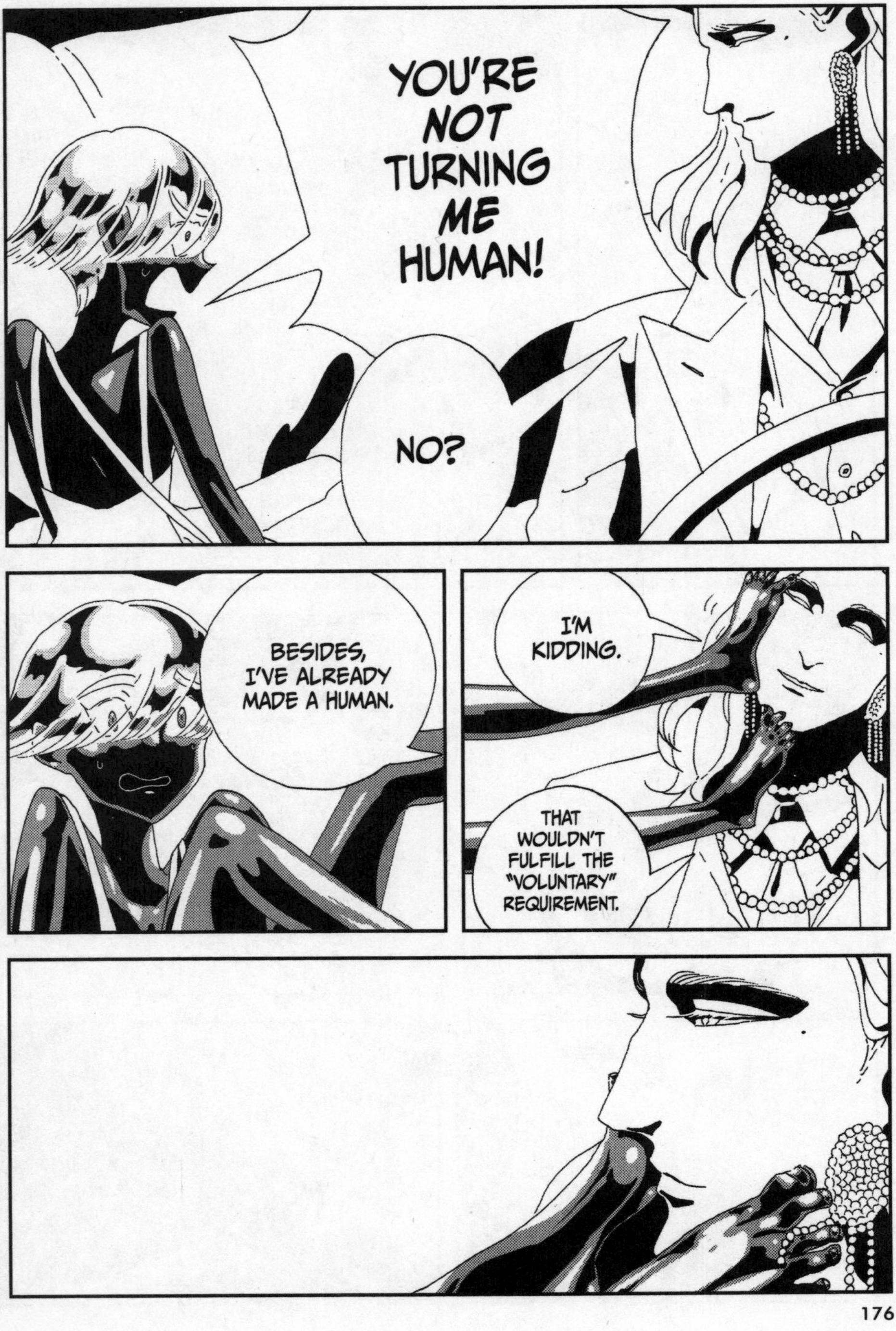
YOU'RE NOT TURNING ME HUMAN!
NO?
I'M KIDDING.
THAT WOULDN'T FULFILL THE "VOLUNTARY" REQUIREMENT.
BESIDES, I'VE ALREADY MADE A HUMAN.

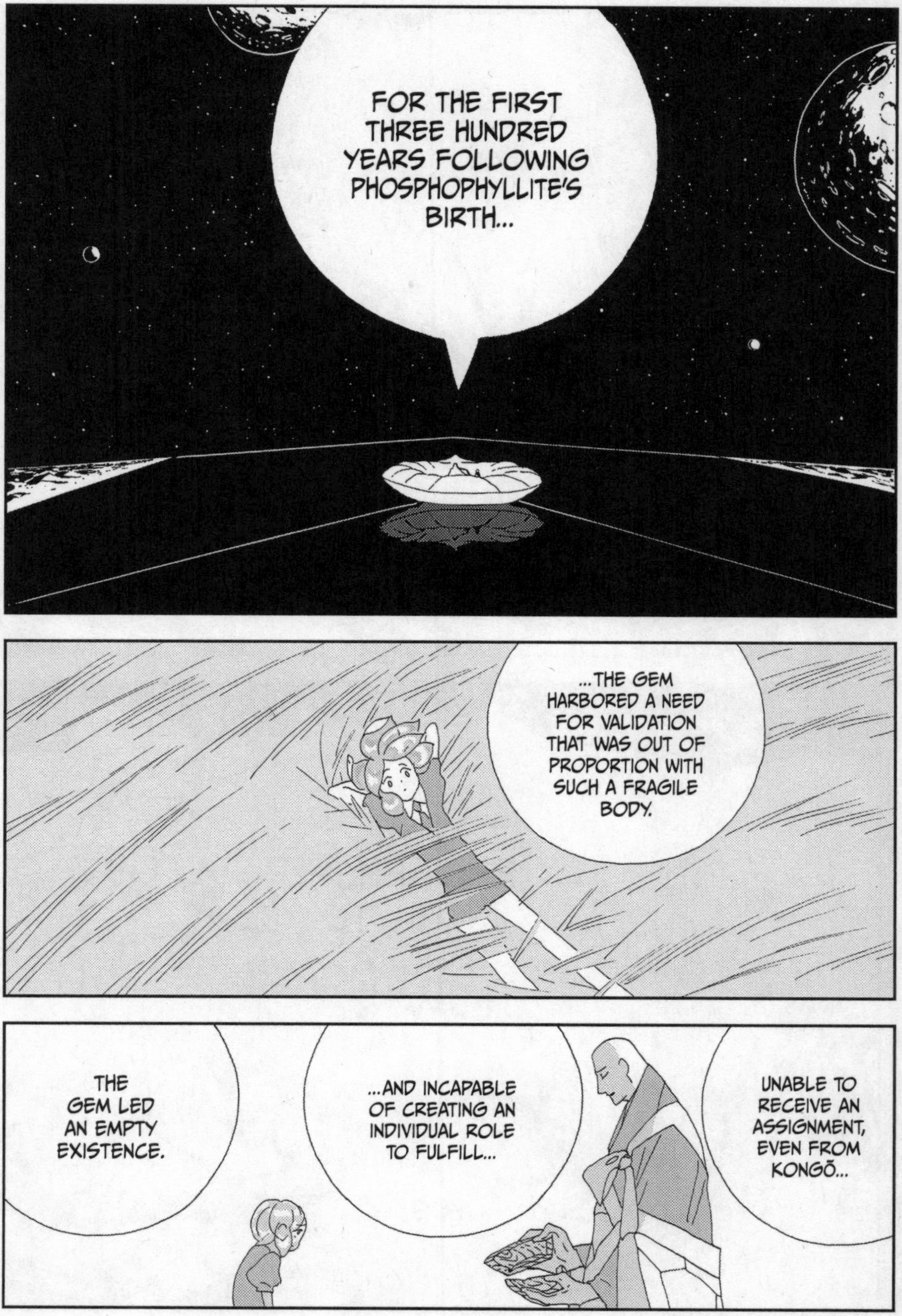
FOR THE FIRST THREE HUNDRED YEARS FOLLOWING PHOSPHOPHYLLITE'S BIRTH...
...THE GEM HARBORED A NEED FOR VALIDATION THAT WAS OUT OF PROPORTION WITH SUCH A FRAGILE BODY.
UNABLE TO RECEIVE AN ASSIGNMENT, EVEN FROM KONGŌ...
...AND INCAPABLE OF CREATING AN INDIVIDUAL ROLE TO FULFILL...
THE GEM LED AN EMPTY EXISTENCE.

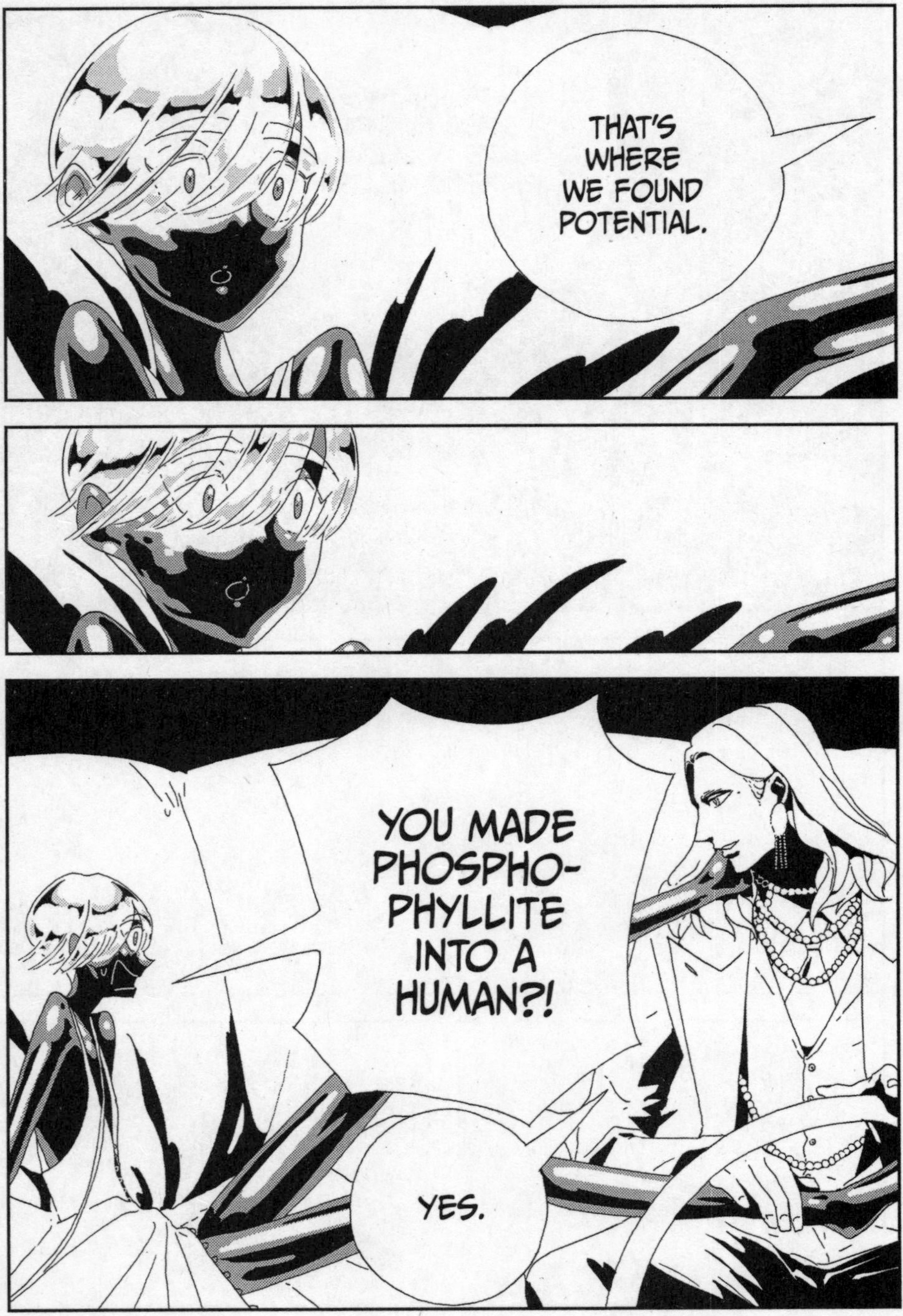
THAT'S WHERE WE FOUND POTENTIAL.
YOU MADE PHOSPHO-PHYLLITE INTO A HUMAN?!
YES.

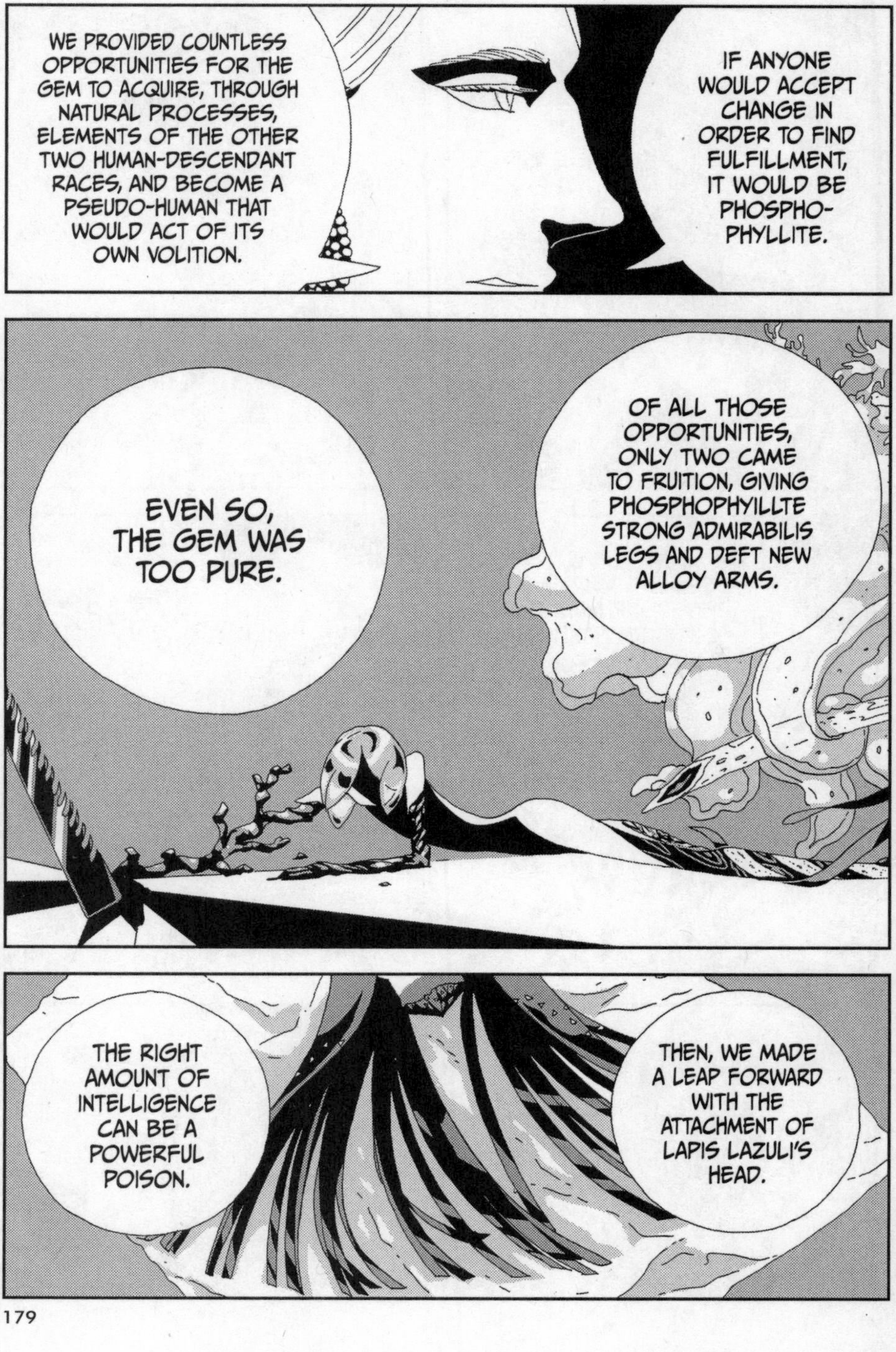
IF ANYONE WOULD ACCEPT CHANGE IN ORDER TO FIND FULFILLMENT, IT WOULD BE PHOSPHO-PHYLLITE.
WE PROVIDED COUNTLESS OPPORTUNITIES FOR THE GEM TO ACQUIRE, THROUGH NATURAL PROCESSES, ELEMENTS OF THE OTHER TWO HUMAN-DESCENDANT RACES, AND BECOME A PSEUDO-HUMAN THAT WOULD ACT OF ITS OWN VOLITION.
OF ALL THOSE OPPORTUNITIES, ONLY TWO CAME TO FRUITION, GIVING PHOSPHOPHYILLTE STRONG ADMIRABILIS LEGS AND DEFT NEW ALLOY ARMS.
EVEN SO, THE GEM WAS TOO PURE.
THEN, WE MADE A LEAP FORWARD WITH THE ATTACHMENT OF LAPIS LAZULI'S HEAD.
THE RIGHT AMOUNT OF INTELLIGENCE CAN BE A POWERFUL POISON.

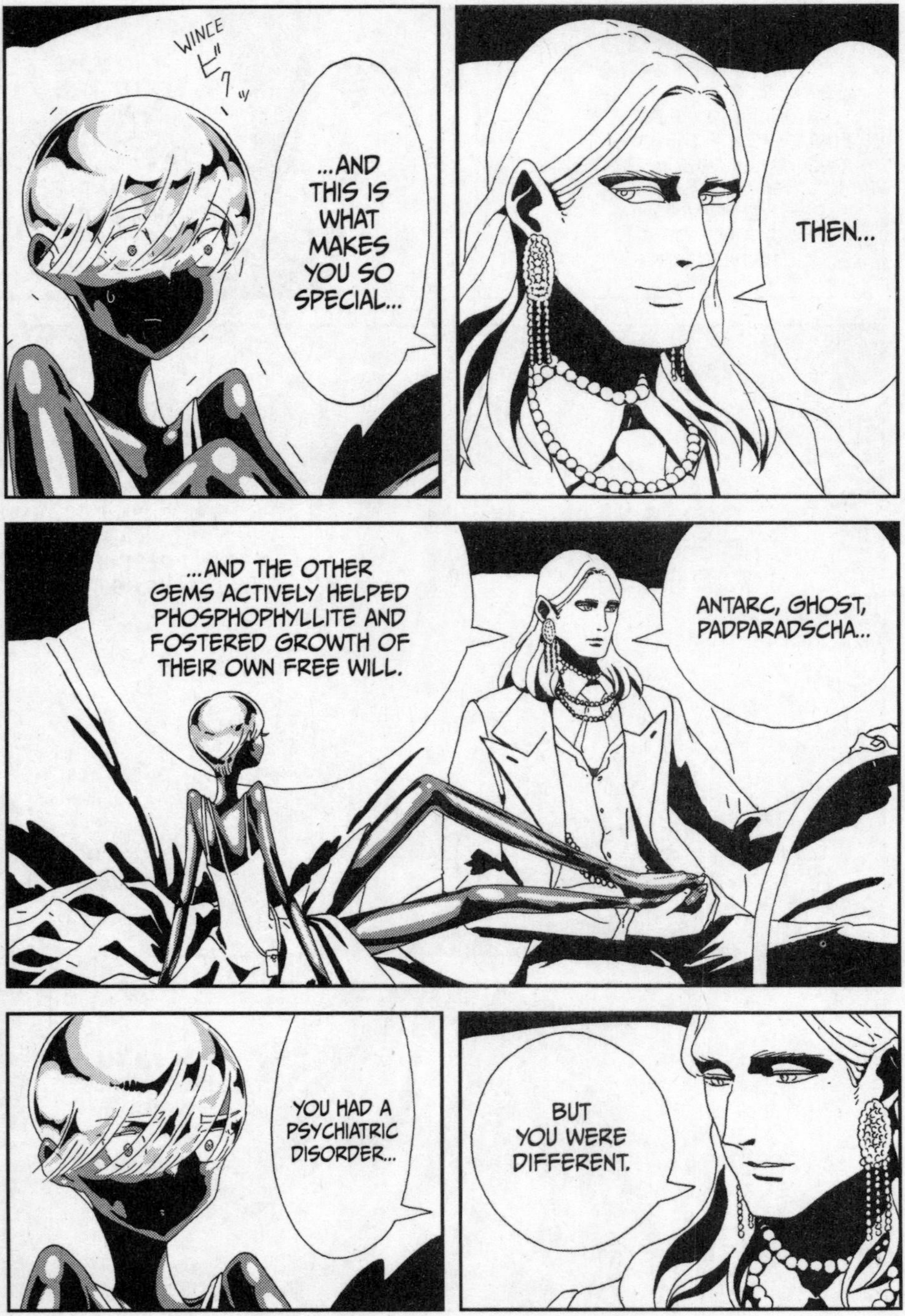
THEN...
WINCE ビクッ
...AND THIS IS WHAT MAKES YOU SO SPECIAL...
ANTARC, GHOST, PADPARADSCHA...
...AND THE OTHER GEMS ACTIVELY HELPED PHOSPHOPHYLLITE AND FOSTERED GROWTH OF THEIR OWN FREE WILL.
BUT YOU WERE DIFFERENT.
YOU HAD A PSYCHIATRIC DISORDER...

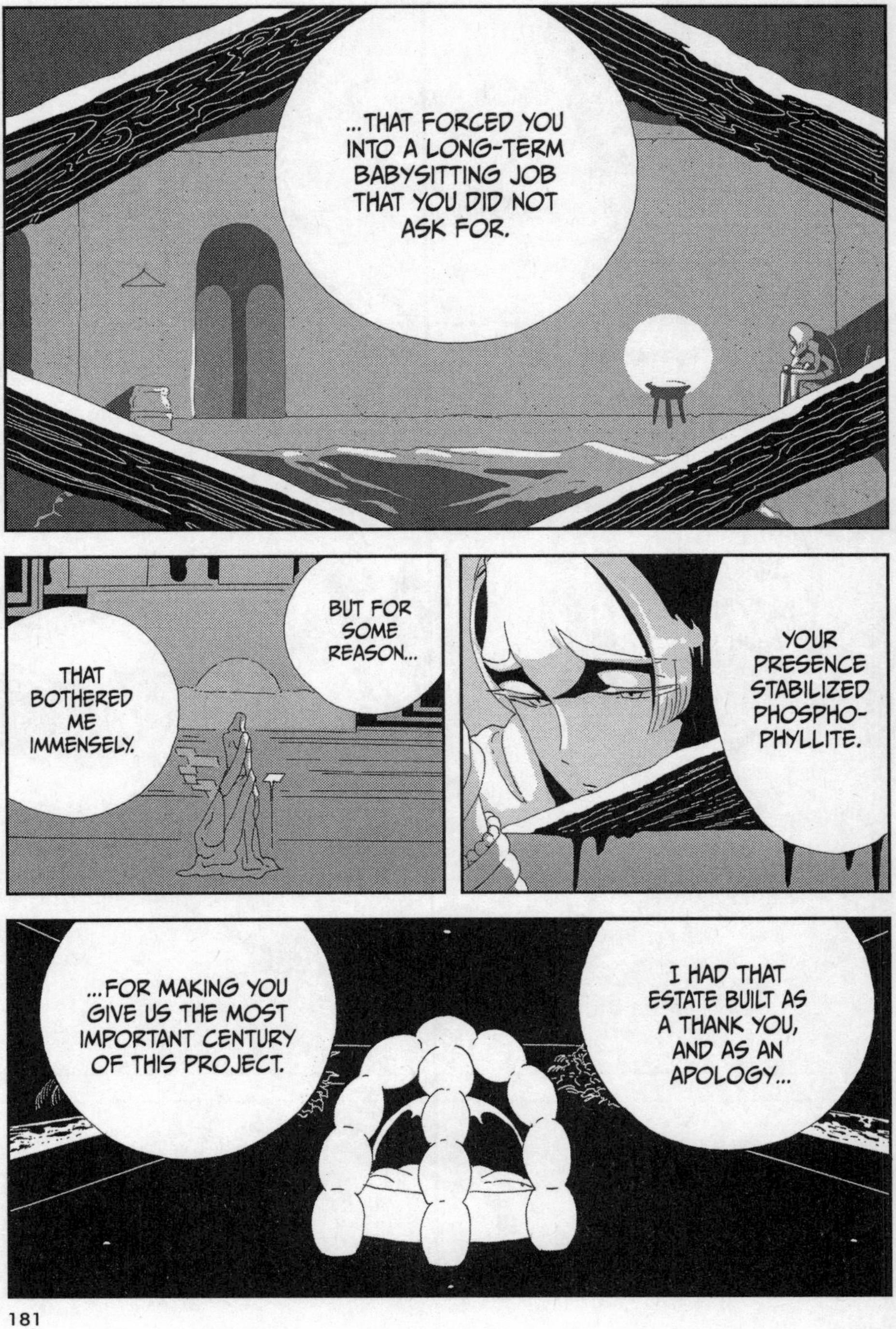
...THAT FORCED YOU INTO A LONG-TERM BABYSITTING JOB THAT YOU DID NOT ASK FOR.
YOUR PRESENCE STABILIZED PHOSPHO-PHYLLITE.
BUT FOR SOME REASON...
THAT BOTHERED ME IMMENSELY.
I HAD THAT ESTATE BUILT AS A THANK YOU, AND AS AN APOLOGY...
...FOR MAKING YOU GIVE US THE MOST IMPORTANT CENTURY OF THIS PROJECT.

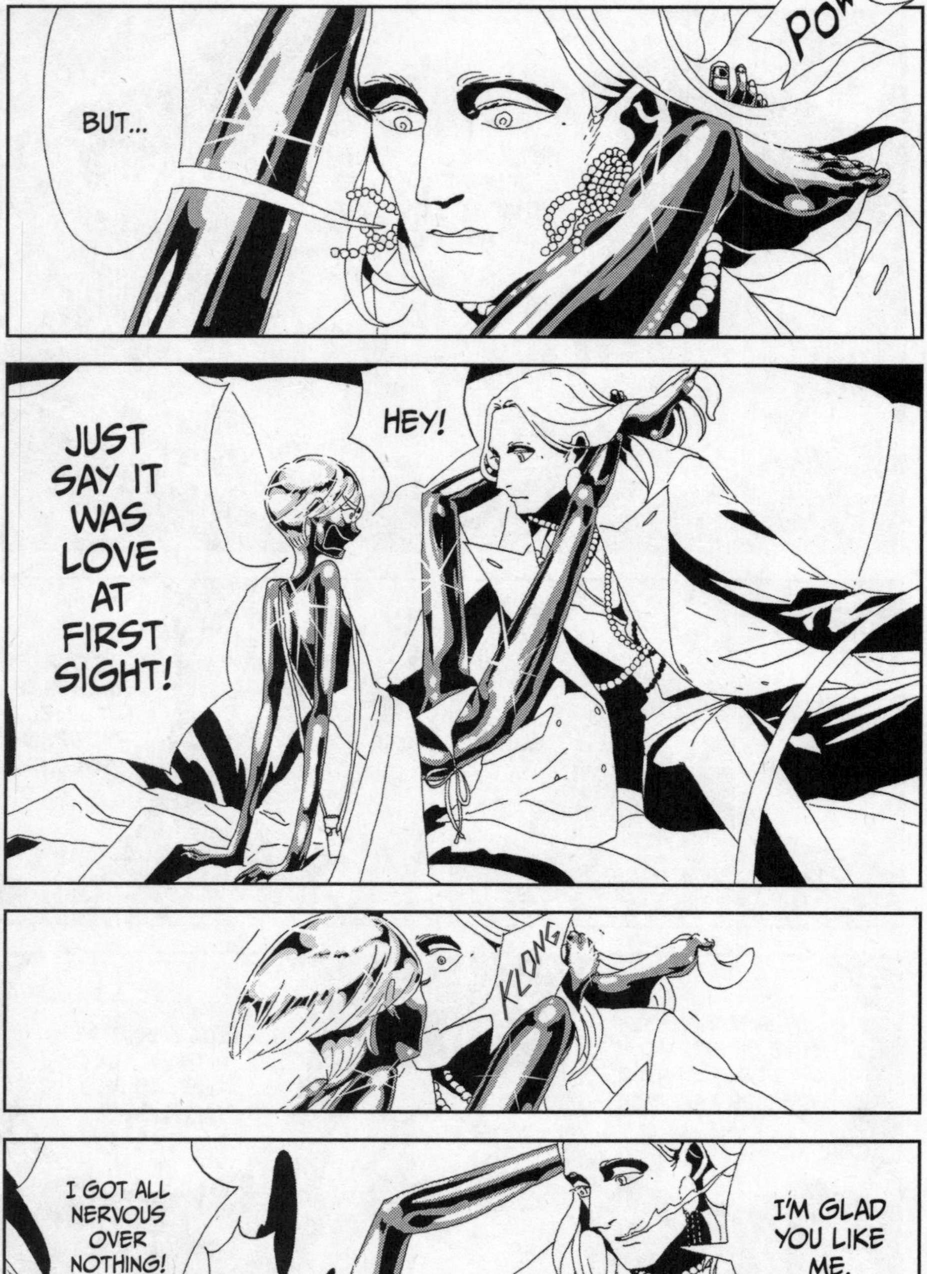
POW
BUT...
HEY!
JUST SAY IT WAS LOVE AT FIRST SIGHT!
KLONG
I'M GLAD YOU LIKE ME.
DAMMIT.
I GOT ALL NERVOUS OVER NOTHING!

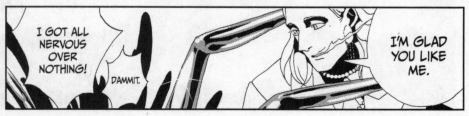

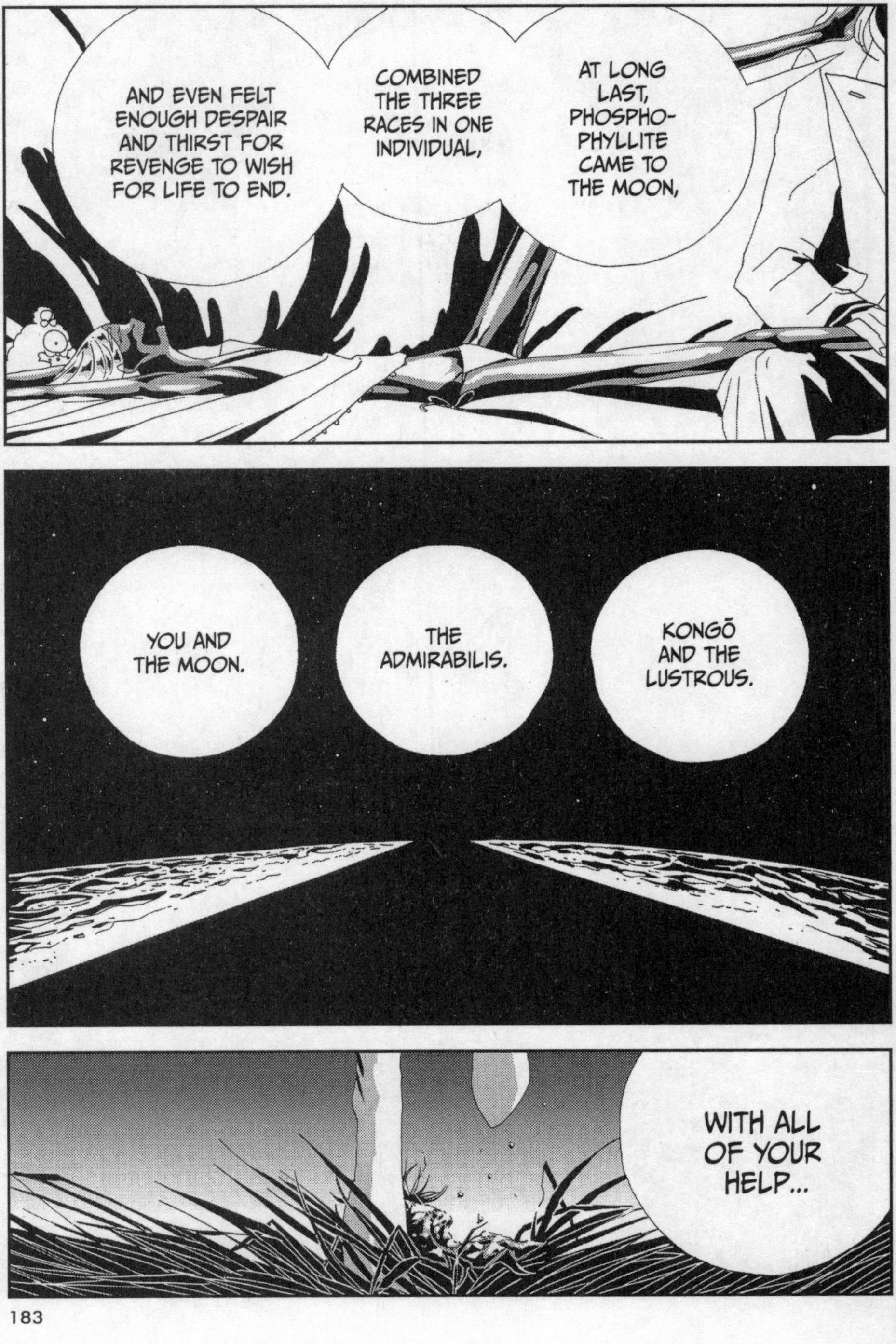
AT LONG LAST, PHOSPHO-PHYLLITE CAME TO THE MOON,
COMBINED THE THREE RACES IN ONE INDIVIDUAL,
AND EVEN FELT ENOUGH DESPAIR AND THIRST FOR REVENGE TO WISH FOR LIFE TO END.
KONGŌ AND THE LUSTROUS.
THE ADMIRABILIS.
YOU AND THE MOON.
WITH ALL OF YOUR HELP...

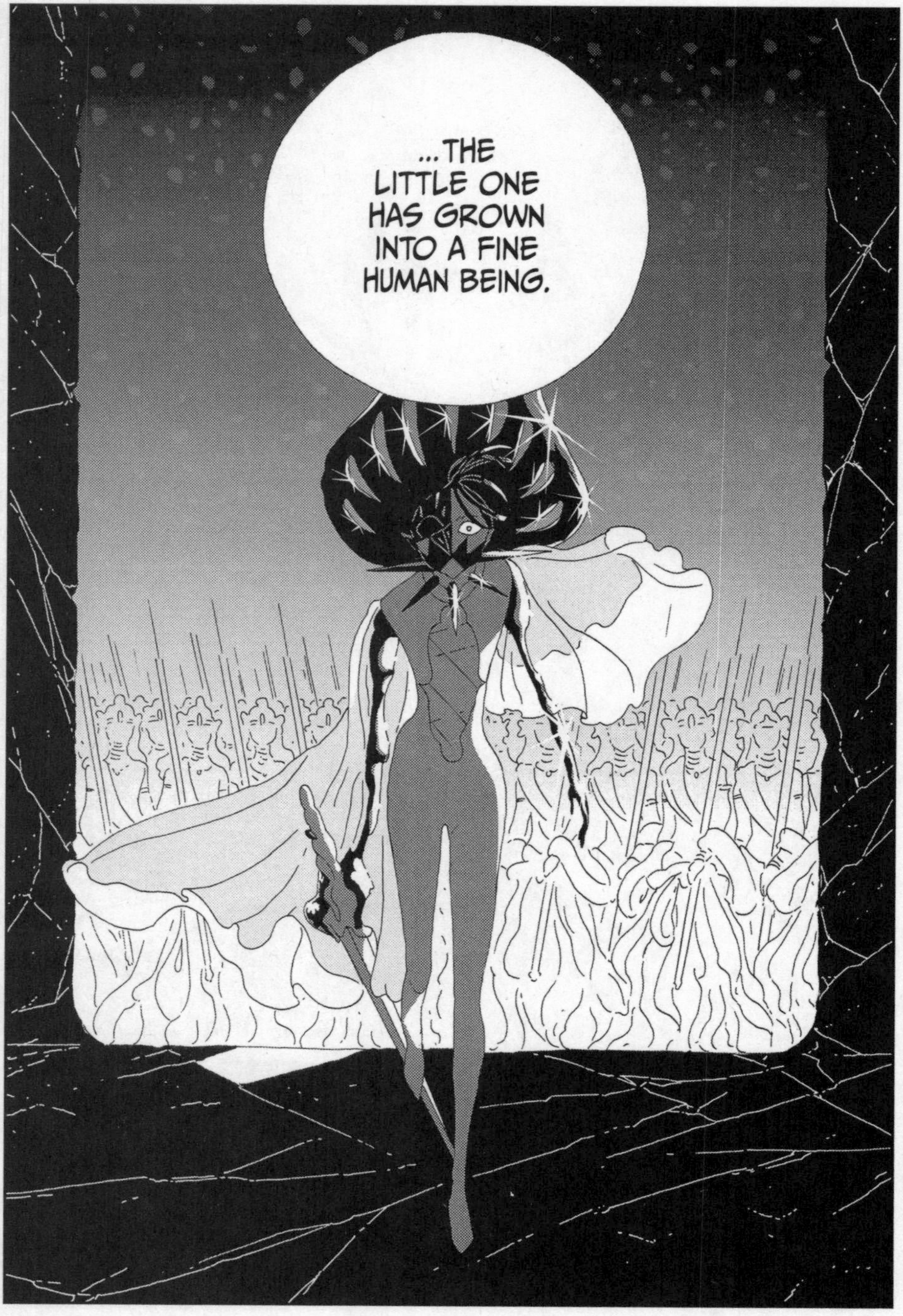
...THE LITTLE ONE HAS GROWN INTO A FINE HUMAN BEING.

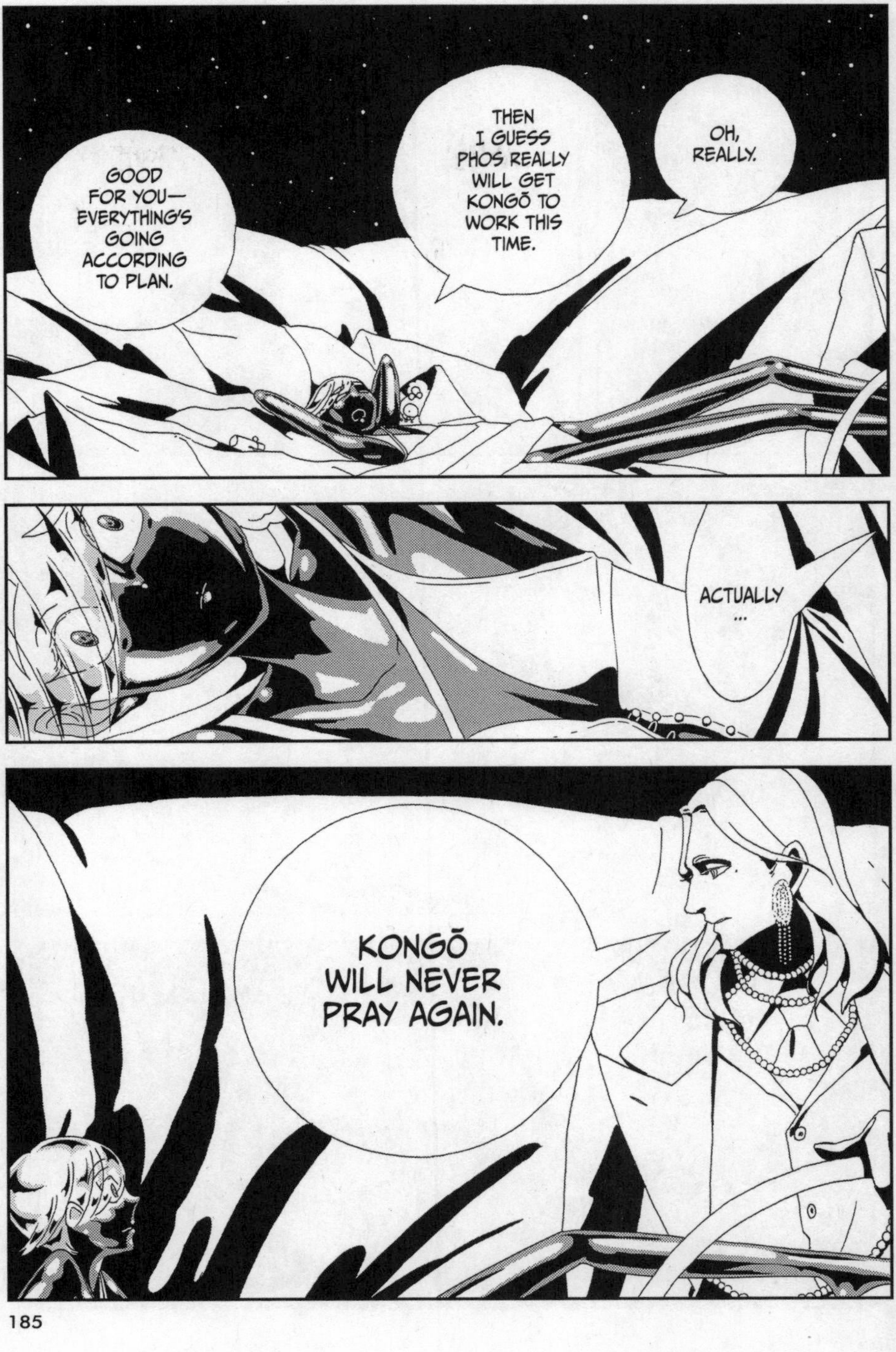
OH, REALLY.
THEN I GUESS PHOS REALLY WILL GET KONGŌ TO WORK THIS TIME.
GOOD FOR YOU—EVERYTHING'S GOING ACCORDING TO PLAN.
ACTUALLY...
KONGŌ WILL NEVER PRAY AGAIN.

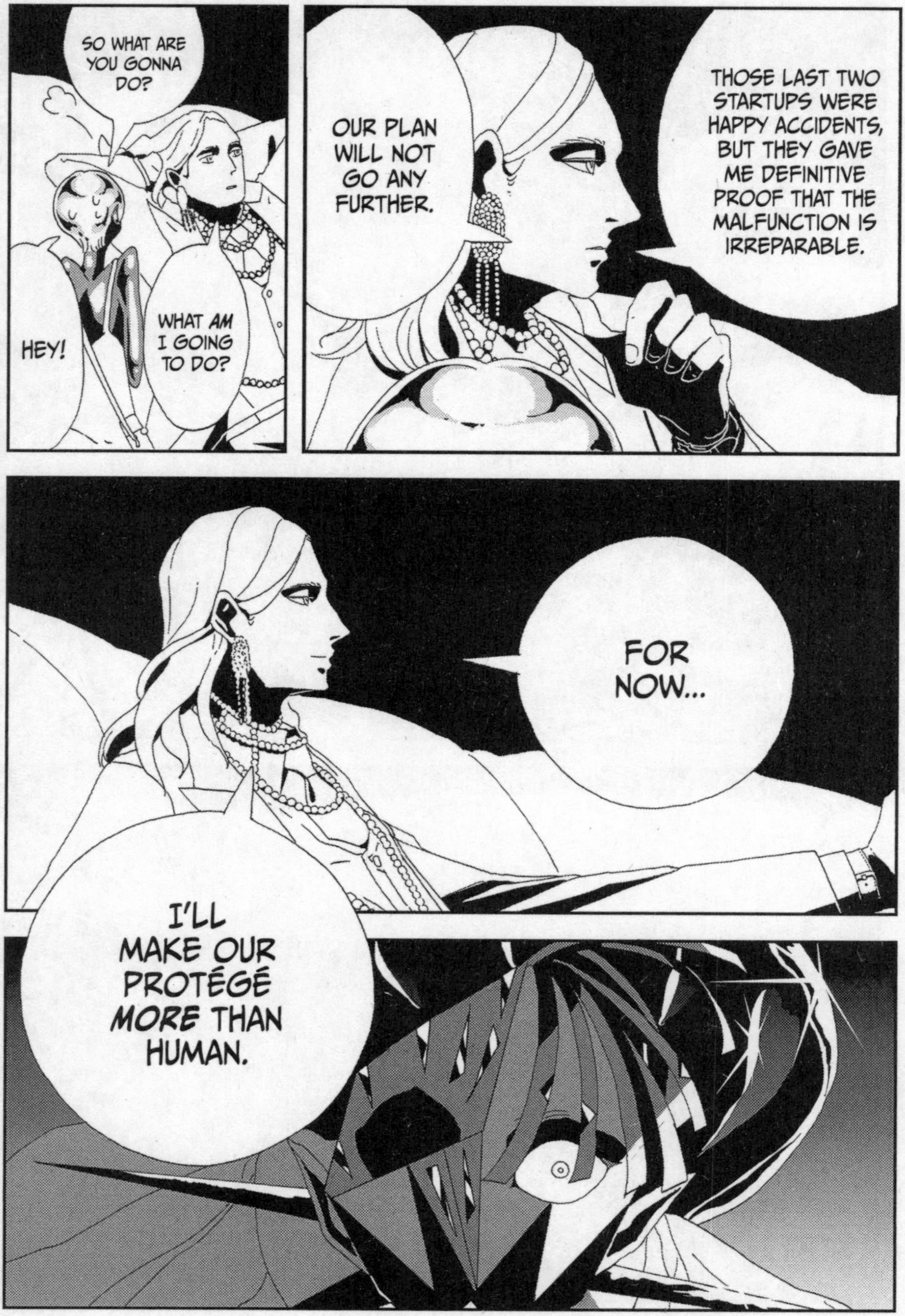
SO WHAT ARE YOU GONNA DO?
HEY!
WHAT *AM* I GOING TO DO?
OUR PLAN WILL NOT GO ANY FURTHER.
THOSE LAST TWO STARTUPS WERE HAPPY ACCIDENTS, BUT THEY GAVE ME DEFINITIVE PROOF THAT THE MALFUNCTION IS IRREPARABLE.
FOR NOW...
I'LL MAKE OUR PROTÉGÉ *MORE* THAN HUMAN.

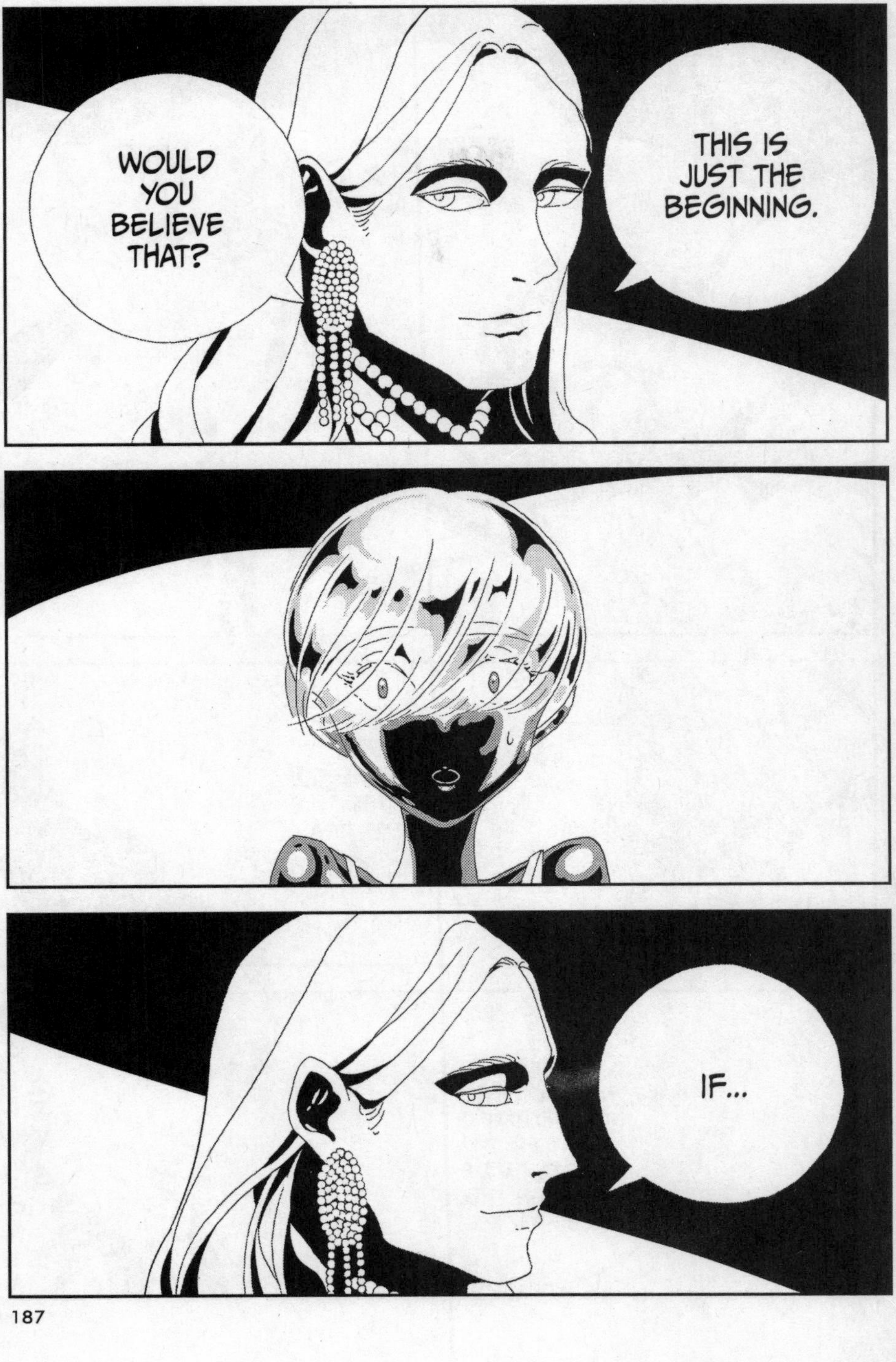
THIS IS JUST THE BEGINNING.
WOULD YOU BELIEVE THAT?
IF...

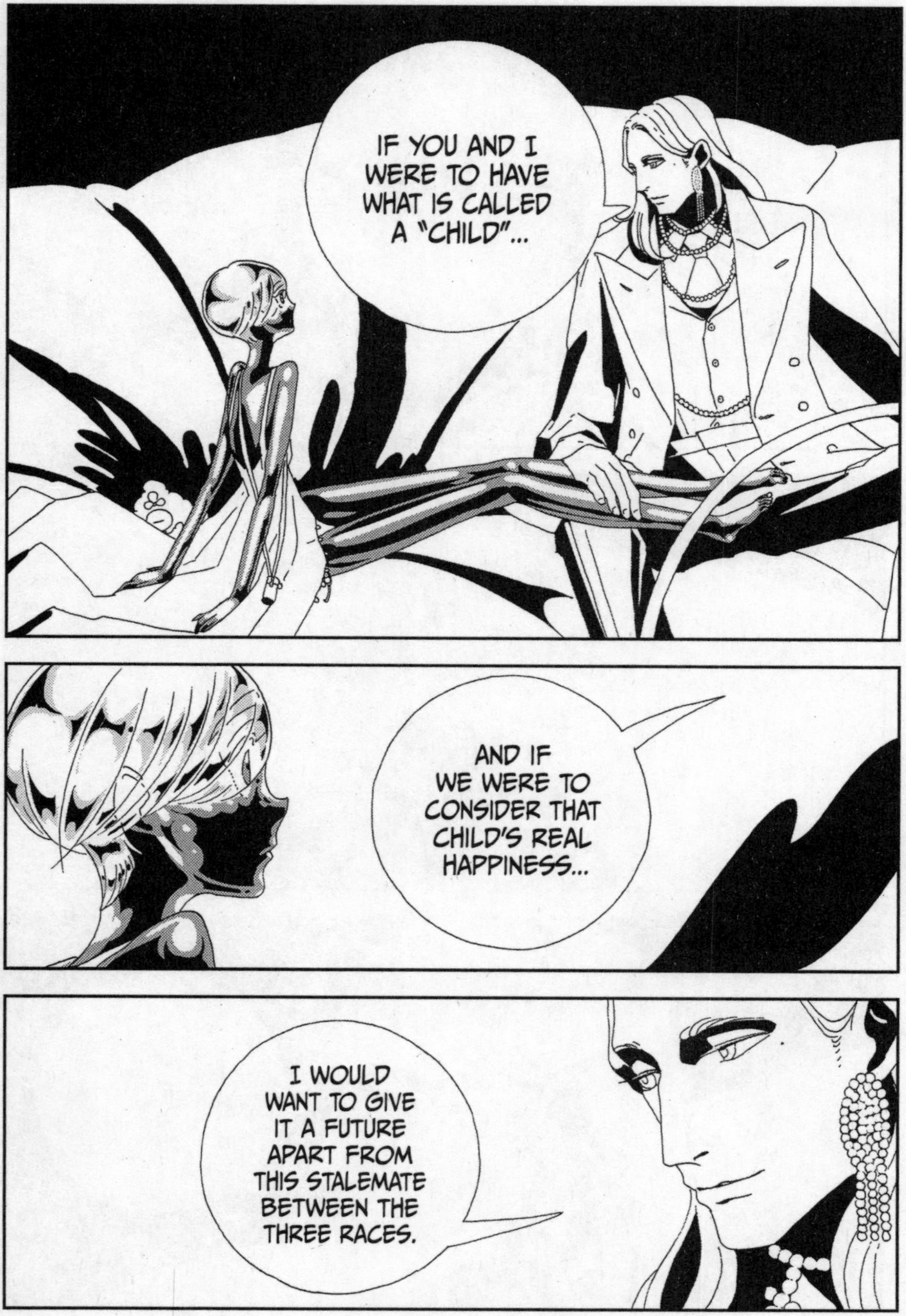
IF YOU AND I WERE TO HAVE WHAT IS CALLED A "CHILD"...
AND IF WE WERE TO CONSIDER THAT CHILD'S REAL HAPPINESS...
I WOULD WANT TO GIVE IT A FUTURE APART FROM THIS STALEMATE BETWEEN THE THREE RACES.

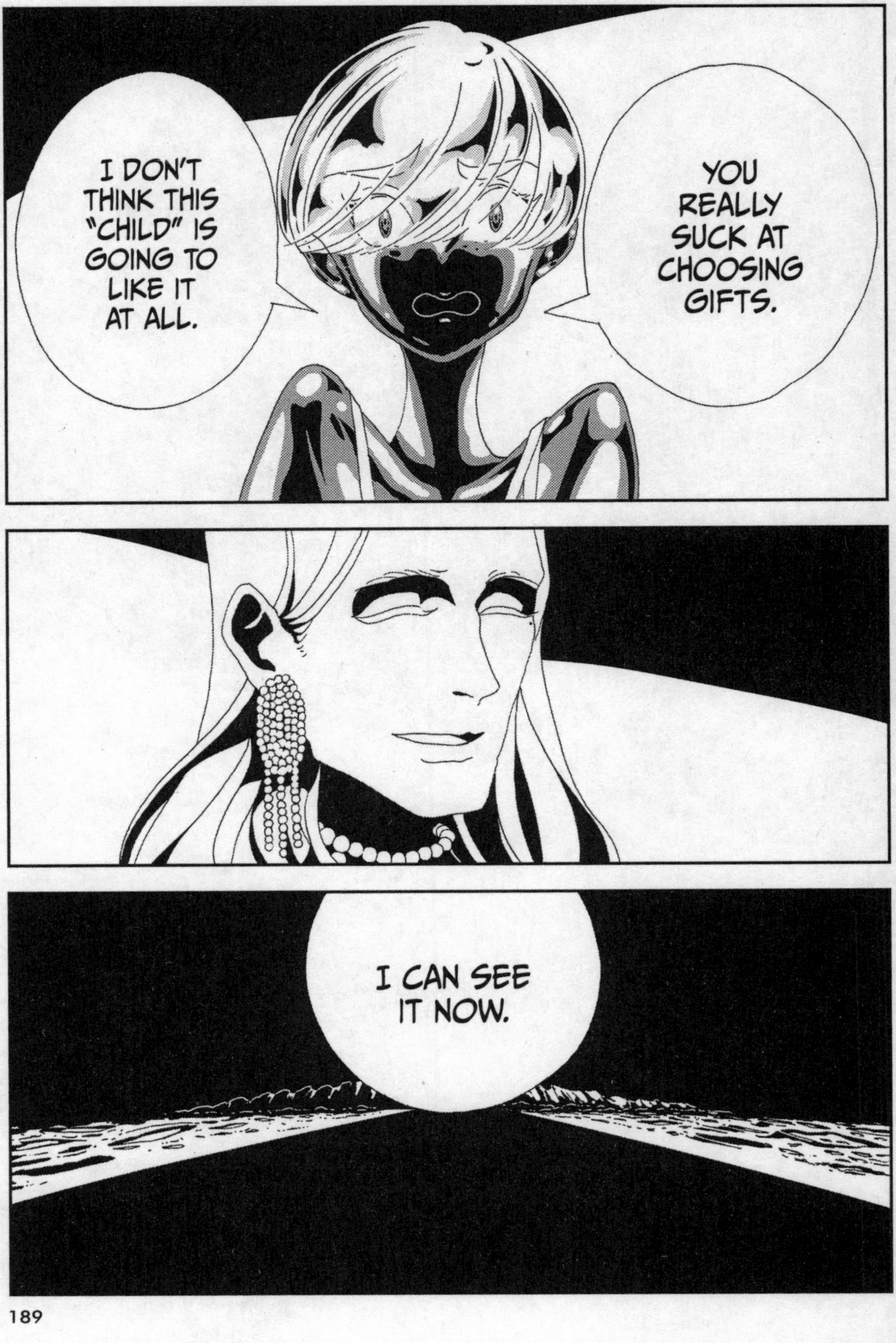
YOU REALLY SUCK AT CHOOSING GIFTS.
I DON'T THINK THIS "CHILD" IS GOING TO LIKE IT AT ALL.
I CAN SEE IT NOW.

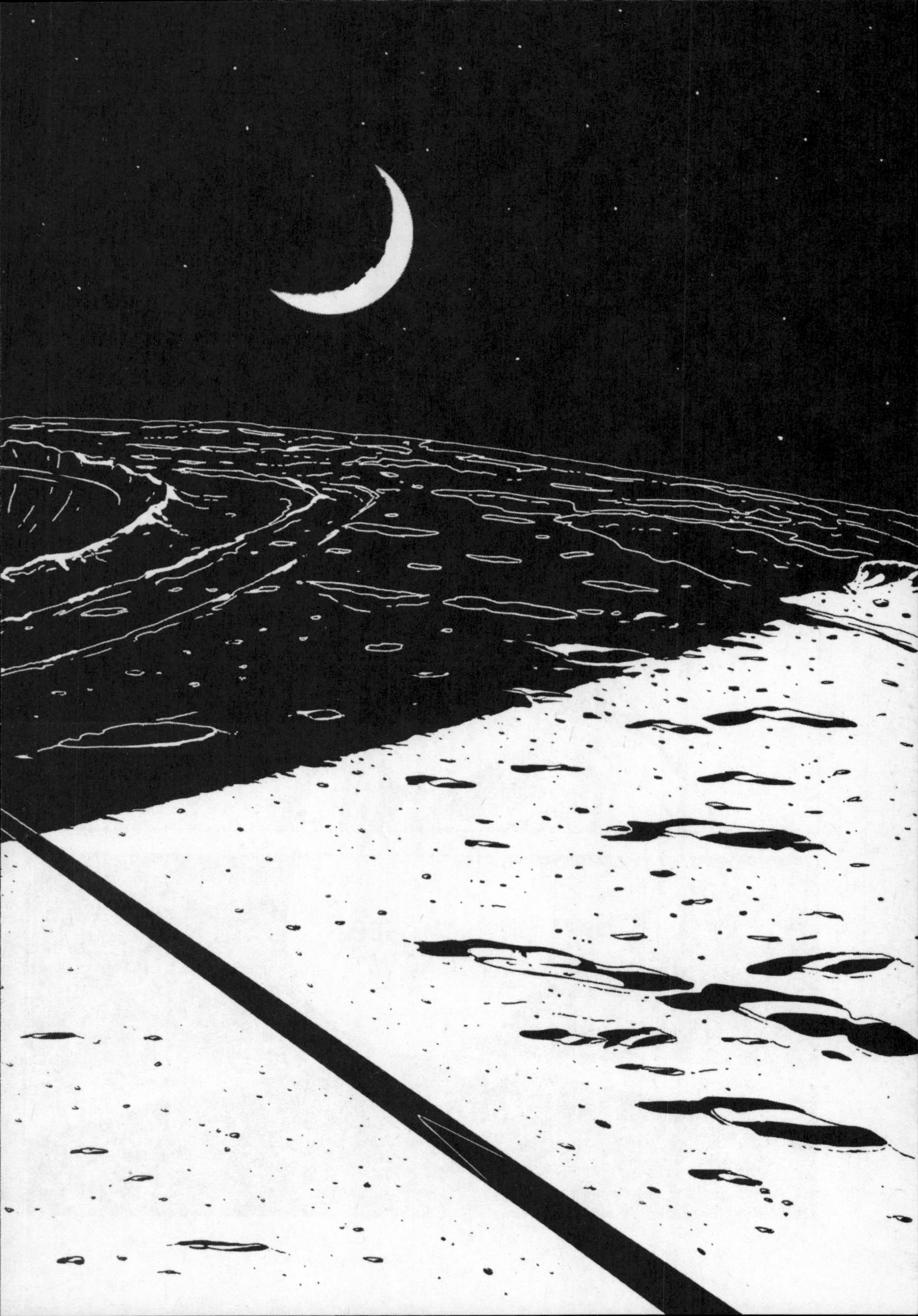

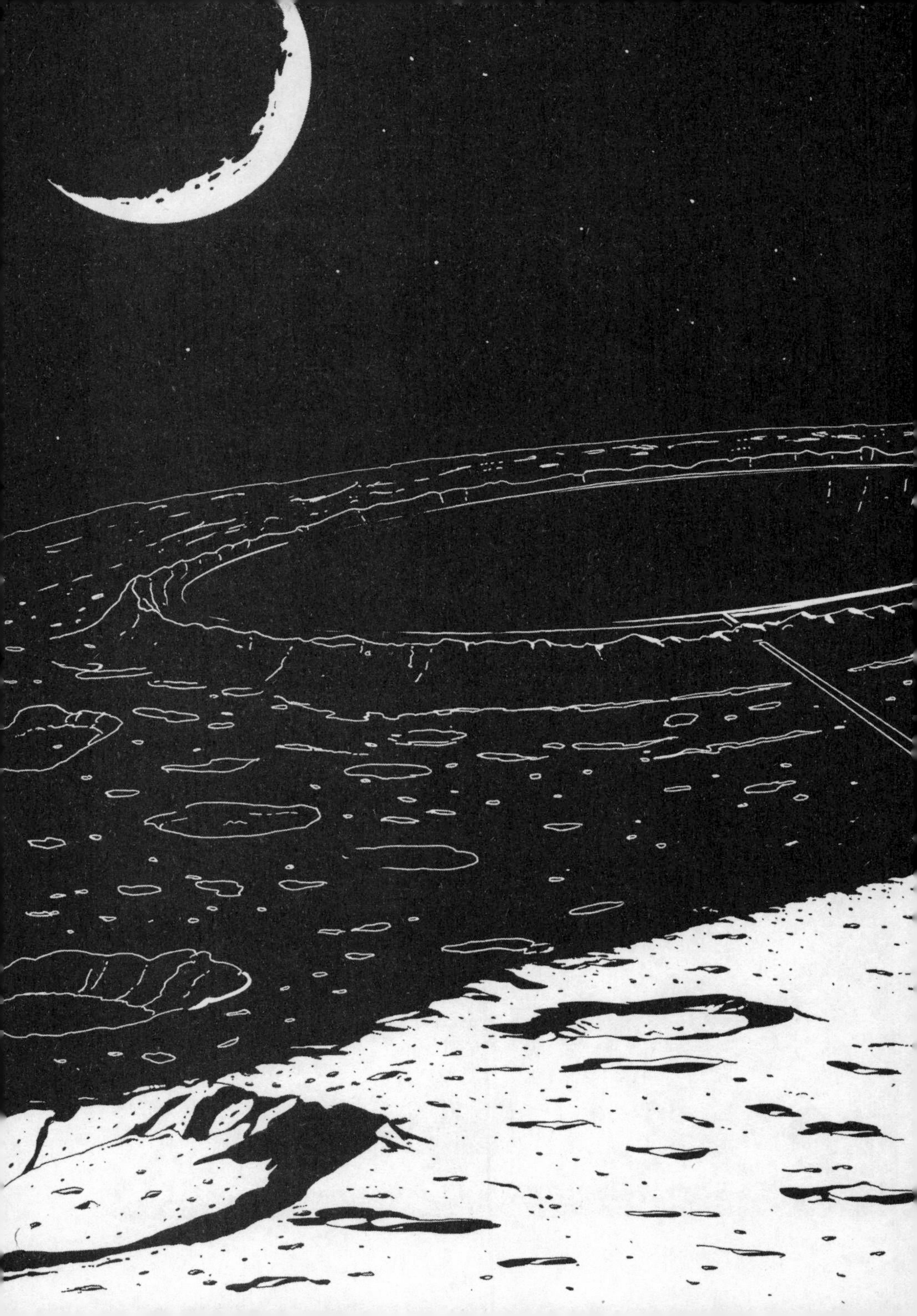

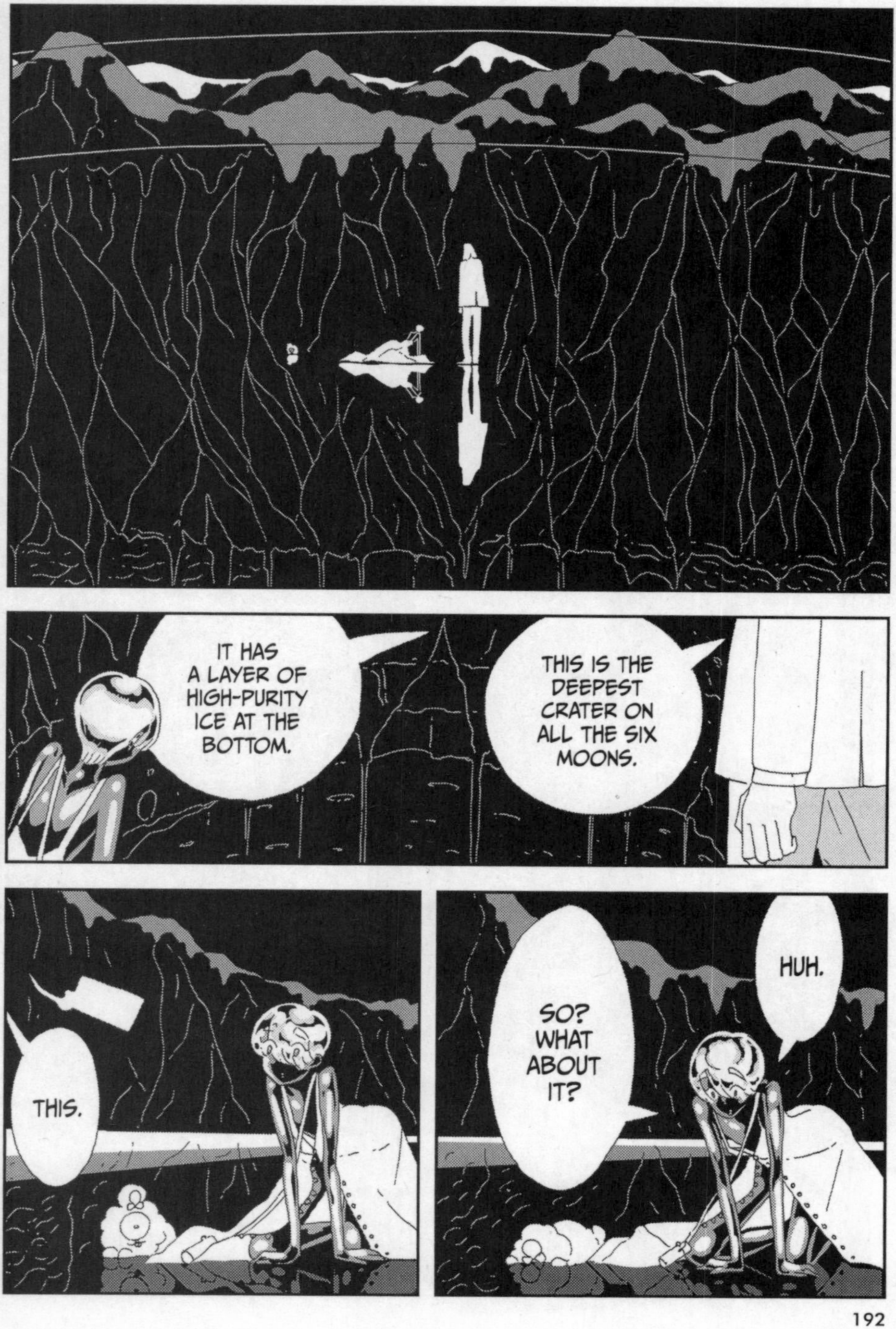
THIS IS THE DEEPEST CRATER ON ALL THE SIX MOONS.
IT HAS A LAYER OF HIGH-PURITY ICE AT THE BOTTOM.
HUH.
SO? WHAT ABOUT IT?
THIS.

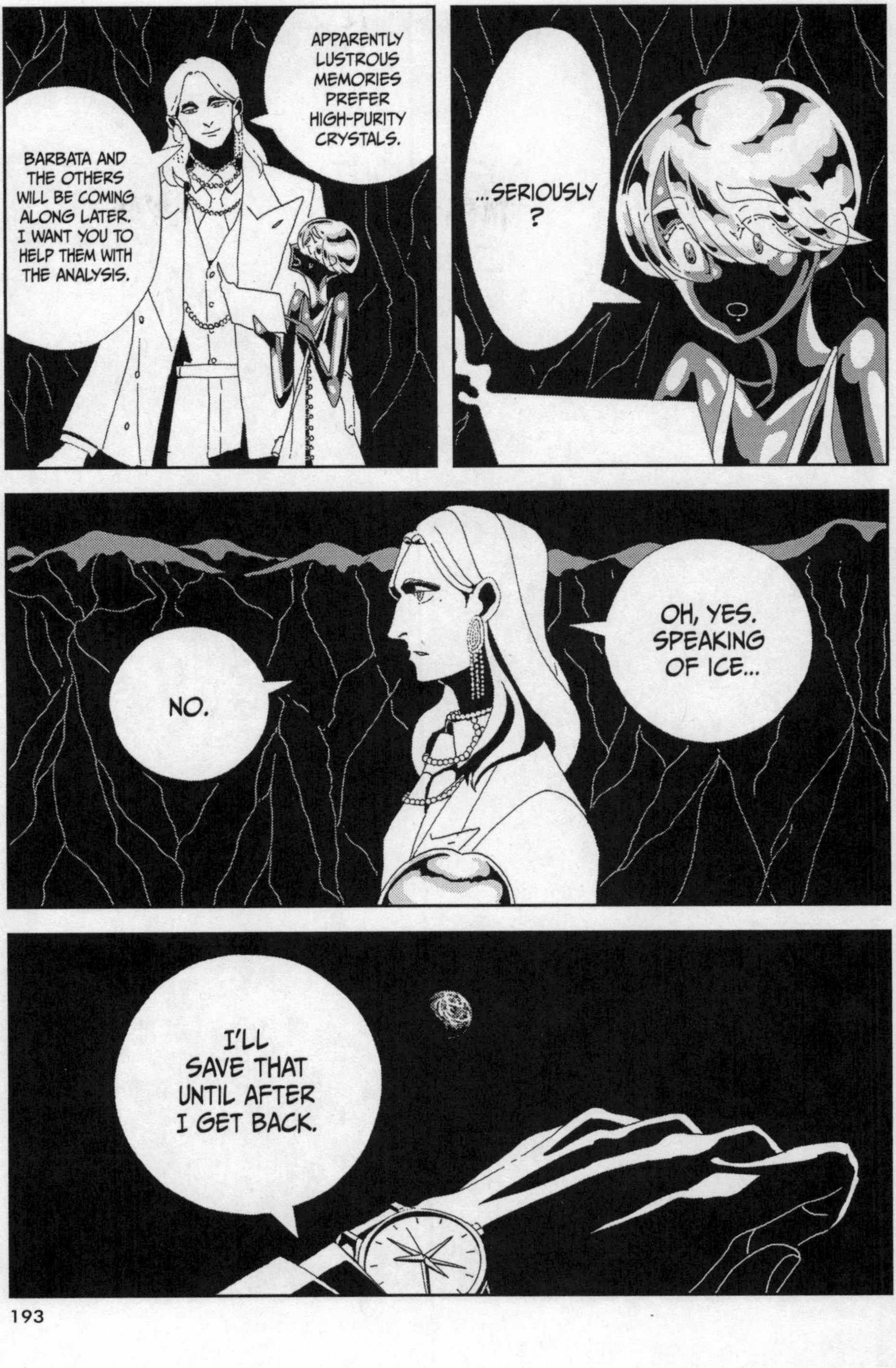
...SERIOUSLY ?
APPARENTLY LUSTROUS MEMORIES PREFER HIGH-PURITY CRYSTALS.
BARBATA AND THE OTHERS WILL BE COMING ALONG LATER. I WANT YOU TO HELP THEM WITH THE ANALYSIS.
OH, YES. SPEAKING OF ICE...
NO.
I'LL SAVE THAT UNTIL AFTER I GET BACK.

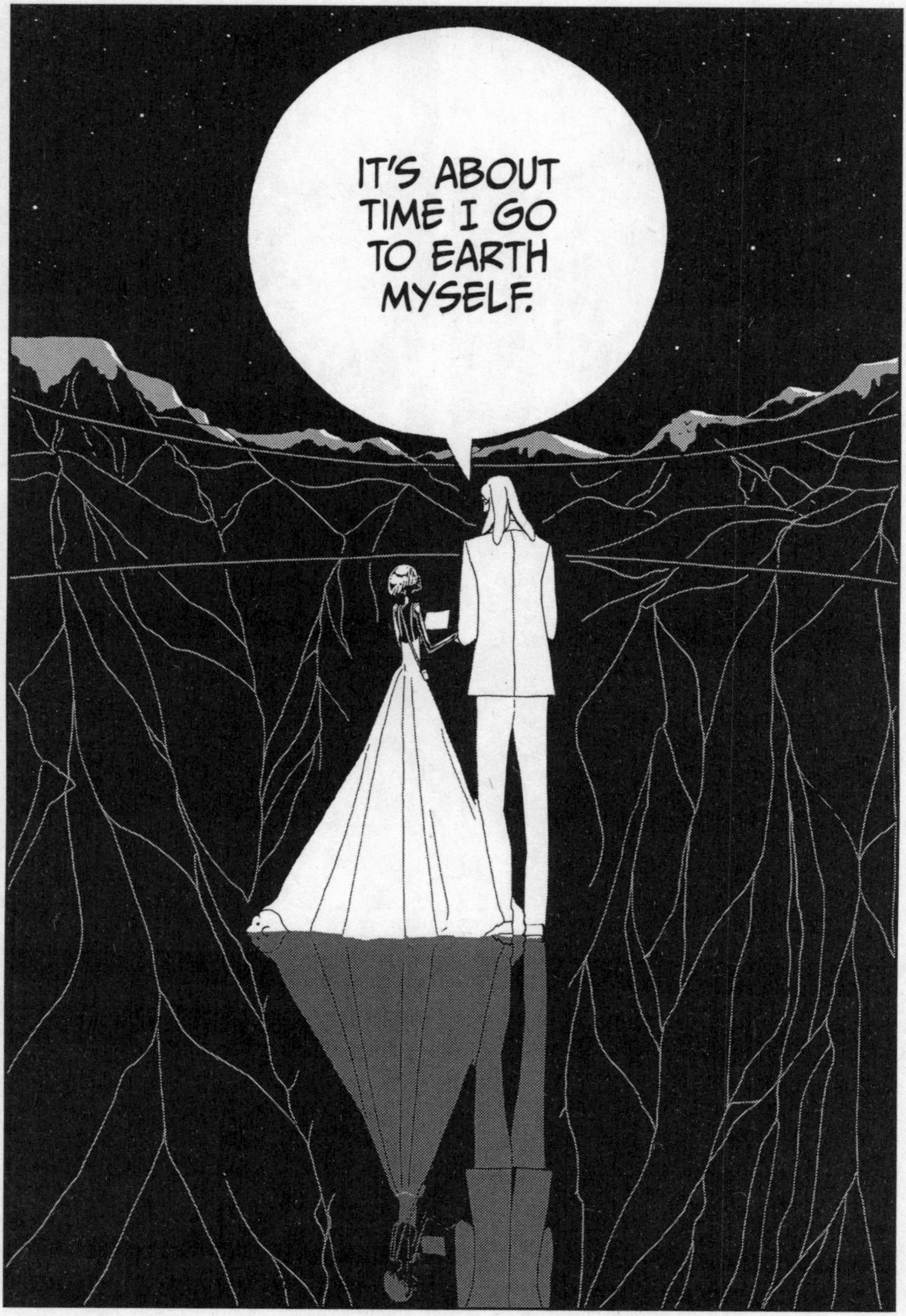
IT'S ABOUT TIME I GO TO EARTH MYSELF.

CHAPTER 88: Nature, Experiments, Future END

LAND OF THE LESS AGED

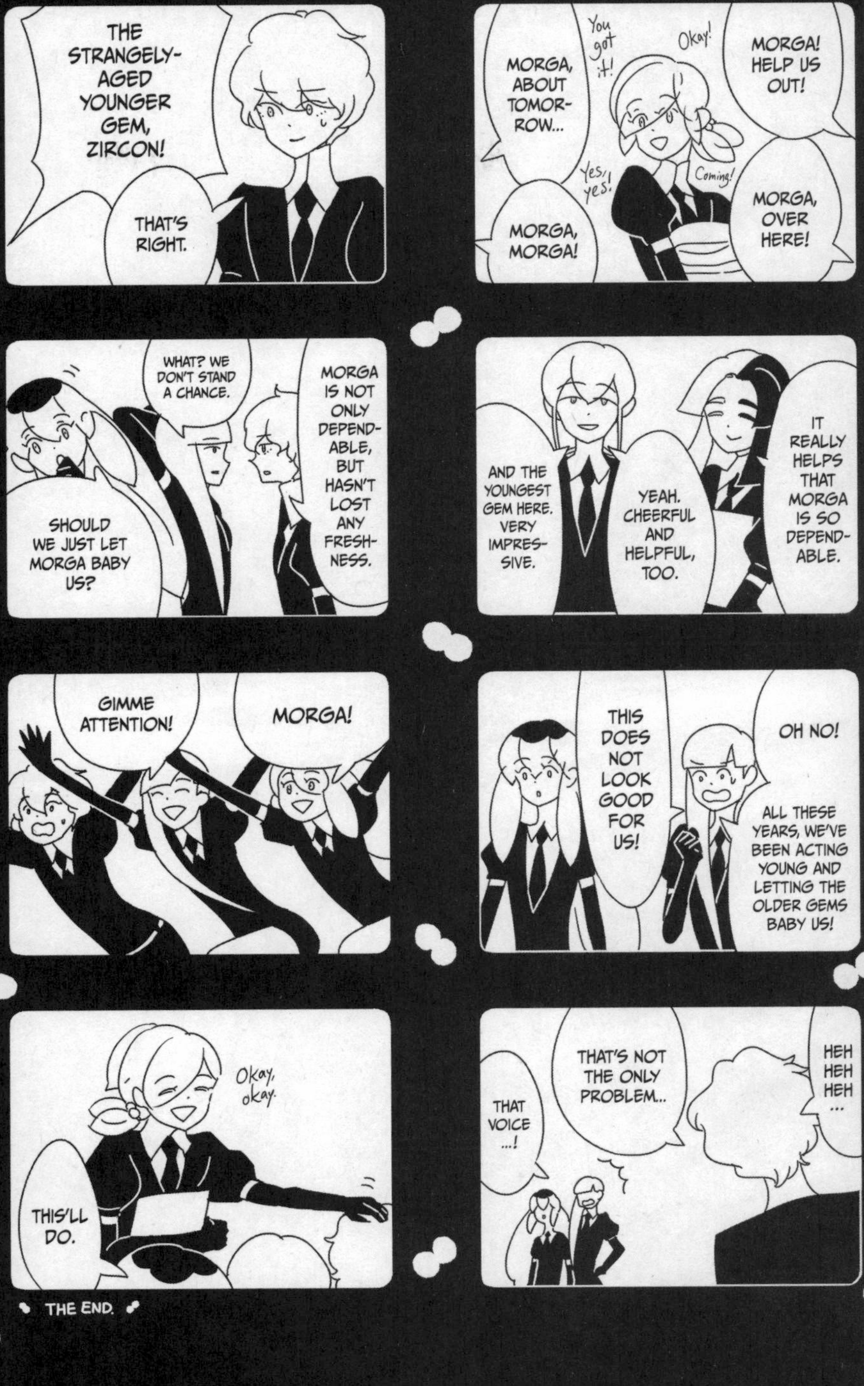
MORGA! HELP US OUT!
Okay!
You got it!
MORGA, ABOUT TOMORROW...
MORGA, OVER HERE!
Coming!
Yes, yes!
MORGA, MORGA!
IT REALLY HELPS THAT MORGA IS SO DEPENDABLE.
YEAH. CHEERFUL AND HELPFUL, TOO.
AND THE YOUNGEST GEM HERE. VERY IMPRESSIVE.
OH NO!
ALL THESE YEARS, WE'VE BEEN ACTING YOUNG AND LETTING THE OLDER GEMS BABY US!
THIS DOES NOT LOOK GOOD FOR US!
HEH HEH HEH...
THAT'S NOT THE ONLY PROBLEM...
THAT VOICE...!
THE STRANGELY-AGED YOUNGER GEM, ZIRCON!
THAT'S RIGHT.
MORGA IS NOT ONLY DEPENDABLE, BUT HASN'T LOST ANY FRESHNESS.
WHAT? WE DON'T STAND A CHANCE.
SHOULD WE JUST LET MORGA BABY US?
MORGA!
GIMME ATTENTION!
Okay, okay.
THIS'LL DO.
THE END.

TRANSLATION NOTES

PAPA *page 32*

Here, Goshenite addresses Padparadscha as *aniki*, a term that can be used to address someone you respect as an older sibling. The translators felt a nickname based on Padparadscha's name could convey a similar sentiment.

APPEAL TO A HIGHER POWER *page 173*

The term translated here to "appeal to a higher power" is *tariki hongan*, which literally means "sincere wish for outside power." It refers to a concept in Buddhism and other faiths that enlightenment, salvation, etc. comes not from one's own efforts (*jiriki*), but must be granted from an outside power, such as Buddha.

LAND OF THE LUSTROUS

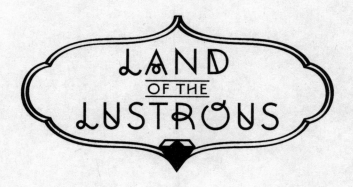

JAPANESE EDITION INSIDE COVER GALLERY
Volume 11

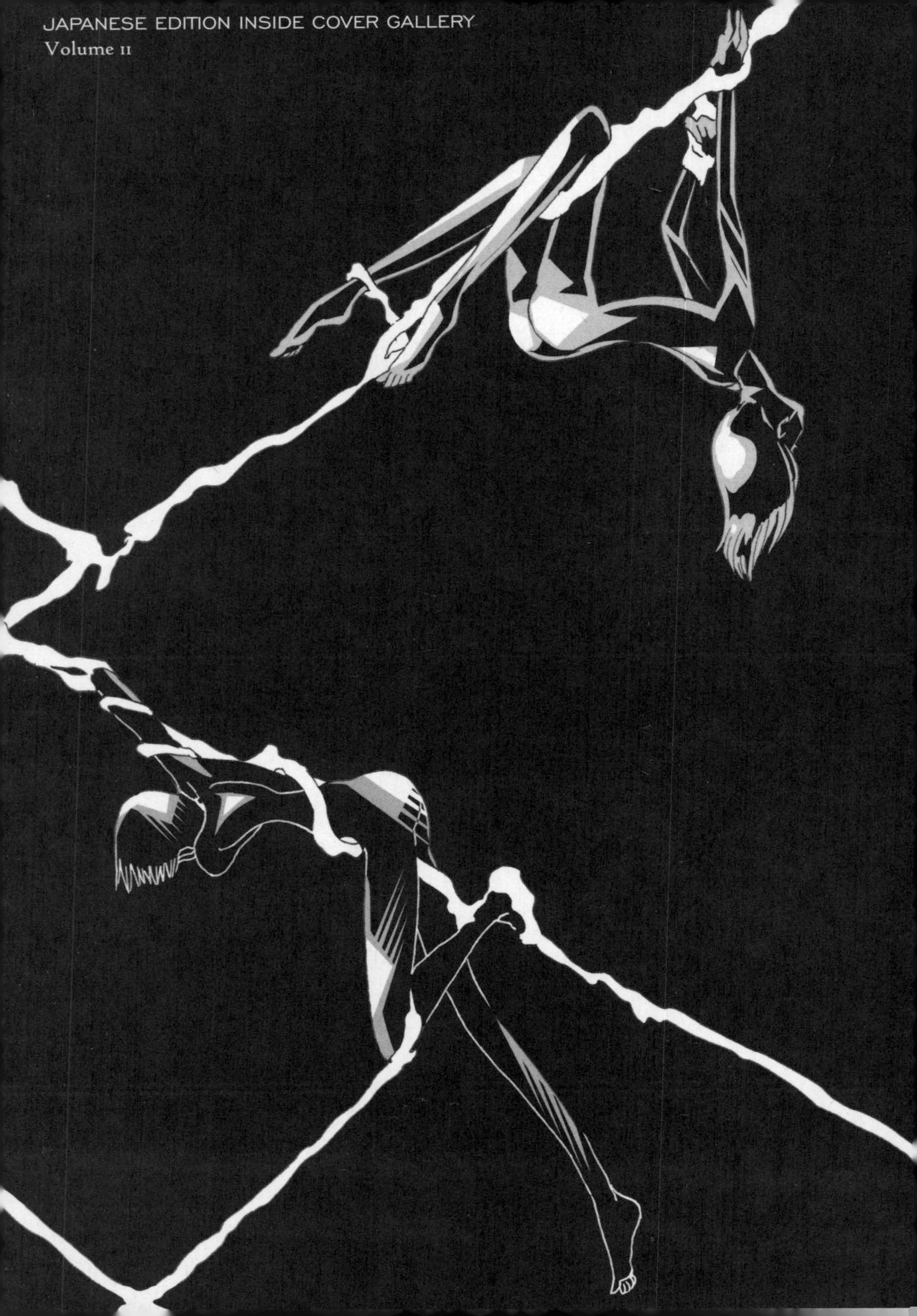

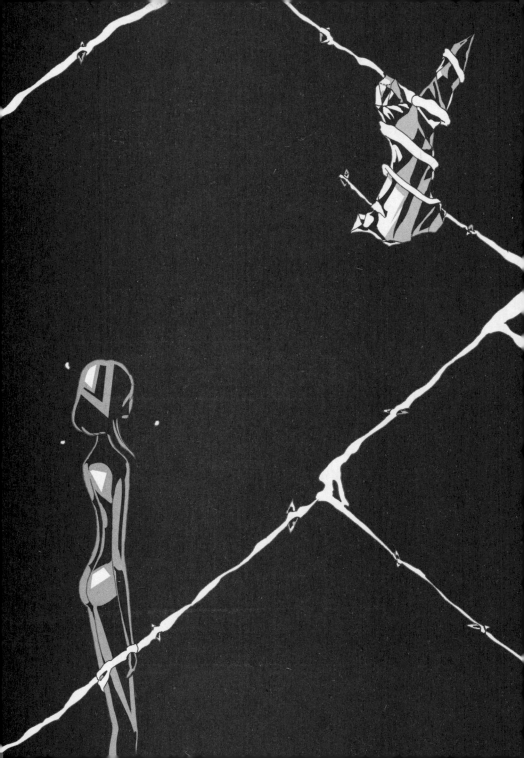

Young characters and steampunk setting, like *Howl's Moving Castle* and *Battle Angel Alita*

Beyond the Clouds © 2018 Nicke / Ki-oon

A boy with a talent for machines and a mysterious girl whose wings he's fixed will take you beyond the clouds! In the tradition of the high-flying, resonant adventure stories of Studio Ghibli comes a gorgeous tale about the longing of young hearts for adventure and friendship!

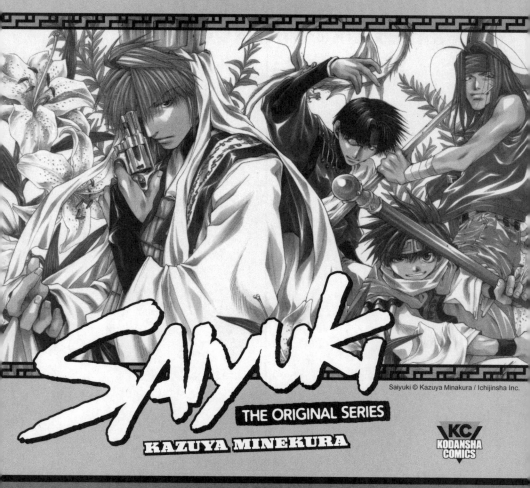

THE SWEET SCENT OF LOVE IS IN THE AIR! FOR FANS OF OFFBEAT ROMANCES LIKE *WOTAKOI*

Sweat and Soap © Kintetsu Yamada / Kodansha Ltd.

In an office romance, there's a fine line between sexy and awkward... and that line is where Asako — a woman who sweats copiously — meets Koutarou — a perfume developer who can't get enough of Asako's, er, scent. Don't miss a romcom manga like no other!

A SMART, NEW ROMANTIC COMEDY FOR FANS OF *SHORTCAKE CAKE* AND *TERRACE HOUSE*!

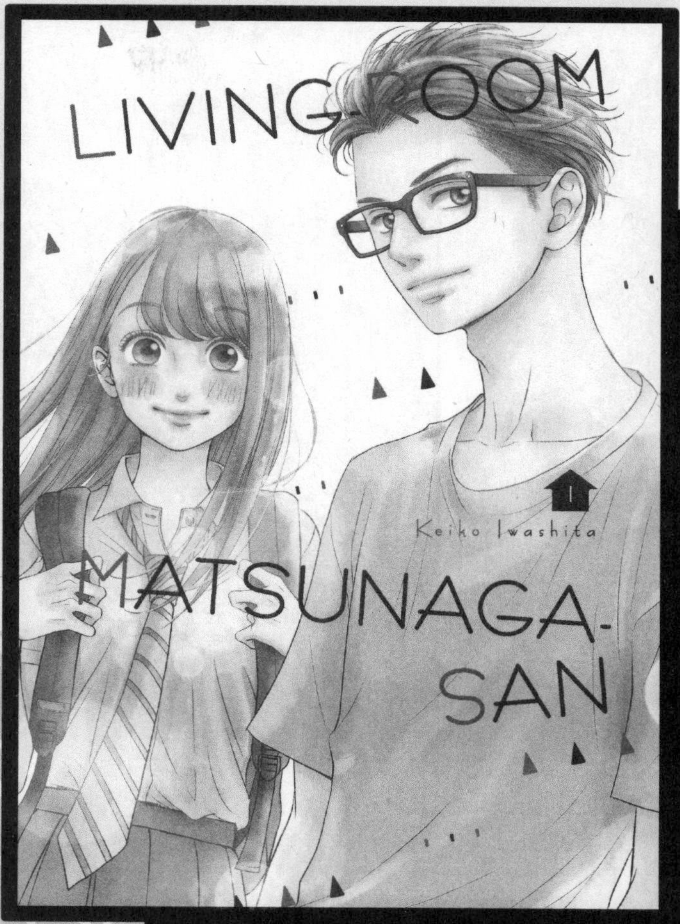
LIVING-ROOM
1
Keiko Iwashita
MATSUNAGA-SAN

A romance manga starring high school girl Meeko, who learns to live on her own in a boarding house whose living room is home to the odd (but handsome) Matsunaga-san. She begins to adjust to her new life away from her parents, but Meeko soon learns that no matter how far away from home she is, she's still a young girl at heart — especially when she finds herself falling for Matsunaga-san.

Knight of the Ice

Yayoi Ogawa

Knight of the Ice ©Yayoi Ogawa/Kodansha Ltd.

SKATING THRILLS AND ICY CHILLS WITH THIS NEW TINGLY ROMANCE SERIES!

A rom-com on ice, perfect for fans of *Princess Jellyfish* and *Wotakoi*. Kokoro is the talk of the figure-skating world, winning trophies and hearts. But little do they know... he's actually a huge nerd! From the beloved creator of *You're My Pet* (*Tramps Like Us*).

Chitose is a serious young woman, working for the health magazine *SASSO*. Or at least, she would be, if she wasn't constantly getting distracted by her childhood friend, international figure skating star Kokoro Kijinami! In the public eye and on the ice, Kokoro is a gallant, flawless knight, but behind his glittery costumes and breathtaking spins lies a secret: He's actually a hopelessly romantic otaku, who can only land his quad jumps when Chitose is on hand to recite a spell from his favorite magical girl anime!

KC
KODANSHA
COMICS

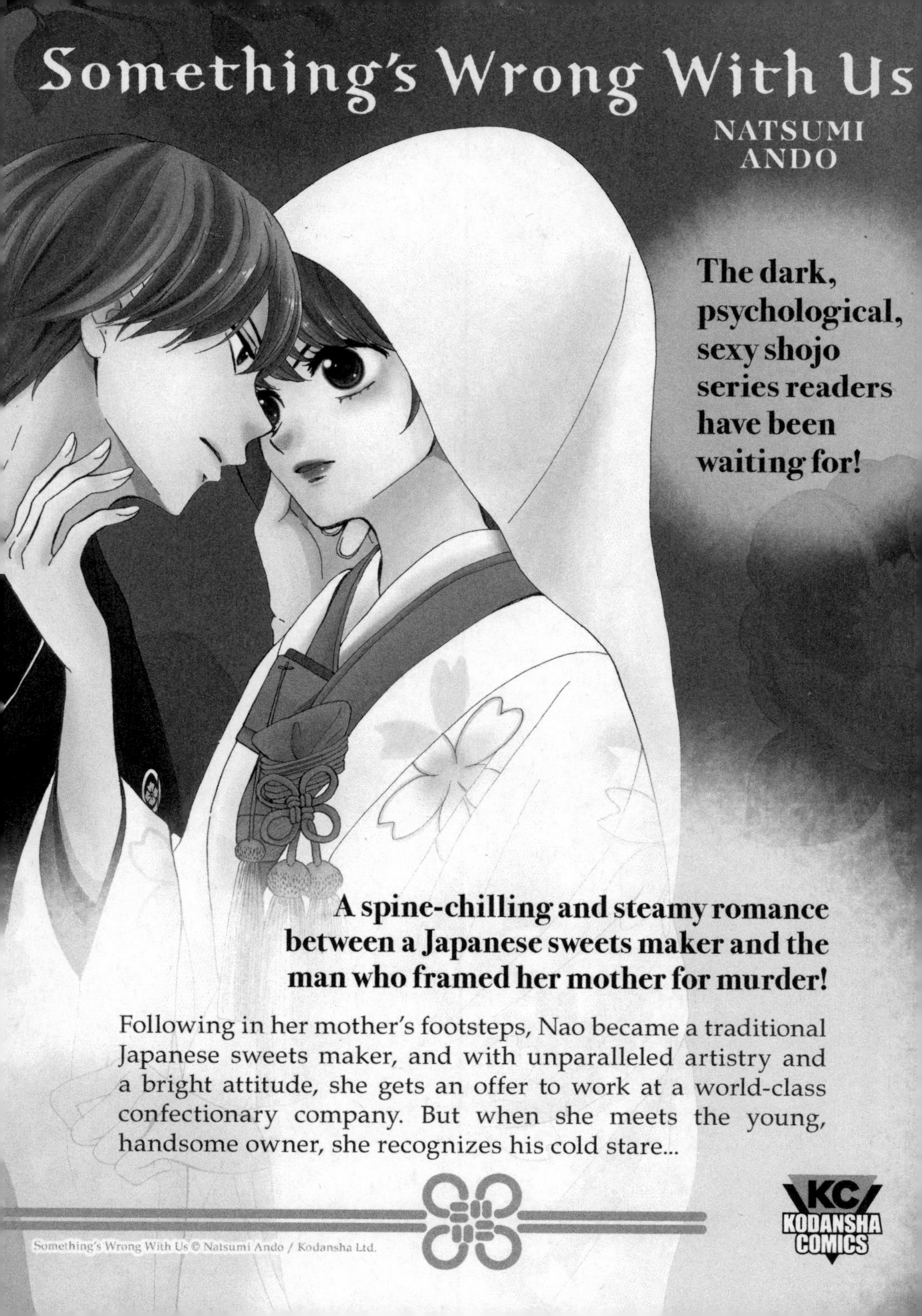
Something's Wrong With Us
NATSUMI ANDO
The dark, psychological, sexy shojo series readers have been waiting for!
A spine-chilling and steamy romance between a Japanese sweets maker and the man who framed her mother for murder!
Following in her mother's footsteps, Nao became a traditional Japanese sweets maker, and with unparalleled artistry and a bright attitude, she gets an offer to work at a world-class confectionary company. But when she meets the young, handsome owner, she recognizes his cold stare...
KC KODANSHA COMICS
Something's Wrong With Us © Natsumi Ando / Kodansha Ltd.

CUTE ANIMALS AND LIFE LESSONS, PERFECT FOR ASPIRING PET VETS OF ALL AGES!

For an 11-year-old, Yuzu has a lot on her plate. When her mom gets sick and has to be hospitalized, Yuzu goes to live with her uncle who runs the local veterinary clinic. Yuzu's always been scared of animals, but she tries to help out. Through all the tough moments in her life, Yuzu realizes that she can help make things all right with a little help from her animal pals, peers, and kind grown-ups.

Every new patient is a furry friend in the making!

PERFECT WORLD

Rie Aruga

A TOUCHING NEW SERIES ABOUT LOVE AND COPING WITH DISABILITY

An office party reunites Tsugumi with her high school crush Itsuki. He's realized his dream of becoming an architect, but along the way, he experienced a spinal injury that put him in a wheelchair. Now Tsugumi's rekindled feelings will butt up against prejudices she never considered — and Itsuki will have to decide if he's ready to let someone into his heart...

"Depicts with great delicacy and courage the difficulties some with disabilities experience getting involved in romantic relationships... Rie Aruga refuses to romanticize, pushing her heroine to face the reality of disability. She invites her readers to the same tasks of empathy, knowledge and recognition."
—Slate.fr

"An important entry [in manga romance]... The emotional core of both plot and characters indicates thoughtfulness... [Aruga's] research is readily apparent in the text and artwork, making this feel like a real story."
—Anime News Network

KC KODANSHA COMICS

SAINT ☆ YOUNG MEN

A LONG AWAITED ARRIVAL IN PREMIUM 2-IN-1 HARDCOVER

After centuries of hard work, Jesus and Buddha take a break from their heavenly duties to relax among the people of Japan, and their adventures in this lighthearted buddy comedy are sure to bring mirth and merriment to all!

"Brilliant...the physical comedy and facial expressions will make you literally LOL."

—Sam Humphries
(host of *DC Daily*;
writer, *Green Lanterns*,
Legendary Star-Lord)

Saint Young Men © Hikaru Nakamura/Kodansha Ltd.

THE WORLD OF CLAMP!

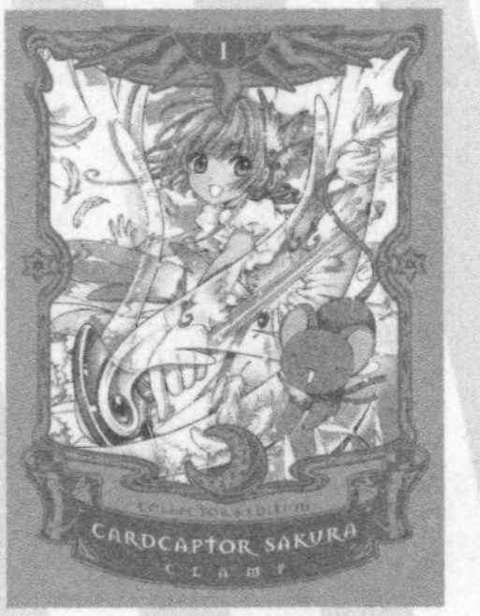
CARDCAPTOR SAKURA
CLAMP
Cardcaptor Sakura Collector's Edition

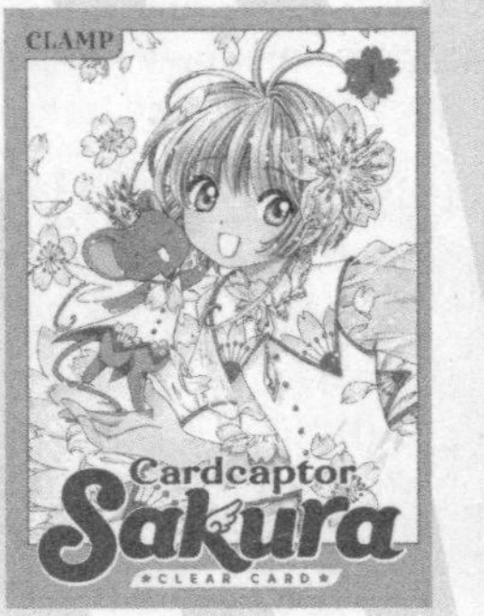
CLAMP
Cardcaptor
Sakura
CLEAR CARD
Cardcaptor Sakura: Clear Card

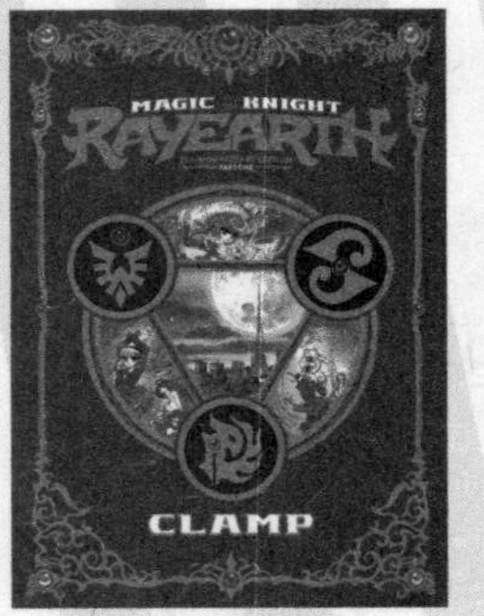
MAGIC KNIGHT
RAYEARTH
CLAMP
Magic Knight Rayearth 25th Anniversary Box Set

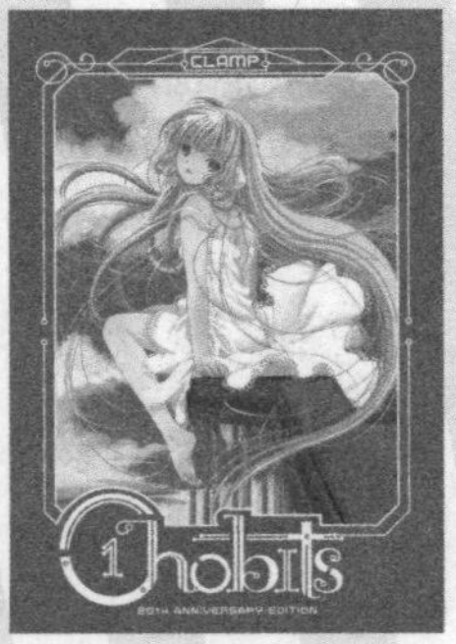
CLAMP
1
Chobits
Chobits

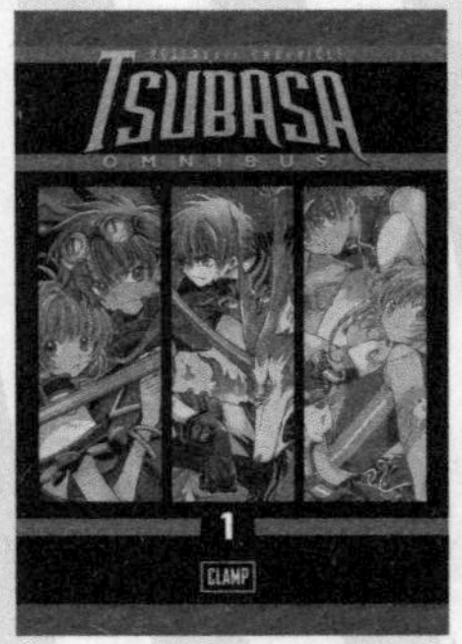
TSUBASA
OMNIBUS
1
CLAMP
TSUBASA Omnibus

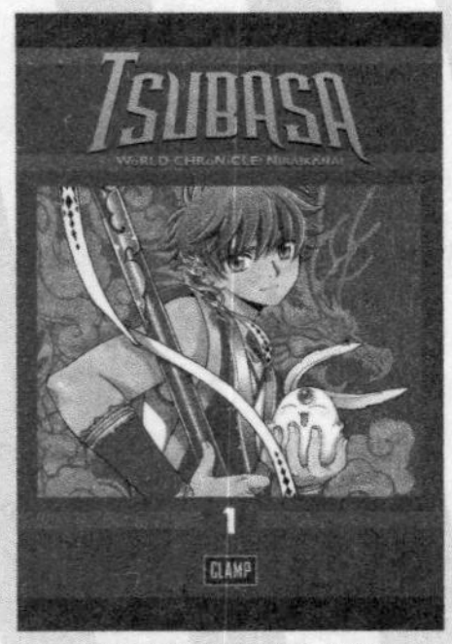
TSUBASA
1
CLAMP
TSUBASA WoRLD CHRoNiCLE

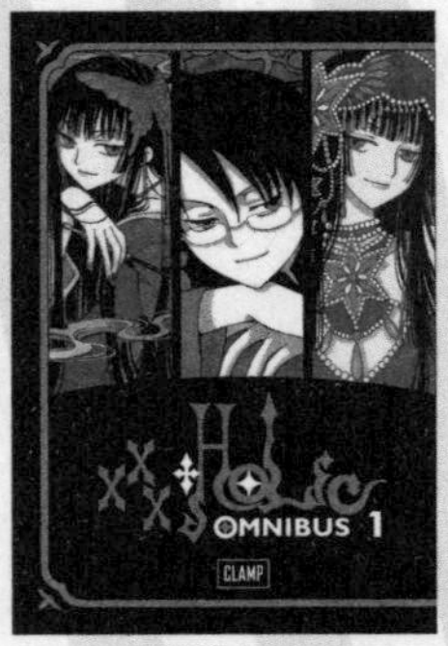
xxxHOLiC
OMNIBUS 1
CLAMP
xxxHOLiC Omnibus

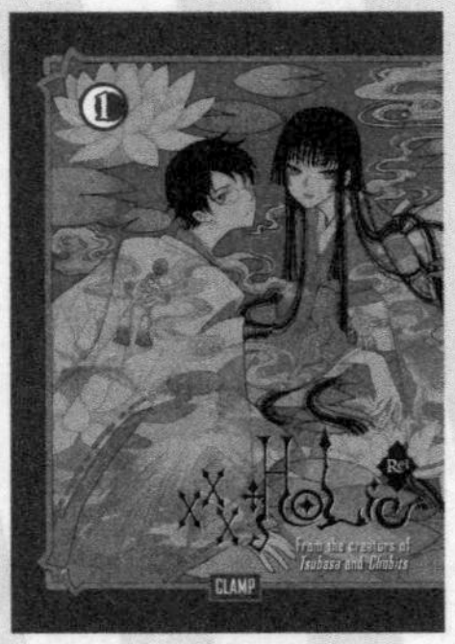
1
xxxHOLiC
CLAMP
xxxHOLiC Rei

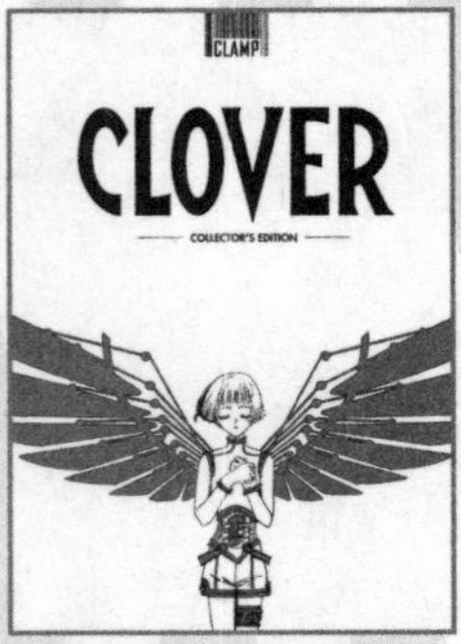
CLAMP
CLOVER
CLOVER Collector's Edition

KC KODANSHA COMICS

Kodansha Comics welcomes you to explore the expansive world of CLAMP, the all-female artist collective that has produced some of the most acclaimed manga of the century. Our growing catalog includes icons like *Cardcaptor Sakura* and *Magic Knight Rayearth*, each crafted with CLAMP's one-of-a-kind style and characters!